Cultural Critique

98

Winter
2018

Review Essays

EDITORIAL STATEMENT

Cultural Critique provides a forum for creative and provocative scholarship in the theoretical humanities and humanistic social sciences. Transnational in scope and transdisciplinary in orientation, the journal strives to spark and galvanize intellectual debates as well as to attract and foster critical investigations regarding any aspect of culture as it expresses itself in words, images, and sounds, across both time and space. The journal is especially keen to support scholarship that engages the ways in which cultural production, cultural practices, and cultural forms constitute and manifest the nexus between the aesthetic, the psychic, the economic, the political, and the ethical intended in their widest senses. While informed by the diverse traditions of historical materialism as well as by the numerous critiques of such traditions from various parts of the globe, the journal welcomes contributions based on a variety of theoretical-methodological paradigms.

Cultural Critique appears four times a year. General issues, including essays, book reviews, and thematic sections, as well as entire issues devoted to special topics, are regularly published. The editors welcome the submission of freestanding essays, special issue proposals on topics of interest to the journal, as well as reviews of relevant, new, and not-so-new books.

Cultural Critique Books is the companion series of the journal. It seeks to attract work by those scholars across the humanities and social sciences who continue to draw inspiration from, and seek to contribute to, the theoretical movements and debates so long nurtured at Minnesota. Book proposals should be addressed to one of the three editors at: *Cultural Critique,* Department of Cultural Studies and Comparative Literature, 235 Nicholson Hall, 216 Pillsbury Drive S.E., University of Minnesota, Minneapolis, MN 55455-0229, U.S.A., or via email to cultcrit@umn.edu.

WILLING TO DIE

ADDICTION AND OTHER AMBIVALENCES OF LIVING

Dana Seitler

I get world sick every time I take a step

—*Broken Social Scene*

I love you, baby,
Can I have some more?

—*Neil Young*

When I was a heroin addict, I used drugs both to achieve what Jacques Lacan has characterized as the "jubilation" one experiences when we seem to coincide with our ego-ideal and to produce a positivity out of my increasing sense "of fragmentation, of rupture, of breaking up, of lack of adaptation, of inadequation" (1975, 38). I was drawn to heroin because it promised that sense of plenitude to which we all ostensibly aspire, when all the while it was really increasing the distance between my feeling of imaginary wholeness and what Kaja Silverman has described as "the body in bits and pieces" (45). I was not the narcissistic subject gazing into my rippling image in the water below, but rather the watery image itself, looking up at me-as-subject and experiencing the realness of the unreal that may be one way to describe the mentally diffuse state of intoxication. Or, to put this another way, I came to inhabit, and to idealize, the alterity that always undergirds subjectivity, but from the inverse of the reflective apparatus.

I am deliberately using the identificatory phrase "heroin addict," despite Eve Sedgwick's salvo against that particular pathologization, for a number of reasons (130–42). First, addiction felt like an identity in ways I want to underscore; it was not a transparent sign of my personhood but that which I attached myself to as a way to inhabit the incoherence of my identity (a deranged strategy, to be sure, but all strategies of ego affirmation are). Second, the term "addiction" seems a better one to me than "compulsion" or "habit" (although I like those too), precisely because it implies each in its own meaning: an addict uses drugs habitually, for example, but also compulsively. "Habit," the term Sedgwick prefers because of its de-pathologizing potential, suggests an inclination for a regular and regulated occurrence or pattern of behavior; compulsion, that you can't help but perform a certain act. So addiction is a habitual, compulsive attachment to an object of desire or way of being in the world. The psychic component is key here, and one of the reasons I am turning to the language of psychoanalysis to explain the experience of addiction, because psychoanalysis is so good at placing emphasis on forms and expressions of psychic confliction. But, as Sedgwick points out, addiction is also a social phenomenon whose construction as such limits the set of options for understanding the feelings, inclinations, and tendencies that make up personhood, for what were once seen as discrete actions or practices now get redefined as pathologies. Thus Sedgwick: "In the taxonomic reframing of a drug user as an addict, what changes are the most basic terms about her. . . . She is propelled into a narrative of inexorable decline and fatality, from which she cannot deimplicate herself except by leaping into that other, even more pathos-ridden narrative called *kicking the habit*" (129).

My own addiction did not follow this inexorable trajectory. It was not the stuff of movies or after-school specials in which drug use leads to an increasingly fast downward spiral or a place called "rock bottom" (though this is not a completely inaccurate genre: one of my friends died of a heroin overdose, others had to be rushed to the emergency room to have their stomachs pumped, and still others turned to Narcotics Anonymous and other rehabilitation centers and techniques in various attempts to "get clean").[1] But this was not my story. Or not exactly. I was very careful with the amount I used, doling out little bits throughout the day, only allowing a touch more in the evenings. While I could not get out of bed in the morning without it, I was perversely *measured* in my destructive attachment to this object of my desire. I could not stop using—the physical dependency had taken over—so the project became one of how to successfully manage my addiction (still receive high grades, accomplish my work tasks on time, keep my secret safe); and, for the most part, I did.[2]

It may seem a serious misconception to claim my efforts were somehow successful, but I never received less than an A grade for a college or graduate course or missed attending a single class—although many of my interpersonal relations were, unsurprisingly, a total mess. Of course, we can consider this need to manage a part of the compulsion, not its mysterious outcome. This is because, for me, drug use was in large part a form of fantasy *and* a form of control, which is to say the form the fantasy took was one of self-discipline that had paradoxically emerged out of, and coexisted with, a space of radical mental disorientation. Heroin provided a sense of comfort and well-being in which many of my unmanageable daily anxieties could be managed. This is not to claim that this was easy to maintain: it was painful and debilitating, and involved psychic and bodily forms of disintegration. But it also augmented my sense of social and sexual difference in ways that felt expansive and resistant. I was in a highly competitive college and then graduate school, whose various scenes of normativity did not just feel socially constraining—cliques and judgments and people who said unthinkingly homophobic things—but also were unattractive to me as scenes of being. I didn't fit in, but I also didn't want to. My turn to drugs was, therefore, not a wholly melancholic one; I had long ago discovered a geek drug subculture in high school and college that felt like, and I experienced as, a better, because more broken, social scene for my own inverted idealizations of personhood (groups of intelligent, overachieving misfits like me who got straight As, cared about politics and ideas, listened to punk rock, and snorted lines over the weekend). From the point of view of psychoanalysis, I was motivated, as a function of drive, by the promise of collective euphoria *and* personal control, and by my overvaluation of alienation as the pivot on which both turned.[3]

In *Beyond the Pleasure Principle,* Freud proposes, "The aim of all life is death" (1961, 32). We all hold an unconscious desire to die, to return to an "early state of things," but this wish is largely tempered by the life instincts, by eros, which is what keeps us from succumbing to the depths of trauma, though not always (30). In Freud's view, self-destructive behavior is an expression of the energy created by the death instincts. But death is more than a wish for the destruction of the biological organism's integrity, it is also what suspends the principle of individuation working in the self. Being willing to die, in whatever form that takes (both conscious and unconscious), is a fundamental part of the shaping of identity, in which our imaginary idea of wholeness is propped up by an equally forceful desire for our undoing.

Ultimately, then, my heroin addiction belongs to a psychoanalytically banal, unsurprising fantasy of living at risk. To be sure, heroin use afforded me a number of things within this schema: to inhabit my awkward difference from the normative as something positive, to use alienation as an affective strategy of self-affirmation, to be-for-death in a way that, if only temporarily and in various states of anguish, was not so much mitigated by but helped fuel a desire for a different life, or possibility of living. Addiction thus enabled a certain enactment of, or engagement with, my constitutive lack—what Lacan calls "being-for-death" (1977, 114). It enabled an apprehension, and living out, of the dissolution of personhood that always exists anyway. For Lacan "every drive is a death drive" because every drive pursues its own extinction; it is not as much a matter of our impulse toward desubjectivization as toward our constitution as persons in relation to everything we know—and don't know—we can never become (844). Every drive involves the subject in repetition, is the motor by which we are compelled to return to traumas of the past but also the nothingness at the center of our sense of self, which is to say every drive is an attempt to go, in Freud's language, *beyond the pleasure principle,* to the realm of excess *jouissance* where pleasure and pain, enjoyment and suffering, are experienced as interchangeable.

I wanted to embrace my "being-for-death," not approximate my ideal imago; or, to put it another way, my ego-ideal was self-consciously nonnormative. I was cathected to genres of self-in-other that were "dark" and "subversive": when I was twelve my favorite movie was *Christiane F (Wir Kinder vom Bahnhof Zoo,* 1981*),* I grew up to write enthralled college essays about Carolee Schneemann's "Interior Scroll," and thought William S. Burroughs was a genius.[4] I wanted to experience bodily and psychic disintegration, not protect myself from knowledge of it, or so the fantasy went. But what kind of fantasy is really at work here? The promise that you won't experience pain if you can manage your own forms of risk is certainly an aspect of it, and a comforting one at that. But the innumerable forms of relation one forges in the midst of (so-called and actual) destructive behavior is not adequately accounted for in most narratives about addiction or other forms of risk that we may or may not deliberately cultivate. Because addiction in particular is so powerful (psychically, physically, emotionally), you have to reject it absolutely in order to survive it. The idea that I am implying here that it somehow made me cool is delusional (and I mean this in the Lacanian sense: it is a fundamental misrecognition).[5] But this makes it very difficult to think through, let alone theorize, one's relation to the risk of death in any other than deleterious ways. You seem irresponsible—and / or unethical—if you think about death, or actions that bring you to its brink as anything other than tragedy (perhaps because it always, in part, is).[6]

In *No Future,* Lee Edelman embraces the death drive as a political metaphor, seeing it as a potential mode of refusal of the heteronormative compulsions that the fetish of the child represents in the space of "reproductive futurity" (14). In part, this does describe what I thought I was doing during the period of my addiction (outlaw sex, outlaw drugs, outlaw politics, yada, yada). But it also fails to account for the real damage that occurs when the metaphor becomes manifest, and for the *various* accounts—psychic, political, experiential, personal, but also atypical and constructed—that inform risk and other forms of compulsion. Even my narrative here is simply that: an attempt at producing in coherent form something that is fundamentally incoherent. My "truths," in the generic form of confession as I am presenting them, are constructions of truth, ways of organizing my past in order to make it useful, readable, *manageable,* and so just another extension of what addiction was for me in the first place: a fantasy of self-management that things like stories allow us to form and tell.[7] As Foucault has argued, as much on behalf of a critique of psychoanalysis and its positing of the psyche as a priori to the social as on behalf of a theory of the diffuse institutionalization of power, "Not only will you confess to acts contravening the law, but you will seek to transform your desire, your every desire, into discourse" (21). And yet, I turn to personal narrative here for a number of reasons. First and foremost, I offer it as an intervening model in current and historical frames for addiction that either result in its sentimentalization, criminalization, or othering. I employ what could be called "critical memory," or a reflective and theoretical use of personal narrative, to suggest an alternative method of reading nonuniversally about suffering and ambivalence.

Taking Foucault's proviso into account, then, I want to ask how we can track or articulate the affective, social, and imaginary attachments generated by forms of self-destruction, of "being-for-death," without the alleged solipsism of the psychoanalytic model. If what I have written above has been a self-serving narrative that ultimately denies the radical instability of personhood in the guise of talking about it, how do we think beyond the variously contaminated, variously mediated zones of fantasy, desire, and identification? Specifically, how do we account for habitual compulsions like addiction?

Karen Kopelson has argued for the possible emancipatory properties of drug use: "Precisely because these lived, embodied practices are among the most derided, dangerous, and (often literally) 'outlawed' manifestations of excessive female desire, their interpretation can be productively, seditiously mobilized to postmodern feminist ends" (2).[8] In part, Kopelson is responding to arguments like Susan Bordo's in *Unbearable Weight* that indict postmodern feminist theory for its dismissal of "the real body" and thus for its celebratory investments in the symbolic dimensions of protest and resistance without consideration for women's actually lived lives (along the way arguing how eating disorders that seem to function as forms of "embodied protest" actually serve the regulatory ideals of the social order). I find Kopelson's suggestion that we account for addiction as a "lived ontological protestation" compelling but ultimately unsustainable. One might ask: Is suffering worth it? Or, following Lacanian thought, if addiction is just the same kind of suffering as that at the heart of being, how much suffering can one take? Are there less agonistic ways of living in and/or responding to the world? I have no answer to this question, but one way to address it might be to think together the distinct, but also always overlapping, relations between lived experience and narrative expression, between willful acts of self-obliteration and identificatory desire, and between negation and form, where we can begin to glimpse the innumerable disorganizations that inform who we think we are. This also might mean moving away from psychoanalysis and its focus on drives as psychic conditions of personhood toward theories of affect as actually felt, and thus nonuniversal, experiences.[9]

It may well be that accumulating stories of being-for-death that adjudicate between psychoanalytic and affective understandings of personhood may be one way to go. After all, my narrative has company. There is Oscar Wilde's Dorian Gray, who drifts from opium den to opium den, reveling in the temporal suspension of his otherwise lost personhood. Wilde explains, "Dorian, having led a life of mere sensation and pleasure, tries to kill conscience, and at that moment kills himself" (Hollan and Hart-Davis, 430). There is also Nick Cage's character, Ben Anderson, in *Leaving Las Vegas* (1995), a dissipated hero whose alcoholism stands in as an allegory for life itself, insofar as we understand life as being-for-death as I am suggesting: "I came here to drink myself to death," he announces in a Las Vegas motel, and it seems as if, until that moment, he has never really lived. In Ben's attempt to disaggregate himself from his own body and history, jubilation and pain intermix until the two become indecipherable from one another.[10] This is not so different from Lacan's contention that the aim is not to limit the destructive impulse of the death drive (you can't) or to mitigate the desired unification with the ego ideal (you can't) but to enact a rupture from this unity desired by eros, a unity that is fundamentally narcissistic and imaginary once it is connected to the projection and introjection of the idealized self image during the mirror stage. But can you?

In Edith Wharton's *The House of Mirth* (1905), enacting such a rupture comes at the cost of both addiction and death. In the narrative, Lily Bart's susceptibility to all sorts of addictive and self-undermining behavior becomes clear early on. First of all, she can't seem to get enough tea: "Lily smiled faintly at the injunction to take her tea strong. It was the temptation she was always struggling to resist. Her craving for the keen stimulant was forever conflicting with that other craving for sleep" (306). Second, readers not only witness her total lack of restraint when playing bridge but also her flouting of feminine decorum when she visits Selden's apartment alone, which she knows will get her into social trouble: "Why must a girl pay so dearly for her least escape from routine?" she laments (14). This self-destabilizing behavior culminates in Lily's addiction to "chloral," the shortened name for chloral hydrate, often prescribed to women suffering from insomnia in the nineteenth century. By the early twentieth century, increasing concerns about various forms of addiction—from chloral hydrate to morphine to cocaine—unsurprisingly tended to cluster around women and people of color, often considered the "weak links" of Western modernity. This concern eventually culminated in the Harrison Narcotic Act of 1914, less a prohibition than a law for the orderly distribution, and taxation, of opium, morphine, heroin, and other drugs either in small quantities over the counter or in larger quantities with a physician's prescription (Hickman 2007; Zeiger, 2008). In a version of what Susan Zeiger calls "morphinomania," Lily's use of the drug is *not* legal, for she has stolen the prescription from her former employer, Mrs. Hatch, which had been "obligingly furnished by that lady's chemist" (Zeiger, 37; Wharton, 305).

In part, Lily's increasing desire for chloral continues the association between late nineteenth and early twentieth-century women and excessive consumption (of fashion, luxury, and now drugs) such that the consuming woman emerged as the figure of the compulsions and imperatives of capitalist modernity par excellence. But her drug use is also more than this. Lily's addictive condition of being stands against the equally habitual, and coercive, thought patterns of her social world. But this "resistance" to prescribed life is tentative and unintended. Just like her craving for tea *and* sleep—to be simultaneously alert and unconscious—Lily's relation to both the self and the social is profoundly ambivalent. She wants to be in the world (awake, alert, caffeinated) and to be out of it (asleep, amnesiac, stoned). Hers is a wish to be and do two things at once: to resist and conform, to pay attention and dissociate, to ensure one's place in the world and reside within the "republic of the spirit" (to borrow Selden's quaint phrase for social autonomy and personal integrity that he uses to judge Lily, but never adheres to when it comes to his own choices for living) (Wharton, 67).

Lily's conflicting impulses lead directly to the chemist on Sixth Avenue. At first, she plays the drug user's familiar game of feigned avoidance: "She had meant to take another street . . . but today her steps were irresistibly drawn toward the flaring plate glass corner" (Wharton, 304–5). The whole scene is described within the terms of a drug deal: "Over the counter she caught the eye of the clerk who had waited on her before, and slipped the prescription into his hand" (305). And she waits, fretting and anxious about the attainment of her source of pleasure: "The nervous dread of a refusal, or even of an expression of doubt, communicated itself to her restless hands as she affected to examine the bottles of perfume stacked on the glass case before her" (305). Finally, after a warning from the chemist not to overdose, she gets what she wants: "The mere touch of the packet thrilled her tired nerves with the delicious promise of a night of sleep" (305).

Lily's attachment to chloral signals her other attachment to personhood as a condition of ambivalence. She is always stuck in the middle of choices she constructs as opposing: the promise of social notoriety and financial abundance in her calculated, but never actualized, marriage to Percy Gryce on the one hand or ordinary living with Selden on the other, which also amounts to a choice between utter boredom or love. She insists on utter boredom in thought, but on love in action, and the compromise keeps her suspended between two places until she no longer has any choices left to make. Except to get high. "In the sleep which the phial procured, she . . . sank into depths of dreamless annihilation from which she woke each morning with an obliterated past" (312). Chloral hydrate wipes the slate of ambivalence clean. It kills her past, it kills her; approximate death brings complete relief. Annihilation and obliteration become her refuge and her survival. But chloral doesn't only produce an approximate death: "The drug gave her a momentary illusion of complete renewal from which she drew strength to take up her daily work" (312). Indeed, "The only hope of renewal lay in the little bottle at her bedside" (314). Lily's little nightly deaths turn into forms of morning time rebirth. She can obliterate the past by forgetting it; she can restore the self by annihilating it. This is a particular kind of fantasy about being able to live as if you had no past, a fantasy that allows for a different scene of the self, and enables Lily to temporarily avoid her predicament as a failed feminine subject of late modernity: "The little bottle was at her bedside waiting to lay its spell upon her" (341).

Perhaps Lily's new bedside companion also replaces her futile romantic relations with Selden. As Dale Bauer argues, "Drugs, not sex, take the place of [Wharton's] tragedies of alienation" (118). But Lily's relation to drug use does not only solidify or even bring about this alienation. That was happening in her social world anyway. Lily experiences narcotic dependency as a new way of relating, this time to herself, that neither her social scene nor Selden affords her. After all, her extreme attachment to chloral not only provides extreme relief, but extreme pleasure, no matter how dangerous or self-destructive we may perceive that pleasure to be. Lily and I have this in common: we used drugs not to die, but to live, or at least to live differently—in a way we fantasized as unconstrained by social norms. The target of Lily's self-love is, therefore, no longer her ego-ideal. The social norms and standards that she has, up until this point, internalized as her own no longer serve to condition her relation to self. Instead, she has overvalued a particular substance that brings with it a promise of oblivion—a refusal of self, a resistance to being. Thus she uses chloral not to forgo intimacy with Selden (that refusal belongs to him), or even, finally, to repudiate her social world (that refusal belongs to them), but to inhabit the increasingly painful incoherence of her personhood.

We can, in fact, understand Lily's drug use as a response to what she has been performing all along—her coherent self ("Why could one never do a natural thing without having to screen it behind a structure of artifice?" [14]). For her, this kind of performance is a necessary survival skill. She knows what her social scene wants and she gives it to them: whether folding invitations for Judy Trenor, keeping George Dorset occupied to all hours of the night so his wife can carry on an illicit affair, or memorizing facts about Americana and performing elegant domestic chores, like serving tea in the middle of otherwise public domains, like a train, to lure the boring Percy into a marriage contract. Look at me! I am exactly who you think I am—except when I'm not.

From Selden's derisive perspective, "her simplest acts seemed the result of far-reaching intentions" where "even her weeping was an art" (1, 74). Unwilling to admit his own complicity with the social scene that he enjoys disparaging, Selden is only partly right. Lily, quite consciously, transforms "the simplest acts" into "far-reaching intentions" because, for her, these are skills for living. Mostly, though, Selden just doesn't get it. This is because he invests too much power in the will with little understanding of the differential pressures accorded to men and women at the start of the twentieth century (a thing Selden doesn't grasp but Edith Wharton assuredly does). He speaks of his ideal of "the republic of the spirit" as if it were a tangible possibility for anyone who wills it when, in practice, he can only claim his own membership because the gender norms of his social world sanction it. The same membership is not available to a single, unmonied woman, and so Lily must perform her coherence in order to survive.

The pièce de résistance of this performance occurs when Lily poses in a tableau vivant of Sir Joshua Reynold's painting *Mrs. Lloyd*. Lily consciously displays her "flesh-and-blood loveliness" by "selecting a type so like her own that she could embody the person represented without ceasing to be herself" (141). "Her unassisted beauty" blows Selden away. "For the first time he seemed to see before him the real Lily Bart . . . that eternal harmony of which her beauty is a part" (141). Thinking of himself as some kind of radical autonomist, Selden doesn't just ooze with sentimentality, he insists on placing Lily within a sentimental script that he can then refer to as natural. Lily plays into this script as a way to showcase her own body as representative of the beautiful. As her greatest value, her beauty is what she must learn to convert into an exchangeable commodity. Assuming his own perceptive insight, Selden merely confirms the script.

Chloral alleviates the stress and exhaustion this kind of performance produces. It enables a detachment from the extraordinary burden of having to be a person in the world. "It was so seldom that she could allow herself the luxury of an impulse!" (14). And yet, this ultimately fatal form of tentative resistance only serves to shore up Lily's shattered psyche. "The next day pressed close upon her, and on its heels came the days that were to follow—they swarmed about her like a shrieking mob. She must shut them out for a few hours; she must take a brief bath of oblivion" (342). What Lily needs most of all is a state of unconsciousness, one that can act as compensation for the lack of pleasure or solace elsewhere.

I have a good friend who once asked me if I ever wished I could go into a temporary coma. Yes, I answered, yes I have. Another friend found this nonsensical—why would you want to do that? The first friend responded: because then you would not be responsible for all your failures; you're in a coma, *so it's not your fault*. And so I was only being partially honest when I claimed earlier that both Lily and I used drugs in order to live differently, to forge a more habitable condition of being. True, but not only. There is also this other pressing fear—of the future, of failing, of incapacity—that one is trying to forget, to will away, which the approximate death of intoxication feels like it might make possible. This is another kind of profound ambivalence that *The House of Mirth* traces: the relentless vacillation between self-aggrandizing thoughts and a stunning sense of worthlessness that the drug addict often experiences. Think here of Lily's sense of the "two beings" that gnaw at her psyche: "one drawing deep breaths of freedom and exhilaration, the other gasping for air in a little black prison-house of fears" (66). This core ambivalence is less a movement back and forth between two opposing affective poles than an emotional simultaneity—a dialectics of the equally pressing desires for affirmation and negation.

Foucault has famously claimed that there is no resistance without power: we could also say, no pleasure without distress. Leo Bersani's early work instructs on as much. He characterizes pleasure as an "unrepresentable psychic shattering" and explains that an "irremediable privacy of masochistic jouissance" lies at the center of our psychic lives (1986, 114). What this means is that there is always an undermining of self at work in the self because pleasure is also always an unpleasure too—what Bersani calls a "pleasurable-unpleasurable tension" (34). For Bersani this should be considered a "good thing" because it disrupts the fantasy of the solidity of being, a fantasy that tends to fund all sorts of other oppressive investments in the legible—the legibility of gender and sexuality, especially. This is where Bersani famously disagrees with Judith Butler's early arguments about gender performance. Using the example of the leather-clad gay man who emerged as a masculinist icon within 1980s and 90s queer culture, Bersani discusses how gender performativity—even of the sort that exploits gender norms by wearing them deliberately and resistantly—does not undermine but makes a cultural and sexual necessity out of fetishized ideals, in this case that of robust masculinity. Instead, we should redirect our attention to the moments when one abandons these organizing norms, where (in orgasm, say) one risks pleasure and the death of self pleasure might bring, because with that death comes the collapse of the categories of gender and sexuality that so dangerously sustain the regulatory imperatives of life. Thus Bersani: "If the rectum is the grave in which the masculine ideal of proud subjectivity is buried, then it should be celebrated for its very potential for death" (1988, 222). Bersani is talking about the function and politics of gay male desire in the age of AIDS, but the kinds of desire that one can read in the logics of addiction are inexorably tied up with the experience of shattering and intense agitation that he describes. Addiction, in this sense, may be seen as a structure of desire. But if we are "always already" in some state of agitation (perhaps some more than others), is it possible to conjure a less dangerous form of desublimation?

Theorists such as Bersani and Edelman compellingly isolate and critique the idea of life as the central category of politics, an ideology that depends on trying to exclude from the social order the negativity of the symbolic. But what happens when approximate death gets real? I was lucky. I found a way to survive addiction. Wharton does not grant Lily the same fate. Her psychic shattering becomes literalized in a well-known deathbed scene. Perhaps this is because death, as both an allegory and a form of narrative closure, is the only means to make psychic shattering representable in the realist novel of manners. The critical question as to whether Lily commits suicide, in this context, seems moot because, on the one hand, she was already dead (in the sense of the emotional toll her social exile takes) and, on the other, she kills herself every time she takes a dose.[11] On this particular night, "she had long since raised the dose to its highest limit, but tonight she felt she must increase it. She knew she took a risk in doing so; she remembered the chemist's warning. If sleep came at all, it might be sleep without waking" (Wharton, 342). Lily enters a space of no longer caring, of emotional dislocation: "The physical craving for sleep was her only sustained sensation" (342). When the chain of signifiers that make up the ideal of personal and social coherence to which she clutches begin to unravel, when the idea of ever living comfortably within the social fold is revealed as an impossible fantasy, Lily becomes decaptivated from and by the world objects to which she has formerly been bound. Only more intensified states of sensation are left to remind her she still exists: "She lay very still, waiting with sensuous pleasure of the first effects of the soporific" (343). And yet intensity yields a kind of erasure, of compounded already deadness that relocates Lily within the space of fragmentation that she can now experience as willed rather than imposed:

> She knew in advance what form [the drops] would take—the gradual cessation of the inner throb, the soft approach of passiveness, the very slowness and hesitancy of the effect increased its fascination; it was delicious to lean over and look down into the dim abysses of unconsciousness. Gradually the sense of complete subjugation came over her, . . . she yielded to it, sank into it, and slept. (343)

Plunged into the irreversible space of drugged-out slow time, Lily inhabits being-for-death as her final jouissance. "The sense of complete subjugation," the "soft approach of passiveness," and the "delicious abyss" of unconsciousness that chloral produces make the desire, pleasure, and, perhaps, Bersani's "irremediable masochism" involved clear, but it is also a very difficult way to think of feminine subjectivity. The description of Lily's bliss of intoxication smacks of all those things we, as feminists, want Lily to be able to react against: the social dictum to be nothing but passive, the idea of an external power to which we must yield as if devoid of agency, the mandate that to do so may be, finally, the only way to feel better. But submission in this scene is not to her social class and their norms of sexuality and femininity but to everything chloral allows Lily to achieve: rest, for one thing, but also the capacity to step outside the bounds of her incapacity. In Lily's annihilation of selfhood, she negates not the self but the social stranglehold on subjectivity that has left her in a condition of near-total impoverishment.

Just before overdosing, Lily signs her name on a check to Gus Trenor, to whom she owes a great deal of money in exchange for which Trenor tries to extract sexual favors. Lily settles her debts, balances her accounts, and, when these final acts of literal self-assertion are complete, escapes from language entirely. By signing the last of her money away with her name on a check, Lily drives herself out of the world. But just prior to, and as a component part of, this escape, she grasps at "some word she had found that should make life clear" between her and Selden, a word that "lingered vague and luminous on the far edge of thought" (Wharton, 343). In a moment of narrative simultaneity, Selden thinks the same thought as he travels to Lily's home the morning of her death: "He had found the word he meant to say to her" (344). He is, of course, too late to share this word with either Lily or the reader (Lily dies before she has a chance to vocalize hers), but we are nonetheless informed that, as Selden kneels beside Lily's dead body, "there passed between them the word which made all clear" (350).

What might this word be? When I teach this text to undergraduates, they want the word to be "love," as if that utterance holds the promise of redemptive closure, a happy ending in the face of the unresolvable narrative predicament death signifies. But Wharton's refusal to narrate the word on which such potential closure hinges brings to a point the narrative's point about ambivalence. On the one hand, this final union of Selden and Lily signals an intersubjective consciousness in which, at the same moment in time, the same word appears to them as a shared one. On the other hand, the clarity the word is said to provide never materializes linguistically; it remains as "vague and luminous on the far edge of thought" as Lily's initial vision of it.[12] Wharton does not lament this lack of manifestation as much as she uses it to underscore the relationship between the desire to articulate the self and to erase it completely.

Just prior to Lily's final night, she considers a visit to Selden in which she will confess everything to him in the hope that such an act of confidence will bring them closer together. Lily's elation over this idea increases rapidly until "the thought of confiding in him became as seductive as the river's flow to the suicide" (183). Putting the self *into* language becomes the same thing as taking the self *out* of it. The evanescence of this (not actually) shared word signals that Lily, in her death, may have accomplished something. For to die, ultimately, is the only way Lily can stop being a text, and thus a projection of Selden's fantasy of feminine perfection. Lily's separation from utterable language consummates what her addiction began: a withdrawal from the perils of meaning and being.

The House of Mirth is an important case study about how the objects in which we invest our psychic energy can also destabilize us. Freud might say that these strategies of cathection increase the displeasure they are intended to circumvent. Lauren Berlant puts it this way: "Your desire misrecognizes a given object as that which will restore you to something that you sense effectively as a hole in you" (2012, 76). What this means is that we are willing to do things over which we have only partial, and maybe no, control, and thus it also speaks to the inadequacy of the existing frames that tend to structure analysis of addiction.

Take, for example, *Intervention*. In 2006, A&E began airing this wildly popular reality television series about addicted individuals and their families who try to help them. This is where I met Audrey, a self-identified heroin addict who describes her addiction as a "slow suicide," where every time she uses she thinks, "I might die this time, but I don't know if I really care." *Intervention* regularly features extreme cases of addiction, where viewers encounter people like Audrey and learn about their childhoods, situations of trauma, exhaustion, and need. Every episode culminates with a group confrontation by family and friends, orchestrated by a professional counselor, who ends the session with the question: "Will you accept this gift of rehabilitation today?" Although *Intervention* ostensibly attempts to normalize addiction for lay audiences and to promote recovery efforts, it ultimately frames suffering as something that takes place elsewhere: in a cordoned-off space with an exceptional individual (Biressi and Nunn; Oulette and Murray; McCarthy).[13]

In Audrey's episode, we watch as she injects heroin into her arm in a friend's bathroom. Afterward, she moves slowly over to the mirror above the sink, alternating between nodding off and looking at her reflection. She moves closer and closer toward the mirror until she and her reflection become one, literally kissing one another. This is a Lacanian moment if there ever was one, and yet, instead of peering into the mirror and discovering there her ego ideal, Audrey instead melds with the image of her narcotic dissolution. She looks up to the camera and murmurs, "I wish I had the words to explain the feeling that I have . . . the satisfaction." Audrey's stumbling reverie is hard to watch, but it does provide an important glimpse into desire's aggressivity, and perhaps even our shared condition of psychic disturbance that variously and unpredictably produces becomings and unbecomings. Heroin use guarantees her suffering and, simultaneously, allows her to experience a form of pleasure that she links, in her actions, to physical and emotional abandonment. Lacan might describe this as a salient example of the pleasure/displeasure complex that comprises desire: "The outer extremity of pleasure is unbearable to us" (1992, 80). Audrey's feeling of satisfaction, then, is not reducible to satisfaction. It illuminates an entire complex of pleasure, disturbance, and the conflicts of desire—our simultaneous desire to live and die, to be whole and undone, to be in and out of control.

What this means (or what it meant for me) is that when you make the decision to stop using a particular drug, you not only have to live the rest of your life without the object to which you have turned for your greatest relief, release, and pleasure, you also have to live your life as if this fundamental aspect of your personhood—this being-for-death that has operated as your primary drive for so long—were not there. But dismissing, or bracketing, this aspect of psychic and social behavior means ignoring what has made you feel like a person. Even more than that, it means disavowing the impossible situation of the desiring subject. If we have come to accept that we are not rational, self-present, indissoluble agents in full control of ourselves (and I am not at all optimistic that we have, such is the strength of the reigning model of possessive individualism), then perhaps what we can learn from what Wharton calls "broken life" is that the desire to inhabit the alterity of subjectivity, and the pleasure of doing so, may be a compulsive, habitual desire without a cure (183).

~

Me, Lily, and Audrey: three women, three narrative forms. Whether autobiography / memoir, literary realism, or reality television, each genre has as its aim the production of a truth effect. One way to read each would be to say that these are formal strategies that serve to define addiction as a practice of suffering and, therefore, to place addictive behavior in a sentimentalizing frame, a frame that simultaneously upholds the addict's predicament as the space of the tragic real. But what we also witness in these stories are quests for joy in which the unprocessed and uncontainable field of emotion that comprises and exceeds the self is intensified in an unending cycle of reprieve and reprise. These are narratives that suggest the propinquity of life and death. None of them should be taken at face value, but taken together they instruct us on how the capacity for violence against the self stands in confused relation to desperate efforts to feel more intensely and to not feel anything at all, and that this capacity might not be present elsewhere, but everywhere present.

I have deliberately intermingled these narrative forms and genres because doing so has allowed me to demonstrate an at-least-century's-long obsession with addiction as a site of intractable meaning and expression. At stake, though, is not simply recording the addiction narrative's long history in the United States. In the end, my "real" lived experience stands in solidarity with Lily Bart's, as well as with the users on *Intervention,* because what we have in common—what links us across time and narrative—is an unyielding desire for anxiety-free environments in which intoxication's promise of capaciousness makes sense of our sense of not-belonging, is at least one way a community of alienation might forge itself. But does accepting as constitutive the wish of becoming undone—and its attendant pleasures of alleviation and promises of a less-lived life—mean acquiescing, more than figuratively and allegorically, to our being-toward-death? Have I written myself into a corner in which less agonistic relations to self and world are unimaginable? I hope not. In James Baldwin's "Sonny's Blues," the narrator says to his heroin-addicted brother in one of the story's many poignant insights into the burden of living: "I don't want to see you die trying not to suffer" (87). But the inverse may also be apropos: Lily, Audrey, and I spent a lot of time suffering so as not to die.

Dana Seitler is associate professor of English at the University of Toronto. She is the author of *Atavistic Tendencies: The Culture of Science in American Modernity* (2008). She just completed her second book, *Lateral Aesthetics: Gender, Sexuality, and the Queer Politics of Art in Modern American Fiction* (forthcoming). Her current project, *I'm Dying To!: Essays on Self-Destruction*, focuses on the aesthetics of refusal and renunciation in suicide plots and addiction narratives in American fiction.

Notes

1. Sedgwick's desire to shift to the language of habit from the more pathologizing term "addiction" has a lot to do with the metaphors of health and hygiene that stand as addiction's opposite. "Getting clean," the vernacular phrase for withdrawing from a drug dependency, intends literally to describe the cleansing of the body of a toxin, but also figures forth a constitutive association between addiction and contamination.

2. In this sense, my addiction more precisely follows the narratives of self-control usually attributed to bulimia and other eating disorders. See Berlant 2011, 95, in which she names the temporality of obesity "slow death."

3. If we, according to Lacan, can never achieve the nonobject of desire (desire for "nothing to be named"), our drive to do so is what may bring us in relation—both to our imagined selves and to all of its compensatory substitutes: our selves-in-others (1978, 261).

4. *Christiane F.* was first a book, published in Germany in 1979 under the title *We Children of Bahnhof Zoo*, and then, in 1981, a film, both of which document the musician and actress Vera Christiane Felscherinow's struggle with heroin addiction in West Berlin in the 1970's. "Interior Scroll" was an art performance in which Carolee Schneemann stood naked on a table, painted her body with mud, and slowly extracted a paper scroll from her vagina while reading from it. The first Burroughs I read was not *Naked Lunch* or *Junky*, but the *Cities of the Red Night* trilogy (1981–87), and I would walk around campus citing passages from it I knew by heart.

5. In Seminar III, Lacan emphasizes the significance of the analysand's account of her delusion, for the delusion is a form of discourse and a part of the process of idealization, what he describes as "a field of signification that has organized a certain signifier" (1997, 121). Freud, in his work on Schreber, puts it this way: "What we take to be the pathological production, the delusional formation, is in reality the attempt at recovery, the reconstruction" (2003, 71).

6. Of course, context also matters. My addiction is what gets referred to in Facebook parlance as a "First World problem" (i.e., a white, middle-class narrative of suffering that could never compare to more coercive, less "voluntaristic" conditions of suffering).

7. Drug addiction and recovery memoirs are a veritable industry, producing a host of best sellers and consolidating a genre that always promises to share an "unflinching look" into a "harrowing experience" shared by individuals "who looked into the abyss" but are eventually able "to step back from the edge and reclaim life," to collect a few book jacket descriptions. See Clegg; Carr; Karr; King; Weaver; Marlowe.

8. In many ways, Kopelson's argument squares with Sara Ahmed's feminist project on willful subjects, where she argues, "To be willing to cause unhappiness can also be how we immerse ourselves in collective struggle, as we work with and through others who share our points of alienation. Those who are unseated by the tables of happiness can find each other" (8).

9. José Esteban Muñoz has called this the "crypto-universalism" of both psychoanalysis and some affect (676).

10. There is a much longer literary and cinematic history of addiction narratives than I could possibly account for here, one that stretches from Thomas De Quincey's *Confessions of an English Opium Eater* (1821) and Edgar Allan Poe's "The Black Cat" (1843) to William S. Burrough's *Junky* (1953), Lisa Cholodenko's *High Art* (1998), Steven Soderbergh's *Traffic* (2000) and beyond. Especially pertinent for me is Jean Rhys's *Good Morning, Midnight* (1939) and her alcoholic narrator: "I have been here five days. I have decided on a place to eat in at midday, a place to eat in at night, a place to have my drink in after dinner. I have arranged my little life" (9).

11. I owe this insight to two sources: Eric Cazdyn (2012), who discusses how various minoritized and problem subjects are "already dead"—that is, in a state of suspension in which they have been killed by the inequalities of global capitalism but are yet to actually die—and a conversation at the 2013 MLA Convention with Lauren Berlant who responded to my desire to explain Lily's suicide as an attempt to deimplicate herself from the binding language of the social by saying: "But isn't she already dead?" For a discussion about whether Lily commits suicide, see Wharton's letter to a doctor friend, where she writes: "A friend of mine has made up her mind to commit suicide & has asked me to find out . . . the most painless & least unpleasant method of effacing herself." On the second page of the letter, Wharton reveals that her "friend" is in fact a fictional character appearing in the pages of Scribner's, and explains, "I have a heroine to get rid of, and want

some points on the best way of disposing of her." Later she asks: "What soporific, or nerve-calming drug, would a nervous and worried young lady in the smart set be likely to take to, & what would be its effects if deliberately taken with the intent to kill herself? I mean, how would she feel and look toward the end?" (McGrath).

12. Perhaps for this reason, Gavin Jones reads Lily's last narcotic reverie as the moment when she "finally loses the ability to represent herself" (100).

13. McCarthy explores reality television as an object through which to assess the biopolitical rationalities of neoliberalism and, in particular, "the ways trauma works in the service of self-governing, as part of neoliberalism's outsourcing of state functions into the private realm" (21).

Works Cited

Ahmed, Sara. 2010. "Feminist Killjoys (And Other Willful Subjects)." *Polyphonic Feminisms: Acting in Concert*, 8, no. 3 (Summer): 1–8.

Baldwin, James. 1995. *Sonny's Blues.* New York: Penguin.

Bauer, Dale M. 2003. "Wharton's 'Others': Addiction and Intimacy." In *A Historical Guide to Edith Wharton*. Ed. Carol J. Singley, 115–45. Oxford: Oxford University Press.

Berlant, Lauren. 2011. *Cruel Optimism*. Durham: Duke University Press.

Berlant, Lauren. 2012. *Desire/Love*. New York: Punctum Books.

Bersani, Leo. 1986. *The Freudian Body: Psychoanalysis and Art*. New York: Columbia University Press.

Bersani, Leo. 1988. "Is the Rectum a Grave?" In *AIDS: Cultural Analysis/Cultural Activism*. Ed. Douglas Crimp, 197–222 . Boston: MIT Press.

Biressi, Anita, and Heather Nunn. 2005. *Reality TV: Realism and Revelation*. New York: Columbia University Press.

Bordo, Susan. 2003. *Unbearable Weight: Feminism, Western Culture, and the Body*. Berkeley: University of California Press.

Carr, David. 2009. *The Night of the Gun*. New York: Simon and Schuster.

Cazdyn, Eric. 2012. *The Already Dead: The New Time of Politics, Culture, and Illness*. Durham: Duke University Press.

Clegg, Bill. 2012. *Ninety Days: A Memoir of Recovery*. New York: Little, Brown.

Edelman, Lee. 2004. *No Future: Queer Theory and the Death Drive*. Durham: Duke University Press.

Foucault, Michel. 1990. *The History of Sexuality, Volume I: An Introduction*. New York: Vintage.

Freud, Sigmund. 1961. *Beyond the Pleasure Principle*. New York: Norton.

Freud, Sigmund. 2003. *The Schreber Case*. Trans. Andrew Weber. New York: Penguin.

Hickman, Timothy Alton. 2007. *The Secret Leprosy of Modern Days: Narcotic Addiction and Cultural Crisis in the United States, 1870–1920*. Amherst: University of Massachusetts Press.

Hollan, Merlin, and Rupert Hart-Davis, eds. 2000. *The Complete Letters of Oscar Wilde*. London: Henry Holt.

Jones, Gavin. 2009. *American Hungers: The Problem of Poverty in U.S. Literature, 1840–1945*. New Jersey: Princeton University Press.

Karr, Mary. 2009. *Lit: A Memoir*. New York: HarperCollins.

King, Heather. 2006. *Parched*. New York: Signet.

Kopelson, Karen. 2006. "Radical Indulgence: Excess, Addiction, and Female Desire." *Postmodern Culture* 17, no. 1 (September): n.p.

Lacan, Jacques. 1975. *The Seminar of Jacques Lacan, Book I*. Ed. Jacques-Alain Miller. Trans. John Forrester. New York: Norton.

Lacan, Jacques. 1977. "The Function and Field of Speech and Language in Psychoanalysis." In *Écrits: A Selection*. Trans. Alan Sheridan. London: Tavistock.

Lacan, Jacques. 1978. *The Seminar of Jacques Lacan, Book II: The Ego in Freud's Theory and in the Technique of Psychoanalysis*. Ed. Jacques-Alain Miller. Trans. John Forrester. New York: Norton.

Lacan, Jacques. 1992. *The Seminar of Jacques Lacan, Book VII: The Ethics of Psychoanalysis*. Trans. Dennis Porter. New York: Norton.

Lacan, Jacques. 1997. *The Seminar of Jacques Lacan, Book III: The Psychoses*. Ed. Jacques-Alain Miller. Trans. Russell Grigg. New York: Norton.

Marlowe, Ann. 2000. *How to Stop Time: Heroin from A to Z*. New York: Anchor.

McCarthy, Anna. 2007. "Reality Television: A Neoliberal Theater of Suffering." *Social Text* 25, no. 4 (Winter): 17–42.

McGrath, Charles. 2007. "Wharton Letter Reopens a Mystery." *New York Times*, November 21.

Muñoz, José Esteban. 2006. "Feeling Brown, Feeling Down: Latina Affect, the Performativity of Race, and the Depressive Position." *Signs* 31, no. 3 (Spring): 675–88.

Oulette, Laurie, and Susan Murray, eds. 2004. *Reality TV: Remaking TV Culture*. New York: New York University Press.

Sedgwick, Eve Kosofsky. 1994. "Epidemics of the Will." In *Tendencies*, 130–42. New York: Routledge.

Silverman, Kaja. 1996. *The Threshold of the Visible World*. New York: Routledge.

Weaver, Allison. 2008. *Gone to the Crazies*. New York: Harper Perennial.

Wharton, Edith. 2000. *The House of Mirth*. New York: Signet.

Wilde, Oscar. 2007. *The Picture of Dorian Gray*. New York: Norton.

Zeiger, Susan. 2008. *Inventing the Addict: Drugs, Race, and Sexuality in Nineteenth-Century British and American Literature*. Amherst: University of Massachusetts Press.

RELIGIOUS STUDIES' MISHANDLING OF ORIGIN AND CHANGE

TIME, TRADITION, AND FORM OF LIFE IN BUDDHISM

Ananda Abeysekara

Most of religious life works quite well without "critique" because most of life does.

—*Talal Asad,* interview in the *Bulletin for the Study of Religion*

Every use is first of all use of self: to enter into a relation of use with something, I must be affected by it . . . ; in the using of something, it is the very being of the one using that is first of all at stake.

—*Giorgio Agamben,* The Use of Bodies

The modern (postcolonial-minded) narrative of religion is a critique of the problem of time, in that it "separates" *(krinein)* origin *(arche)* from change. Central to this narrative is the idea that religion or religious life, as something that belongs to history, changes. Change is assumed to be history's "force of movement." It is often difficult for a modern scholar to narrate the story of religion without the paradigmatic notion of change.

But is this critical narrative of religion as self-evident as is often assumed? I think not. The idea of history-time that guides this narrative is based on a "decision." Decision in this narrative effects an "incision" (i.e., cutting into) or "excision" (i.e., cutting out) of the origin of religion's time from its change. Thus, a closer look at this narrative reveals an unquestioned relation between decision and critique.[1] Decision simply becomes "critique." That is, decision-critique—from the Greek heritage of the word *krino*—seeks merely to "separate" the problem of origin from change, a problem that haunts our secular politics and temporality.[2] This "decisive critique" turns out be a kind of "decisionism" that is caught up in the paradox of deciding that which cannot be decided. In such decisionism, it becomes difficult to think the inseparability between life and its "form." This necessarily prevents us from thinking about tradition itself in other ways than the distinction between origin and change.[3]

In this essay, I try to think how this critique of time works in very different postcolonial-minded texts on religion, particularly those by scholars of Buddhism such as Anne Blackburn, Steven Collins, Donald Lopez, and Richard Gombrich.[4] These texts, which are informed by different theoretical-political orientations, present contrasting conceptualizations of time and life in modern and premodern Buddhism. Nonetheless the texts produce a common problem of temporality by way of seeking to separate the point of origin from successive changes of religious life within history. The problem we find in this narrative is not restricted to the area of Buddhist studies or religion. The problem remains in how we understand history-time as a particular secular object of study and critique. Thus the examples of texts (in terms of essentialist and antiessentialist critics of history) discussed here help us understand the problem of the secular practice of critique and the assumptions that such practice takes for granted about history, tradition, religion, and life itself. To that extent, my interest is not in what critique is, but how critique *works* in the secular practice of time and life.[5]

This general problem can be found in the way the modern narrative of religious life, as something that exists and changes in history, is assumed to be governed by critique. For the antiessentialist critic, the division between origin and change is crucial to determining how religion or religious life changes in history. For the self-proclaimed essentialist, the nemesis of the antiessentialist, the same separation of origin from change is crucial to defending the very idea of "origin." My argument is that the antiessentialist critique of origin cannot undermine the essentialist's argument for origin, because both are informed by the same critical decision of time and life that takes the separation between origin and change to be empirically axiomatic.[6]

My aim here is only to ask questions about the aporetic difficulties that the modern critique runs into in deciding on the question of religious life and time in the above way. The aporia of the modern critical narrative of religion helps us ponder a not-often-posed question about why "most of religious life works quite well without 'critique' because most of life does" (Asad 2014a). The question that becomes possible then is how we may think about such life inseparable from its "form"[7] without the modern decisive critique of time. The form of life, as we will note, is difficult to think without the idea of a discursive-embodied tradition, which does not figure into the historical narratives of religion.

CRITIQUE, DECISION, AND INDISTINCTION OF "FORM OF LIFE" IN RELIGIOUS TRADITION

The distinguished political philosopher Giorgio Agamben argues in a fascinating work titled *The Highest Poverty: Monastic Rules and Form-of-Life* that modernity cannot grasp the inseparability of the "form of life." In examining a body of "peculiar literature" on monastic rules that emerged in the fourth and fifth centuries of the Christian era, Agamben argues that the "life" and "rule" that bound monastic communal living and practice question "the very substance of the rule as a norm separate from life. . . . The form of the law is the monk's very form of life. . . . Through the concept of form, rule *(forma regulae)* and life *(forma vivendi)* enter into a threshold of indistinction in the monk's practice" (60). It is this "indistinction," its "absolute undecidability," Agamben argues, that "modernity has shown itself to be incapable of facing and that our time does not seem to be at all in a position to think" (60, 145). The "form of life" was never available for "appropriation" as a "property" but only for "common use." That question of the form of life involved in part the Franciscan labor to separate the idea of lawful ownership of property from its de facto use, the use of goods from any right to them.[8] So Agamben asks, "What ontology and which ethics would correspond to a life that, in use, is constituted as inseparable from its form" (145)?[9] "Our time" cannot grasp the indistinction that constitutes this form of life because it already grants the separability between "human action and norm, 'life' and 'rule,' without which the political and ethical-juridical rationality of modernity is unthinkable" (4).

Talal Asad (1993) has intervened to consider a similar question about the form of shared life in his examination of the grammar of the disciplinary practices in the medieval Christian and the modern Islamic worlds.[10] There is something that often goes unnoticed in

Asad's otherwise well-known work. It may appear at first glance that Asad's is a mere "genealogy" of religious practice, but it is hardly a historical narrative of how religious practice and life "change" in particular times and places. Asad seeks to think the question of the form of life against the modern narrative of religion in a specific sense. Asad examines how the form of (shared) religious life constituted by the grammar of the practice of distinctive abilities, dispositions, and virtues (passions) *necessarily* depended on the resources of an organized community with a specific "program," within the "coherence" of a discursive-embodied tradition.[11] The coherence of tradition was sustained by particular "limitations," themselves made possible by bitter arguments and disputes within obligatory relationships of power, which render such a tradition authoritative and effective.[12] The relation between the form of life and tradition is not available for apprehension via the modern concept of temporality. It is a mistake to understand the discursive arguments about what concepts and practices constitute the authorized form of life as a mere alteration or preservation of an already-existing, self-evident orthodoxy within the genealogy of a tradition.[13] Part of Asad's concern is with how the disciplinary practices of virtue, which cannot be "so easily varied" in a tradition (79),[14] are "transformed" into symbols of "readable text" in modernity, with the early- and late-modern notions of "prudence" and "change" taking precedence over the concepts of discipline and tradition.

Asad sees the modern transformation and representation of the form of disciplined life into symbols linked in particular to the notion of "critique"—from Kant's critique to anthropological and literary practices of criticism (e.g., the Rushdie Affair). Such critique tends to regard the form of religious life—haunted by the modern questions of the "inner" self-detachable from the "outer" life that needs representation[15]—as something to be shaped by doubt, questioning, and criticism. Part of the legacy of this critique belongs to "an Enlightenment prejudice that counterposes 'tradition' to 'change' and 'reason,'" religious life to "regular" life. But Asad contends, "Let us be clear . . . on the matter of criticism: *no regular life* . . . can be practiced if it is continually subjected to 'doubt,' questioning, and even confusion" (264–65). "Life is essentially itself. Only the part of it that can be narrativized may be said be 'made up' like a story by an artist" (290). My point is that the modern narrative of religion based on decision-critique is heir to the division between something we understand as "regular life" and religious life—that is, the division between "life" and its "form."[16]

Today humanities scholars would hardly want to be associated with the legacy of the Enlightenment prejudice that religion or tradition is opposed to change. Indeed, essentialism has become a bad word in the humanities. But much of the critical narrative of religion—be it an explicit rebuttal of the Enlightenment prejudice or not—that tries to locate change in the history of religious life creates different theoretical problems, making it difficult to consider the question of the form of life. This is because that narrative of change, based as it is on separating origin from change, relies on a critical decision about what constitutes time ("force") vis-à-vis religious life. This modern decision of time obscures how the form of life works in a discursive tradition.

CRITICAL DECISION OF FORCE ("MOVEMENT") IN RELIGION AND TIME

We can find in play such a critical decision of time in the interesting work *Locations of Buddhism: Colonialism and Modernity in Sri Lanka* by the historian of Buddhism Anne Blackburn (2010).[17] Positioned as a critique of "generations of postcolonial and anticolonial scholarship," the text claims to consider anew the problem of the relation between religious life and change ("force," or "movement").[18] It claims to take "a new approach to colonial history" in order to rethink Buddhist life and practice in nineteenth-century colonial Sri Lanka. This approach, it is said, refutes the "attractive simplicity of arguments for an unprecedented 'sea change' in Buddhist practice during the British colonial period" (200). At the outset, then, this seemingly new approach to history is billed as an attempt to decenter the very idea of (colonial) change through which the relation between religious life and modernity has supposedly been told.

To do so, the text makes a decisive distinction between the "force, and the limits, of colonial power" and "local human agency," marked by "deep historical roots" of the "social logic and intellectual creativity of Buddhist life" (xiv, 211). The text calls our attention to the "force . . . of colonial power" only to underscore the "limits" of that force in "remaking local lives" (xiv).[19] The force of colonial power was limited so as not to create a "sea change" in the local agency of Buddhism with "deep historical roots," which, by definition, cannot be easily uprooted or moved. So the nineteenth-century Buddhist monastic world of monks (like Hikkaduve Sumangala) is said to have maintained "elements of deep historical roots" with the precolonial Buddhist past, independent and free of the force of colonial power (143, 200).

But this distinction between colonial power and local freedom is injudicious at best, as it takes colonial "power" (as "force") to be something negative. Colonial power is negative because, as we shall see, it is assumed to be governed by obvious "limits." On the basis of this negative notion of power as force opposed to freedom, the text repeatedly calls attention to the importance of recovering the (widely criticized) idea of "human agency."[20] The text's story hangs entirely on making explicit the presumed distinction between the force of colonial power ("sea change") and the historical roots of religious life (local agency). So force equals change, and roots equal "locations" of local agency (hence, *Locations of Buddhism* as the title of Blackburn's book).

But how clear or tenable is the distinction between the force of colonial power (change) and the deep historical roots of local life (agency and freedom)? The text takes power and freedom to be axiomatically opposed.[21] Here I am not interested in criticizing this notion of agency except to note that the appeal to it depends in part on the failure to think of power as "capability" that is not the embodiment of some internal potentiality already opposed to external coercion. Power as capability to do things in a particular way, to connect to the "truth of it," depends on how one *encounters* authority within a living relationship, where one "lives in a compelling truth, inhabits a relationship with someone who is at once internal and external."[22] What I want to note is that in order to recover local agency in opposition to the external force of colonial power, the text must decisively determine the question of the effect (i.e., change) of colonial modernity on local life (xi, 210). Here the logic of the argument runs into numerous theoretical problems. This is because the text has to determine not just the effect of colonial modernity on religious life but "degrees" of that effect (change) as well.

> If we are to understand the degree to which and the ways in which British colonialism influenced Lanka and wider South Asia, we need to look closely at the habits of thought and modes of affiliation that characterized

> particular persons and smaller-scale social groups during this period. This is really the problem of trying to understand the local social logic and intellectual creativity of the lives fashioned in the context of colonialism. Colonized people were affected by imported ideas and social forms in different ways, and to very different degrees, depending on their circumstances and inclinations. (xiv)

Note what is being said here: To determine colonialism and its effect (change) is to determine the relation between cause and effect. It is through this determination that the "limits" of colonial power are discerned. This is why Blackburn, like many other scholars, claims that colonialism did not "wholly" affect local practices (215). But this task is nearly impossible. To discern the limits of colonial power, one must discern the limits of the extent of colonial modernity. But the determination of the limits of colonialism is hardly possible because, as much literature has demonstrated, colonialism's reach never remained within merely visible limits. Its effects could never be understood as those that merely remained within identifiable boundaries. Yet the text treats arbitrarily the effects of colonialism's limits as if they were self-evident—hence the claim that "colonized people were affected by imported ideas and social forms in different ways, and to very different degrees, depending on their circumstances and inclinations." To claim that colonized life in local history was "affected by imported ideas . . . to very different degrees" is to assert the empirical availability of that effect on life. This, along with the claim that colonialism did not completely "determine" or displace the local practices, creates such a broad, indiscriminate standard for what constitutes a colonial effect on subjectivity (196).

Strangely, the determination of this effect depends on delimiting the relation between not just "circumstances" but also "inclinations" of colonized agents. The circumstances of colonial modernity (force) are contrasted with inclinations of local agency (freedom).[23] Again, colonialism simply becomes a readily apparent power of which colonized people can be independent because of individual "inclinations"—hence the claim that monks "retained a degree of independence in the face of French and British imperial designs on Southern Asia" (143). Confounding the distinction, the text tells us that to determine this relation between cause and effect in colonial modernity is to "discern [note the decisive sense of that word] the human choices, and the play of intellect and sentiment, that characterized one way of being Buddhist" (xv).

To decide the effect of colonial modernity by contrasting the force of its power to "human choices," inclination, intellect, or sentiment is simply not feasible.[24] After all, colonial modernity—if it is to be understood as a circumstance—is not something in which human beings can make mere "choices" as one can make choices in a circumstance whose effect or extent can be fathomed. Surely Blackburn is not suggesting that we understand the circumstances of colonialism as if they were the circumstances of rainfall, with a particular extent, in terms of a measurable area of coverage and level of saturation that can cause one to make choices in terms of inclination or sentiment. After all, the relation between colonial modernity and its effect on choices and inclinations of human beings is not the same as a description of the following sort of circumstance and its effect: "It rained to such an extent or degree yesterday that it discouraged one from going outside and prevented air travel." My point here is that one cannot decide on the distinction between the force of colonial power (change) and local life (agency) that the text does without such an impossible logic.

Yet the distinction between the force of colonial power and local agency is meant to offer a new concept of religious change, critiquing the old historical designations of time and change (e.g., "traditional" versus "modernist").

> Given the deep historical roots of many of the models and idioms on which [the monk] Hikkaduve relied in the course of his long career, some will be tempted to say that he represents "traditional" Lankan Buddhism in the face of Lanka's rapid modernization under British rule. We should, however, attempt to avoid this error. Quite apart from the fact that the long, *internally dynamic*,[25] contentious history of Lankan Buddhism in the precolonial period makes the isolation of a single set of forms as "traditional" a matter of present-day intellectual preference rather than accurate historical representation, it is perhaps useful to recognize that the word "traditional" is essentially an empty term. It is filled only as the antithesis of whatever is specified as "modern" or "modernist." (211, emphasis added)

These local "models" and "idioms" of religious practice, even if models can be ascribed to datable historical sources, do not lend themselves to being readily apparent empirical examples of a new concept of time—"deep" history—that constitutes an alternative to the old narrative of change. After all, can one determine the extent of something called deep history? That is, can one determine history's depth in terms of a span, even if one thinks of history in the sense of days, weeks, months, years, or centuries? More precisely, how much depth would, say, five centuries constitute as opposed to two or three centuries, and can this depth be determined? My point is that this decisive determination of time (i.e., what constitutes change in religious life) that is supposedly based on empirical evidence becomes possible only by the self-evident opposition between power (force) and the local life (agency).

I have tried to suggest above that the text claims to think anew about the relation between local religious life and change in colonial modernity, but it does not satisfy that claim. The text's attempt to decenter the idea of (colonial) change in the configuration of local life is a product of a decision about what is and is not "force"—a decision based on an a priori notion of local life (the idea of some internal dynamics of agency opposed to external force). A double irony: As this critique claims to separate colonial force from local life and time, it imposes a secular notion of agency on such life, and it does so through decision itself—the very notion of external "force" it wants to separate from the presumed internality of local life and time. Here the scholar's sheer decision to separate the colonial force from local life is assumed to be a critique that already inheres within the interiority of religious life itself. We shall soon ask if this decision-critique, which is meant to be a critique of the old problem of origin and change—a critique we find in other works—can be the kind of "political" criticism that it claims to be.[26] This critique ultimately situates the idea of tradition within the logic of temporality that animates the distinction between origin and change.

DECISION BECOMES CRITIQUE: MODERN CRITIQUE OF THE COLONIAL "MODERNITY" OF TRADITION AND TEMPORALITY

Let me discuss how this decision of time, the sovereignty of its empirical certainty, ironically decides what cannot be ultimately decided. The problem of this decision remains at work in the constant attempt to criticize the problem of origin and change in the study of religion. Such critique attempts to think of religion as something that neither remains static ("original Buddhism") nor remains subject to just any change (force of modernity). This critique is in turn assumed to have a specific political purchase, for it quickly disavows—as critics often do today—the "truth" or "essence" of religious identity in history.

Such a critique of time animates an impressive work that some would hardly consider postcolonial at first glance: Steven Collins's *Nirvana and Other Buddhist Felicities*. With a call at the outset for a "need to historicize" religious life and practice (xiii), Collins's text seeks to put aside Weberian claims about the separability of religion from politics—that is, the separation of religion from history.[27] Such separation, we are told, "inevitably leads to a divorce between 'original' or 'true' Buddhism and the vicissitudes of human nature and social life" (56, 417).

> Much of this debate seemed to assume that the issue is to find out the truth about "original Buddhism," "what the Buddha taught" (and hence, often enough, what Buddhism "teaches," essentially and ahistorically). This is a quest I have explicitly disavowed. From the perspective of this book, in which the Pali imaginaire constitutes an aspect of Buddhist ideology in the civilizational history of Southern Asia, the articulation of order to be found in Pali texts is necessarily both cosmological/soteriological and social.[28] But looking at the matter this way does not mean that all one has to do is search, empirically, for views of society and politics in Pali texts and then assemble them in some coherently organized form. This would be, again, to treat the texts, or (as is often the case) passages within them conceived separately as "proof-texts," simply in a documentary fashion and to forget that texts also have work-like aspects, which supplement material realities imaginatively in a critical or reflective, sometimes deliberately inconclusive and open-ended, way. Irony, *inter alia*, escapes the essentialist. (417–18)

Things become more complicated for this nonessentialist critique of time as it has to cautiously navigate the question of time's origin versus change. Collins claims to disavow any quest for the time of an "original" Buddhist identity.[29] Still, he identifies something called "traditional Buddhism" that, from the third century BC onward, "remained, for the most part, a stable ideological *force* until colonialism and modernity began to introduce irrevocable changes into the Buddhist culture in the nineteenth century" (57–58, emphasis added). Colonial modernity is seen here as an external counterforce of change against the internal force and stability of local life. Despite such inevitable modern vicissitudes, we are told, with a curious bracketing, "in the day-to-day lives of [Thai] peasants away from cities (especially Bangkok, a place where *modernity is all too clearly visible*), the aspirations and fears characteristic of [this] traditional Buddhism remain in *force*" (60, emphasis added). I emphasize the recurring word "force" to note how the idea of internal force is opposed to the force of colonial modernity that is "all too clearly visible" in Bangkok.

Note how remarkably similar this is to Blackburn's critique of time. Before external colonial modernity, the history and life internal to traditional Buddhism "remained, for the most part, a stable . . . force." That internal force can remain "stable" because it has within its *own* movement of change, its own dynamism. But the internal force can remain stable only until it is made unstable by something external (e.g., readily visible colonial force) at some point in time—hence the notion of "irrevocable changes" made by colonial power.[30]

This clearly is an indiscriminate verdict on what constitutes change versus stability.[31] This verdict already expects the reader to believe that whatever sociopolitical "change" occurred in the so-called traditional Buddhism within its history—from the third century BC onward, *before* colonial modernity—always belonged to its internal "force," which kept life within it stable. The internal life remained stable, despite its internal force (dynamism), until the external force of colonial modernity made irrevocable changes. This is in part because Collins assumes a priori a notion of *stability* vis-à-vis change without ever showing how what counts as stable is made possible by power.[32]

Again, my point is not empirical, and I am surely not claiming that colonialism did not produce certain changes in colonized cultures. Historians might argue that the time of what is called traditional Buddhism cannot be so easily characterized as something that remained internally "stable . . . until" the arrival of colonial modernity. This determination of what constitutes historical change is possible only because of a distinction between what is internal force and what is external force that is visible a priori to the scholar. The force of change here becomes truly forceful only with colonial modernity. Thus, the distinction between local force (stability) and colonial force (change) constitutes a judgment that does not reflect an empirical actuality.

Can one think of religion and its relation to times in terms of the distinction between force and stability without already turning religious life itself into a "subject" and an "object," the very outcome that scholars like Collins want to avoid since they readily disavow the very notion of an origin? After all, to disavow the identity of a "true" or an "original" religion is to deny it an objectivity that can have "remained" unchanged since its origin. And this is why even though Collins claims that Thai peasant religion remains in force despite modernity, he swiftly qualifies that statement as not being meant "to perpetuate an Orientalist myth about a changeless East, floating dreamily and aimlessly down the sea of change with a kind of idiotic mystical grin" (59; cf. Blackburn's notion of "sea change"). Collins wants only to suggest, so as to avoid determining an essentialist subject in terms of what "'Buddhism' was or is" (57).

Strangely, an undecidability constitutes this decisive critique of the relation between Buddhist life and time, stability and change. We are told decisively that one cannot decide on the origin and truth of Buddhism, because doing so presupposes what Buddhism "was or is" in essentialist and ahistorical terms. "It is certainly possible," writes Collins, "to present speculative accounts of what early Buddhism was, and even to make guesses, as to 'what the Buddha taught'" (55). This of course hardly accounts for why Buddhists make authoritative and essential statements about something called "what the Buddha taught" and why the practice of such language is not "speculative." The use of such normative markers by Buddhists is part of specific conditions of power that make them intelligible or not intelligible to those who are invested within those conditions, with specific dispositions. But, given his empiricist history, Collins is not interested in "speculative accounts" or the conditions of their use. Indeed, his account explicitly refuses to reply on Buddhist ideas themselves about time or nirvana. Collins astonishingly claims to "construct an account of nirvana which does not rely on Buddhist presuppositions" (101).[33] He is concerned with the general notion of the "ongoing" history of Buddhism. Even as Collins speaks of how much in the ongoing history of Buddhist life has remained in force, he still claims not to decide what Buddhism was or is. But he cannot avoid such a decision in the end. Even though there can be no "divorce between . . . Buddhism and the vicissitudes of human nature and social life," one cannot, according to Collins' argument, simply leave religious life to the force of history, a force not part of the internal force that constitutes the stability of Buddhist life. Thus the untenable claim that the Thai peasant religion still remains in force despite the force of "all too clearly visible" modernity in Bangkok. On this reasoning, ultimately Buddhist life in modern Bangkok would not really amount to "Buddhism" as Collins projects it.

The problem here is that the adjudication of what constitutes internal force versus external force is a judgment of how native Buddhist life is governed by its own internal self-critique (i.e., force of stability), which, by some curious reasoning, is separable from external force. Buddhist life (possessed by its own critique) is assumed to be not easily subject to the force of colonial modernity, notwithstanding the irrevocable colonial changes. This is why both Collins and Blackburn—along with a host of other scholars—object to the story of the colonial modernity of religion that anthropologist Gananath Obeyesekere narrated in terms of the emergence of "protestant Buddhism" (cf. Scott 1999). As some other scholars of Buddhism warn, one should "avoid attributing too much *force* to the 'West' (or Christianity, or protestant assumptions, or Orientalism) in the changes to Theravada Buddhism which occurred in the nineteenth century" because that would have the "ironic effect of once more denying any voice to 'Orientals' (Hallisey, 48–49; see also Holt; McDaniel). But determining what constitutes "too much force" of the West is surely an interminable task, but this is what the postcolonial critique of the problem of time is expected to do as it seeks to decide the undecidable: the question of force vis-à-vis religious life in tradition.

My point is twofold: The critique of the notion of an origin in religion on the one hand and the force of colonial modernity on the other is the work of a decision by the scholar; at the same time, it is a critique of the very possibility of religious life in modernity. That is to say, this decisive critique (once again, with all the force of that term) tries to just separate what is called the history of religious life—that is, force internal to it—from change—force decided to be external to it.[34]

To be clear: I am not implying that critiques of the concept of origin, or of colonial modernity and the irrevocable changes it produced within cultures, are not worthwhile. Nor am I denying distinctions like "internal" and "external" that are debated in a given religious tradition. My point is that, based on the scholar's logic of decision, these critiques seek to arbitrate the relation between time and life in terms of distinctions such as external and internal that are assumed to be ready-made or empirically visible. They are neither empirical nor decidable in the way they are presented as objects of critique. Such critique cannot constitute the kind of "political" criticism that postcolonial critics expect it to be.

At the same time, I think it is important to ask about the differences in the forms of sensibility, disposition, capability, and affectivity that religious and secular power authorize, and how those differences have to do with the distinct social–political institutions, programs, and relationships in which they are made possible. But those differences cannot be understood by way of a division between the internal time of religious life already opposed to an external power or force (of modernity). The problem is that the scholars of religion have paid less attention to the concept of a discursive tradition. They have not thought about how the form of shared life works within the coherence of such a tradition and why it can set aside the unending exercise of determining temporal change different from the problem of origin. A discursive tradition, constituted by specific modes of competing arguments, and the kinds of affective practice and disposition they seek to authorize, in specific historical situations and relations of power, is not best captured by the above postcolonial critique of time. What matters in a discursive tradition are not so much how things change in its history but what forms of affective practice and sensibility, opposed to others, are rendered possible by persuasive, rival arguments. It is in these situations that we can ask how such arguments bring into view the questions of what past texts, ideas, institutions, and authorities that they can appeal to or challenge so as to advance distinct modes of reasoning. The notion of decisive critique that is assumed to be "internal" to Buddhism in general does not exist ahead of these arguments in a discursive tradition.

DECISION'S UNDECIDABLE SEPARATION BETWEEN ORIGIN AND CHANGE IN TRADITION

Below I briefly examine the argument of a wholly different modern text on the question of the origin of religion and the question of tradition that haunts it—a text that presents an aporetic problem that the above postcolonial critique can neither respond to nor resolve. To set the stage for the discussion, let me note how this critique works in the work of the prominent postcolonial historian of Buddhism Donald Lopez, *Buddhism and Science*. Here, as he attempts to think about the history of Buddhist practice, Lopez makes a more decisive contrast between life and change, religion and modernity, by a coup de theatre—a coup de force, as Derrida would say. In *Buddhism and Science,* as in his previous work, Lopez offers a historical account—which is supposed to be a critique—of how, for the last 150 years, modern (Western and non-Western) enthusiasts of Buddhism sought to construct compatibility between Buddhism and modern science, either to validate Buddhism as a "philosophy" or to banish modern science as something already to be found in the wisdom of an ancient guru like the Buddha. At the end, Lopez claims to sound only a cautionary note about the "price" one has to pay for attempts to "see Buddhism as ever modern." The attempts to see Buddhism as ever modern are attempts to rationalize and demythologize certain seemingly irrational mythical practices (e.g., Tantric meditation) of the premodern Buddhist world—mythical aspects that rationalists see as later developments or deteriorations of an original pure religion.

At stake in Lopez's analysis is the question of origin and change itself, which he has to tackle carefully. Despite his obvious disquiet with modern rationalizations that lead to a "loss" of premodern religious practice, Lopez (very much like Collins) insists that he does not wish to "pronounce what Buddhism should be, and what it cannot be" (216). Given its "history," as though one cannot interfere with the force of its own movement and change—a history that rationalists too acknowledge—Lopez asserts that he can only try to "understand what Buddhism has been" (216). He therefore says that one "cannot keep Buddhism from changing, attempting to remythologize the demythologized." Lopez makes the qualification, as Collins does, that he does not want to "suggest that Buddhism has an essence, as many apologists for Buddhism and science have sought to identify." But he still cautiously distances himself from simple antiessentialists: "At the same time, those who would account for the adaptability of Buddhism by recourse to some facile claim that Buddhism has always been anti-essentialist run the risk of allowing Buddhism to be everything, and nothing. It is neither" (216).

One can find much to think about in the fascinating history of the modernity of Buddhism that Lopez provides, but despite the claim not to pronounce or decide anything, he ends up deciding exactly what he seeks to avoid. As he makes the contrast between essence and time—that one can only "understand what Buddhism has been" and cannot stop it from "changing"—he still pronounces that one cannot allow Buddhism to be "everything, and nothing." Remarkably, it is through that pronouncement that Lopez can disown the arbitrariness of the pronouncement itself, in the name of what cannot be pronounced or decided (i.e., "what Buddhism should be"). What is decided or pronounced is ultimately claimed to be unpronounced: Buddhism has no essence, but it cannot be anything and everything. Lopez can oscillate between the two claims by making a decision that he claims not to have made, based on a contrast between origin and change that he takes to be natural. That is, Buddhism has a history, but it cannot have an essence, because religion is always what it "has been," something that cannot be stopped from changing.[35] But at the same time, it cannot be "everything, and nothing."

This contrast between origin and change is not simply tautological, assumed to make possible a decision (that the author claims not to make) about why Buddhism cannot be anything and everything. But the problem of origin and essence can never be set aside without running into tautological problems that a contrast between origin and change creates—a contrast that historians like Lopez can make by the coup de force of a decision. Part of the problem is Lopez's unreflective assumption that the appeal to the idea of history eradicates the problem of essence, which preempts the space for understanding how the relation between time and practice works within the discursive tradition of Buddhism.

Ultimately Lopez runs into a paradoxical problem. The decisive distinction between origin and change turns out to be undecidable or indecisive. Consider the remarkable move he makes at the end of *Buddhism and Science,* a move that undercuts all his senses of Buddhism as a historical thing. In a move to set the modern Buddhist rationalists straight once and for all, Lopez abruptly cites a text from what he calls the "oldest collection of texts" in the Pali canon. In so doing, he remarks (facetiously?), "The Buddha should have the last word" about such seemingly irrational things as his having superhuman powers. Note that these are things that modern rationalists have trouble fitting into their modern view of Buddhism as a "philosophy." Lopez then quotes a short passage (loosely translated) from what is said to be one of the "oldest" collections of texts, called the *Mahasihanada Sutta*, from the Pali canon.[36] This text says that the Buddha declared that anybody who denies that he possesses superhuman powers "will wind up in hell" (the seemingly damning English indicative "will wind up" sounds nicer in Pali!).

Regardless of whether Lopez is attempting to be humorous, the sudden citation of a text from the "oldest" collection of the Pali canon implicates Lopez in all the problems of origin that he wants to avoid as a good historian. To cite that text as if it constitutes by itself some evidence, as if the text explained or communicated a direct sense of its own authority by giving the Buddha the "last word," Lopez has to trespass all the limits of history he has already enforced.

This brings up the question of how the "citation" of authoritative texts works within the tradition of Buddhism. The citation of such texts is never simply an innocent and "free" activity that anyone can simply do without lifting the cited text from the conditions of practice of particular dispositions and sensibilities within the limits of a discursive tradition. One can already hear a rejoinder: Of course, as scholars (McDaniel) have shown admirably, Buddhist monks and nuns in Theravada countries do use, quote, or "cite," canonical texts in their teachings, writings, sermons, speeches, and the like. But, scholars like Lopez know very well, monastics use and cite such texts within the daily activities and practices that constitute the form of life they live (cf. Lempert for Tibetan monastic citations and debates of texts) in distinct relationships of power.[37] More precisely, when monastics do cite such texts, they do so not to "communicate" some knowledge or evidence about the authority of the text, as if they were speaking to an audience to be convinced of a subject (such as the Buddha's supernatural powers). The "audience" to whom monastics "speak" when they cite or quote such a text in specific conditions (i.e., in their sermons or teachings) is already *disposed* toward accepting what is being said (e.g., that the Buddha possesses supernatural powers) before the authority of the antiquity of a text is ever mentioned. When one is disposed toward the virtuous practice (that is, the "how") of composed listening to a sermon (on a given subject matter such as the virtue of giving), one is *brought* into an affective position or mood in which one *can* accept what is being said.[38] (This is of course not because of "faith" or "belief.")[39] Thus monastics speak about such matters to those who are disposed toward listening to them not by seeking to establish the authority of a single text—or even its antiquity. In such forms of practice, the speaker-monastic is practicing the virtue of preaching and teaching as much as the audience is exercising the virtue of listening. Even if monastics were to authorize a text from the canon in terms of its antiquity, such authorization would not be separate from the practice of virtuous-disposed listening to sermons in which the text's authority is accepted. Had Lopez sought to think about how the time of the form of life is to be found in the embodied practice of dispositions, necessitated by distinctive relations of power in a discursive tradition, he could have asked different questions about temporality irreducible to the distinction of origin and change.

What I want to emphasize is that the ways in which the practice of the dispositions, sensibilities, and affectivities of life work within the discursive tradition are not constituted by a modern "critical" representation of life, involving some fine separation between the old and the new, origin and change. The practice of the dispositions of Buddhist life and the discursive tradition in which it becomes possible are hardly devoid of the questions of time, motion, and "change," but they are not based on the modern division of time.[40] But the critical division of time that modern scholars use as a theoretical tool to identify and represent change in the history of religious life only takes them back to the problem of having to repeat the claim that Buddhism has no essence or origin. The problem of essence and origin is not confined to the study of religion. Even though "essence" (or "essentialism") has become a bad word in the humanities, its problem is presumed to be readily resolved through a logic very similar to that found in postcolonial studies' self-evident opposition between origin and change. But this contrast cannot help us understand the indistinction between form and life in the temporality of a discursive tradition. Thinking about the form of life in such a tradition is preempted by the idea of change separated from the origin of time.

CRITIQUE'S DECISION ON TIME VERSUS A MODERN TEXT ON ORIGIN AND TRADITION

In this section, I want to show more specifically how the postcolonial critique of the problem of time runs into aporetic difficulties. To do so, I read a modern text entitled *What the Buddha Thought* by Richard Gombrich that defends the very notion of origin (original religion) opposing change ("tradition"). The text is "modern" in that it relies on the same logic of history that postcolonial critique of time produces. Once again, there are many ironies here. This text presents a "historical" account of religion that contests the notion of force-change that the above postcolonial critique sees as part of the history of Buddhist life. Yet this text views the history of Buddhism to be nothing but a history of origin from which it cannot be separated. In this sense, the text is meant to be an explicit reproof of the antiessentialist critique.

I take the example of this text to show that the postcolonial critique of time cannot damage the theoretical problem that undergirds the text. This is because the postcolonial critique assumes that it has resolved the problem of origin by the historicist logic of change, separate from origin. My reading of the text is not interested in empirical matters, and it teases out only the theoretical problems related to questions about time, critique, and tradition.

The author of *What the Buddha Thought,* Indologist Richard Gombrich, has, by his own admission, become the nemesis of antiessentialist historians of Buddhism today. Ironically, Gombrich calls the "method" of his text "historical." He does so because he wants to understand the Buddha's "thought" as being true to the original contexts of the Buddhist canon (which he says was written in Sri Lanka in the first century BCE). The Buddhist canon, for him, marks the locus of the original religion of the Buddha. This original Buddhism is opposed to the "tradition" (of the later commentaries, set in place by the fifth century AD monk named Buddhaghosa, which have been followed by Theravada Buddhists to the present day). At the very outset, then, the text makes a decisive critical separation between two histories: the history of original Buddhism and the history of tradition.

What makes this text distinctive among many studies in the humanities today is its audacious allegation against tradition, against the force of tradition's uncritical movement and indeed separation from its origin, leading to what Gombrich calls "massive failures of understanding" the Buddha's original message (195). This allegation has far-reaching political–ethical implications, as it calls into question the validity of the entire tradition of the Theravada life. Here the life of tradition becomes a counterfeit of origin. My question here is this: Can the antiessentialist critique that finds the problem of Gombrich's text to be readily apparent respond to its allegation against tradition without merely arguing that the history or tradition constitutes "change"?

My answer is that the antiessentialist postcolonial critique cannot respond to it, because *What the Buddha Thought* operates on the same historicist logic that informs the antiessentialist critique. That is, Gombrich's text already grants the possibility of change in history. It is on the basis of that logic that the text defends the idea of an origin that it knows to exist.[41] Both the antiessentialist critique and the text take the division between origin and change to be self-evident. Without that division, the antiessentialist critique cannot question the notion of origin; nor can the essentialist argue for that notion. Central to that division is the question of determining what constitutes "force" (change) in time.

My point is that, to respond to the text, whose theoretical problem haunts the postcolonial historicist critique and, by extension, our secular politics, one has to dispense with the assumption that the division between origin and change, essence and history exists out there, self-evidently (and empirically), as an object of knowledge. In what follows, I want to show that the problem of the division between origin and change in this text, as it operates by way of two other conceptual divisions, helps us ask a different question about religious life and time beyond the antiessentialist critique.

DIVISION BETWEEN KNOWLEDGE AND BELIEF, METAPHOR AND LITERALISM

There are in the text *What the Buddha Thought* at least two related critical divisions or separations—critical in every decisive sense of the word critique—that make possible the text's defense of the division between origin and change. These two divisions are related to each other insofar as they are both presented as transparent objects of knowledge.

The first is the division between knowledge and belief. The second (based on the first) is the division between metaphor and literalism. It is with the second division that the text makes the central allegation against the tradition's historical change, the force of its movement from origin.

To make these divisions, the text attempts throughout to construct a relation between Buddhism and its possible universalizability. We are told that the "thought" of the Buddha "belongs in the same class as Plato, Aristotle, the giants who started Western philosophy." The Buddha's thought, which can be thought and understood, should have universal appeal, beyond the confines of its religious world. The Buddha's "ideas should form part of the education of every child, the world over, and this should make the world a more civilized place, both gentler and more intelligent" (1). The text does not make clear in what sense it speaks of the idea of "thought."[42] What does become clear, however, is that this concept of religion as universalizable "thought" preempts the space for historical religious practice and change that are necessarily embedded in particular social and political relations. The universalizable thought cannot change, as it is something to be "understood" across space and time and not necessarily to be lived and practiced.[43] On this view, a religion like Buddhism becomes a secular object of thought and knowledge available to everybody "the world over." This universalizable knowledge of religion is contrasted with "belief," which supposedly does not belong to the domain of knowledge and understanding. The text emphasizes the overarching importance of the concept of "understanding" in Buddhism with the charge that tradition "failed to understand" the Buddha's original message in a distinct way. Tradition failed to "understand" its origin because it failed to discern the supposed distinction between metaphor and literalism central to the founder's thought (78).

To make this division between metaphor and literalism, the text must account for and separate the ideas that it claims involve "belief" from the original thought. The text must do so to sustain its argument about the universalizability of religion, as what can be universal cannot quite make space for particular religious beliefs. So the text translates such ideas—for example, "law of karma"—into a distinctive modern Christian language by saying that they require a "leap of faith" (28; see also n. 39 to this essay).[44] My point here is that to talk about belief is to authorize a particular kind of knowledge opposed to it. This sense of knowledge is critical to the governing division between metaphor and literalism.

Consider an example that sharpens the focus on the organizing role that the concept of knowledge plays in the text. In keeping with its attempt to separate what is deemed not "pragmatic" (i.e., supernatural beings in Buddhism) from the locus of Buddhism's origin, the text makes an astonishing propositional claim—in a gesture perhaps more evocative than that of the modern figure of Robinson Crusoe: "We probably cannot know whether he [the Buddha] really believed in such beings as gods and other spirits" (164).[45] Again, my interest here is not in empirical questions about this.[46] My interest is in pointing to one of the governing theoretical problems that this separation between knowledge and belief extends—a problem which, I have been arguing, the postcolonial critique cannot quite resolve.[47]

Note that the notion of knowledge opposed to belief plays an organizing role in the text in a particular sense. For the text, knowledge is what is *communicable*. In that sense, the locus of origin (original "pragmatic" Buddhism, as opposed to belief) must always communicate its "meaning" "purely," across time, "the world over" (hence the possibility of religion's universalizability). We are therefore told that the Buddha's "purpose was to purely convey meaning, and anything that was to impede communication was to be discarded" (148). According to this view, whatever follows the locus of origin (tradition) has to equal communication and meaning. That equation is crucial to what the text understands as knowledge. In light of this equation, something called belief cannot play any role in the original religion since belief is assumed to be not communicable knowledge.

The problem of belief is part of the secular narrative of religion, where belief, in relation to the question of authenticity, comes to be understood as a matter of "choice" reinforcing "the idea of an autonomous subject" (Asad 2012a, 43; see also 1996b). My point is that the separation of knowledge from what is called religious belief already seeks to apprehend "belief" as an object of knowledge itself. There is no preexisting boundary between knowledge and belief; rather, it is the scholar's claim to the condition of knowledge—"we probably cannot know whether he really believed"—that makes belief a critical object of knowledge, making the boundary between them seemingly natural.

Better put, it is the knowledge claim about belief that renders the condition of knowledge—that is, the question of whether one can know something about belief—possible in the first place. And this logic of the separation between knowledge and belief in turn makes possible the distinction between the metaphorical and the literal.

Recall that the text's categorical allegation against tradition: tradition failed to understand original Buddhism because it failed to understand the distinction between metaphor and literalism. As I suggested above, one cannot respond to this allegation against tradition by resorting to the claim that tradition represents change. To respond to the allegation, one has to operate within the pregiven division between origin and history (change). This division between origin and change is a division between form and life itself. It is within the division that one can explain change in religious life as particular kinds of form in history. The form becomes a mere example of change identifiable in the historical narrative of Buddhism. But this fails to examine how form constitutes life, and how life itself comes into view in its form within living relationships of power and discourse. I have tried to suggest that what is central to the division between origin and change is the notion of critique-decision. *What the Buddha Thought* relies precisely on such a notion of critique-decision to authorize the division between metaphor and the literal. For the text to allege that tradition misunderstood original Buddhism is to suggest that tradition lacked a "critical" knowledge of its original history or time. That is, tradition lacked "critique."

This is where an important question arises about whether critique (as decision and vice versa) has any place in religious life and regular life in general. This question can help to challenge the modern secular assumptions about the supremacy of critique that is meant to guide life itself. I shall return briefly to this question at the end of the paper.

Now, Gombrich constructs the division between metaphor and literalism by reading a canonical text called the *Tevijja Sutta*. To begin with, we are told that the Buddha used metaphors extensively in his conversations with people and that in the *Tevijja Sutta,* the use of metaphor is crucial. Tradition missed the boat by misunderstanding how this foundational text uses a particularly significant metaphor (80–84). Buddhist history itself is supposed to begin in this text, we are told, because in it the Buddha supposedly separates himself from another *origin*—that of the Brahmanical tradition. (Note that this is how the classic story that Buddhism is self-evidently a different "world religion" from Hinduism can also be told.)[48] So it is a story of one origin against another origin. Insofar as original Buddhism separates from another origin, critique is assumed to mark the very beginning of Buddhist life.

According to *What the Buddha Thought,* tradition misinterpreted the foundational canonical text *Tevijja Sutta* with "disastrous consequences," missing its simple message about love and compassion (as the way to nirvana, after whose attainment one will not be reborn). In other words, this new Indian religion did not teach some "profound" doctrine beyond human comprehension. Yet tradition missed it, because it did not understand how the original teaching of the Buddha turned a key literal Brahmanical idea—that of "companionship with the brahma" (Brahma-sahavyata)—into a metaphor. For Brahmins this notion of companionship with the Brahma is the ultimate goal in the texts known as the Upanishads. The implication is that tradition did not recognize the problem because it was not critical enough to separate that metaphor from literalism. That is, tradition lacked critique to separate metaphor from literalism. (Note again that this is the exact opposite of the antiessentialist critique that sees critique as part of the internal historical force that makes up the tradition of Buddhism.)

How, precisely, did tradition fail to separate metaphor from literalism? Gombrich explains. In the canonical *Tevijja Sutta,* the Buddha has a dialogue with a Brahmin interlocutor. The Buddha first "pokes fun" at other Brahmins who claim to teach the way to the "brahma-world." The Buddha then claims that he too knows the way to that world.[49] (Note that the Buddha does not say that the Brahma-world does not exist.) The Buddha then says that a person who meets him and listens to his teaching "renounces the household life and *keeps all the rules of conduct and morality*" (81, emphasis added). Such a person who renounces then "dwells," pervading "every direction with kindness, compassion, sympathetic joy, and equanimity"—termed elsewhere "dwellings of the brahma" (Brahma-viharas). This, the Buddha says, is the way to companionship with the Brahma, the ultimate goal in the Upanishads.

But note something crucial here: the word "nirvana" is nowhere mentioned in this dialogue! The central argument that Gombrich's text makes is that the Buddha, in his dialogue with the interlocutor, uses the term "brahma-world" as a "metaphor" for nirvana. But, we are told, tradition misunderstood this. It took the Buddha's metaphor literally. Tradition assumed that the metaphor referred to some exoteric idea of "super heaven."[50] Could this be?

Note the impossible move by which Gombrich's text makes the division between metaphor and literalism to determine what the metaphor really stands for.[51] The Buddha took the literal idea of the Brahma-world ("super heaven") and turned it into a metaphor. (This is because, we are told, the Buddha had to take Brahmanical ideas like the "cosmology literally—but only for his own didactic purposes" [89].) And the interlocutor Brahmin, who becomes convinced at the end of the dialogue that the Buddha really does know the path to the literal Brahma-world, *inexplicably* has to accept that the Buddha is really using the literal phrase as a metaphor for nirvana. But the Buddha does this without ever using the word "nirvana"! How could this be?

Note the warped, dizzying logic of this claim: The interlocutor brahmin has to know that the metaphor stands for the literal, which, however, really is a metaphor, but not quite a metaphor because it really stands for the literal. Here we can no longer tell what the literal or the metaphorical is. Yet, according to Gombrich, the Buddha, who has complete liberty to take Brahmanical ideas literally for didactic purposes, clearly and directly *communicates* the "meaning" of the literal to the Brahmin (who is interested in the literal) with the idea that one can know the literal by way of the metaphorical! Poor tradition missed this difference between the metaphorical and the literal. Are there any grounds for believing this allegation against tradition?

For simplicity's sake, take this example: A man who wants to go to California has lost his way. He knows he must go west. Then a stranger says that he can point the way to the west. But the stranger actually means "east" by *west*, which he doesn't tell the lost person. Miraculously the lost person "gets the metaphor" and then happily makes his way to North Carolina! Perhaps all this alternation between the literal and the metaphorical makes sense to Gombrich, but we might be relieved to learn that "tradition" avoided going down that rabbit hole. In other words, it is not such a bad thing that tradition did not use the modern sense of critique (to separate metaphor from literalism).

CONCLUSION

My aim in reading Gombrich's narrative of origin was not to point out the untenable division between metaphor and literalism on which it is based. Rather, it was to point out that his defense of origin, with its allegation against tradition, raises a broader question about the problem of critique that is essential to the modern narrative of religious life in terms of that hauntingly inescapable separation of origin from change. Note that Gombrich's fundamental accusation is that tradition—that is, historical life, which supposedly moved away from its origin—misunderstood its origin because it lacked "critique." By definition, tradition failed to remain filial to its origin because it failed to critically separate metaphor from literalism. This logic of critique is essential to the modern understanding of the problem of time based on the division between origin and change.

I have argued that the antiessentialist critique cannot respond to Gombrich's essentialist critique, to his defense of origin that the former invariably finds problematic. The problem of how tradition lacked critique cannot be solved with the argument that tradition, its life, represents "change" (history). Such an argument is possible only through the very critique that views time through the logic of separating origin from change. I have argued that both the essentialist and antiessentialist critiques are based on the same logic of decision-critique that already grants "change" (force) in the history of religious life; the history of religious life is always a history of change from origin. My point is that within this narrative of change in the history of religious life, neither critique can consider the inseparability of "life" from its "form," leaving the very idea of tradition itself at the mercy of the haunting secular problem of time.

I am not suggesting that it is impossible for scholars to speak of "changes" in the history of religious life, but that question of change has to be understood in relation to the emergences of particular modes of arguments that authorize distinctive forms of practice and affectivity in particular times, constituting the coherence of a discursive tradition. How such forms of practice and discourse come into view within distinct relationships cannot be reduced to mere examples of identifiable change within the history of religious life. My point is that the logic of history we find in the above narratives of religion is based on a critique that can identify the "point" of change only through that problematic separation *(chorismos)* of origin from change.[52] That separation, I have argued, is based on a decision that takes the ideas of both "origin" and "change" to be self-evident, one as the contrary of the other. I have noted the aporetic difficulties that such a decision runs into as it often seeks to decide the undecidable, leading to indecision about what constitutes change (force). Yet it is that undecidability that passes for a decisive critique here.

Central to both critiques—those arguing for and those against change in contrast to some origin—is the assumption that religious life in history must be governed by critique. For the essentialist, critical historical life is that which remains filial to its own origin, knowing how to divorce itself from successive change in history. On the contrary, for the antiessentialist, historical life changes precisely because life moves, within the "force" of its own internal history (unless the internal force is disrupted by external forces). Here critique becomes a matter of deciding what constitutes force within a particular notion of life.

My suggestion is that the problem of the essentialist's accusation against tradition, to which the antiessentialist cannot respond, poses a question that can reorient the modern preoccupation with the relation between secular critique and life. If the central accusation is that critique was absent in tradition (i.e., that religious life within history was not self-conscious of its origin, was unable to separate that origin from what changed), a response to it cannot be just the opposite claim that tradition is critical insofar as life within it changes. Yet this is deemed the only effective response by the antiessentialist against the essentialist. Thus, the two critiques produce an aporia, making it impossible to consider the question of the form of life in Buddhist tradition.

Once we begin to set aside the determination of (religious) life in terms of the problem of disentangling origin from change, we may begin to ask why critique does not play the kind of organizing role in life that scholars often assume it does.[53] The idea that religious life works quite well without critique can help us consider the indistinction between two supposedly separate things called religious life and "regular life." This is because critique, contrary to what secular critics often assume, does not figure into the practice of "regular life." So Talal Asad asks to think why "most of religious life works quite well without 'critique' because most of life does." The challenge here is to think how the form of life works within a discursive tradition, without secular critique—that is, determining the form of life through the historical narrative that understands and indentifies time by way of the division of origin and change. The necessary connection between life and its form can help us think more carefully what we mean by tradition itself. The form of life embodied within a tradition, where time itself is *encountered* in a habituation of activities, is not reducible to the modern concept of time. The form of life in a tradition has implications for thinking about the very tension between moment and temporality, purposeful action and repetition of religious practice.[54] But the decision of time in the modern narrative of religion precludes us from doing so.

Ananda Abeysekara teaches in the Department of Religion and Culture at Virginia Tech. He is the author of *Colors of the Robe: Religion, Identity, and Difference* (2002) and *The Politics of Postsecular Religion: Mourning Futures* (2008). His current research deals with religion, politics, temporality, and tradition in Theravada Buddhism.

Notes

I thank the following colleagues and friends for their comments on drafts of the article: Joseph Walser, Talal Asad, Nirmala Salgado, Ruth Mas, Brian Britt, Justin Thomas McDaniel, Aaron Ansel, Stephen Berkwitz, Lucia Galvagni, and Nick Copeland. I also thank two anonymous readers of the journal for their helpful comments. I presented some of these ideas in a talk I gave at the University of Colombo in July 2016, and I thank Prema de Silva and Sandagomi Koperahewa for organizing it.

1. I have commented briefly elsewhere (2010) on the relation between decision and critique in terms of Foucault's discussion of Aristotle's *kairos*, "decisive or critical moment," in particular. On Aristotle's notion of critique as decision, see Heidegger 1998. On the relation and tension between moment and temporality in Aristotle, see Heidegger 2009; also cf. Murchadha. Derrida (1995b) often says that a decision is always made in the "instant" and that it constitutes madness, sometimes with reference to Kierkegaard, who says the "instant is madness" (cf. Bennington; also Blanchot; Derrida 2010).

2. Note how the problem of origin remains "critical" to the contemporary American media narratives of the connection between time and particular events

of (terrorist) violence. Such narratives often take the form of a sentence like: "This attack . . . is the first, since . . ." Here the preposition "since" marks an origin ("the first") related to another origin-time. The grammar of it is such that each origin is unique and simultaneously transcends itself as it connects to another origin. By connecting to a previous origin, the new origin, to which the "since" refers, already evokes a destination.

3. Hannah Arendt claims that the problem of origin acquires a new sense in the contexts of the French and the American Revolutions. "The modern concept of revolution, inextricably bound up with the notion that the course of history suddenly begins anew, that an entirely new story, a story never known or told before, is about to unfold, was unknown prior to the two great revolutions at the end of the eighteenth century" (1963, 28). Arendt goes on to say, revolution constituted a "hiatus between end and beginning, between a no-longer and a not-yet" (205). "It is in the very nature of beginning to carry with itself a measure of complete arbitrariness. . . . The beginning has, as it were, nothing whatsoever to hold onto; it is as though it came from nowhere in either space or time. For a moment, the moment of beginning, it is as though the beginner had abolished the sequence of temporality itself" (206). Arendt (1977, 140) says that modern revolutions that marked the crisis of the modern present were "gigantic attempts . . . to renew the broken thread of tradition" tied to the Roman foundations of political authority. In *On Revolution,* as elsewhere, Arendt wants to think how the capacity to begin anew marks particular broken times. But Arendt "does not attend to the resulting paradox: to the extent that what is new actually marks a beginning, it also initiates a tradition. It could be said, therefore, that the repetition of beginnings in modernity represents an enduring aspiration for continuity that is continually betrayed—an unhappy yearning for tradition that eludes one" (Asad 2015, 184). On the conflicting sense of beginning as the capacity for freedom in Arendt's thinking, see Kang.

4. My comments pertain largely to the problem of temporality in the works by scholars of Theravada Buddhism. My comments on the work of Donald Lopez, a scholar of Tibetan Buddhism, have only to do with a part dealing with that problem with the tradition of Theravada Buddhism. However, for the sake of clarity, let me make one exception here to note that how I think about the question of temporality vis-à-vis origin is different from how a historian of Mahayana Buddhism, Christian Wedemeyer, tries to problematize the "quest for the origins" in his recent study of Tantric Buddhism. For Wedemeyer, a "normative position on what 'real' Buddhism is" guides the quest for origins. He writes that "one can only identify the origins of a thing if one has already defined what that thing most essentially is; conversely, identifying the most essential nature of a historical thing is generally made with reference to its origins" (31–33). As we will see, the problem of origin cannot be set aside with the claim that it produces an essentialized object. Part of my argument is that this orthodox critique of origin-time precludes us from understanding how life is constituted by its form, within the "coherence" of a tradition. I thank Justin Thomas McDaniel for directing me to Wedemeyer's work. On how the antiessentialist critiques of time fail to notice that all origins (and indeed the very idea of origin) are always and necessarily retroactive, see Walser 2015.

5. On how the problem of critique cannot be solved by distinguishing "critique" from "criticism," see the exchange between Asad and Butler (Asad et al.). Butler chides Asad for supposedly not knowing the difference between critique and criticism. Butler does make this distinction by a logic of decisionism itself and claims that critique is that which is found in the works of figures such as Adorno, Benjamin, Spivak, et al. In Asad's response, what Butler fails to note is how different forms of power make critique possible. That is, one cannot simply say what critique is, opposed to criticism, but has to think how critique is informed by power, in what material conditions. Critique and criticism cannot be so easily separated in "practice." But Butler's desire to separate the two makes it difficult to understand, for example, how "international finger-wagging and many of the North's legal, financial, and military interventions are together designed to promote the conditions of possibility in which, ideally, everyone can govern themselves. These material interventions *are* critique" (143–44).

6. Note that, as Aristotle argues, a separation between *arche* and motion-movement ("change") is possible in mathematics but not in "physics"—i.e., as far as physical beings and things are concerned. Mathematics is concerned with that which "shows itself" through "separation" ("extraction," or *chorismos*) of something from its own place *(chora)*. In his reading of Aristotle (*Physics*.2.2–3; *Physics*.4.1; *Metaphysics*.14.5), Heidegger writes: "The *mathematikos* takes something away from its own place. . . . The mathematical is not in a place." Things become "objective" in this mathematical separation-extraction. "The mathematical as such is removed from beings characterized by motion. . . . The mathematical, i.e., a point, is 'extracted from beings insofar as they move.'" In extracting, the mathematician "discerns" and "cannot be subject to any mistake." Here "everything is in order." So "*chorismos* has a justifiable sense in mathematics, but not where it is a matter of determining the *archai* of *beings*," because "in every category of physical beings there resides a determinate relation to motion." Here the *archai* of things and their motion cannot be divorced. Thus, Aristotle likens those who take "Ideas" as things that can be disclosed in language *(logos)* to mathematicians who simply "extract" something from its own place removed from motion (Heidegger 1992, 69–71).

7. For Aristotle, "form" or "look" *(eidos)* is that in which the life-world comes into view, shows itself, as one *encounters* the world. Thus Aristotle makes a clear distinction between *idea* and *eidos*. In fact, he goes so far as to say that *idea* is *eidos*, "a front against Plato." For Aristotle, "matter" *(hyle)*, which already has the "ability" *(dunamis)* for this or that, is not prior to "form." The genuine relation that matter has is not so much to "work" *(ergon)* through which something (e.g., a house) may be produced or completed. Matter shows itself initially in its "form," the form in which something (e.g., a house) is anticipated for living. That is also the "outline" or "figure" *(schema)*. "The *schema* is to determine what sort of thing is in the look" (*On the Parts of Animals* 1.640b; qtd. in Heidegger 2009, 152–55, 207–9; 1995, 118; 1998, 217). Thus, according to Aristotle, "that which is to be addressed is primarily the look of a being that is there at each moment, and that has its look, insofar as

it has a look. The stuff-matter, that which the being that is there and that is in question consists of, is never to be addressed in itself" (*Metaphysics* 7.10.1035a; qtd. in Heidegger 2009, 153). Also on how *eidos* is not a "species . . . of a higher type," see Heidegger 1995, 41–58). Note that this form of the life-world for Aristotle was not connected to a "common life." Agamben (2013, 11) argues that Aristotle, who spoke of the city as "a perfect community" (*koinonia teleios*; 1252b29) and "living together" (*syzen*; 1278b22) in the *Politics* does not mention anything called a "common life" *(koinos bios)*. According to Cassian, Agamben writes, "the monastery, like the *polis,* is a community that intends to realize 'the perfection of the cenobial life.'" But "the cenoby does not name only a place, but first of all a form of life." This is why Cassian makes a distinction between the cenoby as a form of life and the monastery as place of residence.

8. This is against Pope John XXII, who declared that "there is no difference between *ius* and *licentia* ('right' and 'permission') and that therefore there cannot be for the Franciscans *licentia utendi* separate from *ius utendi.*" The Friars Minor, Ockham argues that "for the Brothers have permission to use things for a time other than a time of extreme necessity *[pro alio tempore quam pro tempore necessitatis extremae],* but they do not have any right to using at all except for the time of extreme necessity; therefore permission to use is not a right of using." So according to Ockham, "wearing shoes depends on a dispensation from the rule in case of necessity; not wearing shoes is the form of life" (qtd. in Agamben 2013, 114). For Agamben, in this "neutralization of law" where the Franciscans "recover a relationship with the law (natural, not positive)" in the case of extreme necessity, they remain simultaneously "outside and before the law." "They seek to neutralize law and at the same time to assure themselves an extreme relationship with it" (111–16).

9. For more on this concept of use, in relation to the form of life, see Agamben 2015.

10. Agamben draws in part on Wittgenstein to think about the indistinction between norm and action, rule and life; for Wittgenstein (202), "'following a rule' is a practice. And to *think* one is following a rule is not to follow a rule. And that's why it's not possible to follow a rule 'privately.' Otherwise, thinking one was following a rule would be the same thing as following it." Much of Asad's work is also informed by Wittgenstein's thinking about such a form of life, always with attention to the "grammar of concepts" and practices in religion and secularism. In *Genealogies,* Asad is interested in understanding how the forms (of discipline, liturgy, confession, penance, labor, monastic writings by figures like Hugh of St. Victor and Bernard of Clairvaux, and practices like *nasiha* [giving advice]) constitute the form of life lived by medieval monks within an organized community and modern Muslims in places such as Saudi Arabia, often thought to suffer from the lack of "critique"—that is, the lack of the separation between religion and politics. Understanding how life is constituted by its form helps to set aside the secular assumptions about the possibility of religious life separated from "politics." There is no pregiven boundary between religion and politics from which religion can be critiqued.

11. In my understanding, the shared life of a tradition requires the repetition of habitual practices that cannot be taken for granted because there can be no uniform "identity" that constitutes an uninterrupted line of temporal continuity within a tradition. Habitually lived life is never the mere repetition of the "old" (past) within a tradition. For a wonderful account how habitual repetition works in the practice of religious life, particularly in terms of the figure of conversion, see Scherer. Scherer argues that the idea of conversion as a final act that marks "an instantaneous transformation of the self" (65) and that has defined the canonical narratives of it does not attend to how conversion is an ongoing process of repeated, habitual practice. For Scherer, St. Augustine understood conversion as something that one is never done with in life.

12. As Asad (2015; also see 2012b) understands it, "Tradition is singular as well as plural. For subjects there are not only continuities but also exits and entries. Tradition accommodates mistakes as well as betrayal; it is not by accident that 'tradition' and 'treason' have a common etymology" (169). I want to emphasize the point that such discursive-embodied tradition, singular and plural, requires the "coherence" of a shared life. "Whatever coherent sense the idea of 'sustained unity' has, it comes not from common sentiment but from the shared life of a tradition—and even that does not preclude bitter disagreement among those who follow the same tradition, and mutual accusations of taking what is contingent for what is essential and worth defending to the last. The disputes themselves, however, make for a kind of unity" (195). The modern critique of time makes it difficult to grasp the ways in which coherence constitutes the conditions for the very possibility of the shared life of a tradition. Elsewhere I (2003) have attempted to show how tradition aspires to discursive coherence in conflicting and violent disputes centering around binding and contested relations of power that bring into view the questions of what can authoritatively count as Buddhism, tradition, and politics in modern Sri Lanka.

13. I can only note that Gillespie's (2008) richly detailed work *The Theological Origins of Modernity* fails to interrogate the problem of origin itself, thereby failing to think about the relation between theological ideas and modernity, and the supposed changes and transformations that mark that relation, in terms of a discursive tradition. The idea of theological origins of modernity is meant to capture the relation between modernity and religion as a certain kind of tradition, but the story provided falls short of a genealogy that can attend to the complicated temporality of a discursive tradition. Ultimately, Gillespie's story of modernity becomes kind of a seamless, temporal string on which seemingly theological ideas merely hang. Or, as one reviewer (McClure) put it, the temporality of the narrative is marred by "the repetition of a silent 'and then,' 'and then,' 'and then.'" (This sense of temporality can be found in sentences such as "Hobbes' view that God is infinite and unimaginable is remarkably similar to that of Ockham" [248].) This parataxis is unfortunately what is assumed to constitute a tradition.

14. This is despite "different" conditions and differences in specific practices and reforms—e.g., penitential practices and labor in medieval monastic life. For

example, as Asad writes with regard to Cistercians' rendering liturgy inadequate to the cultivation of the virtue of humility and adopting instead manual labor, "Such historical reforms indicate the texts comprising the programs were capable of variant readings. But it is important to note that alternative readings were not made at random, that they depended on institutional conditions. Indeed, it can be argued that it was the establishment of new disciplines that defined new readings as authoritative, rather than the other way around" (147).

15. Asad discusses some of the ways these separations began to appear in the context of the Renaissance concerns and, more specifically, in the writings of Francis Bacon. Asad contrasts them to the practice of sacramental confession, where a division between "inner" self and "outer" self as something detachable and representable was not possible. That is to say, working on one's soul (i.e., sinful thoughts) was not some individual mental introspection but necessarily involved practices of humility and obedience that could be done *only* within a structured community, with distinct "programs" of discipline, sustained by relations of power binding the abbot and monks to each other.

16. My thinking about this question of life also owes to Derrida's (2009) criticism of Agamben's earlier work on "bare life," and Heidegger's (qtd. in Derrida 2009, 305–6) own claim that "only for those who are stubborn in their head [or fool-headed] is life merely life" *(denn Eigensinnigen ist Leben nur Leben)*. On an interesting attempt to think about the question of life, see Anidjar.

17. In general, Blackburn claims to critique Chakrabarty's (2000) idea of the "disjuncture of the present with itself" in colonial modernity.

18. Heidegger (1998, 190) discusses the problem of the modern understanding of force, "movement" *(Bewegung)*, and change, which can be found in the secular narrative of religion. In his line-by-line reading of Aristotle's *Physics* 2.1, he states that "today, with the predominance of the mechanistic thinking of the modern natural sciences, we are inclined both to hold that the basic form of movement is movedness in the sense of motion from one position in space to another; and then to 'explain' everything that is moved in terms of it." This is only "one kind of movedness among others" for Aristotle, and it cannot be equated with modern ideas of change or "alteration" different from some origin, or change in terms of movement from one location to another. "A plant that is rooted 'in place' grows (increases) or withers (decreases) [auxesis-phthisis]. And conversely, something that moves insofar as it changes its place can still 'rest' by remaining as it was constituted. The running fox is at rest in that it keeps the same color; this is the rest of non-alteration, rest without *alloeosis*. Or something can be moved in the sense of withering and yet at the same time be moved in still another way, namely, by being altered. On the withering tree, the leaves dry up, the green becomes yellow. The tree that is moved in this manifold sense of *phusis* and *alloeosis* is simultaneously *at rest* insofar as it is the tree that *stands* there." These are all "overlapping 'appearances' as types of movedness," which helps us gain insight into what Aristotle calls "change" *(metabole)* (190–91). Today when we speak of "change in weather" or "change of mood," we mean "alteration." But for the Greeks, the "essential

core" of what is called change is that in which "something heretofore hidden and absent comes into appearance" (191). Similarly something produced—e.g., a chest from wood—is changed *(moved)* in its production from wood only insofar as it shows ("rests" and stands) itself (*as* the chest now). This is why for Aristotle "rest is a kind of movement" (189; cf. Heidegger 2009, 212–13). Essentially, this is Aristotle's response to Plato's not allowing "being" to have anything to do with movement (1992, 2009). Plato includes movement among the five "stems," or origins *(gene),* of being. So movement only "participates" in being (1992, 379–85). More clearly, for Plato "The chest *has* wood. Wood is an idea. . . . The chest *participates* in wood." This is why for Plato, a chest or a chair made from wood is an idol, *eidolon,* because something is "deficient" in its mode of being (2003, 25–26, 39). But for Aristotle "the chest is not wood" any more than "the statue is not the bronze." The chest is "'wooden,' remotely." That is, "wood in itself is not at all there in the chest. But the *chest* is there." The wooden chest is a different way of wood being there (2009, 204, 251; cf. Aristotle, *Metaphysics* 7–9; Heidegger 1992, 374). The relation between "wood" and "wooden" is not separable in terms of *arche* and change—that is, wood is not something that merely changed into a chest. This is because to *begin with,* wood has the "potentiality" or "appropriateness" for being made into a chest or something else. What is appropriate for this or that already has its end within itself *(entelecheia),* which is the "essence of movement" (*Physics* 3.1.201b4f; Heidegger 1992, 216–19). Insofar as is it is there ready for this or that, "wood is in movement." Similarly, "a stone that falls and a plant that grows: In this looking-thus, *kinesis* is there in a specific mode. The chest is not chest and *in addition* wood. The stone is not stone and *in addition* movement. The stone *does not participate* in the movement. . . . The stone is mobile like the chest is wooden" (2009, 212, 204). Heidegger (1998, 209) says that it is a mistake to understand (e.g., as Kant did) Aristotelian notions of *hyle* (e.g., "wood") and *morphe* (e.g., "wooden" chest) as "matter" and "form." *Morphe* is how that which is absent in itself comes into "appearance" or presence. "In the 'vinegar' lies the nonappearance, the absencing, of the wine" (1992, 219, 227). Thus the modern narrative of religion and change does not take into account the multiple, complex ways in which the relation between time and force (movement) works. On a genealogy of "force," from Aristotle's *dunamis* and *energeia* to Hegel's *Kraft,* Freud's "drive" *(Trieb)* or "force" vis-à-vis Heidegger's idea of Dasein as essentially a "drive," and Schmitt's decisionism, with connection to the modern "force of law," to Heidegger's own decisionism and Benjamin's notion of force, see Heidegger 1991; 1988; Derrida 2001; 2010; and Agamben 2005.

19. A similar story about the temporality of "internal dynamics" in which the "agency" of Buddhists "who collectively constituted themselves and their world" cannot be ceded to "a singular, external force of colonialism or modernity" in Burma is found in Turner (4–5). Turner wants to demarcate unmistakably the agency of Burmese Buddhist life and its "moral community" under colonialism. "Membership in the moral community responsible for the Buddha's sasana ["dispensation"] under colonialism gave people a new sense of moral agency. They now

held in themselves both the responsibility and the power to shape their world" (108). Ironically the Buddhists are now uncritically assigned a liberal notion of "responsibility . . . to shape their world" even as they are said to embody some agency internal to their own "Buddhist worldview" and history.

20. The literature on the problem of agency vis-à-vis (religious) life is extensive (e.g., Asad 1993; 1996a; 1996b; 2000; Scott 2004; Mahmood; Mandair; Salgado; Britt). But postcolonial historians of Buddhism (e.g., Walters 1995; King; Walters and Colley; Hansen; McDaniel; Turner) insist on recovering native agency and voice as having political and ethical implications. Numerous reviews of *Locations of Buddhism* failed to even notice this problem with the text.

21. This opposition between power and freedom has been refuted, most notably by Foucault. For Foucault power is not opposed to freedom but makes freedom possible, in that power does not negate but authorizes and enables particular forms of being and capability. Thus, for example, "slavery is not a power relationship when a man is in chains, only when he has some possible mobility, even a chance of escape" (342). Thus, something called "human agency" cannot be separate from power. A good deal of well-known scholarship has shown that (colonial) power must not be understood in the negative sense of power that scholars like Blackburn give it.

22. In a memorable response to his critics about power and authority in a religious tradition, Asad urges us to think of power not just as "struggle," which is part of it, but as "capability." Capability is not the realization of internal potentiality clashing with external forces but is something embedded in a network of authoritatively binding and living relationships of persons, discourses, and things, where one can act in certain ways. Where power authorizes such capability, beyond the "language of command," "an encounter, not a communication, lies at the heart of authority." In such an encounter, one does not merely interpret a compelling truth that is made obvious to one through some signs but "connects to the 'truth' of it" and transforms oneself in "that *moment* . . . that subjects her to its authority." That moment marks a "beginning," where one is "struck" by what one did not notice before. "Like someone love-struck, she lives in a compelling truth, she inhabits a relationship with someone who is at once internal and external" (2006, 212–13).

23. This talk of human "inclinations" vis-à-vis agency and freedom can be traced to at least one strand of the European liberal tradition represented by John Stuart Mill in his text *On Liberty*. Thus, the notion of agency used in this postcolonial scholarship is oblivious to its entanglement in the modern, battled-out genealogy of liberty—from Hobbes, Locke, Bentham, Mill, to others. (I am indebted to Quentin Skinner's work here [1998; 2002; 2008].) The genealogy of what it means to exercise one's own unhindered ability to act freely has competing conceptions, with distinct historical shifts in uses, and they cannot be pinned down to a singular definition. The uses of course include and exclude—and so enable and disable—particular kinds of action and behavior, all the while seeking to organize collective lives. This is the trap that one falls prey to when one is unaware which version of it in history, employed in particular debates, that one is using (or not using). The

genealogy of agency becomes more complicated in contemporary capitalist uses of it. Think, for instance, what notion of agency is being endorsed in expensive and incessant drug advertisements run by pharmaceutical companies to sell drugs (aptly named Abilify), with a particular accent on the kind of autonomous ability and freedom that they are supposed to afford. This is even as the advertisements already aim at guiding the people to make a choice about a given drug while promoting a universal sense of freedom and independence.

24. This opposition of colonial power to local "human choices . . . and sentiments" ignores how power itself is necessary to the authorization of choices, sentiments, and affectivities in different conditions. One way to think about this is to understand the differences in the practice of sentiments, feelings, and emotions within religious and secular power, which would not allow one to merely posit a native inside and colonial outside. Viswanath's study of how the outcaste agricultural laborers became a "problem" in nineteenth-century colonial South India helps to complicate nicely such division between power and sentiments. She shows how the debates about the caste problem among high-caste land owners, missionaries, and colonial civil servants helped to define the "religious rights" respecting the feelings and sentiments of the "Hindus." These debates eventually restricted what the state can do about the plight of the suffering laborers within the "public" domain of law, limiting that plight to the vagaries of the sympathetic humanitarianism within the "social." In general, we need to pay more attention to the contrasting practices of affect in religious and secular power. Mandair illustrates this contrast by discussing how the colonial regime that sought to discover the lost centrality of direct communication between mind (the individual) and God (the divine words in the Adi Granth) continuously deemphasized the place of emotions and feelings in the practice of Sikhism in India. What was dismissed was the importance of the practice of feelings and emotions in the musical performance of the text Adi Granth in the Sikh community. The hymns of the text, set according to their measure (rag) and rhythm (tal), were sung in a dance-performance, producing distinct feelings and moods, affecting the "lyrical interpretation of the text." Feelings did not produce some "auto-affection" in the individual self. "Unlike reflective thought, feeling cannot merely return to itself and thereby affect itself" (361–62). Here sentiments and feelings are not products of some psychological interiority. In the secular–legal use of it (in the case that Viswanath discusses), "religious sentiments" were seen to indicate something of the Indian interior self in which the colonial state could not legally intervene and hence put in place a politics of "religious neutrality." This is an instance of how the division between feeling and doing comes about in modern power. "Having felt [sympathy for a cause as missionaries did for the problem of caste or abolitionists did for slavery], one need not do" anything about it (Festa 2009, 33). For more on the practice of emotions in secular and religious power, and the different kinds of subjectivity and propensity they produce, see Asad 1993; 2014b; Hirschkind 2006; Festa 2006; 2009; Moyn. For more on the difficulty of locating the relation between the modern practice of emotions and "secular body," see Asad 2011 and Hirschkind 2011. In a

remarkable study, the French historian Alain Corbin shows how the new practices of bodily sensibility to foul odor and air as a substance that could cause disease, facilitated by hygiene programs for olfactory vigilance, brought about specific social–political transformations in late eighteenth-century France. It would be interesting to think how this modern "form of life" (Corbin's words) differs from the form of life in premodern traditions.

25. This usage of "internally dynamic" obviously takes colonialism as an a priori Western "outside" from which the internal native agency has to be insulated. The colonial outside that supposedly corrupts native agency is assumed to have an origin and an end that can be identified, whereas the internal agency has "long" been diverse and contentious within itself. The very notion of an "outside" with its contagion as well as an "inside" with its dynamics is a binary that the text brings to its data, not a binary that it gleans from the data, because colonialism as an outside is established a priori as a negative power. Needless to say, the internal and the external are constructed by specific persons in specific arguments in a discursive tradition, and they do not remain out there for representation. As Asad (1986a) pointed out long ago, in a discursive tradition, specific persons, located in specific historical conditions and institutions, vie for positions of authority not only to distinguish what is and is not internal to such a tradition but also to decide who gets to distinguish them. Think about the medieval Christian debates about "the contrast between the demands of the law and the formation of a virtuous will," centering around the problems in the practice of penance and "true repentance," with conflicting discursive interventions in those problems by figures such as Peter Abelard, Bernard of Clairvaux, and Hugh of St. Victor (Asad 2003, 159–65); or think about the questions about how the Franciscans' concept of the "form of life," with its claim of poverty, dealt with conflicts with the church doctrine and hierarchy through arguments that they sought to "reclaim a *life* and not a *rule*"—that is, "to propose not some new exegesis of the holy text, but its pure and simple identification with life, as if they did not want to read and interpret the Gospel, but only live it" (Agamben 2013, 93–94). It is a mistake to take these arguments as tokens of an a priori inside (as an "internally dynamic" antithesis to an already-opposed outside), when it is precisely a question of the internality or externality being authorized within such a tradition. The "coherence," effectiveness of a tradition is aspired to through such arguments (Asad 1993, 29, 153, 164, 200–236; 2015). See also Salgado on how a tradition authorizes such distinctions in the debates about the "status" of nuns in Theravada Buddhism. On a study of the differences between premodern and modern practices of religious life in very different arrangements of power, marked by the secular transformations of the Shari'a law in Egypt, see Agrama.

26. Blackburn intends her project to be "humane" and "political."

27. Like Blackburn, Collins here claims to break with a generation of scholars who talk about Buddhist "modernism," such as Alexander David Kneel, Heinz Bechert, Kitsiri Malalgoda, Richard Gombrich and Gananath Obeyesekere, and George Bond.

28. That is, the Pali imaginaire was not all about minority practices or ascetic practices like celibacy that monks lived, seeking to attain nirvana; it also formed part of a civilizational imaginaire of Buddhist practices by "ongoing collectivities."

29. Again, while my comments are only concerned with the question of the theoretical object of religion vis-à-vis time and origin in this text, some readers have asked what one is to make of Collins's discussion of "repetitive time" and "non-repetitive time" *within* Pali Buddhist texts. Collins of course notes that "'other cultures' do not have another, deeply 'other' way of existing in time" (239). Contrary to other theories of time, he says that repetitive and non-repetitive time that exists in other cultures can also be found in Buddhist texts, particularly in terms of their references to the idea of nirvana, the final "ending" in Buddhism. Thus he writes that "representations of time will obviously vary from place to place, from time to time, across different social strata at one and the same place and time, and indeed in one individual for different purposes (subatomic physicists, astronomers, and farmers can all celebrate anniversaries, enjoy sunsets, and feel grief at funerals). The truth—indeed the truism—that the repetitive and non-repetitive modes of time exist simultaneously, always and everywhere, seems to me to be so monumentally obvious that it becomes difficult to see how the mystifications of theologians like Augustine and Eliade could ever have succeeded in obscuring it" (239). This claim may seem reasonable at first glance. But the problem here is not just that Collins wants to identify two *kinds* of such universal time in Pali doctrinal and other "historical" *(vamsa)* texts. This division of repetitive time and non-repetitive time becomes an exercise in figuring out their *meanings* that supposedly already exist in those texts. The problem is that it ignores how time is (or statements about nirvana within those texts are) *encountered* in a form of life, being put to particular *uses,* within specific disciplinary programs and practices, in binding relations of power, producing specific dispositions and sensibilities, which hardly have any place in Collins's text. In such uses of time, one cannot identify two kinds of time, no matter its complex formulation, without already presupposing their universal meanings. This is why Collins can make propositional statements like, "The claims I have made about nirvana providing the sense of an ending in both non-repetitive and repetitive time are true, I think, of the whole range of Buddhist literature and ritual" (256).

30. Again, part of the problem with Collins's general account of time (within Buddhist texts as well) is that time ultimately turns out be a thing, a cognitive "phenomenon" that is *named*. Collins tries to register a brief complaint about how Augustine supposedly mystifies time, but he does not say how Augustine does so. Notably Augustine writes: "What, then, is time? I know well enough what it is, provided nobody asks me; but if I am asked what it is and try to explain, I am baffled" (*Confessions,* bk.11, sec. 14). The problem with what Augustine says, Wittgenstein notes, is that "something that one knows when nobody asks one, but no longer knows when one is asked to explain it, is something that has to be *called to mind.* (And it is obviously something which, for some reason, it is difficult to call to mind)" (89). As Wittgenstein goes on to point out, one does not call to mind

phenomena. Rather one can describe statements about the "'*possibilities*' of phenomena" (90). Collins claims that he tries to say nothing but what the "texts" say, but his identification of "endings in repetitive time" and "endings in non-repetitive time," for example, with their meanings "true . . . of the whole range of Buddhist literature and ritual" located, turns time into a phenomenon named, one that one may try to call to mind (after reading his text). Once time is viewed as a phenomenon abstracted from any possible dialogic setting or situation of encounter, it already becomes mystified, needing to be explained as to what it is. In how time is encountered in the descriptions of activities, in the past, present, and future, in how one describes what one did, does, and plans to do, time is to be found in an activity itself.

31. This starkly differs from the Aristotelian notion of "force" or "potentiality," which one cannot speak of as remaining stable. To say that something like Buddhism remains stable is to grant in advance its possible unstableness, its possible fall. It is useful to state briefly Heidegger's (1998) argument here about the Greek relation between "being" and "stability," or "the stable." The Greeks "address being as the stable *[das 'Ständige']*. 'The stable' means two things. On the one hand, it means whatever, of and by itself, stands on its own, that which stands "there;" and at the same time 'the stable' means the enduring, the lasting. We would certainly not be thinking like the Greeks if we were to conceive of the stable as what 'stands *over against*' in the sense of the objective. Something 'standing over against' *[Gegenstand]* is the translation of the word "object." But being can be experienced as objects only where human beings have become subjects. . . . For the Greeks human beings are never subjects, and therefore non-human beings can never have the character of objects (things that stand-over-against)" (188–89).

32. For a critique of the idea of "stability" and its assumptions about "durability," in contrast to how *stabilitas* worked in the practice of heresy and power in medieval Christianity, see Asad 1986b.

33. Collins claimed so because he ruled that "any notion of eternal bliss, whether timeless or endless, Buddhist or Christian, or of any other kind, cannot coherently become an object of imagination articulated in narrative" (133). But, even if we set aside the absurdity of writing a 684-page book on a not-really-Buddhist-nirvana, Collins's conception of time that excludes as incoherent both Buddhist and Christian senses is based entirely on the unquestioned authority of the modern Western philosophical presuppositions of Bernard Williams, according to whose requirements there can be no notion of eternal time "articulated in narrative." Collins's granting "logical and conceptual priority to the world he inhabits" and losing the "Buddhist sense of nirvana" led the critic David Burrell to write: "So while the account of nirvana may be free of Buddhist presuppositions, it is hardly exempt from modernist reductive accounts of the telos of human existence but displays a form of unconscious ethnocentrism and cultural hegemony quite at variance with the touted sophistication of the work" (294).

34. Scholars like Collins never tire of stressing the importance of history in Buddhism, but they have thought less carefully about how the relation between

history and tradition works within it. Note that Collins not only makes divisions like internal and external force vis-à-vis Buddhist time but also makes other transhistorical divisions claimed to be internal to the Buddhist tradition itself. In the same text (1998, 284), Collins makes a distinction between "systematic thought" and "narrative thought" in the Buddhist texts. The systematic thought is "a static arrangement of ideas, which are connected by logical and not temporal relations; its narratives, whether the overall master-text or the stories told in actual texts, are by necessity temporally structured." The problem with such a distinction becomes clear when later Collins (2014) has to wonder how other things (like Buddhist "proverbs") can "fit" into this tradition. Here tradition becomes a box into which things can be fitted. Clearly Collins makes such distinctions without thinking how power *includes* and *excludes* particular distinctions of ideas within shifting moments of time, which is necessary to how a tradition works to be authoritative. The scholar's question of how something else can fit into that tradition cannot emerge prior to power and authority. As a counterpoint to the above view of tradition, see David Scott's (1994b) brilliant "Historicizing Tradition," which has been unaccountably ignored by recent scholars of Buddhism. Scott discusses how the Sinhala Buddhists tell stories *[kata]* about ritual practices such as *yaktovil* (which colonial anthropology translated as "demonism," a dark underside of some authentic Buddhism). Scott persuasively shows how these practices work within living relationships of power that seek to make authoritatively Buddhist the grammar of the ritual with distinct concepts, producing specific capabilities, affects, and dispositions such as "startle" *(gasma)* or "fear" *(baya)* toward the *yakku* (malevolent beings). The stories where such grammar plays out seek to produce knowledges about how the Buddha authorized the lay ritual experts *(adura)* to deflect the illnesses *(dosa)* from the human bodies, caused by the energy *(distiya)* of the *yakku* through virtuous commands *(anaguna)*; how the fifteenth-century Buddhist monks like Totagamuve Sri Rahula intervened to authorize it for monastic use; how eventually this monastic intervention liberated the monopoly of the ritual practice by Indian "Brahmanas" and made it possible for Sri Lankan lay experts to take over the practice. Such stories are not part of the authorized narratives like the fifth-century CE chronicle *Mahavamsa,* where the Buddha subjugated the *yakku* during one of his visits to the island. Scott's argument is that one has to pay attention to the *work* of the grammar of intelligibility of such stories, "differently cast, differently emplotted, differently flavored." Such grammar works in "social projects" like *gurukama* (the work of *yaktovil* ritual experts). The social projects like *gurukama* where the stories of *yakku* are told, which compete with the authorized narratives of texts like *Mahavamsa,* constitute the discursive tradition of Sinhala Buddhism.

35. This sense of what "has been" has an Aristotelian heritage, and it cannot be reduced to a notion of a mere past or merely some essence in the sense of *what* was.

36. I am not disputing that this is or is not one of the "oldest" texts.

37. Even though Lopez elsewhere (1998) mentions briefly that the Buddhist texts and the ideas within them (such as the mantra "Om Mani Padme Hum" in

Tibetan Buddhism, whose mystical "meaning" the orientalists and modernists sought to decode and explain) have no independent meanings apart from their "use," he does not elaborate on the idea of use or practice. What needs to shown is how the ideas that modernists find irrational in Buddhist life work in relation to the cultivation of distinct dispositions, capabilities, and sensibilities in distinct relationships of power.

38. The word "disposition" *(diathesis)* has an Aristotelian legacy. Aristotle notes (*Metaphysics* 5.18.1222b) what is distinct about this term. "'Disposition' means an arrangement of that which has parts, either in space or in potentiality or in form. It must be a kind of position, as indeed is clear from the word 'disposition.'" When one is disposed, one is disposed toward a distinct "position," "brought" into this or that mood; for example, when one is brought into "fear." It is "the manner and the mode" *(hexis)* in which one finds oneself in a mood (*Rhetoric* 1.2.1369b35), having being brought into it, and the "affects" *(pathe)* of it characterizing being in such a mood. When one has a disposition to fear, one is in a definite position about "what matters to" one, where one has the "ability to be sent into fear," which is not a mere state of mind. One is brought into fear by something or someone "definite," where the threat is something that is "happening" to one "now" (*Rhetoric* 2.4–5; Heidegger 2009, 167; 173–74). "Fear must have the character of the *near*, something impending" (169). "*Being-afraid* must be characterized as an *oiesthai*. One who is brought into fear must once 'believe' the definite thing that threatens him, threatens *him*" (173) (cf. Wittgenstein, 473: "The belief that fire will burn me is of the same kind as the fear that it will burn me"). A mood (fear), in which one may remain not composed, itself becomes the possibility of being composed (courage). "It is a question of *taking hold of courage*." Courage is the possibility of being composed in relation to fear. "Being-out-of-composure *is itself related to being composed, hexis*" (Heidegger 2009, 116, 175). Heidegger (175) notes that "the possibility of being composed in relation to fear"—that is, that "fear has, as a determinate *pathos*, the possibility of a hexis"—is alluded to by Augustine's "thesis": *initium sapientiae timor Domini* [The beginning of wisdom is the fear of the Lord]. For Heidegger, such dispositions as fear, anxiety, and joy are not "psychic experiences" or just "bodily states," they "also belong to the characteristic being of beings, of human beings" (133). Marjolein Oele informs me that for Aristotle (in *Categories* 8), "dispositions *(hexeis)*, conditions *(diatheseis)*, and affections *(pathe)* all operate on a qualitative spectrum, with *hexeis* the most stable and long enduring ones, with *diatheseis* slightly less durable, and with *pathe* the most fleeting ones" (personal communication with author). To my knowledge, the questions of how the practice of dispositions works in Buddhism have not received much attention from scholars. Scott (1994a) argues that postcolonial anthropology failed to examine how the "disposition to . . . ('demonic') experience is produced and affected as an appropriate response, in particular conditions, to music and dance" in the practice of the ritual of *yaktovil* in the Sinhala tradition of Buddhism. Such dispositions are to be found within the formations of a "specific cultural habitus" among the Sinhala Buddhists (126). Scott shows, inter alia, how the "disposition

to fright" involves the conditions of "being alone" *(tanikama)* that *touch* the body and self of the person said to be affected and afflicted by the malevolent glance of the *yakku* (malevolent beings) (60; also see Jeganathan on how fear works precisely as a social disposition to masculinity and is not a condition of a preexisting emotion like shame). Also see Desjarlais on how particular dispositions work in the ways that the Yolmo Buddhists in northcentral Nepal live out sensory biographies. On how dispositions produce distinct emotions and affects (remorse, humility, fear of God) in the practice of penance and bodily pain in medieval Christianity and the practice of listening to sermons in modern Islam, see Asad (1993) and Hirschkind (2006). Note that the practice of virtuous dispositions, and even the "failure" to attain them, with moral defects as particular "inabilities," can only take place within distinctive programs, centering around the coherence of a *living* tradition whose authority is constituted by obligatory relationships (Asad 1993, 158; 2012).

39. Some scholars (e.g., Gombrich, 28) claim that Buddhists' acceptance of such ideas as rebirth depends on *saddha,* or a "leap of faith." But such an argument already translates Buddhist life into a modern Christian idiom, making the leap of faith the condition of such acceptability. This is how modernity turns religion itself into a "belief." Note also the existential connection between "belief" and "fear" (see n.38). On how belief worked in the practice of Latin Christianity, see Asad 2012a. Asad provides a fascinating example of a young woman named Aude Fauré who was brought before the inquisition because she could not say *credere in Deum.* She could not say it not because she challenged the doctrine of the body of Christ but because of her "own incapacity" to see "in the Eucharist anything but bread." This incapacity reflected her "*anguished relationship* to God." The point is that her "own incapacity" involved "distinctive social and political relationships [that] articulated distinct sensibilities" (46–47).

40. Note that the questions of "change" and "motion" are already in the connection between disposition and emotion and affectivity. But that connection is not a mere causal relationship where one leads to another. Thus in the medieval Christian practice of remorse, "the emotion is . . . not the cause of a changed disposition but its condition" (Asad 1993, 162). Interestingly, the ways the ideas of *metabole, kinesis,* and *alloeosis* ("alteration" or "qualitative change")—along with other concepts like *dunamis* and *energeia*—are intertwined in Aristotle's thinking about how sensations are produced, in relation to the "*being of living things*" (Heidegger 2009, 132; *Metaphysics* 4.21), are not graspable through our modern language of change vis-à-vis time and motion. Generally, Aristotle grants that "sensation . . . depends on a process of movement, or affection from without, for it is held to be a sort of change of quality. . . . Let us speak as if there is no difference between being moved or being affected and being active." "For the unlike is affected, and when it has been affected it is like" (*On the Soul* 2.5.417b). But what is affected or acted on *(paschein)* is not just an "alteration"—where something produced "underlies alteration . . . or being-reversed . . . white-black or sweet-bitter" (2009, 131)—or it is a different kind of "alteration," where the potential is acted on by the actual.

Thus, Aristotle says, "the expression to 'be acted upon' has more than one meaning. It may mean either the extinction of one of two contraries by the other, or the maintenance of what is potential by the agency of what is actual. For what possesses knowledge becomes an actual knower by a transition which is either not an alteration of it at all (being in reality a development into its true self or actuality) or at least an alteration in a quite a different sense." Aristotle gives the example of someone who "knows" or has knowledge about something definite. "Hence it is wrong to speak of a wise man being 'altered' when he uses his wisdom, just as it would be absurd to speak of a builder as being altered when he builds something" (*On the Soul* 2.5.417b). According to Heidegger (2009, 132), *paschein* has the character of *soteria* (saving). Where even something harmful happens to one, "the occurring itself, as happening, does not need, without qualification, to have the character of the harmful, that of *phthora* ['perishing' or 'passing away']." But "something occurs to me such that this experiencing or undergoing has the character of *soxein* [preserving]. By way of something encountering me, occurring to me, I am not annihilated, instead I myself come into the genuine state, namely, the possibility that was in me now becomes genuinely real." But, "as opposed to this *metabole* through which the *hexis* [constitution, or having] is saved, is brought precisely to that which it should be, there is a kind of *paschein* that has the character of the *steretikon* [the privative]. Something happens to me, by which I lose the *hexis*, for example, becoming-old. *Pathos* is, therefore, that which deprives me of a matter, and a preserving, saving—preserving in the sense of safe keeping, of raising to a higher, genuine being of *energeia*." To emphasize the sense of motion involved here, Heidegger says that "*Hegel* took the phenomenon of *soxein* from Aristotle in the expression 'sublation' *(Aufhebung)*." For more on this question of *pathos*, and if its connection to "salvation" is the rule or the exception in Aristotle, see also Oele 2012a; see also 2012b. I mention this here to note that the ways that dispositions and affectivities work within "life" in the very different examples above are not reducible to the division between origin and change that goes into our modern thinking about time and life in religion.

41. One may make a different argument (Derrida 1995a) about this text's quest for origin: the text seeks to produce an archive of religion only to presuppose ironically the "breakdown" of the memory of the *arche* itself. But that is not my argument.

42. Note, for example, that for Hegel God in Christianity is the "highest thought" that cannot be thought (Mandair, 137). In Hegel's schema, Christianity always ranks higher than Indian religions in particular, because of its "consistent" passage through history, which he denied to other religions. Thus, this idea of religion as "thought" has a modern Christian genealogy.

43. The foremost place the idea of "thought" given in this text is another indication of the larger problem of origin and change. Thought in modern Western philosophy, as Wittgenstein reminds us, is assumed to begin in the *inner* self, separable from its *outer* expression—i.e., speech or writing. One of his targets here is William James, who claims that thought is possible without speech (342). This privilege, for example, may be found in the simple idea that when one writes a

letter, one merely looks "for expression" for their thoughts (335). The ideas about the cognitive inner self as the origin of thought can take other propositions: I speak to myself, silently; when I imagine or see an object, I "have *got* something which my neighbor has not" (398); or I experience pain (as something private) unique to myself, which others don't have. I heard a version of this proposition at a panel discussion where the participants found it amusing that Sri Lankan Buddhist monks can "go into great detail" in their sermons about topics like the pain of child birth without having experienced it themselves. The participants wondered how "somehow it works because people sit and listen [to the monks], vigorously nodding their heads." Or, such ideas as private thought or pain can take more simple propositions: "I see," "I hear," "I am conscious." For Wittgenstein, one can treat such things as "thought" as a separate "incorporeal" process only if one can "distinguish the grammar of the word 'think' from that of, say, the word 'eat'" (339). Or, as he writes: "Now sentences like "I see, "I hear," "I am conscious" really have their uses. I tell a doctor 'Now I can hear with this ear again,' or I tell someone who believes that I am in a faint 'I am conscious again,' and so on" (416). What this shows is that the idea of origin as a prior interior cannot be sustained as it cannot be inferred from the use of the "ordinary language."

44. Other instances of translating them into a secular language: The Buddhist theory of karma teaches "individual responsibility" (195); the Buddha "ethicized" karma and "substituted ethics for ritual" (195); Buddhism does not "flout normal rules of logic" (160) because, contra tradition, such "positive" things as "love and compassion can be salvific" (68); "like Socrates, [the Buddha] put forward a view of his own . . . with appeals to common sense" (165).

45. The proposition that "we probably cannot know whether he really believed in such beings as gods and other spirits" performs numerous theoretical–political gestures, whose grammar I do not have the space to discuss. For one thing, Gombrich is making an impossible claim—impossible because, among other things, the word "whether," by which no claim is said to be not made, as it holds back really claiming anything, eventually turns it into a claim. This claim has greater implications than one saying, "I do not know whether *I* believe" in superhuman beings and ghosts as, for example, Robinson Crusoe does in a distinctly modern fashion (Derrida 2011, 136, 163).

46. Buddhist texts of course make references to the Buddha's conversing with gods and other supernatural beings. Some of his audience consists of such supernatural beings.

47. Scholars like Collins respond to Gombrich's proposition with an equally problematic proposition. Collins says that the "modern scholar" cannot ask such questions about the Buddha because he was "a legendry figure (who we cannot be certain actually existed)" (2018, 21). Elsewhere I (forthcoming) have argued that this suggestion privileging a particular notion of "knowledge" effectively reduces Buddhist attitudes to gods and spirits to mere "belief."

48. In a different context, on how modern scholarly works try to separate Buddhism from Brahmanism (and by extension, Hinduism) in terms of the propositions

that "Buddhism teaches x," particularly the doctrine of "no-soul" *(anatta)* against the Brahmanical idea of *atman,* see Walser 2017. Walser's argument is that the proposition that *anatta* marks the distinction between Buddhism and Hinduism as separate world religions is neither theoretically nor empirically defensible. The idea of "no-soul" is found in less than 10 percent of (more than five thousand) sermons *(suttas)* in the Pali Buddhist canon, and it is not presented as a contrast to the Brahmanical doctrine in any of these sermons. Walser grants that the claims about the oppositions between Buddhism and Brahmanism have been made in the Buddhist tradition, but, as in the canon, they have to be understood contextually within the limits of a discursive tradition.

49. As Gombrich notes, in the *Brhadaranyaka Upanishad* the reference is to the plural "*brahma*-worlds." The Buddha's interlocutor also speaks of the plural "companionship with the *brahmas.*" But in the later *Chandogya Upanishad,* only the singular "*brahma*-world" is mentioned. Gombrich thinks the latter is an "attempt to tidy up." He is wrong to treat such texts as belonging to a single tradition, against which Buddhism can be contrasted.

50. That is, tradition assumed that the one who attains the *Brahma*-world is born into a kind of superheaven—above the heavens, below nirvana—in Buddhist cosmology.

51. The reviewers of Gombrich's book (e.g., Gethin; Harvey) do not take up these problems.

52. Note again that, for Aristotle, one can speak of change within movement only through the "extraction" of the "point" from it, as in mathematics. Thus, for Aristotle, movement is not "a being" but a "how of being-there." "*The* movement is not, is never there!" (Heidegger 2009, 251).

53. On how similar assumptions anchor the modern "critical" study of the Islamic tradition, see Mas.

54. Contrary to prevailing views, Mehta argues that Gandhi's spiritual practice of nonviolence has no instrumental purpose or eschatology because it works on the self without trying to intervene in the world in the way the (state) violence aims at a goal (that is, the absence of violence, peace). Mehta's analysis helps to see how the Gandhian practice turns on its head the tension between moment and temporality, decisive action and repetitive training that constitutes the possibility of the question of life as an object of critique in modern politics.

Works Cited

Abeysekara, Ananda. 2003. *Colors of the Robe: Religion, Identity, and Difference.* Columbia: University of South Carolina Press.

Abeysekara, Ananda. 2010. "The Im-possibility of Secular Critique: The Future of Religion's Memory." *Culture and Religion* 11, no. 3: 213–346.

Abeysekara, Ananda. Forthcoming. "Review of *Theravada Buddhist Encounters with Modernity.*"

Agamben, Giorgio. 2005. *State of Exception*. Trans. Kevin Attell. Chicago: University of Chicago Press.

Agamben, Giorgio. 2013. *The Highest Poverty: Monastic Rules and Form-of-Life*. Trans. Adam Kotsko. Stanford: Stanford University Press.

Agamben, Giorgio. 2015. *The Use of Bodies*. Trans. Adam Kotsko. Stanford: Stanford University Press.

Agrama, Hussein Ali. 2012. *Questioning Secularism: Islam, Sovereignty, and the Rule of Law in Modern Egypt*. Chicago: University of Chicago Press.

Anidjar, Gil. 2011. "The Meaning of Life." *Critical Inquiry* 37, no. 4: 697–723.

Arendt, Hannah. 1963. *On Revolution*. New York: Penguin Books.

Arendt, Hannah. 1977. "What Is Authority?" In *Between Past and Future*, 91–141. New York: Penguin Books.

Aristotle. 1933. *Metaphysics, Books I–IX*. Trans. Hugh Tredennick. Cambridge: Harvard University Press.

Aristotle. 1984. *On the Soul*. In *The Complete Works of Aristotle*. Vol. 1. Ed. Jonathan Barnes. Princeton: Princeton University Press.

Asad, Talal. 1986a. "On the Idea of an Anthropology of Islam." *Occasional Papers*. Center for Contemporary Arab Studies, Georgetown University.

Asad, Talal. 1986b. "Medieval Heresy: An Anthropological View." *Social History* 11, no. 3: 345–62.

Asad, Talal. 1993. *Genealogies of Religion: Discipline and Reasons of Power in Christianity and Islam*. Baltimore: Johns Hopkins University Press.

Asad, Talal. 1996a. "Modern Power and the Reconfiguration of Religious Traditions." *Stanford Humanities Review* 5, no. 1: 1–16.

Asad, Talal. 1996b. "Comments on Conversion." In *Conversion to Modernities*. Ed. Peter van der Veer, 263–74. New York: Routledge.

Asad, Talal. 2000. "Agency and Pain: An Exploration." *Culture and Religion* 1, no. 1: 29–60.

Asad, Talal. 2003. *Formations of the Secular: Christianity, Islam, Modernity*. Stanford: Stanford University Press.

Asad, Talal. 2006. "Responses." In *Powers of the Secular Modern: Talal Asad and his Interlocutors*. Ed. David Scott and Charles Hirschkind, 207–41. Stanford: Stanford University Press.

Asad, Talal. 2011. "Thinking about the Secular Body, Pain, and Liberal Politics." *Cultural Anthropology* 26, no. 4: 657–675.

Asad, Talal. 2012a. "Thinking about Religion, Belief, and Politics." In *The Cambridge Companion to Religious Studies*. Ed. Robert Orsi, 37–57. Cambridge: Cambridge University Press.

Asad, Talal. 2012b. "Muhammad Asad between Religion and Politics." *İnsan ve Toplum* 1, no. 2: 155–65.

Asad, Talal. 2014a. "*Genealogies of Religion*, Twenty Years On: An Interview with Talal Asad." *Bulletin for the Study of Religion* 43, 1: 12–17.

Asad, Talal. 2014b. "Reflections on Violence, Law, and Humanitarianism." *Critical Inquiry* 41, no. 2: 390–427.

Asad, Talal. 2015. "Thinking about Tradition, Religion, and Politics in Egypt Today." *Critical Inquiry* 42, no. 1: 164–214.

Asad, Talal, Wendy Brown, Judith Butler, and Saba Mahmood. 2009. *Is Critique Secular? Blasphemy, Injury, and Free Speech*. Berkeley: University of California Press.

Augustine. 1961. *Confessions*. Trans. R. S. Pine-Coffin. Harmondsworth: Penguin Books.

Bennington, Geoffrey. 2011. "A Moment of Madness: Derrida's Kierkegaard." *Oxford Literary Review* 33:103–27.

Blackburn, Anne. 2010. *Locations of Buddhism: Colonialism and Modernity in Sri Lanka*. Chicago: University of Chicago Press.

Blanchot, Maurice, and Jacques Derrida. 2000. *The Instant of My Death*, by Maurice Blanchot and *Demeure: Fiction and Testimony*, by Jacques Derrida. Trans. Elizabeth Rottenberg. Stanford: Stanford University Press.

Britt, Brian. 2016. *Postsecular Benjamin: Agency and Tradition*. Evanston: Northwestern University Press.

Burrell, David B. 2001. "Review of *Nirvana and Other Buddhist Felicities: Utopias of the Pali Imaginaire*." *History of Religions* 40, no. 3: 293–95.

Chakrabarty, Dipesh. 2000. *Provincializing Europe: Postcolonial Thought and Historical Difference*. Princeton: Princeton University Press.

Collins, Steven. 1998. *Nirvana and Other Buddhist Felicities: Utopias of the Pali Imaginaire*. Cambridge: Cambridge University Press.

Collins, Steven. 2014. "The Varieties of Buddhist Wisdom." Presentation at Humanities Day, University of Chicago, October 18.

Collins, Steven. 2017. "Periodizing Theravada History: Where to Start?" In *Theravada Buddhist Encounters with Modernity*. Ed. Juliane Schober and Steven Collins, 17–28. London: Routledge.

Corbin, Alain. 1986. *The Foul and the Fragrant: Odor and the French Social Imagination*. Cambridge, Mass.: Harvard University Press.

Derrida, Jacques. 1995a. *Archive Fever: A Freudian Impression*. Trans. Eric Prenowitz. Chicago: University of Chicago Press.

Derrida, Jacques. 1995b. *The Gift of Death*. Trans. David Wills. Chicago: University of Chicago Press.

Derrida, Jacques. 2001. "Force of Law: The 'Mystical' Foundations of Authority." In *Acts of Religion*. Ed. Gil Anidjar, 228–98. New York: Routledge.

Derrida, Jacques. 2009. *The Beast and the Sovereign, Volume 1*. Trans. Geoffrey Bennington. Chicago: University of Chicago Press.

Derrida, Jacques. 2011. *The Beast and the Sovereign, Volume 2*. Trans. Geoffrey Bennington. Chicago: University of Chicago Press.

Desjarlais, Robert R. 2003. *Sensory Biographies: Lives and Deaths among Nepal's Yolmo Buddhists*. Berkeley: University of California Press.

Festa, Lynn. 2006. *Sentimental Figures of Empire in Eighteenth-Century Britain and France*. Baltimore: Johns Hopkins University Press.

Festa, Lynn. 2009. "Sentimental Visions of Empire in Eighteenth-Century Studies." *Literature Compass* 6, no. 1: 23–55.

Foucault, Michel. 2002. "The Subject and Power." In vol. 3 of *The Essential Works of Foucault, 1954–1984*. Ed. James D. Faubion, 326–48. Trans. Robert Hurley et al. London: Penguin.

Gethin, Rupert. 2012. "Review of *What the Buddha Thought*." *H-Net: Humanities and Social Sciences Online,* January. https://networks.h-net.org/node/6060/reviews/16095/gethin-gombrich-what-buddha-thought.

Gillespie, Michael Allen. 2008. *The Theological Origins of Modernity*. Chicago: University of Chicago Press.

Gombrich, Richard. 2009. *What the Buddha Thought*. London: Equinox.

Hallisey, Charles. 1995. "Roads Taken and Not Taken in the Study of Theravada Buddhism." In *Curators of the Buddha*. Ed. Donald S. Lopez Jr., 31–62. Chicago: University of Chicago Press.

Hansen, Anne Ruth. 2007. *How to Behave: Buddhism and Modernity in Colonial Cambodia, 1860–1930*. Honolulu: University of Hawai'i Press.

Harvey, Peter. 2011. "Review of *What the Buddha Thought*." *Diskus* 12. http://diskus.basr.ac.uk/index.php/DISKUS/article/view/23/22.

Heidegger, Martin. 1988. *Hegel's Phenomenology of Spirit*. Trans. Parvis Emad and Kenneth Maly. Bloomington: Indiana University Press.

Heidegger, Martin. 1992. *Plato's Sophist*. Trans. Richard Rojcewicz and Andre Schuwer. Bloomington: Indiana University Press.

Heidegger, Martin. 1995. *Aristotle's Metaphysics Θ 1–3: On the Essence and Actuality of Force*. Trans.Walter Brogan and Peter Warnek. Bloomington: Indiana University Press.

Heidegger, Martin. 1998. "On the Essence and Concept of Φύσις in Aristotle's Physics B, 1." In *Pathmarks*. Ed. William McNeill, 183–230. Cambridge: Cambridge University Press.

Heidegger, Martin. 2003. *Four Seminars*. Trans. Andrew J. Mitchell and Francois Raffoul. Bloomington: Indiana University Press.

Heidegger, Martin. 2009. *Basic Concepts of Aristotelian Philosophy*. Trans. Robert D. Metcalf and Mark B. Tanzer. Bloomington: Indiana University Press.

Hirschkind, Charles. 2006. *The Ethical Soundscape: Cassette Sermons and Islamic Counterpublics*. New York: Columbia University Press.

Hirschkind, Charles. 2011. "Is There a Secular Body?" *Cultural Anthropology* 26, no. 4:633–47.

Holt, John. 1995. "Protestant Buddhism." *Religious Studies Review* 17, no. 4: 307–312.

Jeganathan, Pradeep. 2000. "Anthropology, Politics, and the Location of a Sinhala Practice of Masculinity." In *Community, Gender, and Violence*. Ed. Partha Chatterjee and Pradeep Jeganathan, 37–65. New York: Columbia University Press.

Kang, Taran. 2013. "Origin and Essence: The Problem of History in Hannah Arendt." *Journal of the History of Ideas* 74, no. 1:139–60.

King, Richard. 2001. "Orientalism and the Discovery of 'Buddhism.'" In *Orientalism and Religion: Postcolonial Theory, India, and "The Mystic East,"* 143–60. New York: Routledge.

Lempert, Michael. 2012. *Discipline and Debate: The Language of Violence in a Tibetan Buddhist Monastery*. Berkeley: University of California Press.

Lopez, Donald S., Jr. 1998. *Prisoners of Shangri-La: Tibetan Buddhism and the West*. Chicago: University of Chicago Press.

Lopez, Donald S., Jr. 2008. *Buddhism and Science: A Guide for the Perplexed*. Chicago: University of Chicago Press.

Mahmood, Saba. 2005. *Politics of Piety: Islamic Revival and the Feminist Subject*. Princeton: Princeton University Press.

Mandair, Arvind-Pal S. 2009. *Religion and the Specter of the West: Sikhism, India, Postcoloniality, and the Politics of Translation*. New York: Columbia University Press.

Mas, Ruth. 2012. "Why Critique?" *Method and Theory in the Study of Religion* 23, nos. 4–5: 389–407.

McClure, Kristie M. 2010. "Reflections on Michael Gillespie's Theological Origins of Modernity." *Review of Politics* 72, no. 4: 697–704.

McDaniel, Justin Thomas. 2008. *Gathering Leaves and Lifting Words: Histories of Buddhist Monastic Education in Laos and Thailand*. Seattle: University of Washington Press.

Mehta, Uday Singh. 2010. "Gandhi and the Common Logic of War and Peace." *Raritan* (Summer): 134–73.

Mill, John Stuart. 1973. *On Liberty*. Indiana: Hackett.

Moyn, Samuel. 2006. "Empathy in History, Empathizing with Humanity." *History and Theory* 45, no. 3: 397–415.

Murchada, Felix Ó. 2013. *The Time of Revolution: Kairos and Chronos in Heidegger*. London: Bloomsbury.

Oele, Marjolein. 2012a. "Heidegger's Reading of Aristotle's Concept of Pathos." *Epoché: A Journal for the History of Philosophy* 16, no. 2: 389–406.

Oele, Marjolein. 2012b. "Passive Dispositions: On the Relationship between πάθος and ἕξις in Aristotle." *Ancient Philosophy* 32, no. 2: 1–18.

Salgado, Nirmala S. 2013. *Buddhist Nuns and Gendered Practice: In Search of the Female Renunciant*. New York: Oxford University Press.

Scherer, Matthew. 2013. *Beyond Church and State: Democracy, Secularism, and Conversion*. New York: Cambridge University Press.

Scott, David. 1994a. *Formations of Ritual: Colonial and Anthropological Discourses on the Sinhala Yaktovil*. Minneapolis: University of Minnesota Press.

Scott, David. 1994b. "Historizing Tradition: Buddhism and the Discourse of Yakku." In *Formations of Ritual: Colonial and Anthropological Discourses on the Sinhala Yaktovil*, 173–203. Minneapolis: University of Minnesota Press.

Scott, David. 1999. "Religion in Colonial Civil Society." In *Refashioning Futures: Criticism after Postcoloniality*, 53–69. Princeton: Princeton University Press.

Scott, David. 2004. *Conscripts of Modernity: The Tragedy of Colonial Enlightenment*. Durham: Duke University Press.

Skinner, Quentin. 1998. *Liberty before Liberalism*. Cambridge: Cambridge University Press.

Skinner, Quentin. 2002. "A Third Concept of Liberty." *Proceedings of the British Academy* 117:237–68.

Skinner, Quentin. 2008. *Hobbes and Republican Liberty*. Cambridge: Cambridge University Press.

Turner, Alicia. 2014. *Saving Buddhism: The Impermanence of Religion in Colonial Burma*. Honolulu: University of Hawai'i Press.

Viswanath, Rupa. 2014. *The Pariah Problem: Caste, Religion, and the Social in Modern India*. New York: Columbia University Press.

Walser, Joseph. 2015. "The Classification of Religions and Religious Classifications: A Genre Approach to the Origin of Religions." *Culture and Religion* 16, no. 4: 345–71.

Walser, Joseph. Forthcoming. "When Did Buddhism Become Anti-Brahmanical? The Case of the Missing Soul." *Journal of the American Academy of Religion*.

Walters, Jonathan. 1995. "Multireligion on the Bus: Beyond 'Influence' and 'Syncretism' in the Study of Religious Meetings." In *Unmaking the Nation: The Politics of Identity and History in Modern Sri Lanka*. Ed. Pradeep Jeganathan and Qadri Ismail, 25–54. Colombo: S.S.A.

Walters, Jonathan, and Matthew B. Colley. 2006. "Making History: George Turnour, Edward Upham, and the 'Discovery' of the Mahavamsa." *Sri Lanka Journal of the Humanities* 32, nos. 1–2: 135–67.

Wedemeyer, Christian K. 2012. *Making Sense of Tantric Buddhism: History, Semiology, and Transgression in the Indian Traditions*. New York: Columbia University Press.

Wittgenstein, Ludwig. 2009. *Philosophical Investigations*. Trans. P. M. S. Hacker and Joachim Schulte. Oxford: Blackwell.

A GLOBAL "WE"?

POETIC EXHORTATIONS IN A TIME OF PRECARIOUS LIFE

Walt Hunter

In his analysis of Charles Baudelaire, Walter Benjamin shows that late nineteenth-century European poetry's retreat into a radical individuality is a response to changes in capitalism—in particular, new temporalities of machine work and "shocks" by the crowd (161). This essay brings together two poets, Sean Bonney and Myung Mi Kim, who write under conditions in which that crowd has disappeared. The hortatory mode used by their poems takes its ethical and political force not from the shock of encountering the crowd but from realizing that crowds themselves are in jeopardy. While some contemporary hortatory poems draw on historical norms of lyric poetry, my concern here is not the Anglophone lyric per se; the ballads and experimental open forms of poetry I look at below also reshape the rhetoric of calling, inviting, pleading, and cursing. Written from, and in tension with, centers of economic and political power in the United States and UK, these poems uncover a specific historical relation between contemporary poetry in English—in Kim's case, English and Korean—and the politics of the crowd. To orient these poems in relation to global capitalism today is to underscore the extent to which global capitalism renders its crowds precarious, capable of disintegration by informalized labor conditions, dispersal by a militarized police and a securitized state, or cooption by the politics of communitarianism and expulsion. In response to the globally induced vulnerability of collective life, the poets in this essay desperately conjure a globalized "we," a crowd to come.

Neither poet lays claim to an explicit, thematized "we," however. Suspicious of the totalizing and potentially totalitarian politics of the "we," both of them develop instead a formal and stylistic procedure for culling and gleaning the material that they include in their poetry.

I use the metaphor of commoning to describe this poetics, taking my cue from the titles of the two poetry collections in this essay, Bonney's *The Commons* and Kim's *Commons*. Their materials are never simply equal fragments juxtaposed across gulfs of difference, but, as the terms "gleaning" and "commoning" both imply, ones scored by economic precariousness and marked by historical and racialized positions of inequality. Nor are they the remnants of a high European tradition, preserved in modernist bricolage against their ruin. The porousness of the poem to its different materials varies in degree from Bonney to Kim, depending on the unique possibilities granted by their chosen forms. The conditions and locations in which the poems are situated are ineluctably specific: Bonney's cuckoo sings ballads about British and U.S. networks of finance; Kim's fractured and reconstituted Korean and English syntax is embedded in the violence of war and displacement. But both poets reinvent the forms they use through the poetic enactment of gleaning. In this way, the commoning of diverse poetic leftovers becomes the stockpile that powers a collectivity yet to come.

The invitation to a crowd is not so much marked by the imagination of a particular set of figures in Bonney and Kim as it is by their innovations within the hortatory modes of summoning, calling together, and inciting. The rhetoric of exhortation has been reinvigorated in contemporary Anglophone poetry written under global conditions of vulnerability, exile and migration, radical uncertainty, and expulsion from social life. Hortatory rhetoric is closely related to the trope of apostrophe, which Jonathan Culler argues "makes its point by troping not on the meaning of a word but on the circuit or situation of communication itself" (1977, 59). Epideixis, or the convention of praise that is constitutive of Greek lyric poetry, can often be combined with exhortation: *The Song of Songs,* for instance, balances devotion with invitation: "come, my beloved, / let us go out into the fields" (105). Aristotle, in the *Rhetoric,* notes that praise has the tendency to slip quickly into exhortation: "To praise a man is . . . akin to urging a course of action" (35). As early as Sappho and as late as Claudia Rankine, exhortation is one of the most recognizable ways that Greek, European, and Anglophone poetry talks to strangers, extending its intimacy to what the poet Jorie Graham calls "regions of unlikeness."[1] Exhortation is thus one of the rhetorical strategies that specific strains of poetry take toward the world as they attempt to call forth a collective "we" through the poem, a "we" of displaced, oppressed, exiled, and vulnerable lives.[2]

Earlier readings of poetic sociality by Walter Benjamin and Theodor Adorno help to situate a contemporary hortatory poetics. Benjamin and Adorno examine a relation between the "I" of a poem and the "we" that is shaped by the altered material conditions of capitalism. For Benjamin, the "we" is the figure of the crowd, while for Adorno the "we" is shorthand for society. Benjamin's "On Some Motifs in Baudelaire" (1939) argues that modern capitalism is based on the encounter with "shock" and its deflection by the consciousness (161). Benjamin draws a set of analogies between machine work, crowds, and gambling: "The shock experience which the passerby has in the crowd corresponds to the isolated 'experiences' of the worker at his machine . . . the reflexive mechanism that the machine triggers in the workman can be studied closely, as in a mirror, in the idler . . . the jolt in the movement of the machine is like the so-called *coup* in the game of chance" (177). A new sense of time connects the worker, the member of a crowd, and the gambler: in Baudelaire's world, Benjamin argues, "each operation [is] screened off from the preceding operation" (177). Benjamin argues that this process of "starting all over again" is inimical to the creation of experience that stretches back in time, which we perceive as the "aura" that surrounds the objects of our memory (179, 186). Since the aura is no longer accessible as long experience over time, Baudelaire's lyric grants its power instead to immediate experience, to the eyes that "have lost their ability to look" (189). In such a context, to write lyric at all requires a cost, which for Baudelaire is "the disintegration of the aura in the experience of shock" (194). In Benjamin's analysis, lyric poetry continues to be written, but only by acquiescing to the loss of the particular social and material conditions that had once accompanied it.

For Adorno, poetry occupies an even more strained relationship to the language of capital. In "On Lyric Poetry and Society" (1957), Adorno argues for an "immanent" approach to lyric that avoids reducing its social efficacy to a set of political concepts or themes (39). The explicit social themes and concepts of a poem are only evidence of its debasement, distortion, and subsumption under capital (38). Adorno maintains that, instead, the social is "imprinted in reverse on the poetic work" (39): "The less the work thematizes the relationship of 'I' and society, the more spontaneously it crystallizes of its own accord in the poem" (42). As Robert Kaufman explains, "The lyric poem must work coherently in and with the medium—language—that human beings use to articulate objective concepts, even while the lyric explores the most subjective, nonconceptual, and ephemeral phenomena" (363). This argument allows Adorno to steer between two social interpretations of a poetic "I." By denying that the "I" speaks from an external vantage point on society, he separates the poetic subject from that false image of an individual who has somehow escaped from "utility" and the "weight of material existence" (39). And by insisting against the thematization of the social, he prevents the "I" from becoming the mouthpiece of already-existing concepts. Thus Adorno claims that "in the lyric poem the subject, through its identification with language, negates both its opposition to society as something merely monadological and its mere functioning within a wholly socialized society" (44).

Benjamin's essay begins with a hypothesis that modern European poetry receives a poor reception because of a "change in the structure of . . . experience" (156). He turns quite deliberately not to philosophy, but rather to Baudelaire's poetry itself to try to find out what this change might be. The "decisive, unmistakable experience" confronted by Baudelaire's lyric is the shock of "having been jostled by the crowd" (193). Today, much U.S. poetry directs itself to a "change in the structure of experience" as well. Yet the changes registered by the poems below are the erosion, rather than the "shock" and "jostling," of sociality. The disposition toward the social modeled by some contemporary poets does not draw into the poem an oppressive encounter fraught with responsibility, as some ethical models propose, so much as it manifests as a side-by-side, adjacent, or contiguous relation. The poetry in this essay is responsive to the global condition that Judith Butler describes as "unchosen cohabitation" and the accompanying ethical commitment "to an equal right to inhabit the earth" (145). While contemporary capitalism fictionalizes social life in terms of corporate personhood or agonistic competition over scarce resources, one strain of recent poetry enacts on the level of poetic form the jostling, prickling, energizing sensations of proximity to heterogeneous others. The poets I consider here use poetic language to summon forth a crowd that would be impossible to represent as either a homogeneous totality or something imperiously "other." In this way, their poetry aligns itself with the "precarious," a term I borrow in order to emphasize both the fragility of these collectivities and their position outside waged labor, political representation, and economic security.

Research in political, economic, and social thought demarcates the current period of globalization as a "new historical phase," an "age of precarity" (Berlant, 193). "Precarious life" and "precarity" have appeared more and more frequently as political, philosophical, and ethical terms that refer to contemporary conditions of life under specific forms of insecurity, including "the shrinkage of the social welfare state, the privatization of what had once been publicly held utilities and institutions, the increase in state, banking and corporate pension insecurity, and the ever more 'flexible' practices of contractual reciprocity between owners and workers" (192). These changes have also been accompanied, most recently, by the increasing financialization of commodities, which exacerbates the pressures put on local markets for food and other everyday items.[3]

Discussions of precarity are shaped by Paulo Virno, who describes precarity as "the chronic instability of forms of life" (87); by Pierre Bourdieu, who examines the "absolute reign of flexibility" (97); by Judith Butler, who considers precarious life as a common ontological vulnerability on the basis of which we might found a tentative solidarity; by Isabell Lorey, who analyzes the normalization of precarity as an aspect of neoliberal governmentality; and by Guillaume le Blanc, who analyzes precarity as the social vulnerability created by economic and political oppression. These philosophies of precarity are complemented by the sociologies of labor undertaken by Saskia Sassen and Andrew Ross, who analyze the increasing role of sweatshops, free zones, and exploited workers in the global economy. While some discourses of globalization emphasize the placelessness of the "information economy," Sassen directs attention to the precarious bodies of workers whose labor supports the global city, especially women of color and immigrants. The precarious subject of "material conditions, production sites, and activities bounded by place," the subject moving through "counter-geographies of globalization," confronts contingency, difficulty, risk, and expulsion from social norms (257, 264).

As a term that describes the period following the independence of former colonies, the implementation of Cold War underdevelopment, and the crises of U.S. legitimacy as a world hegemon, precarity knits together global changes in economic relations, aesthetic perception, and the social production of collectivities. Precarity is particularly important for understanding the poets in this essay because it calls attention to the disintegration of sociality. As Franco Berardi argues, solidarity is hard to imagine under a regime of financial speculation and cognitive labor, because "the work process is no longer based on a community of workers living together in a factory day after day, but instead takes the form of an ever-changing recombination of time fragments connected in the global network" (118). At the same time, precarity has served as a rallying cry that draws together disparate groups into a common struggle against neoliberal globalization. As Lauren Berlant notes, movements of the precarious seek "to forge transcategorical alliances (trans-local,-national,-class,-legal,-sexual, etc.) against the fading of social democratic institutions and toward the invention of new communities of care and political belonging" (270 n.2). In this sense, precarity refers not only to a general state of ontological vulnerability but also to specific global political movements of the present.

The theorization of precarity by Berardi, Butler, Berlant, Sassen, and others is helpful because it undermines celebratory narratives of globalization that focus on a hypermobile capitalist elite. At the same time, the overdetermined figure of the precarious challenges analyses from the Left that privilege the factory floor as the site for labor activism. Arguments about precarity can be situated in the broader context of social–scientific analyses of economic globalization undertaken by proponents and critics of deregulation, privatization, and speculation. By now, the costs of careless pacing, deliberate hypocrisy by certain global players, and the adoption of neoliberalism as a political ideology are glaringly evident.[4] Older arguments that economic globalization might ameliorate poverty and inequality have been refuted by careful attention to the disagreements over what these terms mean and how they are measured.[5] While methodological differences certainly continue to exist—what poverty line to use, whether to measure inequality within countries or between countries—research across the disciplines bears out the claims that neoliberal policies exacerbate inequality, poverty, and precariousness. As Robert H. Wade notes, "What is striking is how little, rather than how much, the 'developing world'—outside of East Asia—has caught up with the West after 65 years of deliberate 'development'" (2017, 137). One widely publicized concession from global development institutions in this respect is the International Monetary Fund's June 2016 report, "Neoliberalism: Oversold?" The report blames short-term capital flow liberalization and austerity policies for both exacerbating inequality and undercutting growth (Ostry, Loungani, and Furceri, 41).

The term "precarity" draws out elements of the historically specific configuration of capitalism and insecurity that faces contemporary poets when they try to imagine a "we." Recent poetry collections by the English poet Sean Bonney and the Korean American poet Myung Mi Kim bring together hortatory rhetoric, poetic calls to gather, with the vanishing spaces that they name "commons." Far from a nostalgic return to a world without capital's enclosures, their poetry encompasses a wide range of strategies for energizing a fragmented and precarized social body. At moments, both these poets are explicitly critical of capital, finance, militarization, and neoliberal politics. Often, however, they explore vulnerability more obliquely. For Bonney and Kim, poetic imagination is one place to look for global solidarity, for a "new social ecology," and for collective agency (Berlant, 193). These poets revalue poetry as the medium through which a collective takes shape or, as Kim puts it, as a "provisional location" designed "to mobilize the notion of our responsibility to one another in social space" (111). As a racialized and financialized global capitalism forecloses the possibilities for sociality and solidarity in dramatic ways, Bonney and Kim explicitly align themselves with poetic traditions, from Whitman and Baudelaire to Ashbery and Rankine, of finding oneself in the midst of a crowd. Confronted with the pressures of adjacency and proximity to others, their poetry creates the literary equivalent of a commons: a shared "meditative space," to recall Claudia Rankine's phrase, that subverts the hierarchies of power reproduced in other forms of discourse (Rankine and Hoover).

Although the language and syntax they use are quite different, the notion of the commons developed in both shares certain qualities.[6] Neither poet lays out a thematic program or a set of slogans for social solidarity or collective political subjectivity. David Harvey underscores this proleptic or anticipatory commons, emphasizing that "the common is not, therefore, something extant once upon a time that has since been lost, but something that, like the urban commons, is continuously being produced. The problem is that it is just as continuously being enclosed and appropriated by capital in its commodified and monetary form" (106). In a formulation that recalls Harvey's, Kim states that a commons is illegible within the "totalizing power of language that serves the prevailing systems and demands of coherence" (110). Within this language, it is a blank space: "______, a word that cannot be translated: it suggests, 'what belongs to the people'" (109). Bonney and Kim both fend off a sentimental, affective call to the commons as the return to an idealized precapitalist condition. To do so, the commons appears only through the operations performed on and by the poem. While Bonney's *The Commons* attacks and interrupts the languages of banking and credit, Kim's poetry focuses on war, displacement, and problems of translation.

Bonney's *The Commons* (2011) represents a contemporary version of the poetic curse that hectors, blames, eviscerates, scorns, hates, and condemns.[7] At the same time, his poems perform a kind of gleaning, gathering together lyric songs and popular ballads with a range of other linguistic materials. Bonney's invectives, written after the world financial crisis of 2008 and during the riots in London in 2011, target global finance for its reduction of language, thought, and people to blanks and gasps:

> Meanwhile, in the fast world of banking
> they are thinking in blocks of sound
> blank ones
> reduced to little knots
> of hair & teeth
> we were speaking
> like any gasping swine. (Bonney, 6)

For those who think in blank "blocks of sound," the voices of the precarious are audible only as "gasping swine." To find another language for precarity, and to create a counterdiscourse to that of financial capitalism, Bonney reaches back into the archives of English poetry and song. *The Commons* is a patchwork of citations, from the traditional English song "The Cuckoo Bird" to Arthur Rimbaud's "L'Orgie Parisienne"; from The Velvet Underground's "Heroin" to Frantz

Fanon's *The Wretched of the Earth*; and from a Hackney Council Housing Benefit Form to Shelley's *Prometheus Unbound*. These references are not disguised, but linked, along with YouTube clips and Bonney's own performances, on Bonney's blog, where the poem was first published. In an author's note, Bonney explains that *The Commons* is written to subvert the official language of neoliberal globalization, which identifies the precarious subject of history as a "zombie":

> The work was originally subtitled "A Narrative / Diagram of the Class Struggle," wherein voices from contemporary uprisings blend into the Paris Commune, into October 1917, into the execution of Charles 1, and on into superstitions, fantasies of crazed fairies and supernatural bandits //// all clambering up from their hidden places in history, getting ready to storm the Cities of the Rich //// to the bourgeois eye they may look like zombies, to us they are sparrows, cuckoos, pirates & sirens //// the cracked melodies of ancient folk songs, cracking the windows of Piccadilly //// or, as a contemporary Greek proverb has it, "smashing up the present because they come from the future."[8]

Instead of "zombies" or "gasping swine," Bonney has the resistance to globalization take the form of figures recuperated from songs and ballads: "sparrows, cuckoos, pirates & sirens."[9]

The material disappearance of the commons is registered in dialectical fashion by the collected remnants of older poems, the "cracked melodies of ancient folk songs," and the silent, invisible groups of people they memorialize. By bundling together these estovers of poetic fragments and titles of songs, Bonney's *Commons* reminds us that the high status of poetry in Anglophone literature in the mid-sixteenth century coincides almost exactly with the English enclosure movements begun by the dissolution of the monasteries in 1536.[10] The rhetoric of lament acknowledges the foreclosure of a collective struggle, even as it insists on the adjacency of others:

> moan, now
> on his white bones
> his intolerable name.
> He is the man or woman
> sitting beside you,
> bitter & false & snapped
> inside every nation

such hawks & hounds, such ravens
o bitter statistics
the cuckoo is a pretty bird (11)

Into the space of the absent commons slip the folk songs and figures that serve as so many indices of revolutionary activity. These include the "cuckoo," which, from Jacobite minstrelsy to Wordsworthian balladry, appears to announce a spring that cannot yet be seen or imagined. Many of these anonymous songs, such as "The Cuckoo Bird" or "The Three Ravens," predate the earliest significant period of privatization in the modern capitalist world-system, the passing into law of the enclosure of the commons in the early seventeenth century. They represent much more than "a sentimental space, purely / some kind of folk song" (17). They also provide a crucial reminder that the current period of neoliberalism, financial capitalism, and endless war is a late moment in a four hundred year cycle of economic regulation and deregulation.[11]

Bonney's poetry searches for a relation between a revolutionary poetic language and a revolutionary political subject. The "intolerable name" of precarious life—the global "we" of the contemporary period, the "man or woman / sitting beside you"—cannot be explicitly summoned within the poem:

cold / blows[12] the future
ballads of the
-blank-
my true love (14)

While the poem retains the poetic address to "my true love," the addressee of the "future ballad" appears as a prolepsis, a "blank" that will be filled in later. Perhaps the "blank" is also a musical rest, a withholding of sound or word, a single beat that calls attention to the absence of what might fill it. "The sun has been disconnected," Bonney writes elsewhere: both electricity and poetic inspiration—one traditional symbol of which is the "sun"—have been cut off because of poor credit (6). Nor can the "windows of Piccadilly" be cracked simply by gleaning bits of song and juxtaposing them, rewriting *The Waste*

Land during a different moment of crisis in the modern world-system. In Bonney's poem, there is little to suggest that a viable position exists outside the "prepared vocab" of neoliberalism:

> history is those who sit
> inside their prepared vocab
> the comfortable ones,
> the executioner, especially,
> never utters an articulate sound
> quietly gets on with his work. (22)

Even as the poet screams "slaughter the fascist BNP," much of *The Commons* is specifically about the complicity and continuity between the language of the poem and the language of power (3).

Bonney's poetry launches an explicit critique of the language of neoliberal globalization. But his poems do more than interrupt the circulation of neoliberal discourse. They also perform, in a version of poetic commoning, a recombination of linguistic registers, literary sources, and heterogeneous lexicons. *The Commons* can be understood as an "anti-discourse," to borrow Christian Lotz's term, that frees words to exist in hitherto unknown relations to each other. Lotz writes,

> If it is true that poetic speech inhibits and "brackets" the primary function of language in our everyday world, such as conversation, information, narration, description, and performative tasks, then it is easier to see how poetry not only releases words out of their ordinary connections, but also introduces and builds up new relations. (499)

Lotz builds on Karlheinz Stierle's effort to describe what is "exceptional" about lyric poetry in particular: "[Lyric] is not its own literary genre, but a specific mode . . . that signifies the transgression of discursive schema" (514). The analyses by Stierle and Lotz of lyric as "transgression" and "anti-discourse" are part of a venerable critical tendency to mark the identity of lyric as paradoxical, dialectical, excessive, or simply contradictory.[13]

Bonney dramatizes such an alienation or othering of poetry from its own language. He does this not by foregrounding the materiality of the "aesthetic function" but rather by documenting the poem's own fraught composition, its own making and unmaking:

> the 'reverie' is a
> stop, oppressive line
> "is this is that"
> like a mystical shudder?
> yeh, that's hideous.
> anyway, false, as I was saying (9)

Bonney's hesitation to define reverie or cuckoo or sea or moon relies on a tactic of incessant interruption and self-reference. The appearance of "as I was saying," and the related phrase "ok, say that again," is one of countless moments of self-recognition, self-criticism, and self-revision documented by the poem (3, 11, 18). Other lines remind the poet to insert material that will signal the presence of a contemporary poem: "*-archaic pop reference here-*," "*-archaic credit reference here-*," "*favorite epoch here*," "insert hope & love," "insert world of banking" (3, 6, 10, 22, 25). Holding "the voice of our political poets" up to scrutiny, Bonney finds no room for a straightforward "flip discount menace" that poets might once have hoped to use against "the hounds of capital" (15, 18).[14] A certain rhetorical promiscuity dominates the poem: the times, Bonney suggests, require all of the poet's rhetorical dexterity. Even as it reflects on the limitations of the power of its address, *The Commons* sustains a relatively direct, colloquial style.[15] And even as the poem distances its audience with self-critical reflections on its own making, *The Commons* invites the same audience into the poem with its calls to riot and revolution, as well as its cries and laments.

As *The Commons* rages, blames, and excoriates, the timescale of precarious lives—a transnational "we" that is radically uncertain, constantly vulnerable to interruption, forced to sign weekly or even daily contracts for labor—is revalued as a poetic and political strategy for insurrection. While Bonney criticizes the Situationist directive to "just, like, *détourne* yourself," something like a *détournement*, or a wrenching of words from their habitual meanings, ultimately occurs by the time the poem ends (11). Despite its anxieties about "discount menace," *The Commons* takes up, at moments, positions of pure antagonism—"HAIL SHIT" (26)—that occupy forms of poetic address ("hail to thee, blithe Spirit!") (Shelley, 304). In this manner, Bonney activates "music love abstraction / the twisted branches / at the centre of our lives," all of which "ignite on interruption" (28). Within the incendiary lyricism of *The Commons*, a "we" emerges as those who, by virtue of their precarity, possess the imaginative capacity to seize and interrupt the categories with which they are classified and silenced:

> & we, with our downturned mouths
> are maidens,
> our credit ratings threaded with flowers.
> & we are bleating,
> & we are fucking immense
> shrieking with gibes and curses-(6)

This "we" can only be declared by the poet when the tropes of pastoral are revealed as interwoven with, or "threaded" through, the financialized subject of the speculative economy.

The plural "we" flashes forth in Bonney as a revolutionary subject in the process of being made, of scattering, and of reforming. Bonney's work coincides with riots in the streets of London and with revolutions in the squares of Tunisia, Egypt, the United States, and Turkey, among other sites of protest. In contrast, Myung Mi Kim's *Commons* (2002), written in the United States during the post-9/11 surge of U.S. territorial expansion and military occupation, avoids almost entirely thematic representations of a collectivity, desiring instead to "activate" language's ability "to call into question, to disclose, to make common" (110). As this quotation makes clear, the commons to which the title refers does not exist in the past, susceptible to recovery, but remains to be "made." The fact that Bonney and Kim share a title is more than a matter of coincidence. In both, the making of the commons occurs through a hortatory form that searches for a language of the precarious beyond the "prepared vocab" available. With Kim, however, this hortatory form is anatomized and radicalized through a rigorous attention to the smallest particles of language; to the possibilities of translating between languages; to the discrepant ways that English and Korean index material processes of war, poverty, and displacement; and, finally, to the potential for the poem to make a space for multiple languages while denaturalizing the precedence of a monolithic global English.

A professor at the State University of New York at Buffalo, one of the institutional homes for experimental poets and critics in the United States, the Korean-born Kim investigates the links between destabilizing language and disrupting political or economic structures. She shares with the U.S. avant-garde traditions of L=A=N=G=U=A=G=E poetry an interest in finding the places where referential and nonreferential functions of language jostle against each other.[16] But such a general description of Kim's work threatens to erase its documentation and performance of collective suffering and violence under racial capitalism. It might be more precise to say, with Joseph Jonghyun Jeon, that her collections, from *Under Flag* (1991) and *The Bounty* (1996) to *Commons* (2002) and *Penury* (2009), make visible "issues of historical violence, immigration, and diaspora" by framing them "through linguistic rather than social lenses" (2015, 998). This use of language as the lens through which to encounter history makes Kim's work undeniably elusive, difficult, and austere. The first section of *Commons*, "Exordium," begins with the following passage: "In what way names were applied to things. Filtration. Not every word that has been applied, still exists. Through proliferation and differentiation. Airborn. Here, this speck and this speck you missed" (3). Many of the elements of Kim's defamiliarizing syntax and compositional procedure are already present here. The short paragraph opens with a reference to Adamic naming, as though to draw attention to its own place at the beginning of the book as well. Next, the word "filtration" could be a metaphor for the "way names were applied to things," or it could be an example of a name applied to a thing; the word creates two divergent tracks for interpretation. "Proliferation," "airborn," and "speck" all pick up on the "filtration system," but "differentiation" keeps active the linguistic references in the first and third sentences. It is possible, then, that "proliferation and differentiation" name the processes by which words that have been applied to things in the past cease to "exist." Finally, "missed" supplies a third binding agent by virtue of its vowel and consonant sounds, which recall "exists" as well as the short "i" sounds in proliferation and differentiation.

As this fragment suggests, Kim defamiliarizes and disrupts a reader's acquired ability to discover meaning in a poem by describing how the units of the poem interact. To prevent an attitude of absorption in the text, Kim also includes metacommentary on the writing of the poem itself. This self-consciousness is present throughout *Commons*, but it is especially prevalent in the final section, a paratactic series of notes about her poetic process entitled "Pollen Fossil Record." Here, Kim explains that "*COMMONS* elides multiple sites: reading and text making, discourses and disciplines, documents and documenting.

Fluctuating. Proceeding by fragment, by increment. Through proposition, parataxis, contingency—approximating nerve, line, song" (107). The poems cobble together disparate sources from which Kim gleans a single sound, word, phrase, or sometimes large paragraph. These sources are not given, but they include bald, declarative statements from what would seem to be counterinsurgency manuals; single letters or diphthongs; travel narratives; Da Vinci's notebooks; definitions of fairly obscure words, such as "periplus" or "muo"; songs and lyric poems from both English and Korean traditions; and quotations from the news. Although these programmatic lines from "Pollen Fossil Record" ostensibly describe the book, they also resemble closely, in their own form, the poetry in the preceding sections. "Pollen Fossil Record" is both a key to the rest of the text and an extension of it. Commoning, in Kim's terms, involves a method of "elision" by which incommensurate discourses are conjoined, or by which poetry cohabits space with its "others."[17]

Kim's poems are crowded with elements that resist easy explanations for their simultaneous presence in the poem. Such a fractious assemblage makes it hard to identify a "we," even as a metaphor for the heterogeneous materials in the poem. Instead, Kim's poetry prepares the ground for a genuine "we" by exposing the false universality and the politically produced coherence of existing discourses. Against this, Kim writes that poetry has the ability to grasp the "'particularizable' prosody of one's living" (111). The specific "prosody of living" that Kim dissects and reconstructs through poetry is not prised from BNP (Banque Nationale de Paris) and global finance, as in Bonney's work, but from a globalized English language riven by differential forms of material suffering and expulsion: "What *is* English now, in the face of mass global migrations, ecological degradations, shifts and upheavals in identifications of gender and labor? . . . How to make plural the written and spoken . . ." (110).[18] Kim's "commons" designates the linguistic space for a "plural" English, an English that "belongs to the people" linked together by the shared experiences of global precarity.[19]

To examine the possibilities for a "plural" English, Kim constructs incomplete or deliberately thwarted translations from Korean to English song and back. Frequently in *Commons,* the ghost of a quatrain will appear, as in the poem marked "405":

> Little flower,
> What day is it
> The light stops at glum
> O'clock and *f* (32)

At first, "little flower" might be read as an apostrophe to the flower. The second line could then be the question addressed to it. One thinks here of William Blake's line "Little lamb who made thee" and of the habit certain poems have of apostrophizing the nonhuman. In Kim's poem, the third line supports and elaborates this reading, but then takes a sharp turn from it in the final word, "glum," which, in light of the fourth line, seems to have been substituted for a specific hour. This unexpected adjective, given additional emphasis at the end of a line, casts doubt over the interpretation of the previous two lines: "what day is it" might be a question the speaker poses to herself; "little flower" might be a description rather than an address. Lines one and two may have no necessary relation at all. The temptation to grant a certain poetic license in the fourth line—"glum / O'clock" as some dreary hour—disappears with the single syllable *f*. If "f" stands for "forte," an indication of volume on a musical score, then the reader is given an instruction for how to voice the poem—a self-conscious move that comes as a jolt after the way the initial lines set up a scene. Just as likely, however, "f" introduces an unrelated, nonsignifying sound into the poem and the flickering scene deteriorates further.

I read this passage as a draft of a "bad" translation, allowed to retain its ventures and soundings *(f)* as well as its "mistakes" (glum). At the same time, the passage clearly borrows from a ballad-like form: Kim notes in "Pollen Fossil Record" that she juxtaposes a fourteenth-century Korean *sijo* and "an alliterative English poem from about the same time" and "translates" them simultaneously. She explains her procedure and its stakes in the global:

> It is not the actual translation or even the state of translatability between the two texts that is intriguing but the possibilities for transcribing what occurs in the transversal between the two languages (and, by extension, between the two "nations," their mutually implicated histories of colonization, political conflicts, and so on). What is the recombinant energy created between languages (geopolitical economies, cultural representations, concepts of community)? (110)

In order to render this transversal legible, to explore "how 'English' is made and disseminated," Kim reduces her lyrics to the barest vowels, consonants, and diphthongs, those units of language that, when thrust together, create "recombinant energy." This is the level on which we might locate her own hortatory poetics, her exhortations to build "concepts of community" "between languages." While creating a dissonant music out of translations-in-process, Kim's poetry presents the activities of translation and transliteration as the poetic means by which racialization, differentiation, and dehumanization can be transcribed.

Kim's poems about the romanization of Korean into English, or the representation of Korean using a Latin script, make her practice and critique clearer. The second section of the book, "Lamenta," stages what Kim calls a "rehearsal of listening" in which she raises the questions, "Whose ears are at work? Where does the authority of romanizing reside? How might it be entered into otherwise?" (110). For Kim, a pluralized English—an English spoken by a conjectural "we" created by colonization, war, dislocation, environmental destruction—becomes apparent through a process of mishearing and its consecration in writing. The resulting poem denaturalizes a single authoritative position from which sense can be made.[20] Poem 506 of "Lamenta" generates one of Kim's "transversal" translations:[21]

> ap
——
ac
>
> Pock
>
> *ji-wuat-dah*   erased
jil-eu-dah   shouted
>
> Regarded among penury
Numb pie mum pie
>
> *jip-sae-gi*   *ji-pah-raeng-e*   :   show here
>
> Look at that noise!
Numb pie mum pie (52)

Here, the structure of the poem is reduced to a set of notes and enunciations, carefully arranged on the page.[22] The first set of letters, "ap" and "ac," sets up an initial test for the word "pock," offering different ways "pock" might be heard. Then, the slight mishearing of two words in Korean brings "erased" and "shouted" into imaginative proximity. Similar words pertaining to lack and amplitude, "penury" and "noise," are both heard as the same thing in English; the phrases "regarded among penury" and "look at that noise!" become "numb pie mum pie." Poem 506 presents a drama of garbling and partial legibility, exploring what happens when two phrases in Korean and two phrases in English are transliterated.

Kim's poetry undermines the authority of a single position from which English and Korean sounds might be turned into a romanized form and mutually understood. As one of Kim's "practices in transliteration," poem 506 opens a gap between "standard romanization" and "what [I] might be said to be hearing" (110). The notion of a commons, in this particular case, refers to the room within transliteration to mishear, or to hear multiple things at once. But the poem does more than this. As the "illegible" comes into speech, the elements of a scene scramble into view, although the details of this scene are limited to a set of verbs: to erase, to shout, to show. The "recombinant energy" generated by transliterating these verbs—the "commoning" of sounds together—is one way for the poem to reveal a precarious global subject in the grip of exigency, first shown poor, then seen shouting.

Bonney and Kim generate a poetics that resists privatization and a "totalizing" global English, respectively. I do not wish to minimize the differences between the two, especially since Kim's work makes a unique intervention within processes of racial ascription by undermining the authority of the listener, the translator, and the romanizer. Bonney's incendiary lines, meanwhile, are conducive to modes of performance and to poetry readings in a way that Kim's textual experiments are not: it would be challenging to capture in speech the large blank spaces or the brackets, ratios, colons, and ideograms that appear on many of Kim's pages. Reading them side-by-side, however, adds to critical thinking in global studies, which, over the last two decades, has revisited notions of the commons in the face of precarity, scarcity, commodification, and privatization. As Peter Linebaugh argues, the commons not only demarcates a physical space for grazing, fishing, irrigation, or the gathering of firewood, it also designates a set of lost words, activities, and relations once tied to that space. Linebaugh writes, "The widow's estovers of common is thus the phrase that leads us to a completely different world, a world of use values" (43).[23] Confronted with the necessity of representing a commons in the absence of a language for it, Bonney and Kim write a kind of hypothetical poem that refuses to settle into a completed shape on the page. Calling attention to the process by which the poem is composed, they transcribe the decisions, hesitations, and mistakes that generate the interruptive, recombinant energy of a language of the precarious.

Walt Hunter is assistant professor of English at Clemson University. He is the author of *Forms of a World: Contemporary Poetry and the Making of Globalization* (2018) and the cotranslator, with Lindsay Turner, of Frédéric Neyrat's *Atopias: Manifesto for a Radical Existentialism* (2017). His writing about poetry, globalization, and politics has appeared in *ASAP/Journal, Atlantic, College Literature, Essays in Criticism, Jacket2, minnesota review, Modern Philology, Viewpoint, symplokē,* and other publications.

Notes

I wish to thank the editors and the two anonymous readers for their helpful comments. I also thank Richard Re and Shirley Wong for reading an earlier version of this essay.

1. *Region of Unlikeness* is the title of Graham's 1991 collection of poems.
2. In her work on the "we" in poetry, Bonnie Costello writes against a notion of plurality as "imperial authority or forced consensus," instead suggesting that poetry "often tries to bring into being a particular 'we' that has been obstructed in history" (Costello, n.p.).
3. The 2011 report of the United Nations Conference on Trade and Development states that "the frequent and wide price fluctuations that have been observed in the markets for many commodity groups since 2007, particularly in oil and agricultural markets, have been unprecedented, and in many instances they have no obvious link to changes on the supply side" (*United Nations,* 113).
4. For a concise history of the economics, politics, and culture of neoliberalism, see Centano and Cohen.
5. Studying the positions of "cautious" and "strong" globalizers, the economist Emma Aisbett warns that "much work remains to show which policies can reduce the adjustment costs borne by the poor and maximize the share of the benefits they obtain from globalization" (67). See the work of Robert H. Wade for a thorough examination of the neoliberal argument that economic liberalization has reduced inequality and poverty.

6. In her Nobel Prize–winning research on common-pool resources in Japan, Switzerland, Spain, and the Philippines, Elinor Ostrom criticizes the assumption, popularized by Garrett Hardin in "The Tragedy of the Commons," that the "creation of private property rights . . . is an obvious solution to the problem of degradation" (60).

7. Other recent books of poetry with similar concerns are Rae Armantrout's *Money Shot*, Ariana Reines's *Mercury*, Lisa Robertson's *The Men*, and Keston Sutherland's *Hot White Andy* and *Odes to TL61P*.

8. This description is taken from the home page of Openned Press, found at http://www.openned.com/print/category/sean-bonney.

9. John Bloomberg-Rissman suggests that *The Commons* might be a sonnet sequence, "although its somewhat disjunctive nature allows it to be read straight through as well" (n.p.).

10. For a concise history of enclosure movements and the English state, see Hill.

11. See Arrighi, 1–26.

12. This slash is not a line break but rather inserted by Bonney within the line itself.

13. For more on the historical processes that Virginia Jackson has described as "lyricization," see *The Lyric Theory Reader* (2013), edited by Jackson and Yopie Prins, which contains a set of theoretical sources for the development of a primarily English and European idea of the lyric. Jonathan Culler's *Theory of the Lyric* (2015) examines lyric as a transhistorical genre.

14. As Jacob Edmond argues, "Bonney attends to the way revolutionary writing, if too direct or smooth, can become implicated in the power structures it seeks to overcome" (n.p.).

15. See *The Politics of Poetic Form: Poetry and Public Policy* (1990). In the United States, Steve Benson, Charles Bernstein, Lyn Hejinian, Susan Howe, Bob Perelman, Ron Silliman, and Barrett Watten are a few of the key figures. See also Burt, "Sestina! Or the Fate of the Idea of Form" for a reading of contemporary American poets as having given up on a relationship between poetic form and political formation.

16. Rae Armantrout, in a 1978 essay titled "Why Don't Women Do Language-Oriented Writing?" perhaps puts it best. She writes, "I use that term [language-oriented writing] but I'm suspicious of it, finally, because it seems to imply division between language and experience, thought and feeling, inner and outer. The work I like best sees itself and sees the world. It is ambi-centric, if you will" (Armantrout, 518–20).

17. In *Poetry and its Others*, Jahan Ramazani notes that "a poem faces both inward and outward: it enriches itself on its play of euphonies and dissonances within itself and across an array of earlier poems, and it feasts on, digests, and metabolizes linguistic forms of other kinds" (6–7).

18. Jeannie Chiu suggests that these "attempts to recover individual and cultural histories" challenge "not only essentialist notions of ethnic and racial identity, but also the transcendent 'I' of conventional lyric poetry" (85).

19. Juliana Spahr argues that Kim's work is part of an "emerging formation of a poetry in English that includes other languages." Refusing associations between identity and language, "Kim returns again and again to question the naturalness of English" (1130).

20. This procedure relies on what Lyn Hejinian describes as the "realism of language": "Content is not imposed from without; rather, it emerges from independent initial points in the language itself" (Silliman et al., 470). Charles Bernstein puts it slightly differently, but his point is the same: there is "no logic on which to base the work other than the sense developed ongoing in the actual activity itself" (Silliman et al., 471).

21. Each poem in this section is numbered to fit within a span that individual sections introduce (for instance, 406–24).

22. See also Sarah Dowling's reading of this poem. Dowling situates "Lamenta" within the context of the doubling of immigration to the United States between 1970 and 1990, arguing that the poem captures "the new reality inaugurated by the rapid and dramatic increase of Asian immigration to the United States. Kim does not suggest that the figures she depicts are without legal rights; instead, she demonstrates that inclusion is at once legal reality and a social impossibility" (15–19; 18).

23. In *The Magna Carta Manifesto: Liberties and Commons for All* (2009), Linebaugh traces a history of discommoning and of enclosure, showing the effects of privatization on language, representation, perception, and philosophical ideas of personhood and agency.

Works Cited

Adorno, Theodor. 1991. "On Lyric Poetry and Society." In *Notes to Literature, Volume 1*. Ed. Rolf Tiedemann, 37–54. Trans. Shierry Weber Nicholsen. New York: Columbia University Press.

Aisbett, Emma. 2007. "Why Are the Critics So Convinced That Globalization Is Bad for the Poor?" In *Globalization and Poverty*. Ed. Ann Harrison, 33–85. Chicago: University of Chicago Press.

Aristotle. 2010. *Rhetoric*. Trans. W. Rhys Roberts. New York: Cosimo.

Armantrout, Rae. 2007. "Why Don't Women Do Language-Oriented Writing?" In *In the American Tree: Language, Realism, Poetry*. Ed. Ron Silliman, 518–20. Orono, Maine: National Poetry Foundation.

Arrighi, Giovanni. 2010. *The Long Twentieth Century*. London: Verso.

Benjamin, Walter. 1968. "On Some Motifs in Baudelaire." In *Illuminations*, 155–94. Trans. Harry Zohn. New York: Schocken.

Berardi, Franco "Bifo." 2012. *The Uprising: On Poetry and Finance*. Los Angeles: Semiotext(e).

Berlant, Lauren. 2011. *Cruel Optimism*. Durham: Duke University Press.

Bernstein, Charles. 1990. *The Politics of Poetic Form*. New York: Roof Press.

Bloomberg-Rissman, John. 2011. Review of *The Commons,* by Sean Bonney. *Galatea Resurrects #17* (blog), December 20. http://galatearesurrection17.blogspot.com/2011/12/commons-by-sean-bonney.html.

Bonney, Sean. 2011. *The Commons*. London: Openned Press.

Bourdieu, Pierre. 1998. *Acts of Resistance: Against the Tyranny of the Market*. Trans. Richard Nice. Cambridge: Polity Press.

Burt, Stephen. 2007. "Sestina! or the Fate of the Idea of Form." *Modern Philology* 105:218–41.

Butler, Judith. 2012. "Precarious Life, Vulnerability, and the Ethics of Cohabitation." *Journal of Speculative Philosophy* 26:134–51.

Centano, Miguel A., and Joseph N. Cohen. 2012. "The Arc of Neoliberalism." *Annual Review of Sociology* 38:317–40.

Chiu, Jeannie. 2004. "Identities in Process: The Experimental Poetry of Mei-mei Berssenbrugge and Myung Mi Kim." In *Asian North American Identities: Beyond the Hyphen*. Ed. Eleanor Ty and Donald C. Goellnicht, 84–101. Bloomington: Indiana University Press.

Costello, Bonnie. 2012. "The Plural of Us." *Jacket2*, January 6. http://jacket2.org/article/plural-us.

Culler, Jonathan. 1977. "Apostrophe." *diacritics* 7:59–69.

Culler, Jonathan. 2015. *Theory of the Lyric*. Cambridge, Mass.: Harvard University Press.

Dowling, Sarah. 2015. "Interpolation, Coherence, History: The Works of Myung Mi Kim." In *Nests and Strangers: On Asian American Women Poets*. Ed. Timothy Yu, 15–19. Berkeley: Kelsey Street Press.

Edmond, Jacob. 2012. "'Their Echoes Split Us': Sean Bonney Rewrites Baudelaire and Rimbaud." *Jacket2*, December 3. http://jacket2.org/commentary/%E2%80%9Ctheir-echoes-split-us%E2%80%9D.

Harvey, David. 2010. "The Future of the Commons." *Radical History Review* 109:101–7.

Hill, Christopher. 1967. *Reformation to Industrial Revolution: The Making of Modern English Society, 1530–1780*. Vol. 1. New York: Pantheon.

Jackson, Virginia, and Yopie Prins, eds. 2013. *The Lyric Theory Reader*. Baltimore: Johns Hopkins University Press.

Jeon, Joseph Jonghyun. 2012. *Racial Things, Racial Forms: Objecthood in Avant-Garde Asian American Poetry*. Iowa City: University of Iowa Press.

Jeon, Joseph Jonghyun. 2015. "Asian American Poetry." In *The Cambridge History of American Poetry*. Ed. Alfred Bendixen and Stephen Burt, 978–1002. Cambridge: Cambridge University Press.

Kaufman, Robert. 2004. "Adorno's Social Lyric, and Literary Criticism Today: Poetics, Aesthetics, Modernity." In *The Cambridge Companion to Adorno*. Ed. Tom Huhn, 345–75. Cambridge: Cambridge University Press.

Kim, Myung Mi. 2002. *Commons*. Berkeley: University of California Press.

le Blanc, Guillaume. 2007. *Vies ordinaires, vies précaires*. Paris: Éditions du Seuil.

Linebaugh, Peter. 2009. *The Magna Carta Commons: Liberties and Commons for All.* Berkeley: University of California Press.

Lorey, Isabell. 2015. *State of Insecurity: Government of the Precarious.* Trans. Aileen Derieg. New York: Verso.

Lotz, Christian. 2011. "Poetry as Anti-Discourse: Formalism, Hermeneutics, and the Poetics of Paul Celan." *Continental Philosophy Review* 44:491–510.

Ostrom, Elinor. 1990. *Governing the Commons: The Evolution of Institutions for Collective Action.* Cambridge: Cambridge University Press.

Ostry, Jonathan, Prakash Loungani, and Davide Furceri. 2016. "Neoliberalism: Oversold?" *Finance and Development* 53:38–41.

Ramazani, Jahan. 2014. *Poetry and Its Others: News, Prayer, Song, and the Dialogue of Genres.* Chicago: University of Chicago Press.

Rankine, Claudia, and Elizabeth Hoover. 2010. "Poet Claudia Rankine on Wounds We Should Not Forget." *Sampsonia Way,* November 12. http://www.sampsoniaway.org/literary-voices/2010/11/12/poet-claudia-rankine-on-wounds-we-shouldnt-forget/.

Ross, Andrew. 2009. *Nice Work If You Can Get It: Life and Labor in Precarious Times.* New York: New York University Press.

Sassen, Saskia. 2002. "Global Cities and Survival Circuits." In *Global Woman: Nannies, Maids, and Sex Workers in the New Economy.* Ed. Barbara Ehrenreich and Arlie Russell Hochschild, 254–74. New York: Henry Holt.

Shelley, Percy Bysshe. 2002. *Shelley's Poetry and Prose.* Ed. Donald H. Reiman and Neil Fraistat. New York: Norton.

Silliman, Ron, Barrett Watten, Steve Benson, Lyn Hejinian, Charles Bernstein, and Bob Perelman. 2007. "For *Change.*" In *In the American Tree.* Ed. Ron Silliman, 468–72. Orono, Maine: National Poetry Foundation.

The Song of Songs. 1995. Translated by Ariel Bloch and Chana Bloch. Berkeley: University of California Press.

Spahr, Juliana. 2015. "Multilingualism in Contemporary American Poetry." In *The Cambridge History of American Poetry.* Ed. Alfred Bendixen and Stephen Burt, 1123–43. Cambridge: Cambridge University Press.

Stierle, Karlheinz. 1979. "Die Identität des Gedichts—Hölderlin als Paradigma." In *Identität (Poetik und Hermeneutik 8).* Ed. Odo Marquard and Karlheinz Stierle, 505–52. München: Wilhelm Fink.

United Nations Conference on Trade and Development Report. 2011. New York: United Nations.

Virno, Paulo. 2004. *A Grammar of the Multitude.* Trans. Isabella Bertoletti, James Cascaito, and Andrea Casson. Los Angeles: Semiotext(e).

Wade, Robert H. 2004. "Is Globalization Reducing Poverty and Inequality?" *World Development* 32:567–89.

Wade, Robert H. 2017. "The West Remains on Top, Economically and Politically." In *The Global Political Economy of Rául Prebisch.* Ed. Matias E. Margulis, 135–54. New York: Routledge.

FROM TARGETS TO MATCHES

THE DIGITAL ANATOMY-POLITICS OF NEOLIBERAL SEXUALITY

Andrea Righi

A remarkable trait of our neoliberal societies is that the widespread discredit of political institutions is counterpoised by an unprecedented expansion of power. Power hides behind ultramodern techniques while simultaneously letting traits that look archaic resurface. On one side, we have extensive deployments of digital technologies and metadata analysis that enable pervasive control, while on the other, we have the institutionalization of practices—infringements of fundamental democratic rights such as due process, torture, secrecy of correspondence and so forth—that modern democracies had abolished, at least in principle, long ago. When describing the forms of power that developed with the advent of capitalism, Foucault argues that we should not restrict our attention to the transformation of legal apparatuses, but rather concentrate on what happens to social technologies and to the series of practices and knowledge that comprise a *dispositif*. As he argues in the 1979 lecture "Les mailles de pouvoir," which he delivered in Bahia, Brazil, we should move from a juridical conceptualization of the deployment of power to a technological one. This is Foucault's most timely contribution to the understanding of our present: exploring venues for the disciplining of subjectivities that are affirmative rather than negative, modalities of subject formation that while administrating "things and persons right down to the minutest detail, would neither be expensive nor essentially predatory on society."

In "Les mailles de pouvoir," the two chief historical cases that Foucault uses to exemplify this transformation are the military and sexuality. Foucault is particularly interested in the "techniques of training" of the modern Prussian army and in the emergence of sexuality as the discourse that controls population growth. Both are what he calls "techniques for the individualization of power" that developed methodologies to "monitor *[surveiller]* someone . . . control his conduct, his behavior, his aptitudes . . . intensify his performance, multiply his capacities." The issue of efficacy—that is to say, of the creation of sites of affirmation in which individuals autonomously maximize their existence while optimizing the system as a whole—is truly one of the most pressing problems that neoliberal governmentality presents us with today. Pierre Dardot and Christian Laval argue that neoliberal rationality requires "liberty as a condition of possibility." By this they mean that "to govern is not to govern against liberty, or despite it; it is to govern through liberty" (5, 15).[1] As we know, this system is far from being aseptically positive: blood runs every second the neoliberal machine ticks. There is a deep connection between killing life and expanding it, if only because of the banal fact that the labor of life is also that of death, as Heraclitus would say. But more poignantly, war and sexuality are terms of comparison insofar as they give shape to a system of positivity that wants to code the movement of matter itself by transcribing it into the language of capital accumulation.

To investigate this correlation, I will briefly discuss the technology of neoliberal war, drawing a parallel with the kind of socio-symbolic environment that digital media reproduce; this is particularly the case with a popular locative media matchmaking app like Tinder. To anticipate my conclusions: I contend that both systems of power are undergoing a transformation that mimics life emergent, self-transformative properties (its potentiality, as we will see) while reprogramming and recording its outputs according to a logic of what Matteo Pasquinelli has called "algorithmic governance"—in other words, the political, economic, and "epistemic space generated by algorithms of data mining" (2015).[2] War and sexuality are revelatory of how neoliberalism fashions, in Foucault's terms, "an anatomo-politics, an anatomy that targets individuals to the point of anatomizing them" (n.p.). Although a great deal of work has already been carried out on the epistemological and political implications for modern warfare, scarce attention has been paid to those of the other term of our dispute: sexuality. On the other hand, the growing literature that studies the exhibitionist and permissive outlook of hookup culture and social media seems to be limited to the empiric collecting of scientific evidence—usually restricted to young adults—and to the debate concerning issues of public health.[3] These investigations do not risk, in other words, more general insights at the level of epistemology and what psychoanalysis calls "the register of the symbolic" that I will attempt in the next pages.

A BIOPOLITICAL HORIZON

"Of all these knights and ladies of ancient times . . ." One only needs to recall Virgil's words in canto 5 of Dante's *Inferno* to argue that at the core of Western culture love and war are intrinsically bounded together as two sides of the proverbial coin (*Inferno* 5.71). Achilles had Briseis just like Roland had Angelica, and they were both driven mad by their passion. Further back in time, as Jesse Glenn Gray reminds us, one finds "a familiar Greek myth about the goddess of love, Aphrodite, becoming the mistress of Ares, god of war, whose youth and passion captured her heart" (60). Today, we instinctively reject any unity between the two terms. At the same time, we also tend to forget that these outbursts regularly took the form of violence against women, for in terms of the circulation of desire men historically enjoyed "an acquired right to expropriation without compensation" (Tiqqun). And yet if one looks at pop culture, it is difficult to find a war movie without the redeeming flames of passion glaring amid gun smoke. Usually, love plays an ancillary role. With the big bucks invested in fighting, sentiment works as a kind of subplot with a proleptic value, so to speak. It stands in for the rewards that victory will eventually bring. Consider, for instance, the story of a mainstream film like *Fury* (2015) by David Ayer. In the final days of World War II, Wardaddy Collier's ruthless tank squad finds momentary solace behind enemy lines. In a devastated German village, Wardaddy and his inexperienced soldier, Norman, encounter two German women, who are cousins, and spend a few hours in their house. Here, Norman has a furtive intercourse with the younger woman, while Wardaddy plays family man with the older one. The ephemeral image of an idyllic middle-class life alludes to a happy future in a world without Nazis.[4]

But the *contiguity* of sex and war does not explain what locks them together—in other words, it does not explain their *continuity*. As feminism teaches us, for man, the first objectification of reality is that of the woman. She is at times an object of desire, and at times she turns into the instantiation of the *Other,* whose foreignness he must court, conquer, betray, exchange, sometimes even fear.[5] This so-called theological assumption has longstanding consequences. Bundled with the question of desire of man, which means *by* men but also *for* men, she becomes the other side of the coin of the violent deed par excellence: war. After all, she has always been conjured up as an honorable pretext for war—think obviously of Helen of Troy. More prosaically, women were a conspicuous—and much coveted—part of the spoils of any military victory. In this case, male desire is simply diverted to another kind of symbolic act of possession, another kind of consumption, not the material wealth one seizes but the carnal one.

Let us move a step further and explain this continuity in more theoretical terms. I would like to unpack this knot by laying it out in terms that may seem all too blunt, but the matter at hand would occupy the pages of several volumes. Paolo Virno once argued that whenever we have a definition of what an animal *is* we can detect a theory of sovereignty in the making (2008, 11). In a similar fashion, whenever we speak about the relationship between sex and war we catch sight of an ontology in the making. More specifically, sex and war intersect a power that humankind partakes in and that it cannot quite grasp, transcending the two domains at stake. According to Gilles Deleuze and Félix Guattari, the nexus desiring-production (sex)—which may easily turn into its opposite desiring-destruction (war)—refers to "a nonsexual energy, for which sexuality has merely served as a symbol for an anagogical beyond" (46). This force goes under various names according to the discipline that investigates it—"libido" according to psychoanalysis, "being" for philosophy, and so on. What we can say about it is that it is measureless and imperishable. It involves the "the pure potentiality, the power of self-actualization" (Kordela 2013a, 106). Our biopolitical times mark a specific moment in history where *bios* is raised to a force of production in itself, or to use Virno's definition, where capital realizes virtuality itself—not the product but the potential to produce (2004, 84).

That this horizon directly influences warfare, and as we will see, sexuality too, is reflected in the most interesting developments of war studies. Michael Dillon and Julian Reid indicate that this shift defines what they call "the liberal way of war." They argue that "when species existence becomes foundational . . . in theory and practice, the properties of species life will begin to dictate the terms under which the authority and legitimacy of states will also be expressed and state power exercised locally and globally" (53). This implies a remarkable emphasis on the world-forming qualities typical of biopolitics. More in detail, when life becomes the object of a direct intervention, the modalities through which that very life is organized and organizes itself point toward a unidimensional, almost immanent, shaping of existence. As reproduction of life becomes more deeply inherent to itself, one also notices a peculiar attempt to liquidate the gap that customarily separates the subject (or the agent) from the object, and in the political domain, the ruler from the ruled. Dardot and Laval call it a form of "govern[ing] through liberty" (5), while Dillon and Reid define it as the attempt "to rule by encouraging subjects/objects of rule to rule themselves" (38).

Similarly, it can be argued that smart technology tends to disavow the duplicative and transitive nature typical of symbolic structures. This does not mean that reality, or whatever is represented, disappears, but rather that the digital holds the promise of "simulating a thing so effectively that 'what it is' becomes less and less necessary to speak about" (Galloway, 13). This argument goes beyond the usual discourse on how the society of simulacra liquidated reality. Take for instance the case of a branch of research in molecular biology called synthetic biology. This discipline pledges to study and redesign biological systems by nominally eliminating any organismal intervention in vivo. Microscopes, autoclaves, and petri dishes with samples will be soon neatly stored in the Cabinets of Wonder of the University because, so they hope, software programs will provide nearly all experimental data for analysis and testing. The unidimensional structure of smart technology implies an incredible generative capacity that is productive rather than hermeneutic, for as Alexander Galloway argues, "The matter at hand is not that of coming to know a world, but rather that of how specific, abstract definitions are executed to form a world" (23). This is why we can also argue that the smart era is fundamentally asymbolic—that is to say, it is more interested in modeling and reformulating rather than designating or representing the reality at hand.[6]

THE BALLISTIC EYE

Computing life also means effectively performing its fluid and unexpected nature. Where the goal is suppressing lives, this ultimately means producing weapons that are responsive and adaptive to the nature of the enemy. Because of its epistemological consequence, theorists who do not usually deal with military studies have dedicated a great attention to the notion of the target. Here scholars have emphasized the significance of contingency, opportunity, and the tendency for abstracting (dematerializing) reality by casting it as something utterly locatable, virtual, and thus manipulable (Chow, 21–38; Weber, 5–7). The point here is to reformulate a topography that can engender its own existence—in other words, that is capable of self-actualization. We can call it a "datascape," or digital *chronotope*: an infrastructure based on location and predictability of time and space.[7] These are the fundamentals a modern army needs to surveil, analyze, and take action on different forms of life. The technological capacity of transforming the world into a map that is searchable but also smart—that is to say, which is capable of autonomously producing feedback information and enabling action—goes hand in hand with the rise of asymmetric warfare. Here military confrontation is not determined by the clash of two armies but by incursions against smaller, difficult-to-track units (Chamayou, 52–59). As the modern battle turns into a global hunt, the most effective weapons are seemingly unmanned surveillance and incursion aircrafts, what we normally call "drone technology."

These devices constitute a further development of the modern approach (photography) to reality that finds in vision its vanishing point or outermost peak of opaqueness:

> Despite the image's kinetic attributes, the camera obscura allowed the movement of matter to be contained enough to become the subject of contemplation. With long range, visually prosthetic weaponry, a similar containment occurs, but with an altogether different goal. Rather than contemplation, manipulation and obliteration become the effects of both containment and observation. With such weaponry, to see the target is to destroy the target. (Bishop and Phillips, 28)

The idea that this optic technology provokes a type of physiological blindness is probably attenuated by the fact that something else intervenes in the localization of the target. As Harun Farocki argues, the kind of images produced in prosthetic war "do not represent an object, but rather are part of an operation," which is processual and involves duration (17). In addition, the functioning and actual application of this technology is less smooth than common parlance likes to admit. It rather registers the mysticism of what Benjamin Noys calls drone "theological metaphysics," a specific characteristic of neoliberal power based on the expansion of the scopic as the space for disembodied and godlike human control (2). In reality, the distance between the thing and the visual apparatus is still not immediate. The reason lies precisely in the flux of information that is recorded, and that must be analyzed and made instrumental to individuate a potential enemy and receive authorization to execute the attack. This is why, as for any other system that involves big data, the army analyst must isolate anomalies (or regularities) from the data flow to detail predictive behaviors. This operation costs time and comes with a burden. After all, "anomaly detection," Pasquinelli writes, "is the mathematical paranoia of the Empire in the age of big data" (2015).[8]

This said, it is not difficult to imagine a perfected version of a remotely piloted aircraft system equipped with an enhanced level of quasi-immediate recognition—for that matter, arms that enable pilots to execute the strike as they perceive the enemy are already available to the U.S. Army (Bishop and Phillips, 28–31). In this sense, one could talk of a weaponized eye; the latter seems to observe and kill precisely in order to observe and kill as if enthralled by such a complete form of contemplation that it embodies the structure of a drive, the scopic drive to be precise. In the drive, the question of truth is irrelevant, for it is the very dynamism of the movement that constitutes the latter.[9] This is a distinctive quality of contemporary technology that has consequences for sexuality as well. The structural element of this scopic system is that annihilation seems to have turned into a goal independent from any final objectives. For similarly to the optic apparatus that once in place cannot but keep gazing, drone technology seems to incorporate a self-propagating goal that transcends the military victory on the field. Ironically, these attacks exponentially increase recruiting capacities for insurgents. Drone war may deliver conflicts without casualties for the American army but, at the same time, it sets up the stage for a strategy according to which war cannot be won (Chamayou, 60–72). A prey that shall not be ultimately seized, an opponent that cannot be conquered—it is not only that prosthetic war must reshape itself according to the emergent behavior of life. The endless nature of this system of power also echoes the modus operandi of capital: endless accumulation. To shed light on these relationships, one must look more closely at the economic–symbolic complex, particularly at the rationality of capitalism and its current neoliberal mutation.

CAPITALISM AS A CULT ACCORDING TO WALTER BENJAMIN

A fast-growing literature has attempted to map the symbolic transformations produced by neoliberalism.[10] Here, I want to explore this post-Lacanian line of thought and connect it to a note by Walter Benjamin, in which tendencies of early liberal capitalism already prefigure the extent to which they become dominants under neoliberalism. I begin with the issue of *anxiety* and its relation to the mechanism of *debt* to sketch the main characteristics of contemporary life. When, as in modernity, the subject is delivered over to his or her subjectivity as a supposedly empty and nonqualified dominion—one that is utterly manipulable—what emerges is not so much the mighty figure of an all-powerful subject but the more fragile, besieged individual of contemporary society. The reason for this condition is quite intuitive. In reality, the social imperative that commands self-affirmation creates anxiety—a relentless condition for the subject—for it orders a satisfaction that is structurally unachievable because it is built precisely on a lack of order, on excess. Therein we encounter the other side of this unanswerable call for self-realization—that is to say, a specular mechanism of infinite movement: it is the liability that exceeds the confines of individual life of contemporary economic crisis. This is one of the mechanisms that feeds what Maurizio Lazzarato calls "the economy of debt," which further implements this form of self-imprisonment via "the creation and development of the power relation between creditors and debtors." Debt is not an unfortunate accident, but rather it "has been conceived and programmed as the strategic heart of neoliberal politics" (27). In Foucauldian terms, debt is not based on the prohibitory force of the law, but rather it "leaves you free, and it encourages you and pushes you to act in such a way that you are able to honor your debt" (31). Needless to say, these procedures realize enormous profits for the elite leaving to the rest the grim reality of never-ending work. No wonder several symptoms of an existential anxiety are clearly visible among the population.

Most obviously, it is the precariousness and increasing pressure of accountability of today's life that produces a widespread anxiety.[11] But at a more profound level, a society based on positive injunctions also creates a vacuum for the subject's self-realization, as it lacks any definite criterion. Industrial democracy was a society built on some level of measurability; notwithstanding how unequal this ratio was, a distinct sense of exchange between bestowing work and remuneration was still perceptible. Likewise, there was a difference between working and nonworking time, or between work and nonwork space—even though the latter was already characterized by consumerism as a nonproductive activity that indeed produced value. One of the side effects of present impossibility in determining clear ratios between working and nonworking time—what postworkerist thought called the decline of the law of value that regimented industrial democracy—is precisely this: a ubiquitous anxiety for the ungraspability of the very grid of representation that supported symbolization.

In a short note on capitalism as religion, Benjamin already alluded to this process, showing how early twentieth-century production accommodates a further radicalization that we now see fully in effect under neoliberal biopolitics. He argued that capitalism is a religion that has a specific structure. It is a "cult that makes guilt and debt pervasive. Capitalism is probably the first instance of a cult that creates guilt, not atonement" (288, translation modified). Why is capitalism a religion and to what extent is this spiritual dimension connected to debt? One way to explain the religious essence of capitalism is that it articulates a set of beliefs, conducts, and cultural imaginary that inserts transcendence—that is, limits and boundaries that used to rule and ground representation—into the human (Kordela 2013a, 4–5). As a modern form of representation of the infinite, capitalism recodes into the human domain the natural flow of life by subjecting it into goal-oriented philosophies such as "utilitarianism" (Benjamin, 288). According to Benjamin, "Capitalism has developed as a parasite on Christianity in the West, not in Calvinism alone" (289, translation modified). I believe Benjamin is arguing here that capitalism is grafted on a topological assumption that has a clear lineage. The Jewish representation of the law "consign[ed] God to the place of the unrepresentable" (McNulty, 11). The Christian tradition, on the other hand, reintrojected the structural dimension of the principle of order into the human through Christ as the incarnation of the Son of God.[12] But Christianity still promised redemption through earthly deeds. Catholicism provided that through the promise of paradise while Calvinism through the concept of grace. Although crucial to the development of capitalism, Calvinism still restricted human activity, at least theoretically, by offering moral precepts and the possibility of expiation. For Benjamin, on the other hand, capitalism enacts a double movement that, as it holds fast to the incarnation of the infinite into human life, it parallels the Nietzschean notion of "breaking open of the heavens by an intensified humanization" (289, translation modified). It thus also pulverizes natural limitedness by setting in motion a law of movement that is abstract and cyclical: the endless accumulation of capital. In this sense, Benjamin states that, in the end, "Christianity's history is essentially that of its parasites—that is to say, of capitalism" (289). Capitalism feeds off the Christian reterritorialization of infinity into the realm of human-makings only to consign transcendence to a goalless dictum of more and more work, thus reproducing that same indebtedness ad infinitum.

In effect, the most radical trait that Benjamin traces in the cultic spirit of capitalism is the idea that its very principle of order is the standard-bearer of guilt. As he writes, the "fourth feature is that its God must be hidden and may be invoked only when his guilt is at its Zenith. The cult is celebrated before an unmatured deity; every image, every representation of it violates the secret of its immaturity" (289, translation modified). For what I said so far, it seems clear that there is no final moment of exhaustion of the debt because transcendence has been erased and folded in human destiny. Hence, the principle of order itself incarnates this vanishing point of unredeemable debt. The excessive nature of reality points to the true but hidden, maturity of this deity. Precisely because of the nonsensical telos of its movement this deity must be clothed into more conciliatory narratives of capitalist self-image: the wealth the entrepreneur produces for the benefit of the community, the risks he takes as he invests his patrimony in production, and so forth. But in reality, Benjamin notes, this deity wants "explosive and discontinuous intensification"; this is a religion that "no longer is a reform of being, but rather its shattering" (289, translation modified).

To recapitulate, I described two technologies neoliberalism currently deploys: a military and an economic one. Both follow a similar biopolitical pattern based on an open-ended principle that optimizes the potentiality of life. And yet this theoretical apparatus barely touches on the other domain—i.e., sexuality and desire—that is coterminous with the latter. I now turn to an analysis of the symbolic structure supported by informationalized society, where digital technology, as Dominic Basulto writes, is "moving away from just curating content, to actually performing artificial intelligence operations on that content" (n.p.). This inquiry will set the framework to consider the case with the dating app Tinder: a type of technology that enables temporary comfort from the transient nature of reality and from the haunting structure of the *other* that invests the sexual domain. What's more, Tinder optimizes this existential complex via a very interesting application of spatial mapping.[13]

THE OTHER AND INFINITE ACCUMULATION

Describing this state of things, one feels almost forced to use a vocabulary that draws from the old Italian autonomist tradition: emphasis toward finding a principle of self-organization and autonomy; the (perverse) drift toward immanence that is obviously used to enhance the system itself; the liquidation of authority in the guise of a privileged point of view that validates what is true, real and so forth; and the rise of a virtual perspective (workerists referred to Marx's term "general intellect") that turns reality into something that is materially operative. As noted, these transformations have direct consequences at a psycho-symbolic level, determining a social order that is antinormative and intransitive, where power is not vertical but horizontally organized via digital, unidimensional forces. Meanwhile in the visual domain, perception slips into opaqueness because of the infinitesimal resolution that prosthetic technology delivers. The implosion of the demarcation between subject and reality, or what I called the asymbolic character of smart technology, clearly echoes transformations in the deep structures of society. In a related manner, many scholars have in fact described the mutation of our social organization by referring to the notion of a post-Oedipal society. From a modern socio-symbolic order based on oppositional and duplicative structures, think of the opposition unconscious vs. conscious, we have shifted to "a world that is not a theater anymore but a market, where representation gives way to exposition . . . seduction to performance, relation with the other to the consumption of the other" (Dominijanni 2014b, 238).

Insofar as conquest is the goal both in war and seduction, however, the *other* of the sexual relation is a more intractable entity than the combatant on the battlefield, especially if one considers how enemies are aseptically liquidated by pushing buttons from a remote location.[14] The question is: In what ways does the paroxysm of absolute perceptive knowledge seek to colonize other life domains that include the interrelational rapport with the *other*? What I am trying to elaborate here is the following: visual prosthetic weaponry develops a theory of knowledge that seeks the object by liquidating it; concurrently, it turns the latter into metadata augmenting the scalability of the system. Couldn't it be that digital technologies that mediate sexual encounters pursue a similar practice, one that by targeting partners aims at keeping the danger of exposure to the *other* at bay? In other words, could it be that the modeling capacity of these technologies individualizes power in a martial fashion precisely by consuming or, as it were, holding the *other* in possession through a dynamic loop of winning over, exhausting, and replacing the latter with always renewed targets of opportunity?[15]

The device of debt and how it manages life is significant for a nonmonetary type of economy, which is to say, for the economy of relation with the *other*. The present work on the self that obliges everybody to be happy cannot elude the problem of *relationality,* not even in the most egotistical mindset. The very issue of desire calls into question a necessary connection to the *other*. This implies the well-known Lacanian definition of the desire *of* the *other* as the desire *for* the *other,* but also *by* the *other*. The last part of this double-binding relation elicits a response. According to Lacan, anxiety is related to the "the capture of the Other in the web of desire," to the fact that "common experience shows that we do not live our lives, whoever we are, without tirelessly *offering* to goodness knows what unknown *divinity* the sacrifice of some little mutilation, whether valid or not, that we impose on ourselves in the field of our desires" (277, emphasis added). This is why, according to Lacan, the gift offered for sacrifice always had to be completely pure: it had to present itself as the reliable legal tender of the symbolic exchange. But this equivalence becomes increasingly problematic in a society that has lost any point of reference. For the anxiety generated by the impossibility of matching with the structure of desire of the *other* cannot count on means that offered stability in the past—that is, under the bourgeois nuclear family, the prospect of conjugal life that gave the lie to this stability.

Industrial society regulated the production of labor power through several institutions whose kernel was reproductive sex, which was actively encouraged and introjected in people's mentality with the usual double standard between the male and female. On the other hand, the new pattern that has emerged with the shift to a postindustrial economy is one in which neoliberalism seems to pursue modes of life in which reproductive sex is tendentially marginal. One of the reasons for this change lies in the fact that the Western economy has outsourced manufacture from the North to the Global South. This relocation involves not only the production of commodities but also the reproduction of labor power. Paul Virilio's turn-of-the-century claims that cyber-sexuality would put in peril "the future of sexual reproduction" by turning "vital copulation . . . into the practice of remote-control masturbation," are clearly off the mark (106; Terranova, 34). I believe that presently we are witnessing the growth of a series of technologies that atomize the social body in terms that are more complex than that of pure abstraction and erasure of the corporeal. These digital apparatuses represent sophisticated ways of folding in the material dimension, precisely because life itself is the target of neoliberalism.[16]

What does it mean that life itself is invested by technology? In other words, what do we mean when we say that life is digitalized, informationalized? The algorithmic element of information society holds the key to understanding how these technologies of power work, mutatis mutandis, in different areas of experience such as the military, the economic, and the sentimental. Douglas Haddow summarizes these points recalling the market crash of 2010, "when the Dow Jones Industrial dropped 1000 points in under a minute, the biggest one-day point decline in history," a downturn that barely made the news "because everything returned to normal a few seconds later." As he explains, this event

> was a turning point, demonstrating that something had changed. That something was that the neoliberals had achieved what communists, socialists, and Christians never could: they made their god real, and in doing so, achieved their utopia. . . . The searches we make, the news we read, the dates we go on, the advertisements we see, the products we buy and the music we listen to [together with the stock market, are] all informed by this marriage between mathematics and capital, all working together in perfect harmony to achieve a singular goal. . . . Like the advent and rise of high-frequency trading, they're part of an optimization trend that leads to a strange brand of perfection: automated profit.[17]

The capitalist use of algorithm is what enables the simulation and valorization of life in its different dimensions. As in the case of the weaponized eye and the digital chronotope, these processes of mathematization replicate the dynamic of the natural, for they reflect the ontological quality of "emergent behavior" and "generative capacities of matter to evolve" (Parisi 2013, 1). Only they pose at their basis the true creed of their guilty deity: accumulation. In effect, smart technology presents a double movement by which the sophistication of the digital aims at enhancing the experiential dimension of the corporeal. Mobile interface technology practices with great precision this strategy. Jason Farman writes:

> Location-based social networks offer a form of intersubjective embodiment that gives participants . . . a sense of embodied integrity that is aware of the self's place as that which is always already situated in relationship to the location of others. . . . The self's identity extends beyond the immediate context and encompasses a much broader socio-spatial sphere. (27)

I contend that we have thus entered a phase in which this relationality becomes a form of individuation of power. How and why? I discussed how the neoliberal reconfiguration of society thrives on indeterminacy—what Benjamin called "shattering of being"—and increasingly produces an exponentiation of anxiety. It is plausible to maintain that new technologies also serve the purpose of administering relations with the *other,* especially in a period of free and permissive sexuality. In keeping with what has been said regarding capitalism as a cult and modern warfare, the relationship with the *other* must also be made smooth and affirmative so as to minimize blockages and restrict possibilities, slowdowns in the acceleration of capital's accumulation. This is why even acute theorists such as Virilio may sometimes fall into the trap of moralism. Reflexes of authentic conjugal life or abstinence seem to oppose power but are in fact simply former devices of capital grown residual.

WEAPONIZING THE SEXUAL MARKET

As argued, ensuring a compatibility with the web of the desire of the *other* is a central issue for our society. Techniques of individualization of power such as Tinder comply with a fundamental role in melding together society by keeping it in a fluid and all-expansive form, one that thrives in reifying anxiety and that bears a specific mark on a similarly atomized and exploitative labor regime (Franklin, 8–9). Tinder is a utility app that uses a GPS system to track the availability of potential matches in a user's immediate area. It is integrated with Facebook and other platforms so that once users generate a profile they are fed with potential matches. These profiles then appear on your mobile phone; you can "like" them, as Facebook jargon says, or pass on them. Swiping right is positive, swiping left is a "no" but it still moves you to the next possible partner. The app incarnates the gamelike essence of courtship and several qualities of game design, such as its aleatory nature, its role-playing characteristics, the attachment it produces, and its emergent gameplay outputs—probably the most interesting characteristic that seems to swerve away from the intended goal of the app.[18] Obviously, it was carefully crafted for that purpose: "The stack of dating-profile photos displayed in the app was modeled after a deck of cards. 'When you have a deck or a pile of cards,' says Sean Rad, co-founder of the Los Angeles–based company, 'the natural urge is to interact with it'" (Stampler, 44). Swiping right is the intended action but it also arrests the perusing motion that aims at the infinite series populating the beyond-space of the off-screen on the left. In other words, it stalls the game. Hence, it is as if the very goal of the utility dissolved in its functioning as the user constantly lives in a precarious balance between the fictional and the real world. Far from being problematic, this is a very productive incongruence, particularly if one considers the sustained growth of its user base (Bilton).

GPS localization allows for an interesting interaction between the fictional and real world, one that incarnates a peculiar modern disposition toward a reality where the object turns into a live target. The parallel with the informatization of modern warfare is blatant. Reduced to the game of chance of libidinal investment, multiplication, and at times consummation, these technologies, however, also provide an interesting take on the algorithmization of life. And yet we must pierce through its all-powerful outlook and see, as Jordy Rosenberg reminds us, "the discourse of molecularization [of sexuality] as a kind of abstract dispossession—or making-waste of the body—that is the condition of a fantasized speculative self-possession." This technology operates in this way by enacting a multi-level strategy. To begin with, the promise of an easy fix to the issue of sex produces a new series of mediations and detours that show an intrinsic normative schema. If this is a game, you need to learn how to play it. So at a personal level it gives the lie to the rediscovering of a more authentic but also easily manageable form of law—that is to say, the rules of seduction and the codification of the impalpability of desire that a series of websites and dating coaches are already reselling to eager users. This provides some comfort against the anxiety that the incredible bulk of contacts and information exchange produces, but it also helps to orient users toward the real goal and not toward the ludo-like dimension of the game. The surrogate of multiple encounters moreover reinforces this semblance of security: through the serialization of the latter, any risk of rejection, exposure to failures in the rapport, and so forth, is minimized.[19] As the obverse or the necessary counterpart of the accountability of the modern subject as debtor, Tinder constructs an idea of life as a limitless investment in the libidinal that promises pleasure.

Second, looking at the materiality of this media, one may also argue that Tinder stands out as yet another advanced experimentation in the capitalization of people's nonlabor time. It announces the belief in an idea of order based on a moveable classificatory system precisely at the time when the old paternal law of prohibition has liquefied. It thus proceeds to expropriate the collective and social dimension of sexuality by transforming it into a mode of production of value. But here something is at stake that is more significant than the rightful concern regarding the immense webometric archive that is in the making and, incidentally, the problem of who will use this information (and how) concerning the most private tastes and feelings of people. What seems like another and more advanced venue for the expansion of subjective self-realization betrays its ambiguous nature. It is the obliterated normativity of the neoliberal order, which "aims to secure a no less total subjection from their participation in a 'win-win' game," to use "the eloquent formula that is supposed to describe professional and social existence" under neoliberalism (Dardot and Laval, 297).

Third, this is also an incipient system of knowledge. The mystery of attraction represents that knowledge: it is what in game theory is called the "value" of the game. Here we assist to the formalizing, via a new series of algorithms, of the "je ne sais quoi" that stirs that particular emotion—be it the sexual passion or the loving attachment to the *other*—which is another instance of the new mode of self-governing that is becoming hegemonic. In other words, this technology implements the typical axiomatic under which the neoliberal self is securitized by a series of individual calculations—in this case suitable lovers—just like a program executes a task by computing at each step variables and possible outcomes. Moreover, it is an experiential dimension in which the individual relates and seems to dominate a world that offers itself as completely available—hence the importance of the geospatial component of its operations. Simultaneously, the fantasy of this omnipotence of the subject is reinforced by mechanisms that shield the latter from rejection. Risk and exposure to the *other* are conveniently neutralized "because you see only matches" (Stampler, 47). And this is where neoliberalism hinges on a superficial rhetoric of progressivism based on equality and freedom. It is the idea that women feel now empowered because they may explore sexuality in a more neutral space where they can be active seekers.[20] To use Peggy Drexler's mainstream journalistic postfeminism: "The math is pretty simple: In the end, what social media dating does is give users—and, most poignantly—women more options. And more options means more freedom, and more power, too" (n.p.).

In taking them one step closer to man's privilege, locative media would thus be emancipatory. But this commonsensical approach is irreflexive of neoliberal governmentality. One should not forget Judith

Butler's warning against the confusion between freedom and hedonism: "The body can be the agency and instrument of all these as well, or the site where 'doing' and 'being done to' become equivocal. Although we struggle for rights over our own bodies, the very bodies for which we struggle are not quite ever only our own" (2004, 21). In the case of feminine and nonmale subjectivity, these modern mechanisms of capture illustrate a rather perverse form of entanglement: "For it is undeniable that that process of self-fashioning that was key in fleeing from the patriarchal norm has been recoded into the market logic," and today's "emphasis on self-ownership and self-determination risks drifting toward liberal and neoliberal individualism if not accompanied by a radical deconstruction of the sovereign subject" (Dominijanni 2014a, 62). As Joan Copjec maintains, the magnifying and enhancing capacity typical of our smart era exposes a kind of predatory predisposition toward the world and the *other* ruled by the assumption that nothing exists "that cannot be exposed to a persistent, prying look." One of the consequences here is a "new desire of transgression" that "originates not in a belief in the existence of another world, but from the belief that what we want in this world always lies behind a barrier which prevents our access to it" (2006, 23). As in the case of war, in sexuality too nothing truly subversive emerges that may jam the ways in which neoliberalism governs via freedom.

The self-feeding mechanism of Tinder resembles a particular kind of fixation, what in another context Jane Elliot called "acts of modeling . . . reflect[ing] the algebraic, abstracting engine of neoliberal microeconomics itself" (88). In effect, the proxemics induced by the app (swiping right or left) inaugurates an interesting physical dimension, a sort of adult lateralization that pushes users to the beyond-structure typical of our economy. The pleasure of matchmaking is constantly destabilized by the searching of what? This is truly the big question. It seems like the scope here is the infinite series that lies beyond, while the original goal that somehow freezes movement in the specific selection recedes in the background, in the archival depth of potential matches. In this sense, we find a particularly instructive incarnation of modern rationality. This is only superficially a binary decision. The user's attention instead is pulled to the side of the infinite. Reading user's tips, one cannot help but notice the continuous recommendation to stay focused on the real goal: matchmaking. What a remarkable contraindication for such a successful dating tool!

Just like the urgency of knowing what's happening online that is typical of our connectionist era, the proxemics of these kinds of technologies is an indicator of something else. It displays what I call a "sacrificial predisposition" that is perfectly in tune with the processes of subjectification that I previously described. We must return to the issue of anxiety for here we encounter a particular mutation of the famous biblical scene of Isaac's sacrifice as retold by Lacan via the commentary of the eleventh-century Rabbi Rashi:

> When Abraham learns from the angel that he is not there in order to immolate Isaac, Rashi has him say: *What then? If that is what is going on, have I thus come here for nothing? I am at least going to give him a slight wound to make him shed a little blood. Would you like that?* (93, emphasis in the original)

This is not a derogatory description of Abraham, but rather, Lacan notes, it points to how we are bundled in the structure of desire of the *other*. The measureless dimension that neoliberalism manufactured, which Dardot and Laval called "self-transcendence," implies an equally excessive structure that inhabits the field of the *other* (282). Abraham may offer the most prized thing he has in life to appease God. But that only works in a system in which exchanges follow a standard of measure. Now that the criterion that guaranteed value has vanished, how are we to cope with the anxiety generated by the *other*? I suggest we have now fallen into a lesser form of sacrifice. These rituals follow the rule of anything is better than nothing. Strictly speaking, given that we cannot repay our debt, we return it in small installments, and this is, in fact, what Abraham attempts to do after the angel intervenes. Because God has refused his sacrifice, Abraham feels that at least a little scratch is needed, that something that secures a minimal covenant must be offered. Our debt, in turn, is unpayable, and no sacrifice will be enough. A small offering that is constantly repeated as in a perpetual ritual may instead keep at bay the *other*, at least for the time being. Little installments but continuous: just like the obsessive refreshing of a Facebook page or the swiping motion through a mobile interface. Checking who is next in the series is a way to cope with anxiety. Anxiety is the anguish of the future; in moving forward through the stack of cards we find a surrogate for the implicit desperation of the individual who is unconsciously besieged by the unknown.

Tinder is advertised as a new matchmaking utility that promises to deliver true love. Yet the game-oriented telos of the app is clearly factored in the very idea of the project. It is objectless. Pleasure is secondary while the endless circulatory movement is essential.[21] For merely contingent reasons, Tinder masks itself in idealistic terms (finding true love), whereas it showcases a distortion of the former that tends not toward desire, but again toward the logic of the drive. Hence, just like capitalism, the image it offers for adoration is that of an immature deity—the romantic aspiration to a final union while it instead drifts toward proliferation and acceleration of movement itself. Slavoj Žižek made the argument that "drive . . . stands for the paradoxical possibility that the subject forever prevented from achieving his Goal (and thus fully satisfying his desire), can nevertheless find satisfaction in the very circular movement of repeatedly missing its object." This mode of being enacts "the self-enclosed loop of a circular repetitive movement [that] replaces infinite striving" typical of desire (360). What is the difference between desire and the drive? It is not only that desire sustains itself by missing the object, and as such remains frustrated, but that far from being an autotelic process in which the subject affirms itself in a kind of self-presupposing mode, through desire the subject undergoes an ecstatic suspension in which the latter is "involved in the Other, de-centered through its identifications which neither excludes nor includes the Other in question" (Butler 2010, 114). In falling back onto the drive instead, the subject reaches a perverse satisfaction precisely in not capturing the object and establishes a self-form that is not reflexive anymore, but rather obstinate in its movement forward. And this is said to be true for new technology in general, where "the movement from link to link, the forwarding and storing and commenting . . . is circulation for its own sake" (Dean 2010, 121).

Endlessly moving forward like the weaponized eye of drone war, this technicization of sexuality also draws another interesting parallel with neoliberal warfare. As argued, drone warfare does not only rely on direct recognition of the target to act but must also compile a study of patterns and anomalies to render informative the enormous amount of data that it accumulates. In locative sex, participants engage in similar strategies. On one side, the codifying of a specific likeability that one needs to achieve in order to be successful can be described as a veritable self-profiling. It is as if by indexing one's persona, participants facilitate the immediate recognition of the target to be pursued. Eventually patterns are established, and the development of a microknowledge of set behaviors provides a reliable infrastructure for the targeting. This formula for seduction meets at the convergence of the user and the screen of his or her mobile phone; meanwhile, human encounters are pulverized in the infinitesimal calculation of digital archives. Is this necessarily bad? Not exactly.

Benjamin Noys argues that in order to detoxify us from the mysticism of prosthetic war and smart technology one needs to take seriously this "metaphysics and the desire for a particular kind of subject-less subject" while simultaneously "grasping how these constant transformations can be interrupted, negated, and refused" (15). In mutating toward a drive-form, the subject-less aspiration is instead dispossessed, surveilled, and rendered productive.[22] What's more, a subject-less subject should not be conceived as a well-oiled machine perfectly attuned to the rhythms of capital accumulation. Instantaneous matches and targets—this is the nightmare of an ultimate instrumentalization of the world, of a naturalized nature held fast under the iron heel of capital, and not the legitimate aspiration to vitality, difference, and freedom.

Andrea Righi is assistant professor of Italian and coordinator of the Italian studies program at Miami University. He is the author of *Italian Reactionary Thought and Critical Theory: An Inquiry into Savage Modernities* (2015) and *Biopolitics and Social Change in Italy: From Gramsci to Pasolini to Negri* (2011).

Notes

1. Dardot and Laval remark that the aim is "to achieve self-government by the individual him—or herself—that is, to produce a certain type of relationship to the self" through "an accountable and financial subjectivation" and "by systematically creating competition between individuals" (14).

2. With "emergent properties" or behavior media scholars have tried to capture the quasi-living status reached by technology as it imitates the same germinal, creative, and anomic capacity of life for growth. See Parisi (2013, 1–3) and Terranova (114–15). As the parallel between war and sexuality shows, capitalist subsumption of life comes at a high cost and points to the fact that not everything is smoothly assimilated by a computational process of digitization. See Franklin (89–91).

3. This is seen in the alarmist claims by authors like Donna Freitas or the more health-care oriented work by Hasinoff.

4. The Oedipal implications of this scene are blatant. The abrupt assassination of the two women by the Germans is the turning point for Norman to accept his military duty as a man.

5. As Simone De Beauvoir writes, since the agricultural age, "being naturally different from man, who posits himself as the same, woman is consigned to the category of Other; the Other encompasses woman" (104). See also Boccia (71).

6. This was a point that Jean Baudrillard had already noted when discussing the First Gulf War. As Astrid H. M. Nordin and Dan Öberg write, summarizing the thought of the French philosopher, Baudrillard describes "a situation in which subjectivity, social relations and will are essentially liquidated by operational practices. They are not supplanted by a higher will or a higher purpose. Rather, they vanish into processing entirely devoid of symbolic meaning" (399).

7. Pasquinelli specifies that under this digital horizon "data are not numbers, but *Gestalten*, structures that become image: infinite points that draw the silhouette of a new Singularity emerging against the background of apparently meaningless data" (2016, 254).

8. See also Pasquinelli's notion of the spike, which he defines as "a ruffle along the smooth data space of the intelligence of power" (2016, 257).

9. See Dean (2010, 218–21). This point resonates with Kordela's intuition that it is through the gaze that the issue of infinity reveals itself in neoliberal temporality. She argues that being "infested by infinity," this temporality gives us "the illusion of immortality" (2013b, 285). Similarly, prosthetic war promises immortality thanks to its optic invulnerability.

10. Some of the categories used to define it are: post-industrial society (see Marazzi), society of enjoyment (see McGowan), post-oedipal society or post-patriarchy (see Dominijanni 2014b).

11. For the problem of digital accountability, see Righi (687–89).

12. On this point, see also Weber (22–39).

13. Tinder is a development of an older matchmaking system called Grinder, which was very popular in queer communities. These and other technologies were undoubtedly instrumental to the fight of LGBTQ groups. The extent to which these forms of opposition to heteronormativity may now be diffused by neoliberal anatomo-politics is not the topic of this paper but it is certainly worthy of a larger inquiry. More recently, a number of locative apps (Bumble, TikiTalk, Happn, etc.) have mushroomed following the same optimization drive.

14. One may object that military targets cannot be compared to erotic ones because in war the aggressor has an active role while the targeted combatant does not. In sentimental–sexual seduction, on the other hand, both duelists must be (to a certain degree) active. However, one should consider von Clausewitz's classic definition of armed conflict in *On War* as a reciprocal antagonistic confrontation where positions are equally interchangeable and the passive–active role is only retrospective misrepresentation.

15. Samuel Weber depicts a specular mentality in modern warfare: "The insistence that opportunity be treated strictly as a 'target' that can be seized or missed itself misses the mark, because the mark involved is never simply present but always involved with other marks and other opportunities" (21). More broadly, Seb Franklin argues that "sociality, from the epistemic position that grounds the control era, can be understood only as targeting under the continued impression of free will—a conceptual frame underscored by the fact that the terms *recticle* (gun sight) and *network* share a root in the Latin *reticulum*, net" (166).

16. Although she retains hopes for the circulatory potential of "abstract sex," Luciana Parisi seems to hint at this state of affairs when she discusses the implications of a biopolitical "superfold" that "commercializes the unpredictable (virtual and not the possible) power of mutations marking a new bifurcation between the molecular control of sexual reproduction and the molecular proliferation of bacterial sex" (2004, 26).

17. I wouldn't be so sure about the complete mastery of this episteme if only because of a basic limit that any science encounters—that is to say, the Heisenberg uncertainty principle—which Pasquinelli here reframes in these terms: "In many cases, from military affairs to algotrading and web ranking, algorithms often influence the very field that they are supposed to measure" (2015). Yet, it is also true that genetic algorithms performed substantially better than their human counterparts during the recent financial turbulence provoked by the UK European Union membership referendum. See Cui, Hope, and Zuckerman.

18. On game theory basic features, see Juul. On alternative uses of Tinder, see Stampler (46) and Feuer.

19. This is no less than a revamping of the old bourgeois notion of decor but with a subversive twist: that of the promise of the unleashing of libido in its eternal flux. Following the parallel, one could argue that for high bourgeois thought contemplation and nostalgia stood as the index of reified culture, while the index of contemporary reification turns into the fantasy of happiness framed as endless opportunity.

20. Notice the similarity with "the corporate discourse of empowerment" where, as Agre writes, capture technology "permits work activities to be disciplined through aggregate measures derived from captured information" (117).

21. This seemingly eternal movement is prompted by what Kordela calls *surplus-enjoyment,* for "the biopolitical machinery resolutely shuns eternity and aims instead at proxies that provide only a controlled and safe illusion of eternity" (2013b, 282). See also Jodi Dean, who argues that neoliberalism mobilizes the

"force of loss as an absence of completion or limits. Capital is only capital through the loss of a capacity to be at rest" (2014, 159).

22. I am much more skeptical than Rey Chow who, if I read her correctly, still looks to self-referentiality with a benign eye. It seems to me that neoliberal instrumentalization is one that functions precisely through the "radical intransitivity" that Chow seems to value for its deconstructive capacity (6).

Works Cited

Agre, Philip. 1994. "Surveillance and Capture: Two Models of Privacy." *The Information Society* 10:101–27.

Alighieri, Dante. 1995. *Inferno*. Trans. Mark Musa. Bloomington: Indiana University Press.

Basulto, Dominic. 2015. "Your Life Is an Algorithm, Your Brain Is an Operating System." Big Think. http://bigthink.com/endless-innovation/your-life-is-an-algorithm-your-brain-is-an-operating-system.

Benjamin, Walter. 1996. "Capitalism as Religion." In *Selected Writings*, 288–91. Vol. 1. Trans. Rodney Livingstone. Cambridge, Mass.: Belknap Press.

Bilton, Nick. 2014. "Tinder, the Fast-Growing Dating App, Taps an Age-Old Truth." *New York Times*, October 29. http://www.nytimes.com/2014/10/30/fashion/tinder-the-fast-growing-dating-app-taps-an-age-old-truth.html?module=Search&mabReward=relbias%3As&_r=2.

Bishop, Ryan, and John Phillips. 2010. *Modernist Avant-Garde Aesthetics and Contemporary Military Technology*. Edinburgh: Edinburgh University Press.

Boccia, Maria Luisa. 2014. *La mia vita è la mia opera*. Rome: Ediesse.

Boccia, Maria Luisa, et al. 2009. "Sesso e politica nel post-patriarcato." *Il Manifesto*, September 25.

Butler, Judith. 2004. *Undoing Gender*. New York: Routledge.

Butler, Judith. 2010. "Longing for Recognition." In *Hegel's Philosophy and Feminist Thought: Beyond Antigone?* Ed. Kimberly Hutchings and Tuija Pulkkinen, 109–29. New York: Palgrave MacMillan.

Chamayou, Grégoire. 2015. *A Theory of the Drone*. Trans. Janet Loyd. New York: New Press.

Chow, Rey. 2006. *The Age of the World Target: Self-Referentiality in War, Theory, and Comparative Literature*. Durham: Duke University Press.

Copjec, Joan. 2002. *Imagine There Is No Woman*. Boston: MIT Press.

Copjec, Joan. 2006. "The Object-Gaze: Shame, Hejab, Cinema." *Filozofski Vestnik* 27, no. 2: 11–29.

Cui, Carolyn, Bradley Hope, and Gregory Zuckerman. 2016. "Who Made Money in the Brexit Chaos? Machines, Not Humans." *Wall Street Journal*, June 29. http://www.wsj.com/articles/in-brexit-trading-machine-beats-man-1467158146.

Dardot, Pierre, and Christian Laval. 2013. *The New Way of the World: On Neoliberal Society*. Trans. Gregory Elliott. London: Verso.

Dean, Jodi. 2010. *Blog Theory: Feedback and Capture in the Circuits of Drive*. Cambridge: Polity Press.

Dean, Jodi. 2014. "Complexity as Capture—Neoliberalism and the Loop of Drive." In *Capital at the Brink: Overcoming the Destructive Legacies of Neoliberalism*. Ed. Jeffrey R. Di Leo and Uppinder Mehan, 158–85. Ann Arbor: Open Humanities Press.

De Beauvoir, Simone. 2011. *The Second Sex*. Trans. Constance Borde and Sheila Malovany-Chevallier. New York: Vintage Books.

Deleuze, Gilles, and Félix Guattari. 1993. *Anti-Oedipus: Capitalism and Schizophrenia*. Trans. Robert Hurley, Mark Seem, and Helen R. Lane. Minneapolis: University of Minnesota Press.

Dillon, Michael, and Julian Reid. 2009. *The Liberal Way of War. Killing to Make Life Live*. New York: Routledge.

Dominijanni, Ida. 2014a. "Libertà Precaria." *Femminismo e Neoliberalismo*. Ed. Tristana Dini and Stefania Tarantino, 50–64. Benevento: Nathan edizioni.

Dominijanni, Ida. 2014b. *Il Trucco*. Rome: Ediesse.

Drexler, Peggy. 2015. "Millennial Women Are Taking a Laissez-Faire Approach to Romance." *Huffington Post*, January 30. http://www.huffingtonpost.com/peggy-drexler/-millennial-women-are-tak_b_6578116.html.

Elliott, Jane. 2013. "Suffering Agency: Imagining Neoliberal Personhood in North America and Britain." *Social Text* 31, no. 2: 83–101.

Farman, Jason. 2012. *Mobile Interface Theory: Embodied Space and Locative Media*. New York: Routledge.

Farocki, Harun. 2004. "Phantom Images." *Public* 29:12–24.

Feuer, Alan. 2015. "On Tinder, Taking a Swipe at Love, or Sex, or Something, in New York." *New York Times*, February 13. http://mobile.nytimes.com/2015/02/15/nyregion/on-tinder-taking-a-swipe-at-love-or-sex-or-something-in-new-york.html?smid=fb-share&_r=1&referrer.

Foucault, Michel. 2012. "The Mesh of Power." Trans. Christopher Chitty. *Viewpoint Magazine*, September 10. http://viewpointmag.com/2012/09/12/the-mesh-of-power/.

Franklin, Seb. 2015. *Control: Digitality as Cultural Logic*. Cambridge, Mass.: MIT Press.

Freitas, Donna. 2013. *The End of Sex: How Hookup Culture Is Leaving a Generation Unhappy, Sexually Unfulfilled, and Confused about Intimacy*. New York: Basic Books.

Galloway, Alexander. 2013. *The Interface Effect*. Malden, Mass.: Polity Press.

Gray, Jesse Glenn. 1958. *The Warriors: Reflections on Men in Battle*. Lincoln: University of Nebraska Press.

Haddow, Douglas. 2015. "Life in the Algorithm." Adbusters, January 9. https://www.adbusters.org/article/life-in-the-algorithm/.

Hasinoff, Amy Adele. 2013. "Sexting as Media Production: Rethinking Social Media and Sexuality." *New Media & Society* 15, no. 4: 449–65.

Juul, Jesper. 2005. "A Dictionary of Video Game Theory." Half-Real, November. http://www.half-real.net/dictionary/.

Kordela, Kiarina. 2013a. *Being, Time, Bios: Capitalism and Ontology*. Albany: State University of New York.

Kordela, Kiarina. 2013b. "(Marxian-Psychoanalytic) Biopolitics and Bioracism." In *Penumbra*. Ed. Jöttkandt and Joan Copjec, 279–91. Melbourne: repress.

Lacan, Jacques. 1990. *Television: A Challenge to the Psychoanalytic Establishment*. Trans. Jeffrey Mehlman. New York: Norton.

Lazzarato, Maurizio. 2012. *The Making of the Indebted Man: An Essay on the Neoliberal Condition*. Trans. Joshua David Jordan. Los Angeles: Semiotext(e).

Marazzi, Christian. 2008. *Capital and Language: From the New Economy to the War Economy*. Trans. Gregory Conti. Los Angeles: Semiotext(e).

McGowan, Todd. 2004. *The End of Dissatisfaction? Jacques Lacan and the Emerging Society of Enjoyment*. Albany: State University of New York Press.

McNulty, Tracy. 2009. "Demanding the Impossible: Desire and Social Change." *differences: A Journal of Feminist Cultural Studies* 20, no. 1: 1–39.

Nordin, Astrid H. M., and Dan Öberg. 2015. "Targeting the Ontology of War: From Clausewitz to Baudrillard." *Millennium: Journal of International Studies* 43, no. 2: 392–410.

Noys, Benjamin. 2015. "Drone Metaphysics." *Culture Machine* 16:1–22.

Parisi, Luciana. 2004. *Abstract Sex: Philosophy, Bio-Technology, and the Mutations of Desire*. London: Continuum.

Parisi, Luciana. 2013. *Contagious Architecture: Computation, Aesthetics, and Space*. Boston: MIT Press.

Pasquinelli, Matteo. 2015 "Anomaly Detection: The Mathematization of the Abnormal in the Metadata Society." Talk delivered at the Transmediale Festival, Berlin. https://www.academia.edu/10369819/Anomaly_Detection_The_Mathematization_of_the_Abnormal_in_the_Metadata_Society.

Pasquinelli, Matteo. 2016. "The Spike: On the Growth and Form of Pattern Police." Entry in the catalog for the exhibit *Nervous System: Quantified Life and the Social Question*, Berlin. https://www.academia.edu/23052361/The_Spike_On_the_Growth_and_Form_of_Pattern_Police.

Righi, Andrea. 2017. "The Corpulence of Self-Tracking: The Quantified Self, Derrida, and Writing in the Age of Digital Accountability." *Theory & Event* 20, no. 3: 679–98.

Rosenberg, Jordy. 2014. "The Molecularization of Sexuality: On Some Primitivisms of the Present." *Theory & Event* 17, no. 2.

Stampler, Laura. 2014. "The New Dating Game." *Time*, February 17, 42–74.

Terranova, Tiziana. 2004. *Network Culture: Politics for the Information Age*. London: Pluto Press.

Tiqqun. 2010. *Sonogram of a Potential* [Échographie d'une puissance]. English translation available at Caring Labor: An Archive, https://caringlabor.wordpress.com/2010/10/31/tiqqun-2-sonogram-of-a-potential/.

Virilio, Paul. 2008. *Open Sky*. Trans. Julie Rose. London: Verso.

Virno, Paolo. 2004. *A Grammar of the Multitude: For an Analysis of Contemporary Forms of Life*. Trans. Isabella Bertoletti, James Cascaito, and Andrea Casson. New York: Semiotext(e).

Virno, Paolo. 2008. *Multitude: Between Innovation and Negation.* Trans. Isabella Bertoletti, James Cascaito, and Andrea Casson. Los Angeles: Semiotext(e).
von Clausewitz, Carl. 1976. *On War.* Princeton: Princeton University Press.
Weber, Samuel. 2005. *Targets of Opportunity: On the Militarization of Thinking.* New York: Fordham University Press.
Žižek, Slavoj. 2008. *The Ticklish Subject: The Absent Center of Political Ontology.* London: Verso.

THE PEDAGOGICAL POWER OF THINGS
TOWARD A POST-INTENTIONAL PHENOMENOLOGY OF UNLEARNING

Tyson E. Lewis

Jane Bennett's book *Vibrant Matter: A Political Ecology of Things* has two overlapping and mutually supportive aims. First, she has a philosophical project: to problematize and hopefully overcome a major bias in Western philosophical thinking that separates life and death, activity and passivity, vibrancy and inertness. As counterintuitive as it may seem, Bennett proposes that brute matter exerts its own power that exists below the human world. Focusing on the "vitality" of things means coming to terms with the "capacity of things . . . not only to impede or block the will and designs of humans but also to act as quasi agents or forces with trajectories, propensities, or tendencies of their own" (viii). This philosophical project is linked directly to an overarching political hypothesis. Bennett argues that one of the causes of the destruction of the natural world and the impending ecological disaster is precisely the Western belief that matter is inactive, a mere resource for human consumption. But, if we see matter as vibrant and powerful then perhaps we will not instrumentalize it or uncritically consume it.

Here I do not want to review possible criticisms of these two projects or their underlying assumptions and arguments. Instead I want to bracket off these lines of inquiry in order to expose and think through another project of this book, one which Bennett only indirectly gestures toward but is nevertheless essential for forming a bridge between the philosophical and political poles of her overall aim. This other project concerns the possibility of an aesthetic pedagogy of things—a new educational practice that would route our collective attention away from issues of cultivating human-centered knowledge, skills, and aptitudes toward a perceptual receptivity and attentiveness to things that fall outside our worldly concerns. I call this an "aesthetic pedagogy" first and foremost because it concerns the sensorial dimension of our experience of things—their ability to gross us out, make us feel uncanny, or provoke weird pleasures that emerge when we recognize the secrete lives of things.

Although much more focused on philosophical and political issues, varieties of speculative realism (including object-oriented, vitalist, and materialist incarnations) do have a weak strain running through them that concerns educational questions. Like Bennett, Ian Bogost ends his book *Alien Phenomenology, or What It Is Like to Be a Thing* with a gesture toward the meaning and purposes of education. Critical of STEAM (science, technology, engineering, art, and mathematics) educational policies, Bogost observes that when all art and science are reduced to instrumental ends serving predefined economic functions, then there is no room left in education for the experience of things as such. He writes, "But what if the real obstacle to youthful interest in science arises not from a distaste for mathematics or the natural world but from a latent dissatisfaction with the way science melts the shell of wonder around ordinary objects?" (129). Bogost, like Bennett, sees things as an interruption of anthropocentric (human-centered) educational aims, opening up a space wherein the mere thingliness of the thing can appear in its own right. The goal here is not to reduce things to resources that can be studied in order to improve human worlds. Rather it is to let shine the irreducible material power of things. Of course, such thingly presence can be important for rethinking future political actions, but such actions need to be predicated on a perceptual sensitivity toward the weirdness of things as such.

For both Bennett and Bogost, an aesthetic education in things is essential, yet largely undertheorized. In the rest of this article, I will tease out the complexity of such an education. What is at stake here is an education that does not merely reinforce the human-centered nature of perceptual grasping but rather reveals something about perception itself that is object-centered (or, even better, object-infused). In this sense, things need to be seen as having *pedagogical power* of their own, as nonhuman teachers that do work on our perceptual common-sense orientations and bodily comportments. Instead of human perception shaping how things appear, I want to tell a different story, one where things shape how humans perceive. To do so, I want to turn to that which would seem to be most human: the realm of visual art. Art can reveal how human perception contains within it a nonhuman surplus, an alien presence. As such, art education might have a particularly important role to play in unlearning human perceptual styles while opening up students to the possibility of perceptual restylization (see also Hickey-Moody and Page; Hood and Kraehe).

Thus, art education becomes a particularly important point of struggle in promoting a new relationship between humans and things. When art education becomes nothing more than an adjunct to functionalist approaches to education or a mere mirror for reflecting back the image of the human to itself, then the experience of things as things is replaced by mere curiosity concerning how we as human actors can better ourselves and fulfill our projects using and manipulating things as pieces of equipment.

EDUCATION AND PERCEPTUAL STYLE

Shaun Gallagher and Dan Zahavi present a quick and useful overview of some basic phenomenological structures of perception that underlie human experience and allow those experiences to be recognizable as the kinds of experiences that they are. First and foremost, perception has an intentional structure. Perceptions are about something, and thus are entangled with the world. They also note that all perceptions come frontloaded with meaning. Perception is not simply the appearance of raw data that is then synthesized and organized according to the mind. Rather, perception is itself meaningful, and therefore, perception "*is* interpretational" (8). And this interpretation is context specific, informed by bodily skills, cultural norms, focal practices, and specific social roles that actors play in their worlds. The intentional structure of perception also has spatial and temporal aspects. Spatially, our bodies are anchored and thus limited in what is accessible. In this sense, perception is always incomplete, always perspectival. But precisely because of this, perception is also always anticipatory. Based on our habitual movement and familiarity with the world, perception anticipates certain possibilities, or rather directly perceives certain possibilities as given. Perception plunges us into the world by setting us up to anticipate outcomes that are built up in our motor intelligence. And finally, perception has a foreground and a background, a focal point around which it can be oriented. Perception is, in short, a *composition* of a meaningful, wordly scene.

Here is a simple description that should be familiar to any academic that reveals this basic perceptual structure in action. When I walk into my classroom to teach my seminar, I perceive the table where I place my notes for the day's lecture. I do not perceive the desk as merely a meaningless blob of a certain shape, size, and color. My perception *immediately* presents the table as a specific object: a table. But not only that, it is a table that is recognizable by me as relevant to my work. Based on my specific skills as a teacher, the context of the room, and the orientation of student bodies, I unproblematically link up with the table's use value. Stated differently, the table is a piece of equipment that, to quote Heidegger *(Being and Time),* is ready-to-hand. It comes frontloaded with meaning that I can intuitively plug into without a thought. Mental representations do not have to intercede or direct me in any way—rather the table solicits me to move toward it and place my notes upon its surface. And based on my familiarity with tables as pieces of equipment that support my focal practices as a teacher, I intuitively know that although I do not see them, the table has four legs that are present in their absence in the form of an anticipation that will unfold as I adjust my body by swinging my torso around the corner and plopping myself down upon the chair. In the split second that I entered the room, the room came into a certain focus where the table had a certain phenomenal primacy. My gaze instantaneously gravitated toward it, enabling the entire scene to organize itself into a coherent gestalt. In this sense, the table called out to me as a piece of equipment to "free it up" to be the kind of equipment that it is within a scholarly world, but at the same time, the table's call could only be registered as a call precisely because I had the contextually sensitive skill set to allow the table to appear as equipment in the first place. The resulting fusion is an equilibrium between my focal practices as a teacher and the world. This is the "sweet spot" of perceptual grasping, or what Maurice Merleau-Ponty would refer to as an "optimal" (2012, 316) grasp of a situation.

In short, perception is worldly. We are never outside of the worlds that form the implicit and tacit backgrounds of our actions, and perception is the interface that allows us to hook into and find our equilibrium within worlds. Perception is intentionally directed toward the world in the sense that perception is always already *about* worldly stuff. Without a world, there would be no perception, but without perception such worlds would never be able to be worldly, in the sense of being familiar contexts.

While phenomenologists from Husserl to Heidegger to Merleau-Ponty to Gallagher and Zahavi find the pragmatics of perception useful for enabling us to get along with our lives, it is precisely this *fundamental structure* that poses a decisive problem for thing theorists like Bennett who are concerned with the autonomous, vibrant lives of things. The lives of things are, for Bennett, "irreducible to the culture of objects [in a human world]" and thus posit an "eccentric outside" (5) that is irreducible to either human-centered notions of use or exchange value. Things in their thingliness persist below the level of our worldly purposes, meanings, and values. In other words, things are not simply pieces of equipment to be animated by human agents. Things are *always already animated* by a subtle "thing-power," or a power "of inanimate things to animate, to act, to produce effects" (6).

But here is the rub: Normal everyday perception is structurally set up in a way to censor any attentiveness to such thing-power. As outlined above, perception is intentionally directed toward *the world*. It is always already an interpretation of things as objects within meaningful contexts, focal practices, roles, and traditions. As such, perception is permeated through and through with the texture of the human-centered world (composed as it is of our roles, equipment, purposes, and so forth). Because of this structure, Heidegger finds it practically impossible to penetrate the thingly quality of things. After presenting several possible definitions of the thing, he states, "The unpretentious thing evades thought most stubbornly" (2001, 31). Its "self-contained independence" (31) resists interpretation precisely because of perception's structural tendency toward meaning-rich, worldly appearances. Summarizing, Steven Crowell finds a distinct gap in Heidegger's essay "The Origin of the Work of Art," which begins with the question concerning the thinghood of the thing, yet never seems to answer this opening inquiry, moving off in other directions in order to reveal the truth of equipment and artwork.

The gambit of speculative realists such as Bennett is that things are not merely reducible to their human clothing. Through certain strategies, we can begin to speculate what things are like beyond the combination of mind and body that anchors them firmly in a human world of focal practices, equipment, and roles. If normal perception censors or subtracts the power of things, then we need to undermine the very structures of such perception in order to become attentive to the call of things beyond their cultural, economic, and use values. In particular, if perception is frontloaded with meaning, if it is always already embedded in a world, if it anticipates certain appearances through habituated coping, then these structural facets of perception have to be rendered inoperative or suspended in order for thing-power to enchant us. And to further complicate matters, such an operation must remain within perception itself (as there is no escaping its intentional structure), finding resources immanent to perception that disorient its worldliness.

Indeed, Bennett argues as such. To access thing-power we need a new "perceptual style" (5) that is open to the appearance of the thingness of objects. Or, even more aptly, we need a "cultivated, patient, sensory attentiveness to nonhuman forces operating outside and inside the human body" (xiv). Her interest in *cultivating* a new perceptual style is not merely a philosophical problematic or a political one. Most properly it is educational. In the next section I will see what kind of phenomenological education is needed for the cultivation of a thing-sensitive perceptual style and, in conclusion, speculate how certain forms of art may offer an example of such pedagogy.

FROM PHENOMENOLOGICAL BREAKDOWN TO BREAKTHROUGH: LESSONS IN VIBRANT MATTER

I will begin this section with an overview of two central phenomenologists—Heidegger and Merleau-Ponty—in order to argue that they have missed certain opportunities for thinking through the unique pedagogical agency of things to suspend human-centered worldliness. Here I will present a series of these "missed opportunities" in order to demonstrate the difficulty of theorizing the pedagogy of things and also the ongoing need to address this difficultly head-on with a theory dedicated explicitly (rather than marginally or tangentially) to educational questions of perceptual unlearning. In an effort to begin this project, I will then argue for a new approach to the question of the pedagogy of things, one that turns to the arts for nonhuman educational possibilities. At stake here is moving from the phenomenological interest in learning to an alien phenomenology of unlearning; from equipmental breakdowns to thingly breakthroughs.

For Merleau-Ponty, education concerns the cultivation of a perceptual style that is attuned to the affordances of the world. For example, Merleau-Ponty writes, "Learning to see colors is the acquisition of a certain style of vision, a new use of one's own body; it is to enrich and to reorganize the body schema" (2012, 154–55). Learning is the development of ever-more discriminating perceptual apprehension of what is possible in a world. It is a modification of the body schema that allows fine-grained adjustments, and thus helps us to move toward a state of "equilibrium" (155). Equilibrium is a kind of "knotting together" (148) of self and world into a seamless flow. At this point, Merleau-Ponty offers an instructive example of such embodied learning: "The subject who learns to type literally incorporates the space of the keyboard into his bodily space" (146). Learning offers a kind of alteration of the body and how it hooks up with the world, enabling us to develop increasingly more sophisticated couplings with the equipment that is of importance to our focal practices. This is all fine and good if one wants a phenomenology of what it is like to be masterful at something, but what I want to emphasize is how such mastery is contingent on the disappearance of the thingly quality of things. The keyboard disappears into the background. As my habits become more and more discriminatory and exact, my body and keyboard knot together to form an integrated whole without remainder. Whatever otherness resides in the material thing vanishes into a world oriented toward accomplishing human-centered tasks. The power of learning erases our attentiveness to things as autonomous agents. Returning to my opening example of entering a seminar room and putting my notes on the table, we could say that I do not even perceive a table (as a material surface) so much as a possibility for an action (put-ability, if I can coin a rather clunky term).

Because perceptual education (a) is always already in a world, and (b) causes objects to become transparent (absorbed into the tacit background), perception itself is a pedagogical issue for speculative realists. There is a need for a thingly pedagogy that interrupts the type of learning emphasized by Merleau-Ponty. To manage a first step toward theorizing what such an education might be, we can remain with phenomenology itself for inspiration, and in particular Heidegger's analysis of breakdowns. To begin, we might think of Heidegger's important description of equipmental breakdowns from *Being and Time*. If equipment disappears as we learn how to use it (as in Merleau-Ponty's description of learning offered above), how do we gain access to the structure of equipment? This structure appears in breakdown situations when the hammer is "unready-to-hand" (2008, 104). There are three kinds of attending breakdowns. The first is unusability, as when we are confronted with a broken hammer. Second, there might be a missing piece of equipment, as when we cannot find the hammer we are looking for. And third, we may be confronted with an obstacle, as when there is something in the way of adequately grasping the hammer (distractions from concentrating on the work to be done). In all cases, that which is implicit (the background structure of equipment and its context of use) suddenly reveals itself from within the breakdown situation. What is important here is that breakdowns give us access to the ontological structure of equipment as equipment. In his later work on the thingliness of things, Heidegger returns to this exact point, writing, "The situation stands revealed as soon as we speak of things in the strict sense as mere things. The 'mere,' after all, means the removal of the character of usefulness and of being made. The mere thing is a sort of equipment denuded of its equipmental being. Thing-being consists in what is then left over. But this remnant is not actually defined in its ontological character. It remains doubtful whether the thingly character comes to view at all in the process of stripping off everything equipmental" (2001, 30).

Yet perhaps Heidegger missed something important in his own analysis of breakdowns. Returning to his description of breakdowns in *Being and Time* we notice the following sentence: "Anything which is unready-to-hand in this way is disturbing to us, and enables us to see the *obstinacy* of that with which we must concern ourselves in the first instance before we do anything else" (103). And, "with this obstinacy, the presence-at-hand of the ready-to-hand makes itself known in a new way" (103–4). It is the uncanny and disturbing remnant of presence of the thing in its obstinacy that offers a point of contact with thingliness. As Heidegger says, "first and foremost" the breakdown offers a confrontation with a unique and singular thing in its obstinacy. The brute force of things to affect a response is the first "lesson" of the breakdown, and it is only afterward that the context of the equipmental structure comes to light.

Bill Brown makes a similar point. He writes, "We begin to confront the thingness of objects when they stop working for us: when the drill breaks, when the car stalls, when the windows get filthy, when their flow within the circuits of production and distribution, consumption and exhibition, has been arrested, however momentarily" (4). Moments of breakdown, Brown emphasizes, *teach* us that we are surrounded by things—things that are gazing at us from a distance, from a point external to our worldly endeavors. Citing Fernando Pessoa, Brown further points out that breakdowns are "lessons in unlearning" through which "what we see of things are the things" (2). In this case, the breakdown is explicitly linked not to learning but to *unlearning*. This unlearning opens a perceptual space wherein things can shine forth. In relation to my seminar table, the thingliness of its material power would only become apparent if a breakdown caused me to unlearn my habitual bodily comportment (when I lay down my notes for example, the table collapses).

While leaving room for the appearance of things within phenomenology, Bennett would most certainly argue that this educational reading of the breakdown is problematic because the thing only appears in its obstinacy, or as an obstacle in the course of human-centered worldly activities. The breakdown is a moment wherein a new perceptual style can emerge from an interruption and suspension of the knot tying body and world together, yet this starting point is still too tethered to the very world it negates precisely because the thing is not experienced as a positive power in its own right. Stated differently, the thing is a negative power that resists human-centered goals and purposes rather than as a vibrant and positive presence in itself (without reference to human purposes).

Another possibility opens up through Bennett's analysis. In *Vibrant Matter,* she theorizes a pedagogy of perceptual breakdown in her own educational interpretation of Theodor Adorno's negative dialectic. Bennett argues that a new pedagogy of the negative consists of four educational movements (14). First, there is an intellectual movement that attempts to make our conceptual practices explicit objects of thought. Here, her own philosophical project becomes an educational project in showing and demonstrating the limits of the Western tendency to create binaries that separate and divide the world into active and inactive, living and dead matter. Second, she calls for attentiveness to things—an attentiveness that remains impossible as long as the structure of the binary dominates. Third, there must be an exercise of the utopian imagination to recapture what remains in the gaps of the binary (and thus what has been obscured). And finally, such a pedagogy needs to admit to a little playful or speculative magic. For Adorno, we can never have direct access to the thing, but we can approach it obliquely through indirect, poetic means.

Whereas Bennett might criticize Heidegger's description of the breakdown as merely proposing a negative definition of the thing (the thing in its obstinacy is nothing more than the negation of the world rather than an agentic force), I would like to suggest that Bennett's own reading of Adorno is also problematic. First, her description of Adorno's negative pedagogy, oddly, does not include any agency of the thing to act as a teacher. It seems as though *we* initiate the process of the negative dialectic by reflecting on *our* concepts. Certainly, such concepts contain the trace of the thing in spectral form, but this is nevertheless spectral (rather than material). This kind of internal, self-reflection misses Bennett's own clarion call for the cultivation of a new perceptual style. From a phenomenological point of view, it is highly suspicious that we will ever "get at" the thing-power of the thing by introspection or philosophical critique of categories. Bennett's emphasis on materiality and the body is here oddly absent.

Second, attentiveness to the thing, or what Bennett refers to as "aesthetic" attention (15), is important, but again, her framing of the issue could be read as reemphasizing human intentionality in the process. *We* focus *our* perception toward things thus *allowing* them to show themselves to us. This is problematic precisely because it denies the possibility that the thing can and does *exert its own presence, thus calling us to see or to listen in certain ways.* Our attentiveness does not come first, but is rather the result of the call of things. Or at least they come together simultaneously in a moment of recursive cause and effect. Either way, attentiveness when separated from responsiveness seems to grant agency first and foremost to the human actor over and above the nonhuman actant.

The virtue of Heidegger's breakdown (while flawed) is that it starts from the sudden appearance of the thing that causes a breakdown in the perceptual field and the smooth running of an embodied focal practice. Thus the thing speaks and the body takes notice, resulting in a moment of suspension and inoperativity. This seems much more materialist than Bennett's pedagogy.

What is at stake here are the difficulties in defining an educational logic that can disrupt and disorient the worldly structure of perception in such a way as to let appear thing-power as an autonomous, creative force. Rather than an education in body–world coupling, speculative realism calls for an educational breakdown of this very coupling, enabling a gap to emerge through which things can appear (no matter how briefly or indirectly). Instead of an education that orients us, this is an education that dis-orients us, and thus opens up a new access point for thingly enchantment.

Perhaps the best place to look for such a pedagogy is not in Heidegger or in Bennett's pedagogical formulations, but in Bennett's example of the thing-power of the black plastic glove, oak pollen, dead rat, bottle cap, and stick of wood. The assemblage found in the grate over a storm drain in the Chesapeake Bay issued an enigmatic call that interrupted and suspended Bennett's worldly purposes, shifting her attention away from her daily comings and goings toward another, more mysterious life of things. Some*thing* snagged her eye, dragging her away from her worldly concerns. "It issued a call," she remembers, "even if I did not quite understand what it was saying. At the very least, it provoked affects in me" (4). Notice, the starting point was an embodied, affective experience of responsiveness *and* attentiveness, not an intellectual reflection on philosophical concepts or categories.

Furthermore, this is not simply a negative experience. Because the things are not things found in a context of use or exchange, they are immediately weird and disarming. In other words, the fact that these things have been discarded is important—their materiality is not submitted to worldly purposes. Their presence is not merely an obstruction to achieving a set goal. And because of this they are full of wonderment merely in their being there. The thing-power that was exposed alters the body schema in ways that throw it out of the world, temporarily arresting its tendency toward effortless flow or equilibrium. Here the body has no habituated knowledge to couple successfully with the call of thing-power. A gap opens up in the perceptual gestalt, letting leak in an alien presence that freezes the body, urging it to be attentive to something that it does not understand. Where perception is normally guided by a kind of spatial and temporal anticipation, such anticipations falter, stumble, and barely manage to recuperate some stability. In such instances, we are confronted with a situation wherein it is not simply the hammer that is broken but rather the very perceptual field within which breakdowns are recognized as breakdowns. In this sense, the difference between breakdown and *breakthrough* becomes indifferent.

When one begins from the moment when the thing intrudes (not merely as a piece of equipment but as a thing proper), then perceptual disorientation produces a momentary opening toward thing-power by arresting the "natural" course of perceptual grasping. In this sense, the thing breaks through. What is therefore necessary for an education by things is heightened receptivity to moments where the thing announces its presence as a *teacher-actant*. An education in things is an education *by* things. It is only after the fact that we can intellectually reflect on how certain beliefs and concepts are problematic, or how thing-power can be an active force in a new ecological assemblage.

Furthering the opportunities for the development of thing pedagogy, I will finally turn to art. Below I argue that art can be seen as a resource for cultivating the perceptual receptivity and attentiveness toward things that Bennett desires. Although Quentin Meillassoux has recently called for a turn toward mathematical abstraction as a way to approach an uncorrelated understanding of the earth, I will suggest that art still provides untapped resources for a more materialist understanding of the thing. Meillassoux, like Bennett, seems to privilege intellectual reflection in order to get around a human-centric perceptual style. Yet I want to argue that we need to stay firmly within the realm of the perceptual in order to disorient it and thus open up the possibility of a new style.

THE PERCEPTUAL PEDAGOGY OF THE ARTS: TOUCHING THINGS

As with the previous section, here I will begin with two "missed opportunities" for recognizing connections between art and the pedagogical power of things to interrupt our worldly perceptual style and assert their power to interrupt and intervene in perceptual orientations. In particular, I remain interested in the aesthetics of perceptual stylistics as a surface for things to break through. My goal is not to dismiss figures like Heidegger or Merleau-Ponty but rather to suggest that their interpretations of art can be expanded beyond the human. They argue that art enables us to experience the presencing of world (Heidegger) and how perception is wrapped up in worldly relations with things (Merleau-Ponty). On this view, art crystalizes how worlds emerge *for us*. With art, we see our seeing of the world. Yet what I want to argue is that there are moments in Heidegger and Merleau-Ponty's descriptions that can be read subversively or counterintuitively as indicating the vibrant power of things to imprint their ways of perceiving themselves on our perceptual conventions. In this alternative, speculative realist reading, with art, we see how things see each other. Thus, certain forms of art allow us to eavesdrop on another kind of perceptual stylization that has been adopted as our own, even if it has alien origins.

The question of the aesthetic is already internal to certain strands of speculative realism, perhaps most strongly represented in Steven Shaviro's call for a "speculative aesthetics" (156). With Shaviro, I propose that aesthetic encounters enable us to "act in the world and relate to other things in the world without reducing it and them to mere correlates of our own thought" (156). While Shaviro does not discuss art as such, I would argue that turning to the work of artwork helps concretize his own aesthetic turn in important ways. In this section, I will highlight how phenomenologists highlight the subtle ways in which certain forms of visual arts are not reducible to human-centric perceptual styles but also offer moments wherein the perceptual styles of things jut forth. Such a reading defamiliarizes taken-for-granted aesthetic conventions in order to reveal their object orientedness.

According to Heidegger in his canonical essay "The Origin of the Work of Art," art "opens up a world" (41) or grants a world space in which to appear as a world. Although rather mystical sounding, his meaning becomes clear if we look at his example of the Greek temple. For the early Greeks, a temple "gives things their look and to men their outlook on themselves" (42). The temple organizes Greek life into a coherent whole, gives it meaning through ritual, and frames the landscape around its edifice. It allows things, people, and activities to appear as significant, sheltering traditions and a particular style of being. The work of a great work of art is thus to open up a world.

This work is distinct from the work of equipment. For Heidegger, the materiality of a piece of equipment withdraws in its use, becoming a transparent part of the background. For instance, it is almost impossible to think of the keyboard itself while I am typing these words without interrupting the flow of the typing itself. As a piece of equipment, the keyboard must become absorbed into the activity, effectively concealing its enabling function precisely because of this very functionality. Yet the piece of art does not withdraw its materiality in a similar way. The stone of the Greek temple protrudes, makes itself present. Heidegger writes, "The temple-work, in setting up a world, does not cause the material to disappear, but rather causes it to come forth for the very first time and to come into the Open of the work's world" (45). In this sense, the thingly character of the stone is an active agent in the work of art. This is a positive notion of the earth as breaking through the world, and entering into strife with it. But this breaking through is at the same time a withdrawing or self-secluding. As such, the thing of the earth is always sheltering and concealing. The appearance of the earth is equally its disappearance. Heidegger writes, "The earth cannot dispense with the Open of the world if it itself is to appear as earth in the liberated surge of its self—seclusion" (48). My issue here is not with Heidegger's description of the disappearing appearance of the earth. Such a description, as we shall see below, has great explanatory power. Rather it is with his tethering of this dynamic to human-centered worldhood. If Graham Harman has argued that tool-being has an "unlimited scope, covering all entities, not just narrowly 'useful' ones" (110), then I would like to argue the same point in relation to earth. The dynamic that Heidegger describes between presencing and withdrawing is a phenomenon that happens between all things—all things exhibit a "spontaneous forthcoming of that which is continually self-secluding" (2001, 47). In this sense, I want to argue that Heidegger's description of the earth as a thing that juts forth but only insofar as it recedes is not human dependent. Instead, art lets appear a process that is more diasporic than opening up a world.

We can perform a similar reading with Merleau-Ponty's analysis of the work of art. Perhaps more forcefully than others of his generation, Merleau-Ponty emphasized that the "great achievement" of modern art "has been to allow us to rediscover the world in which we live, yet which we are always prone to forget" (2008, 32). In everyday life, we rarely stop to reflect on the work of perception and its relationship to the world, how we are anchored in the world through perceptual grasping. Yet the paintings of artists like Cézanne "recapture the feel of perceptual experience" and thus *teach* us that "being is not given but rather emerges over time" (41). Indeed, Merleau-Ponty clearly states that art offers a "reawakening of the world of perception" so that "learning to see the world around us" (53) becomes a possibility. The plastic arts in particular can facilitate a certain kind of learning: a learning which enables us to reflect on how our bodies are anchored in a world. In short, art teaches by allowing us to perceive our perception perceiving the world.

This learning is predicated on two chiasmic relations: the visible and the invisible and the gaze of the painter and the gaze of the thing. Instead of positing the invisible as an absolute difference from the visible, Merleau-Ponty points toward their chiasmic intertwining in the moment of perceptual grasping. The invisible is *in the visible*. Paintings reveal that things are not solid beings that are transparently accessible to us through our perceptual grasping. Instead, they are entangled with a vast field of invisible, worldly relations with other things. This color red, for instance, is a "punctuation in the field of red things" (1968, 132) that remains invisible even though it in-forms how *this* particular red appears as red. In addition, another chiasma is at stake in Merleau-Ponty's interpretation of art. The artist's gaze is always met by the gaze of the thing staring back. Merleau-Ponty writes, "Inevitably the roles between the painter and the visible switch. That is why so many painters have said that things look at them" (1993, 129). To see is to be seen. Perception is therefore a meeting of human and nonhuman looks. Here, Merleau-Ponty clearly attributes agentic power to things, which have their own perceptual style. Art is a crossing of these styles. As with my interpretation of Heidegger above, what I want to stress here is how the intertwining of the visible and invisible is not simply about *our* perceptual experience of the world. Instead, I want to speculate that this is a basic, generalizable claim that can be extended to all things and their intimate relations between each other. Further, I would like to push Merleau-Ponty's second analysis further and suggest that things not only look back at *us* but can also look at each other. Art teaches us that our perceptual style is constantly restylized by how things perceive.

In both cases, art teaches, but the lessons it teaches always seem to come back to the question of human worlds and human perceptual grasping of those worlds. Yet if we are to turn to art as one possible source for an aesthetic education in and by things, we need to move beyond these phenomenological descriptions and see art as offering an "alien phenomenology" (Bogost) where things teach us a lesson in alien perceptual styles. We need to speculate that our artistic conventions are translations of the perceptual relations between things and thus are not mere mirrors reflecting us back to ourselves.

To illustrate how this might work, I want to use Merleau-Ponty's description of contour lines as a starting point. Modern painters, on Merleau-Ponty's reading, discovered that "there are no lines visible in themselves, that neither the contour of the apple nor the border between field and meadow is in *this* place or that, that they are always on the near or the far side of the point we look at. They are always between or behind whatever we fix our eyes upon; they are indicated, implicated, and even very imperiously demanded by the things, but they themselves are not things" 1993, 143). The contour line is therefore located at the cusp between the visible and invisible. It demarks at the very moment it disappears. It is not reducible to the thing, yet it is not completely separate from it either. Importantly, the line is neither the result of a human perceptual condition nor a human cultural tradition. Instead it is *demanded* by the things themselves. It is here that we have an opening—one that is slender and almost invisible within the visible of Merleau-Ponty's writing—that gestures toward a thingly interpretation of contours as more (or less) than human.

Here Steven Crowell's analysis of Giorgio Morandi's still-life paintings is insightful and can act as a springboard for further reflecting on the alien nature of contour lines. To summarize Crowell's main point: "Morandi's still lifes are metaphorical representations that are *about* items of equipment, but are crafted in such a way that these items are pictorially displayed *as* mere things. Through these paintings our everyday (though 'withdrawn') understanding of thinghood becomes 'noticeable,' revealed explicitly in the way the painting works to tell us something about its subject" (46). In other words, the thinghood subtending our experience of equipment as equipment is revealed when the basic structure coupling world and perception is suspended. The jugs and vases in Morandi's paintings are oddly mute; they do not call or solicit the viewer in normal ways because they do not embody the structure of worldhood that sutures them to the relational totality of activities, contexts, and practices. In Crowell's words, Morandi makes thinghood visible because he "refuses the well-known techniques whereby still life manifests horizontal connections" (48) of worldhood that link jug to water, water to thirst, thirst to drink, drink to life, life to happiness (as the ultimate "for-the-sake-of" defining human worlds). Through his muted pallet and almost claustrophobic compression of things, Morandi achieves a total abstraction of the everyday. Unlike Cézanne's objects, which give the instantaneous feeling of entities appearing as the kind of entities they are (relative to the human world), Morandi's paintings give the feeling of things jutting out in their material existence beyond human purposes or usages.

One of the key features that conveys the thingly quality of the things is his bold use of contours. And it is these contours that can shed light on how things exist, autonomously, side-by-side one another. Harman speculates, "All objects encounter a sensual realm of caricatures" (2011, 121). In other words, things only interact through a limited set of sensual properties that never exhaust the dark matter (invisibility) of real things. Timothy Morton picks up on this argument, further stating that causality is the "aesthetic dimension" (66) of things. For Morton, one of the central problems of science is the fundamental split between aesthetics and logic (between style and substance). Yet when we return to things, we realize that such philosophical distinctions are indeed nothing more than false problems. Rather than mere icing on an ontological cake, style, according to Morton, is "an elementary aspect of causality" (79). Stated differently, objects affect each other through their appearances. Here Morton describes Harman's concept of vicarious causation in terms of touching. "Touching," Morton writes, "no matter how intimate, involves a necessary aesthetic distance" (73), otherwise quanta would simply fuse with one another. In this sense, things do not simply touch, rather they withdraw from one another in and through that touching. Causality is therefore a stylistic variation of a thing's thingness. As his analysis of touch indicates, formal (aesthetic rather than mechanistic or efficient) causes are located in the *shapes* of things. When Morton claims "causality takes place 'in front of' things" as the way things "talk to one another, apprehend one another, comprehend one another" (66), he is actually describing artistic stylization. In this sense, causality is the *perception* of things by other things. When things perceive one another, there is a causality introduced into the equation—a causality from a distance, a magical, vicarious, aesthetically alluring causality. The thing has a positive presence in its very absence in the form of the touch. Appearing and disappearing are features of how things interact with other things on their own terms. On this reading, appearing and disappearing (visibility and invisibility) are unbound by human perceptual stylization.

Harman and Morton both argue that this essential claim (that causality is formal or aesthetic in nature) is perhaps the most difficult concept in the object-oriented branch of speculative realism—certainly it is the most controversial. Yet I would argue that it is easily understood if we merely pay attention to Morandi's paintings. A still life painted by Morandi is chocked full of things squeezing up against one another, "touching" one another, but only indirectly through the vibrancy of line and color. The things do not merge, nor are they completely isolated, rather, through the miracle of aesthetic appearing, things hold together, draw one another into a compositional unity. They approach one another, nestle into one another, affecting each other's presence, but in that very approach they are perpetually withdrawing from one another. The capability of things to touch is not predicated on a force that exists outside the things (a law of gravitational attraction, for instance), but rather seems to emanate from them, from their styles. As such, touching affords not merely a positive presence to the thing, but a positive, vibrant power to appear as a thing.

In particular, they vicariously touch one another through the abutment of *contours*. As Merleau-Ponty observed, contour lines are neither the things themselves nor something else either. The contour is the *space of* and the *space around* a thing, extending the thing beyond itself (as if a material halo). On this view, the contour is the thing *out in front of* itself. Stated differently, the contour is the paradoxical space where the thing delineates itself only insofar as it touches that which is beyond itself—a zone where the thing touches its own point of dissolve. It is precisely here that the thing withdraws from other things through its touch. The contour is the *making present* of the trace of the thing's withdrawal. For Morton, there is always a rift between a thing in itself and its various appearances. On my reading, the rift which Morton describes is not located in the fissure between essence and appearance so much as in the space of the contour which is a part of the thing and yet not part of the thing—it is the part that is no part, a split between appearance and appearance. In this sense, the contour is the surplus or excess of the thing passing beyond itself without leaving the thing that it is passing. Contours aesthetically express the fundamental insight of speculative realism argued by Morton: "Objects then are always a little bit out of phase with themselves and with one another" (176). The contour line defines the identity of the thing as *this* thing yet also pushes the thing outside itself toward nonidentity. And this nonidentity within identity is the source of aesthetic, formal causality (a causality among things that is also a kind of nonrelational relationship).

On my reading, the contour (thick, black, and bold in Morandi's work) is a *perceptual* space, or a space where things feel one another, where things appear to one another (make themselves present) but only through their withdrawal. In terms of Morandi's painting *Natura Morta* (1956), one contour, as a zone of perceptual touching, leaks into another contour to the point where two things only become distinct things by sharing an *indistinct* contour. The two things communicate across their differences through the aesthetic dimension of the shared contour. In this sense, the "interobjective" (Morton) touching of things *enables* things to touch without merging. This is only possible because the contour reveals an ontological truth about things: that they touch one another because they are out of phase with themselves. Without this ontological nonidentity, things would never touch: they would melt into blobs. But because things withdraw, the contour is able to *translate* one thing into another thing through an (ex)change of information that never fully exhausts the essence of any given thing. The translation of shapes into other shapes is precisely the work of a nonconceptual and noncorrelational form of perceptual grasping. As such, Morandi's contours are not merely an accident of human-centered artistic convention but rather *reveal the aesthetic sentience of things as they teach each other about themselves by presenting caricatures*. The contour is therefore a kind of special, pedagogical device for shifting the human-centered perceptual field outward, beyond itself toward things and *their* particular styles. In this sense, we can extend Morton's ontological appropriation of rhetoric in order to reveal how certain visual styles (contours) are much more than mere cultural conventions: they indicate the alien power of things to restylize the human according to their modes of appearing.

The human audience *unlearns* its perceptual style the moment it recognizes the contour as the way in which things learn from one another. The contour is a thingly breakthrough that is also a simultaneous withdrawal. This is not only an aesthetic phenomenon (vicarious causality) but also a pedagogical phenomenon (a pedagogy of, by, and through things). Here we could trace a counternarrative of art that is on the margins of both Heidegger and Merleau-Ponty—a narrative that suspends the dependency of things on human-centered notions of world. As such, Morandi demonstrates that art is not reducible to learning about intersubjectivity so much as about exposing us to the alien terrain of interobjectivity. His contours are appearances in art of something alien (rather than familiar and worldly). We do not learn from contours something about our perception, rather we unlearn such lessons, and in the process, hold open the possibility for the perceptual restylization that Bennett calls for.

CONCLUSION: A PLEA FOR UNLEARNING IN EDUCATION

When Bennett (20) argues that children are particularly sensitive to the vibrant life of matter (to thing-power), she does not ask the follow-up question: What does education do to this perceptual sensitivity? Here we are reminded of Bogost's warning. Current STEAM policies in education reduce the disciplines to mere adjuncts of a creative economy. There is no longer any room for things as things to appear in the curriculum. And as such, there is no moment for pondering the vibrancy of matter or the aesthetic style of interobjectivity. I thus conclude with a simple suggestion. Instead of lifelong learning (which is the new mantra of the creative industries), perhaps we need an education in lifelong unlearning. While phenomenologists in education have long recognized the importance of experiences of objects for rekindling a "fascination with meaning" (van Manen, 12), they have equally retained the human-centric notion of intentionality that anchors such experiences in the world and in intersubjectivity. The possibility of a "post-intentional" (Freeman and Vagle) sense of unlearning from the aesthetic power of things to dis- orient perceptual styles has not been adequately theorized as an important educational event, especially in the arts. If the arts are to play a role in this education, then they cannot be reduced to the handmaids of science, technology, and math. At the same time, art for art's sake needs to be equally problematized (especially in relation to its latent humanistic assumptions about genius, creativity, and expression). Instead of cultivating either skills needed to be successful in math and science fields or skills to be an educated connoisseur of the products of human genius, art education could focus on questions that direct our attention away from human concerns, purposes, interests, and investments toward the lives of things.

Children's art, in this sense, could be reconceptualized as a form of ontological investigation into the lives of things. The dominance of color fields and thick contours in children's art might not be a coincidence, considering the contour is, on my reading, a particularly thingly aesthetic convention that reveals something essential about how things touch (interobjectivity). In this sense, art curricula can be organized around thingly questions in order to further this ontological investigation by children. What would it feel like to be a thing? What kinds of perceptions would a thing have? If we suspend reference to human purposes, human intentionality, or worldly concerns, what kind of agency remains for things themselves? And how can we translate such questions and artistic experimentations into sensorial forms that speak to human audiences while also interrupting the perceptual stylistics of these audiences?

In these ways, art-based education can foster the aesthetic speculation called for by speculative realists (of all shapes and sizes), but only if we struggle over its fate within the current moment of defunding and cooptation. When we struggle to sustain arts in education, we do so with an understanding that this might be the last place where the natural inclination of children to perceive thing-power can be safeguarded and where things can be respected as pedagogical actants in their own right. In this manner, art classrooms can become the last places in schools where nonhuman teachers can teach and where human students can unlearn.

Tyson E. Lewis is an associate professor of art education at the University of North Texas. His work in educational philosophy, aesthetics, and politics has appeared in journals such as *Cultural Politics, Thesis Eleven,* and *Rethinking Marxism*. Most recently, he has authored the book *Inoperative Learning: A Radical Rewriting of Educational Potentialities* (2017) and has coedited the volume titled *Pedagogies in the Flesh: Case Studies on the Embodiment of Sociocultural Differences in Education* (2017).

Works Cited

Bennett, Jane. 2010. *Vibrant Matter: A Political Ecology of Things*. Durham: Duke University Press.

Bogost, Ian. 2012. *Alien Phenomenology, or What It Is Like to Be a Thing*. Minneapolis: University of Minnesota Press.

Brown, Bill. 2004. "Thing Theory." In *Things*. Ed. Bill Brown, 1–16. Chicago: University of Chicago Press.

Crowell, Steven. 2011. "Phenomenology and Aesthetics, or Why Art Matters." In *Art and Phenomenology*. Ed. Joseph D. Parry, 31–53. New York: Routledge.

Freeman, Melissa, and Mark D. Vagle. 2013. "Grafting the Intentional Relation of Hermeneutics and Phenomenology Linguistically." *Qualitative Inquiry* 19, no. 9: 725–35.

Gallagher, Shaun, and Dan Zahavi. 2012. *The Phenomenological Mind*. 2nd. ed. New York: Routledge.

Harman, Graham. 2010. *Towards Speculative Realism*. Winchester: Zero Books.

Harman, Graham. 2011. *The Quadruple Object*. Winchester: Zero Books.

Heidegger, Martin. 2001. *Poetry, Language, Thought*. New York: Harper Perennial.

Heidegger, Martin. 2008. *Being and Time*. New York: Harper Perennial.

Hickey-Moody, Anna, and Tara Page, eds. 2015. *Arts, Pedagogy, and Cultural Resistance: New Materialisms*. Lanham, Md.: Rowman and Littlefield.

Hood, Emily, and Amelia Kraehe. 2017. "Creative Matter: New Materialism in Art Education Research, Teaching, and Learning." *Art Education* 70, no. 2: 32–38.

Meillassoux, Quentin. 2013. *After Finitude: An Essay on the Necessity of Contingency*. London: Bloomsbury.

Merleau-Ponty, Maurice. 1968. *The Visible and the Invisible*. Evanston: Northwestern University Press.

Merleau-Ponty, Maurice. 1993. "Eye and Mind." In *The Merleau-Ponty Aesthetics Reader: Philosophy and Painting*. Ed. Michael B. Smith, 121–49. Evanston: Northwest University Press.

Merleau-Ponty, Maurice. 2008. *The World of Perception*. New York: Routledge.
Merleau-Ponty, Maurice. 2012. *Phenomenology of Perception*. New York: Routledge.
Morton, Timothy. 2013. *Realist Magic: Objects, Ontology, Causality*. Ann Arbor, Mich.: Open Humanities Press.
Shaviro, Steven. 2014. *The Universe of Things: On Speculative Realism*. Minneapolis: University of Minnesota Press.
van Manen, Max. 2007. "Phenomenology of Practice." *Phenomenology & Practice* 1, no. 1: 11–30.

COLONIALISM AT HOME

COLONIAL SENSIBILITY OF THE SUBURB IN YASUJIRŌ OZU'S *I WAS BORN, BUT . . .* (1932)

Kota Inoue

Kota Inoue, assistant professor of Japanese literature at Washington State University at Pullman, died in December 2016 in a car accident. We worked closely with him on this essay and are very sad that he could not see it in print. Many thanks to his partner, Nancy McLoughlin, and to his advisor, James Fujii, for helping us with the final submission. All of us at *Cultural Critique* are conscious of the terrible honor of bringing out the last publication of a committed, scholarly life, cut short too early.

In the early 1930s, a distinctive film genre emerged in Japan. As its name suggests, the "middle-class film" *(shōshimin eiga)* featured families of white-collar employees in their modern, everyday milieu. Highly successful not only with the middle-class audience but also the general public, it has proved to have a lasting influence on various forms of Japan's visual culture, including the widely popular television melodramas in the postwar period. Mitsuyo Wada-Marciano has argued that the genre was both symptomatic and pedagogical: the new genre reflected the emergence of the Japanese middle class since the 1920s, while the images shown on the screen helped shape middle-class consciousness, and even a normative national identity, among the general population (6). The genre also exposed the precariousness of that emerging national identity. The sensibility of the new genre, much like what Miriam Hansen calls "vernacular modernism," often articulated Japan's ambivalence toward modernity, split between an embrace of the state-sanctioned, fast-paced life of production and consumption and a nostalgia for a mythic traditional past (10–11).[1]

The sound film, which arrived in Japan around the same time the middle-class film emerged, had a close relationship with the new genre as it developed. Their connection is epitomized well by *The Neighbor's Wife and Mine (Madamu to nyōbō)* (1931): the first fully sound film produced in Japan is also generally known as a representative middle-class genre film. The simultaneous appearance of the middle-class genre and sound films is a testament to changing conditions surrounding the film industry and Japanese capitalism at the time. The conspicuous growth of the middle class since the 1920s, a major factor in the birth of the new genre, was a sign that Japan's capitalism was in a mature phase, and large manufacturing and trading corporations with white-collar positions were becoming influential in the economy. Meanwhile, the rise of the sound film signaled the film industry's significant shift into the monopolistic stage, since the hefty expense of sound film production made it difficult for small studios to survive, let alone enter the market.[2] As in other contemporary industrialized nations, the growing concentration of capital in the hands of the few became so pronounced in the early 1930s that the extraordinary economic and political influence of large conglomerates *(zaibatsu)* came under broad criticism and even violent attack from ultranationalists, as exemplified by the assassination of Takuma Dan, the head of the Mitsui Conglomerate, in 1932.

Japanese capitalism, in its monopolistic phase in the early 1930s, not only triggered the concurrent emergence of the middle-class film genre and the sound film but also provided the major impetus for the increasingly aggressive colonialist exploits overseas that led to the Manchurian Incident in 1931 and subsequent, long conflicts in China and elsewhere. In fact, studies of metropolitan societies and cultures in the Euro-American empires suggest that the rise of the middle class in the metropole cannot be discussed without considering colonialism overseas (McClintock; Cooper and Stoler; Kaplan; Hall and Rose). Thus, the middle-class film, in spite of its generally cheerful portrayal of everyday life in mainland Japan, can be rightly placed in the context of Japan's colonial expansionism. Films not overtly propagandistic—like the middle-class film—may form ideological complicity with the Japanese state's imperialist priorities in various ways. As Aaron Gerow demonstrates, for instance, contending discourses on the definition of the early cinema helped "mold not only a film culture but also a populace compatible with an authoritarian state" (15).[3] As Japan's colonial expansionism entered a new stage in the 1930s, what role, if any, did the new middle-class film genre play in shaping subjectivity suitable for the state's imperialist project?

The present essay engages this question by analyzing the cinematic representations of the suburb, the everyday space prominently associated with most middle-class films, as an articulation of colonial relations embedded in the everyday life of imperial Japan. In particular, it will closely examine bodily expressions of the shared assumptions and unspoken rules that shape everyday life in the suburb. It will also analyze a particular mode of sensory perception prompted by the cinematic representation of the suburb. In other words, the essay investigates the representation of the suburb as a set of cultural indices of coloniality inside Japan that Miriam Silverberg calls "colonial sensibility."[4]

At first glance, the suburb and colonialism may appear to be two unrelated phenomena. Yet the juxtaposition offers an opportunity for a critical, theoretical intervention, because, as one critic observes, "To theorize means to produce the relation between two seemingly disparate, isolated, and unrelated elements, then to support rigorously how such a relation works and what such a method opens for intellectual and political life in general" (Cazdyn, 209). This essay attempts to produce such a relation between cinematic representations of the suburb and Japan's colonialism.

The modern suburb in Japan began to proliferate in the 1920s, particularly as the white-collar class grew, and by the early 1930s it gained significant visibility in popular culture as a novel space representing modern values and a modern lifestyle. In many works in the middle-class film genre, including *The Neighbor's Wife and Mine,* the suburb appears as the quintessential modern, middle-class site. The suburb, however, is more than a fashionable backdrop for those films about the dramas of family life. Suburbanization is a process in which the process of capital accumulation reorganizes the geographically peripheral space on several levels, from the physical landscape to the social order and to nonmaterial dominant values and assumptions. The reconfiguration fundamentally alters the orientation of the original, pre-suburb community, transforming it into a set of resources largely to serve the needs of the central city. In fact, one can argue that suburbanization is a process in which an adjacent but independent space that once served the needs of its residents *becomes* functionally marginal and subordinate to the urban core.

This relationship of subordination is identified as colonialism in this essay. It refers to a form of economic dominance in which an existing community with its own economic and social order is incorporated into a larger, exploitative economic system, much like Japan's domination of other Asian nations. When understood as a sign of the accelerating expansionary drive of the metropolitan core, the suburb, in its subordinated position vis-à-vis the city, can reveal much about the impact brought on to peripheral space by the dominant capitalist order. Identifying capitalism's drive toward spatial expansion at the core of colonialism, this essay ascertains these suburban characteristics as indices of colonialism at home, and discusses how representations of middle-class life in the suburb can reveal the degree to which Japan's colonialism manifested itself in contemporary film culture.

The film we closely examine is Yasujirō Ozu's *I Was Born, But . . .* (*Umarete wa mita keredo . . .* , 1932), one of the representative works of the middle-class film genre. The film's narrative unfolds as the protagonist brothers move to a suburb and subsequently face conflict with children in their new neighborhood. The essay first looks at the different logics of power underlying the children's rivalries and locates their roots in different forms of the economy observable in the suburb. It is in the ascendance of certain economic principles reflected in the shifting pecking order among the children that we see an indication of a lopsided power relationship between the suburb and the city. The essay then turns its focus to the bodily discipline of the children. A close look at their internalization of, as well as failure to follow, the disciplinary regimes helps us identify the state authority that permeates the film's suburb as the source of the disciplinary gaze. Considering the mechanism of the gaze further, an analysis of the film's most celebrated tracking-shot scene reveals how the film creates a particular gazing position vis-à-vis the peripheral lands—such as the suburb—that fosters a subjectivity aligned with Japan's expansionism.

TRANSFORMATIONS OF THE EGG, OR CONTENDING LOGICS OF POWER IN THE SUBURB

Ozu's *I Was Born, But . . .*, which followed *I Graduated, But . . .* (1929) and *I Flunked, But . . .* (1930), depicts the challenges two young brothers face at school and home when their middle-class family moves to a Tokyo suburb.[5] Generally regarded as a representative work from Ozu's early career, the film is critically acclaimed and widely praised for its mix of humor and pathos. The protagonist boys' strategies to cope with the new environment in the suburb involve physical and verbal plays and are very entertaining even today. Yet the film also poignantly portrays their disappointing realization that their father is only a white-collar worker who has to ingratiate himself humiliatingly to his boss in order to maintain his career. Perhaps encouraged by the film's subtitle, "A Picture Book for Grown-ups," most critics have commended the film for its "great didactic rigor" (Bordwell, 224).[6]

At the center of the didactic reading of the film is the bitter lesson the Yoshii brothers, Ryōichi and Keiji, learn about their father's less-than-dignified existence in the corporate hierarchy. What makes the lesson particularly distressing for the brothers is their own ability to climb the hierarchical order among the local children. Upon moving to the new neighborhood, they are initially picked on by local bully Kamekichi and his underlings, but they eventually succeed in overtaking the leadership position of the neighborhood children. Proud of their achievement, they cannot accept their own father's subordinated existence. Yoshii's sycophantic attitude toward his boss Iwasaki is especially infuriating because in the children's hierarchy the brothers are clearly superior to Taro, Iwasaki's son. After being spanked by Yoshii for calling him a weakling in protest to his obsequious behavior toward Iwasaki, the older brother Ryōichi angrily declares, "I'm stronger than Taro and I get better grades. If I have to become his underling when I grow up, then I'm not going to school anymore!"

The brothers' idea of who is greater and more powerful is comically and tragically contrasted against the pitiless rules that govern the hierarchical social order among adults. The didactic reading of the film directs our attention to this gap and, in the process, presents two parallel hierarchies as incompatible systems. But while the demeaning and unreasonable corporate hierarchy to which Yoshii acquiesces indeed seems to be monolithic, the children's rules of power are actually varied. Seeking to assert authority over others, different children use different tactics, each of which is informed by a distinct logic of power. The difference between the adults' and children's worlds is also spatially marked: the corporate hierarchy in the film is an urban phenomenon while children's power struggles involve local specificities of the suburb. If the rigid, uncontestable adult hierarchy is a product of the entrenched urban, capitalist relations of production, the changing pecking order among the children indicates something unsettled and fluid about suburban space.

In his analysis of *I Was Born, But . . .*, Alastair Phillips identifies the trains as a symbol of the unsettledness of the film's suburb, arguing that the film's suburban setting is "a form of intermediary location which is signaled by a sense of constant flux provided by the flow of trains in the compositional background of the images" (29). Indeed, throughout the film, commuter trains are constantly seen where the children play. The Yoshii house is also situated along a rail track, and scenes shot in their backyard never seem to fail to include a running train in the background.[7]

The constant, even excessive, appearance of trains in the film aptly reminds us of the central role commuter trains played in shaping Japan's interwar suburbs. Private commuter rail companies in Japan expanded their networks in major cities from the early twentieth century and, in the Tokyo area, particularly after the Great Kanto earthquake in 1923, whose devastating effects spurred new residential developments in the western part of Tokyo.[8] As they grew, the rail companies sought to increase their profit opportunities by strategically diversifying their enterprises into other businesses essential for the lives of their rail passengers who lived along the rail lines—from real estate business to department stores to amusement parks. As the rail networks expanded, the outlying lands with distinctive characters were standardized and homogenized by massive rail capital, and the lives of the people who moved to the new suburbs were also systematically incorporated into the profit-making system of the diversified commuter rail industry.

This accelerating capital accumulation through suburban development in 1930s Tokyo is the material reality of what Phillips identifies as "a sense of constant flux." In a work that analyzes the commodification of subjectivity in the space of commuter trains, James A. Fujii puts the suburbanization process this way:

> As much as [the accelerated commuter rail service] represented the material opening up of land, it was, of course, a "cultivation" of areas not for agricultural purposes, but for conversion and integration into the political economy of the central city. To that end, the rail lines would alter the nature and recalibrate the value of land, first by distance from Tokyo, and later, with the arrival of express trains, by commuting time. The trains, then, helped give new value to space whose use and worth up until then had been determined locally, in the process converting them to commodities with more abstract exchange value. (116–17)

Shaped by these multifaceted business practices of the rail companies, the suburban expansion during the interwar years in Japan was a process in which the power of capital integrated the suburban lands into an urban-centered economy, making small local communities dependent upon the metropolitan center. The conflicts and unsettledness in our film's suburban space are situated in this context of the making of the peripheries.

In *I Was Born, But . . .* , the children's competition over their status is most clearly visible in the fight between the bully Kamekichi and the Yoshii brothers. The rivalry is established on the day the Yoshii brothers move to the suburb. Kamekichi, the leader of the neighborhood children, immediately confronts the newcomers. He asserts his superiority by forcibly taking away a puzzle ring from the younger brother Keiji and sending him away crying. When Ryōichi comes running to avenge his younger brother, Kamekichi attempts to intimidate the brothers by performing a ritual of symbolic killing and resuscitation, an established game among the local children that serves to confirm Kamekichi's dominant status. He picks one of his underlings and makes a hand sign in front of the boy. Upon this cue, the little boy submissively lies on the ground on his back pretending that some mysterious power from Kamekichi's extended arm has killed him. Kamekichi then makes another hand sign, which involves a gesture resembling Christian-crossing, and the little boy is resuscitated and back on his feet again. After watching the demonstration, the Yoshii brothers refuse to obey Kamekichi's cue, and a fistfight ensues but ends inconclusively.

Capable fighters, the brothers soon defeat Kamekichi's five underlings handily in a fight, in spite of the numerical disadvantage, but they know they cannot vanquish Kamekichi physically. At this juncture, the younger brother, Keiji, succeeds in securing aid from Shindon, the boy from the local liquor store who makes the rounds in the neighborhood, taking orders and delivering goods: Keiji assists him in winning an order for some beer from the Yoshii household, and in exchange he persuades Shindon, who is much older and larger, to help the brothers defeat Kamekichi. With this arrangement in place, Keiji provokes a fight with Kamekichi soon after, and Shindon obligingly comes to his aide, physically overwhelming the bully and sending him home crying. The victory establishes the brothers as the new leaders of the neighborhood children.

Both Kamekichi and the brothers rely on physical strength to establish their authority over others, but they ultimately operate on very different logics of power. Physically largest among the children by far, Kamekichi can readily demand his subordinates' obedience, as evidenced in the "killing and resuscitation" game. In addition to his muscular strength, however, he acquires extra power from a unique source: raw sparrow's eggs. He gulps one down in a showy fashion in front of his subordinates before going off to the second showdown with the Yoshii brothers. Later, during a class at school, he again makes a display by swallowing another egg in a provocative gesture directed to Ryōichi. In Kamekichi's logic of power, the special substance he consumes transforms into his physical strength. In its treatment of the egg as a particularly rich nutritional source for enhanced muscular strength, his logic of power is predicated on the use-value of the egg.

In challenging Kamekichi's dominance, the Yoshii brothers employ a different logic of power. As grade school children, they only vaguely understand the meaning of their father's existence as a salaried white-collar worker. But they are already familiar with the temporal structure of salaried middle-class life exemplified by the payday cycle. When they see their mother applying her makeup carefully before their father's return, they understand that a payday has arrived and that the mother is trying to show her appreciation for the breadwinner of the family. They know that she is preparing a small feast. It is this information—today is a payday, and his mother would surely purchase some beer for her husband—that Keiji exchanges for Shindon's crucial aid. The information itself has no inevitable link with Shindon's physical act of hitting Kamekichi, yet the Yoshii brothers can make an abstract equation between the two. While Kamekichi's authority is established by the direct, organic link, albeit partly imaginary, between the egg and his physical strength, the brothers attain their position of power by a strategy based on exchange-value.

The different logics of power employed by Kamekichi and the Yoshii brothers reveal different economies that shape social relations in the suburb. As symbolized by the sparrow's egg, which is harvested and consumed within the community, Kamekichi's use-value-based logic of power is rooted in the local agrarian economy. Kamekichi himself is a local son as revealed by his father's artisan appearance. The occupations of the local children's fathers—undertaker, tailor, and chicken farmer are mentioned—and the presence of some farmers in the fields suggest that the community has the structure of self-sufficiency. In such an economy, people work and live in the same community, and goods are primarily produced, circulated, and consumed in the same locale, possibly with the exception of some cash crops shipped to the city.

A locally oriented economy fosters social relations that are largely marked by a sense of shared communal interests. The localized circulation of goods, information, and capital, as well as the residents' rootedness in the community where both living and working take place, foster tight local cohesion. We see an expression of this kind of societal bond in one scene in the film. In the first confrontation between Kamekichi and Keiji, the youngest boy among the neighborhood children is shown with a sign on his back. When the boy picks up the bread Keiji has just dropped and is about to take a bite, an older boy quickly snatches it away from the little boy. A close-up shot displays the sign, which reads, "This child has diarrhea. Please do not give him food." The sign, apparently written by his parent, humorously reveals that in this suburb people would feed someone else's children and that a sign like this is expected to function as an effective means to communicate among neighbors (and it certainly does, although the older boy's own appetite might also explain his swift intervention). Kamekichi's use-value-based logic of power is a manifestation of these social relations in this close knit local community, where the circulation of goods and human relationships are less mediated by money.

The Yoshii brothers have a different relationship with the local community. Recent transplants from the city center, they are intrigued by Kamekichi's logic of power. They even look for eggs themselves, although they cannot stomach the idea of gulping down a raw sparrow's egg when they finally acquire one. They also adopt Kamekichi's killing and resuscitation ritual to assert their own authority when they take over the gang. Yet their mode of power sharply departs from Kamekichi's because Keiji's crucial pact with Shindon is a skillful application of abstract thinking not bound by its material-based logic of the use-value. What enables the brothers' ascension is their ability to find an equation among disparate events and materials through abstraction, a mental capacity that a capitalist economy demands. In this regard, it is fitting that the information exchanged for Shindon's help—the father's payday—is about a form of wage-earning, a central feature of capitalist economies. In an economy built around exchange-value, the process of abstract equation removes local specificity and uniqueness from a product and turns it into a commodity for wider circulation, thereby opening up the local social formations to a larger, more dominant economy.

In seeking to overcome Kamekichi, the Yoshii brothers utilize their familiarity with abstract transaction and are able to search for a resource outside the local boundaries. When securing the help from Shindon, they essentially rely on their father's economic activity performed in the city—wage earning. The introduction of Yoshii's salary to the children's competition symbolically opens up the local space for organized urban capital that circulates far beyond the city's boundaries. And as the centralized capitalist economy is introduced in the form of the information about Yoshii's payday, its attendant forms of social relations and class structure touch the children's lives: The purchasing capacity of the Yoshii family helps drive Kamekichi out of his leadership position, but the brothers themselves soon have to experience crushing disappointment about their father's salaried status under Iwasaki. What the conflict between the two logics of power among the children reveals is that the older agrarian form of social bonds are being destabilized by the newer political economy emanating from the urban center of industrial production and trade. This encroachment by urban capital, which challenges the agrarian norms and expectations, is at the heart of what is unsettling about the suburb in the film.[9]

Given the unsettling and conflicting dynamics behind the children's competition, it is fair to say that the film's suburban setting is a heterogeneous space. A heterogeneous suburb may strike one as a peculiar idea in the United States, where the prevailing image of the suburb is a homogeneous, middle-class residential enclave. Since the era of Levittowns and William H. Whyte's *The Organization Man*, the suburb has stood for monotonous and conformist middle-class life in the cultural vocabulary and, to a great degree, in academic discourses in the United States. David Harvey, for example, once argued that the division of labor under capitalism creates a distinctive class of white-collar workers whose shared ideology of competitive and possessive individualism produces a mode of consumption conducive to a suburban lifestyle (122). In this view, the suburb is inevitably middle-class and homogenous in nature. This formula of suburbanization certainly holds true especially for the large-scale developments since the GI Bill and the post–World War II economic boom in the United States, but it cannot adequately describe smaller-scale suburban encroachments in interwar Japan. While suburbanization in the United States evokes an image of an empty, uninhabited land turned into a massive tract housing development, incremental, small-scale suburbanization in prewar Japan was a process in which an existing agrarian community outside the city was haphazardly converted into a residential space to satisfy the needs of the city. The outlying land is often already a settlement of some kind. Tensions arise—and children fight—when such existing local social formations are affected by expanding capital circulation.[10]

In the space encroached on by urban capital, the Yoshii brothers succeed in replacing Kamekichi and his sparrow's eggs by acting on their abstract economy. But it is Taro who further advances the abstraction process by transforming the eggs themselves into a more sophisticated symbol of power. As soon as Kamekichi is disgraced by Shindon's intervention, Taro, one of his followers, gives the Yoshii brothers a celluloid strip (presumably of his father's amateur movie) as a token of surrender and deference. Later, when he announces that his father is going to have a screening of his amateur movies, children begin to give Taro sparrow's eggs, asking him to let them see the movies. The Yoshii brothers give him a large one for two admissions, and Kamekichi, though initially unwilling, eventually follows the others. In the process, the material egg empties out its use-value and becomes purely exchange-value for admission to the screening.

The conversion of the egg into a movie admission fee symbolizes yet another defeat for Kamekichi: he not only has to bow down to an abstract exchange transaction again, but also has to literally surrender his source of power to Taro. The exchange transaction is also more advanced than the Yoshii brothers', since Taro's eggs function as something akin to currency rather than random items for barter transactions. The sophisticated abstraction in Taro's logic of power corresponds to the level of capitalist economy with which his family is familiar. Georg Simmel observed that the money economy stands in the closest relationship with what he calls the intellectualist quality that characterizes metropolitan life, a strong drive toward rationalistic approaches to one's environment. He attributed this tendency to the fact that the money economy is built only on exchange-value, which in turn reduces everything to a quantitative level (326). Under this condition, an abstract mode comes to occupy the central place in one's thought process and enables one to engage in an abstract transaction. Taro's economy of the egg has this abstract quality, which is an expression of the logic of capitalism that homogenizes time and space, the drive behind suburbanization.

While Taro does not become the leader of the group by collecting admission fees, behind his money economy is a logic of power that threatens the Yoshii brothers' authority because of its sophistication. Indeed, it is at this screening that their father's sycophantic behavior toward Iwasaki, which is exposed on the screen, publicly humiliates the brothers. As Taro clearly understands, making an offer of an object—such as a film strip—is a form of submission. At the amateur movie showing, it is Taro who extracts such submission from others, including the Yoshii brothers, in the form of the eggs.

The commodification process involved in Taro's economy of the egg echoes the changes that had been taking place in the larger community since the turn of the twentieth century. In the work cited earlier, Fujii examines a short story by Katai Tayama, "Girl Crazy" (1907), in which the protagonist indulges himself in sexual fantasies about the schoolgirls he encounters on his commuter trains. Noting the extremely close yet utterly impersonal encounter with a large number of people inside crowded commuter trains, Fujii argues how such space induces a condition he calls "intimate alienation," which turns the individual into a commodified subject for whom fragmented visual encounters replace meaningful social relations (128). The existing communal bonds in our film's locale are challenged by such disjointed, abstracted subjectivities shaped by one of the constitutive practices of middle-class suburban life—the commute. While the children do not place themselves in the commuter train, Taro's deployment of the economy of the egg suggests that the local social cohesion exemplified by the sign on the back of the child with a digestive condition is now being threatened by the commodified and abstract human relations the mass transit society encourages.

Examined for the underlying logics of power, the children's humorous competitions in *I Was Born, But . . .* begin to reveal the political economy that is shaping social relations in the film's suburban setting. Modern suburbanization is a restructuring of a peripheral land by industrial capital concentrated in the city. In the process a distinct place just outside of an urban area with specific use-value for the local community is transformed into a set of abstract values determined by its role in urban capital accumulation. Movements of goods, people, and money take shape in such a way that the local community is incorporated into a larger circulation of urban capital and becomes dependent on the city. Kamekichi's loss of authority, first to the Yoshii brothers' exercise of a logic of power based on exchange-value, then to Taro's commodification of the egg, highlights this land conversion process in which an existing community in the outlying area is subordinated by the city.

This expropriation of peripheral land is primarily driven by an expansionary form of economic development, but without armed occupation of the land. It does not involve subjugation of racial and ethnic others. And there are no state institutions that plan and execute the expropriation of the land and its resources. Yet suburbanization, in its mechanism of land appropriation, closely resembles colonization. In both cases, a peripheral land is stripped of its own history and autonomy, and is reshaped largely as a useful resource for the industrial capital in the city. What enables such conversion is a cultural consciousness in which a mode of thinking based on abstract equation and exchange renders the "aura" of local specificity obsolete. And in fact, in the case of colonization of a foreign land, it is this abstraction of values and disregard of local specificity that further facilitate various forms of racial and ethnic subjugation.

In his study of the shifting consciousness about the city and the country discernible in English literature, Raymond Williams identifies an asymmetrical relationship between these two forms of human settlements. After examining the system of exploitation most prominently symbolized by the English country house, Williams extends his observation about the asymmetrical city–country relation to the context of emerging industrial capitalism and British expansionism.

What happened in England has since been happening ever more widely, in new dependent relationships between all the industrialized nations and all the other "underdeveloped" but economically important lands. Thus one of the last models of "city and country" is the system we now know as imperialism (Williams, 279).

Here Williams draws together two types of center–periphery relations—city–country and metropole–colony—as two different manifestations of the same uneven capitalist development, and argues that the city and the country are held in an inequitable relationship that is colonial in nature.

The city and the suburb, another manifestation of the unevenness of capitalist modernity, are similarly bound by colonial relations. The more dramatic difference between the city and the country may underscore the unequal relationship more readily, but the suburb's closer ties to the city center on the everyday level makes it easier for us to see the process of capital expansion through the more visible flows of goods and people between the city and the periphery, particularly exemplified by commuting. As a defining factor of the suburb, commuting pointedly reveals the repetitive and abstracting effects industrial capitalism and its attendant technologies have on time and space. Organic time and space are transformed into abstract and interchangeable, uniform modules, and repetitive temporality begins to restructure everyday life, preparing grounds for colonial sensibility.[11]

It should be noted here that railways—modern transportation technology that made punctual but repetitive commuting possible—were no stranger to colonialism. Besides the commuter rail discussed here, the long-distance railway also has played a key role in colonizing distant lands in many regions of the world, in what some call "railway imperialism" (Davis and Wilburn). In the case of Japan, the most well-known example was the nominally private South Manchurian Railway Company, which was an essential organ of the Japanese state for the colonial administration of Manchuria (Kobayashi). But the domestic railway network was also shaped by imperialist wars and rivalries at the turn of the twentieth century. For instance, realizing the necessity of effective war mobilization during the Russo-Japanese War (1904–5), the Japanese state in 1906 moved to nationalize the existing domestic long-distance railways deemed strategically important (Hara, 21).

The suburb's colonial structure—an asymmetrical system of exploitation of a peripheral land aided by abstraction processes—manifests itself in the children's fights in *I Was Born, But . . .* . But the film, made shortly after the Manchurian Incident of 1931, is not without more explicit references to Japan's ongoing imperial expansionism and militarism. For instance, when asked by their father, the Yoshii brothers express their dream of becoming a general and a lieutenant general together, and in the opening scene Keiji playfully salutes his father in the military style from the bed of the moving truck. In the classroom, a calligraphic plaque is prominently displayed with five Chinese characters reading, "Three Brave Human Bombs." It refers to an incident on the Shanghai war front in early 1932 as, following the Manchurian Incident, Japan's aggression toward China escalated. On this occasion, three Japanese soldiers were said to have engaged in a daring suicide mission in order to break the Chinese defense line. The truthfulness of the heroic account was later questioned, but the patriotic story extolling the virtue of self-sacrifice for the empire was enthusiastically embraced by the Japanese mass media in what Louise Young has called "war fever." Commemorating the three soldiers, the calligraphic plaque in the classroom instructs the pupils to be good imperial subjects. Thus, the norms and expectations necessary for Japan's national mobilization are discernible within the everyday cultural practices in the film.

Another but less obvious reference to the empire is the middle-class existence of the Yoshii family itself. In studies of Euro-American colonialisms, various connections between the rise of the empire and the emergence of the middle class have been discussed. For example, Anne McClintock argues that as a foreign, "uncivilized land" is occupied and becomes domesticated in the image of the "middle-class home" in the metropole, the discourse of evolutionary racism, in turn, shapes the domesticity of the emerging middle class by constantly reinforcing such notions as progress and cleanliness through, among other means, the mass advertisement of household commodities (31–36). While the Yoshii family may not exhibit a Japanese equivalence of the Victorian cult of domesticity, the wife embodies "Good Wife, Wise Mother," a slogan the Japanese state adopted in the late nineteenth century in order to ensure the establishment and maintenance of patriarchal domesticity useful for the empire: she puts on makeup on her husband's payday and prepares a special meal, and she modestly advises her husband after the boys' protest against his brownnosing for his boss culminates into an emotional confrontation and spanking. Yoshii's middle-class job also directs our attention to the empire. His company office, which prominently features the telephone—new technology that assisted in effectively moving extracted resources and manufactured commodities throughout the empire—reminds us that the middle-class jobs in the empire often had something to do with the circulation of goods and information among the colonies and the metropole.[12]

The shifting logic of power among the children that we examined is a more subtle but corresponding form of Japan's colonialism in its effects of commodifying local specificities into calculable, abstract units. In what follows, we will take a close look at another way in which the film articulates the colonial structure of the suburb, involving the children's bodies and the film's invocation of a certain viewing position.

THE COLONIAL GAZE IN THE SUBURB

Just as the children's different logics of power reveal the ascendancy of exchange-value in their world, differentiated norms about their bodies and behavior suggest their varying degrees of familiarity with transparent, disciplinary space. Once again, Kamekichi and the Yoshii brothers form an instructive contrast. As soon as the Yoshii brothers take over the gang of children from Kamekichi, the brothers immediately adopt his killing and resuscitation game. Then they have their new subordinates stand in line at attention according to height so that they can perform a military-style inspection, carefully examining each boy's outfit and posture and making them swear their allegiance to the new leaders. Thus, the brothers make every body visible to them as they assert their authority in a space that, mimicking a modern military institution, carries a pronounced sense of order, linearity, and transparency. For the brothers, being in the position of authority entails the ability to discipline the bodies of others.

In contrast, Kamekichi, as an individual shaped by the local, mostly agrarian social order, seems most comfortable in a communal form of play. When Ryōichi comes to the field looking for him in order to settle scores for his rough treatment of Keiji, Kamekichi sits on the grass, animatedly talking to those around him. He gesticulates excitedly, and the competing centers of attention in the frame—the Yoshii brothers in the foreground, wrestling children in the middle, and Kamekichi's circle in the back—create a lively, but rather crowded and chaotic, feel. The disorderliness of this space is enhanced by the fact that, when challenged by Ryōichi to identify himself, Kamekichi has to stand up and push away a couple of boys to confront Ryōichi. Unlike the brothers he does not demand orderly bodies or create visual display of hierarchy, rather favoring a disorganized, jumbled space.

The Yoshii brothers' explicit interest in bodily control in their play becomes understandable when we consider how often their bodies themselves come under scrutiny, especially in school. And such moments of bodily discipline are precipitated by orderly, transparent spaces that make the body visible and observable. At their school, all children are required to stand at attention in the schoolyard at the morning assembly as their teachers watch. In the classroom, with straight, orderly rows of desks, instructions often emphasize proper behavior and body posture over the content of the lesson. In a calligraphy class, for instance, Ryōichi's teacher corrects a pupil's posture without even commenting on the actual writing. Pupils are under constant, close watch by their teachers, and those who do not behave properly are sent out to the hallway and ordered to stand still and maintain a correct posture. In the physical education class, which is little more than a military-style marching drill, pupils stand in formation and are trained to follow the teacher's commands and move their bodies in unison. Once again, the modern regime of bodily discipline in the school's Euclidian space becomes acutely visible on Kamekichi. At the drill practice in the schoolyard, he repeatedly makes the wrong moves. In a classroom scene, he is sent out to the hallway for his egg-gulping demonstration meant to provoke Ryōichi. Even in the hallway, his body is not disciplined easily: he sits on a vaulting box instead of standing at attention, only to receive a reprimanding glare from the teacher.

The transparent Foucauldian space that makes visible and observable—and thus disciplines—children's bodies points to the existence of panoptic authority in the suburb of *I Was Born, But . . .* . The presence of this authority that quietly watches is strongly felt in the most celebrated scenes of the film—all involving matching tracking shots—that humorously and critically underscore the values placed on the disciplined body. The first and best-known scene among them comes at the end of the physical education segment when the pupils in the schoolyard begin marching to the left at the teacher's command. The camera captures the march from the side of the line in a slow rightward traveling shot as the pupils advance leftward. Then, there is a cut to Yoshii's Tokyo office. The camera keeps traveling in the same direction with the same speed, now showing a row of yawning office workers. The camera eventually reaches Yoshii and his colleagues in conversation at the far end of the room, at which point begins a brief office scene. This ingenious juxtaposition of the marching children and the row of bored office workers is generally regarded as a critical comment on the prevalence of "meaningless regimentation[s]" in all sectors of modern societies.[13]

The deployment of the moving camera in this scene, in addition to offering a critique of the mind-numbing quality of school and work, in fact makes perceptible a panoptic, surveying authority that invisibly permeates these places. We will briefly turn to a scene from the contemporaneous French film *Liberty for Us* to underscore this point. The 1931 film by René Clair deftly captures the regimented nature of the modern workplace, in this case manufacturing assembly lines. Two wandering vagabonds briefly experience the affluent but highly ordered life of industrial capitalism, but at the end of the film they happily regain the liberty of their previous vagrant life on the road, unmolested by the regime of control, whether exercised in the factory or in the office. In one scene, one of the protagonists is detained by policemen, ostensibly for idly sleeping in a field, when the camera abruptly cuts to a classroom where a teacher declares to his students, "Work is mandatory because work means liberty." Then the viewer is shown children studying at the desk in rows, cheerfully singing "Work is mandatory because work means liberty!" Presumably, education, at least the kind advocated by the state, helps young people grow into industrious and liberated workers. The camera then cuts—it is not a tracking-shot transition—to a factory assembly line where workers mechanically perform the same small tasks endlessly, thus bridging the school and work as with *I Was Born, But . . . .*

Both films highlight the hollowness of official rhetoric about the virtue of hard work by showing the stultifying reality of the regimented workplace in an age of concentrated industrial capital. *Liberty for Us* even goes one step further and likens the assembly line to the prison. Yet, while the editing with a straight cut and a stationary camera in *Liberty for Us* juxtaposes the school and the workplace in a critical light, the distinctive use of the tracking shot in *I Was Born, But . . .* additionally creates a sense of a surveying authority because of the way the moving camera is deployed.

In the widely celebrated marching scene, no particular character's gaze motivates the camera movement. The camera simply begins to track along the line of marching children in the schoolyard and effortlessly transitions into the office space. The lack of a reverse shot that shows the source of the moving gaze leaves the traveling gaze unattributed and thus generates an uneasy feel. Brian Henderson has characterized Godard's use of an unmotivated long, slow tracking shot as a distancing and flattening technique to demystify the "bourgeois worldview and self-image" projected by composition-in-depth (79–81). While Ozu's use of the tracking shots does not serve to critique bourgeois subjectivity, Henderson's analysis clarifies that an unmotivated tracking shot has a defamiliarizing effect because it evokes a viewing position detached from what is shown. In the case of *I Was Born, But . . .* , the detached viewing position is also a surreptitious one because the expressions of boredom in the office are supposedly to be kept private, yet we witness them. This surreptitious nature of the viewing position gives the gaze a feel of surveillance. And the seamless editing of the two unmotivated traveling shots—unlike the straight cut with a stationary camera in *Liberty for Us*—creates the effect that the same detached, surreptitious observer moves through space and visits the school and the office at will. Thus the moving camera in *I Was Born, But . . .* shows the bodies of school children and office workers as objects of a gaze and simultaneously evokes an omnipresent, clandestine observer that watches them without being seen. This feeling of surreptitious surveillance is also reinforced by the other two tracking-shot transitions—similarly without a motivating gaze—that follows the first.

The connoted existence of the surveying, disciplining authority, particularly given Japan's increasingly expansionist atmosphere after the Manchurian Incident, points to the Japanese state, since the modern regime of the disciplined body is indispensable to the state's imperialist projects.[14] Rather than a personal failing, then, Kamekichi's difficulty with the school's disciplinary regime is a sign of a conflict between the agrarian, communal norms of the body and the increasingly totalitarian Japanese state's claim over it. Likewise, the communal norms of mutual care for the welfare of neighborhood children, embodied by the sign on the boy with a stomach condition, are in conflict with the regime of surveillance that originates in the authority located outside of the community itself.

While the disciplined (and some undisciplinable) bodies of the children thus make us aware that the film's suburb is not disconnected from a structure of power larger than the suburban community, the film also invites the viewer to occupy a certain viewing position implicated in that power structure. The tracking-shot scenes are once again instructive. In the first such scene, the surveying gaze travels from the school to the office in the city without interruption, with the smooth lateral move underscoring the effortlessness of the transition. In the process, the physical distance between the two locations is collapsed. The smooth, mobile transition allows the viewer to experience the two places as an unproblematically related unit of a whole—an effect unachievable by plain cut editing, which would simply suggest parallel spaces. The other two tracking-shot scenes also have the same effect of eliminating geographical distance. The erasure corresponds to the fact that, despite the frequent appearance of trains in the background and the repeated scenes of Yoshii's morning commute, the film never shows him in transit, in the train or at the station.[15] The absence of in-train scenes, as if the repetitious commute is rendered invisible, has the effect of eliminating the physical distance between the suburb and the city from the film.[16]

The lack of in-between space in the tracking-shot scenes and the absence of in-train shots in the film in fact highlight an impact modern high-speed traveling has had on human sensory perception. Railway technology, a major driver of suburban development in Japan, had a critical impact on not only physical reality but also everyday consciousness and space-time perception.[17] In his study on the cultural significance of the rise of the railway journey, Wolfgang Schivelbusch argues that before the dawn of train technology travelers experienced the space through which they journeyed as a living whole. The advent of the railway journey altered the space-time relationship into a more abstract and disorienting one. Travel became a movement between two points, and the singular spatial-temporal presence of the traditional space in between was rendered insignificant (36–38). In the process of railway-driven suburbanization, just as the unique, organic peripheral lands are converted into calculable, abstract values according to the accessibility to the urban center, the intermediary space is in effect made inconsequential. Schivelbusch connects this obliteration of the middle space to the cinematic technology of seeing in the following words: "In the filmic perception—i.e., the perception of *montage,* the juxtaposition of the most disparate images into one unit—the new reality of annihilated in-between spaces finds its clearest expression: the film brings things closer to the viewer as well as closer together" (42). Our tracking-shot scenes' effortless and immediate transition between the suburban space and the city center fittingly captures this new consciousness in a succinct visual language and invites the viewer to a certain viewing position that renders the separate spaces something naturally connected.

And such an imagining of the suburb has a profound implication on the way the metropolitan center's relationship to distant places can be envisioned and collectively understood. As the collapsing of the space between the city and suburb creates a sense of immediate connection between the two locations within the film, the viewer located in the urban theater experiences the images of the suburb as something immediate. Through this viewing position, the viewer is implicated in the lopsided relationship that governs the city and the suburb. Projected from such a position, the gaze at a faraway place, displayed without a sense of distance, bears a mark of power. And this power is not unlike the disciplinary power claimed by the surveying gaze. When the smooth tracking-shot editing opens up a viewing position over the truant Yoshii brothers in the field, the viewer is interpellated into the position and watches the truants clandestinely, thereby assuming identity with the surveying authority.

The collapsed distance between the city and the suburb that signals relations of domination echoes Japan's colonial experience. As Japan integrated formal and informal colonies into its economy, people, goods, and their images from the colonies entered the everyday lives of the Japanese. Silverberg's investigation of the fluid imperial identity during Japan's colonial era, for instance, reminds us that images of the colonized other had a strong presence in publishing and café cultures in the early 1930s. The visual experience of these exotic images in the everyday context, which diminished the perceived distance between the viewer and the colony, was not a benign event without any implication of power relations.

Images of distant lands were becoming a regular part of film-viewing experience amid the aforementioned Three Human Bombs fever. Technological advancement in communication and transportation made it possible to quickly bring images from the war front to be shown in, among other places, movie theaters, which regularly screened newsreels with feature films. Louise Young notes that the Manchurian Incident triggered widespread use of public newsreel showing: "As fast as new film canisters could be flown in from Manchuria, the Asahi and Mainichi screened the newsreels in city parks in Osaka, Kobe, Kyoto, and Tokyo, and circulated the films for additional showings in department stores, elementary schools, and elsewhere throughout the country" (65). Given this practice, the brothers' suburban school is a site where images from the colonial war were projected. And in all likelihood, *I Was Born, But . . .* was also shown in theaters with newsreel images from the war front, in accordance with the film-screening practice of the day. The increased speed with which those fresh images were delivered and the heightened public exposure to those images altered the nature of viewing experience. The sense of immediacy that was generated by new technology and was intertwined with colonial power prepared a viewing position suitable for the Japanese state's imperialist project.

I Was Born, But . . . was made just as the Japanese empire initiated open aggression toward China. The level of enthusiasm with which most imperial subjects supported colonial aggression suggests that an effective imperialist mechanism was in place by that time. One can find a glimpse of such a pervasive system in diverse social strata, from the emperor ideology to the military conscription system. But we can also consider the development of monopolistic industrial capitalism in the interwar years, for it not only built an economic impetus for colonial expansionism but also shaped social and cultural norms and expectations into colonial sensibility. The advanced capitalist mode of production brought the rule of abstract exchange into social organization, which prompted a shift in relations of power. The change was inevitably highlighted in the suburb because, built into a hierarchical relationship with the city by the development of capitalism, it was a space of unevenness in which the older social relations were constantly confronted by the new logic of power. The children's world in the film fittingly captures the resulting tension. Technological advancement and capitalist development also enabled a new cultural imagining of the periphery from the metropolitan center. Peripheral places, suburbs and colonies alike, entered the cultural lexicon as visual images, prompting a new mode of gaze that governed the relationship between the center and the periphery. The gaze interpellated the viewer into an imperial subjectivity, and, when examined as a visual experience of the suburb, *I Was Born, But . . .* reveals this mechanism of subject formation. And the visual experience of the suburb was not isolated from Imperial Japan's larger geopolitical expansion. Only four months after the release of *I Was Born, But . . .*, Tokyo annexed eighty-two surrounding municipalities to become the second largest city in the world, as if to foreshadow Japan's further colonial expansion into Asia.

Kota Inoue, assistant professor of Japanese language and literature at Washington State University, was completing a manuscript exploring the relationship of colonialism to suburban space in "interwar" Japan. Author of several published essays on Japanese imperialism, his most recent work was directed at reframing colonial understanding from ecological considerations.

Notes

I'd like to thank following individuals for their insightful comments that helped me see what I could not see before: Jim Fujii, Yoichi Komori, Michael Cronin, and Nancy McLoughlin.

1. For a view that places this ambivalence in the context of Japan's triadic imperialism, see Inoue, 191–93.

2. Akira Iwasaki, a contemporary film critic, already observed at the time that the rise of the sound film dramatically exacerbated the ongoing concentration of capital in the U.S. film industry (26).

3. For a study of Japan's wartime ideology and the cinematic style of period dramas, see Davis.

4. In Silverberg's words, "Colonial sensibility encompasses the more ephemeral aspects of colonialism—its affect and aesthetics, fantasies and reminiscences, along with its manifestations in material culture, and its embodied representation and self-representation" (qtd. in Sand, 1). Sand also elaborates on it as follows: "Colonial sensibility as kansei can be conceived as a matrix of bodily expressions of the experience of inhabiting a colonial society and, at the same time, as a matrix of affects, unspoken assumptions, and often-unconscious behaviors that are *generative* of colonial relationships" (5, emphasis in original).

5. *I Graduated, But . . .* revolves around the plight of a recent college graduate who cannot find work. *I Flunked, But . . .* depicts idle college students' hilarious schemes to pass graduation exams without studying for them. Because of the job scarcity, those who flunked turn out to be the lucky ones. These three works are set against the background of the worldwide Great Depression. Japan's economic trouble began with a series of bank runs in 1927.

6. Richie remarks that the film "is about children, who innocently reflect the falseness of an adult society. Ozu goes further, suggesting that such innocence cannot continue. Though the film is a comedy, it is a serious one; the two little boys will never again be the same" (215).

7. Thirty distinct running trains are spotted in the film, in addition to two scenes that prominently feature a switchyard with numerous trains.

8. For a broad view of the literary treatment of commuter trains between the Russo-Japanese War and the early 1930s, see Freedman.

9. Elsewhere in modern Japanese literature, a children's conflict also serves to suggest a similar process in which a peripheral space of Tokyo is being transformed and subordinated by the economy of the growing city. See the interpretation of Ichiyō Higuchi's short story "Growing Up" (1895) in Maeda. Maeda argues that the children's fights in the story—which may seem to be simple, juvenile conflicts between rival cliques—are indeed an expression of the tension between the older social formation in the peripheral community, which values communal ties cultivated over generations, and the newer, increasingly dominant norms of life dictated by the more mobile money economy of the growing modern city.

10. It should be noted that an increasing number of scholars now treat U.S. suburbs as diverse space. See, for instance, Kruse and Sugrue.

11. In *I Was Born, But . . .*, three morning commute scenes effectively capture such effects on the temporal and spatial organization of the suburb. In all three, essentially the same events take place in the same place in the same order, with

some variations. Thanks to Ozu's characteristically stylized shot construction and editing, these scenes formally resemble each other, especially with the first two even having almost identical framings, shot order, and lengths, further underscoring the repetitiveness of the commute.

12. I thank Yōichi Komori for pointing out the details of the office and linking them to the growth of the trading industry.

13. See, for instance, Bock, 76; Mellen, 317. The quote is from Bock.

14. The film's own censorship record reminds us of the state's vested interest in maintaining irreproachable images of the school and the family. The censor demanded two excisions from the film. One of them was the scene in which Yoshii tells the boys how he used to get A's for his arithmetic in his youth. One of the boys then asks, "Was that because you gave your teacher gifts?" This intertitle was excised for "negative effects on public moral." In the boy's humorous question, teachers' integrity and parental authority were at stake, and the state had to intervene (Naimusho keihōkyoku, 53).

15. It is not that Ozu did not like filming in-train scenes. In *Days of Youth (Wakaki hi)* (1929), for instance, he effectively used in-train scenes between Tokyo and a ski resort, and *Late Spring (Banshun)* (1949) includes a scene in a commuter train near the opening.

16. On the collapse of distance in film, Wada-Marciano notes, "As cultural production, the cinema in particular enacted modernity's characteristic collision of spaces and temporalities, the spectacle of the unfamiliar and exotic juxtaposed with the everyday. Distant spaces were now brought suddenly within reach of the filmgoer" (17–18).

17. Kirby argues that such perceptual experience, as well as the social and ideological effects, of the railway prepared the U.S. public for the kind of modern subjectivity the silent film would soon help shape.

Works Cited

Bock, Audie. 1978. *Japanese Film Directors*. New York: Kodansha International.

Bordwell, David. 1988. *Ozu and the Poetics of Cinema*. Princeton: Princeton University Press.

Cazdyn, Eric. 2002. *The Flash of Capital: Film and Geopolitics in Japan*. Durham: Duke University Press.

Cooper, Frederick, and Ann Laura Stoler, eds. 1997. *Tensions of Empire: Colonial Cultures in a Bourgeois World*. Berkeley: University of California Press.

Davis, Clarence, and Kenneth Wilburn, eds. 1991. *Railway Imperialism*. New York: Greenwood Press.

Davis, Darrell Williams. 1996. *Picturing Japaneseness: Monumental Style, National Identity, Japanese Film*. New York: Columbia University Press.

Foucault, Michel. 1995. *Discipline and Punish: The Birth of the Prison*. Trans. Alan Sheridan. New York: Vintage Books.

Freedman, Alisa. 2011. *Tokyo in Transit: Japanese Culture on the Rails and Road*. Stanford: Stanford University Press.

Fujii, James A. 1999. "Intimate Alienation: Japanese Urban Rail and the Commodification of Urban Subjects." *differences* 11, no. 2: 106–33.

Gerow, Aaron. 2010. *Visions of Japanese Modernity: Articulations of Cinema, Nation, and Spectatorship, 1895–1925*. Berkeley: University of California Press.

Hall, Catherine, and Sonya O. Rose, eds. 2006. *At Home with the Empire: Metropolitan Culture and the Imperial World*. Cambridge: Cambridge University Press.

Hansen, Miriam. 2000. "Fallen Women, Rising Stars, New Horizons: Shanghai Silent Film as Vernacular Modernism." *Film Quarterly* 54, no. 1: 1–22.

Hara, Takeshi. 1998. *Osaka as "People's Metropolis" vs. Tokyo as "Imperial Metropolis" ("Minto" Osaka tai "teito" Tokyo)*. Tokyo: Kōdansha.

Harvey, David. 1989. "Class Structure and Residential Differentiation." In *The Urban Experience*. Oxford: Basil Blackwell.

Henderson, Brian. 1980. "Toward a Non-bourgeois Camera Style (Part-Whole Relations in Godard's Late Films)." In *A Critique of Film Theory*, 62–81. New York: E. P. Dutton.

Inoue, Kota. 2012. "A Little Story of Settler Colonialism: Imperialist Consciousness and Children's Literature in the 1920s." In *Reading Colonial Japan: Text, Context, and Critique*. Ed. Michele M. Mason and Helen J. S. Lee, 188–208. Stanford: Stanford University Press.

Iwasaki, Akira. 1931. *Film and Capitalism (Eiga to shihonshugi)*. Tokyo: Sekaisha.

Kaplan, Amy. 2002. *The Anarchy of Empire in the Making of U.S. Culture*. Cambridge, Mass.: Harvard University Press.

Kirby, Lynne. 1997. *Parallel Tracks: The Railroad and Silent Cinema*. Durham: Duke University Press.

Kobayashi, Hideo, ed. 2000. *Modern Japan and the South Manchurian Railway (Kindai nihon to mantetsu)*. Tokyo: Yoshikawa kōbunkan.

Kruse, Kevin M., and Thomas J. Sugrue. 2006. *The New Suburban History*. Chicago: University of Chicago Press.

Maeda, Ai. 2004. "Their Time as Children: A Study of Higuchi Ichiyō's *Growing Up (Takekurabe)*." In *Text and the City: Essays on Japanese Modernity*. Ed. James A. Fujii, 110–43. Trans. Edward Fowler. Durham: Duke University Press.

McClintock, Anne. 1995. *Imperial Leather*. New York: Routledge.

Mellen, Joan. 1976. *The Waves at Genji's Door*. New York: Pantheon Books.

Naimusho keihōkyoku. 1932. *Eiga ken'etsu jihō* 15. Reprt. Tokyo: Fuji shuppan (1985).

Phillips, Alastair. 2007. "The Salaryman's Panic Time: Ozu Yasujiro's *I Was Born, But . . .* (1932)." In *Japanese Cinema: Texts and Contexts*. Ed. Alastair Phillips and Julian Stringer, 25–36. London: Routledge.

Richie, Donald. 1974. *Ozu*. Berkeley: University of California Press.

Sand, Jordan. 2013. "Imperial Japan and Colonial Sensibility: Affect, Object, Embodiment." *positions* 21, no. 1: 1–10.

Schivelbusch, Wolfgang. 1986. *The Railway Journey: The Industrialization of Time and Space in the Nineteenth Century*. Berkeley: University of California Press.

Silverberg, Miriam. 1993. "Remembering Pearl Harbor, Forgetting Charlie Chaplin, and the Case of the Disappearing Western Woman: A Picture Story." *positions* 1, no. 1: 24–76.

Simmel, Georg. 1971. "The Metropolis and Mental Life." In *On Individuality and Social Forms*. Ed. Donald N. Levine, 324–39. Chicago: University of Chicago Press.

Wada-Marciano, Mitsuyo. 2008. *Nippon Modern: Japanese Cinema of the 1920s and 1930s*. Honolulu: University of Hawaii Press.

Williams, Raymond. 1973. *The Country and the City*. New York: Oxford University Press.

Young, Louise. 1998. *Japan's Total Empire: Manchuria and the Culture of Wartime Imperialism*. Berkeley: University of California Press.

UBI CARITAS

CHILDREN AND RELIGIOUS CELIBATES

Hailey Haffey

It is perhaps easy to fall prey to the pop-cultural assumption that religious celibacy necessarily indicates a type of peculiarity, or "queerness," that coincides with predatory homosexuality. In April 2011, New Hampshire Republican House Majority Leader D. J. Bettencourt disparaged a critic of his proposed budget—Roman Catholic Bishop John McCormack—by calling him a "pedophile pimp who should have been led away from the State House in handcuffs with a raincoat over his head in disgrace" (Love and Ramer, 1). Bettencourt's riposte came after Bishop McCormack had spoken against the budget to a crowd of protesters, arguing, in line with Catholic teachings on social justice, that the proposal would not do enough for the poor and that "the vulnerable should take priority in our society." According to Bettencourt, however, the bishop didn't have a right to speak for the "vulnerable" and "has absolutely no moral credibility to lecture anyone" (1). A Catholic himself, Bettencourt's response to McCormack's complaint referenced McCormack's previously self-acknowledged failure to use his office adequately to protect victims during infamous sex-abuse scandals that erupted largely under the tenure of Boston's Cardinal Law in 2002. During this period, McCormack allegedly facilitated the notorious practice of dealing with abuse allegations—at least in part—by transferring suspected priests to other parishes. The New Hampshire Diocese avoided legal charges at the time in exchange for its immediate promulgation of strict policies designed to protect children and prevent similar communal failures in the future (1). By his own admission, McCormack made mistakes in his role as a clerical official responsible for preventing child abuse. And yet ten years later, his adversary Bettencourt's style of recalling such mistakes also evokes important questions about the public's automatic associations of celibacy, queerness, and adult–child relationships. As can be seen with the highly quotable (and oft-quoted) tag line "pedophile pimp," contemporary media unfailingly reiterate the idea that relationships between children and religious celibates are inherently unredeemable and sexually dangerous.

These violations of children's physical and psychological well-being are undeniable failures in the Church, and such abuse is the Church's institutional responsibility to mitigate. Nonetheless, I will show, it is not possible to argue statistically that religious celibates pose any more threat to children than do other adults in positions of trust (teachers, coaches, family members, to name a few). Accordingly, we must ask what is being obfuscated by culturally typecasting priests and (sometimes) nuns as predatory above other members of society. We must also differentiate between violating and helpful interactions. In this discussion of age-stratified, religious intimacy, the levels, roles, and uses of sexual awareness, on the part of both adult and child, are key. We should also consider the peculiar commonality of adult religious and children both as, ideally, celibate—according to both church rules and legal standards. Such an analysis, I will argue, reveals that valuable lessons and emotions are overshadowed and displaced by the indiscriminate use of terms associated with child sexual abuse.

The project of this essay is to use assumptions like those motivating Bettencourt's critique as a call for a deeper understanding of the presumed problems between religious celibates and children, and to use the moments in celibate–child interactions to help understand the rhetorical fields surrounding these characters. First, I will look at mass-media investigations into the assumption that a vow of marriage to God actually veils a twisted taste for children. As I will show how the rhetorical strategies of "sex panics" work as red herrings that merely repeat hackneyed and simplistic assumptions about childhood, about the priesthood, and about vocations of religious celibacy in general. This is not at all to say that those who perpetuate public traumas via the secretive policies of Church authority are innocent. Rather, I want to show how any of the clergy's (or other celibates') crimes garner disproportionate attention that distracts from what can become, at times, uncommonly enriching relationships between children and religious celibates. Most critical for this chapter are significant parallels between how heteronormative adult culture treats and constructs children as little celibates, and celibates as children. Consequently, children and religious celibates would seem to have significant ground on which to coidentify. I pose this question: Do we focus on scandals between priests and children because heteronormative adult culture benefits from only allowing the representations of traumatic relations between these groups? I would argue that the constructive similarities between celibates and children are denied by those keeping the party line in ecclesial hierarchies. This disavowal shifts the focus (for the mass media and general public) onto problematic interactions between celibates and children—changes in focus that can function like decoys or red herrings.

In the first half of this essay, I want to look closely at recent public discourse on the association of pedophilia with the Catholic celibate life to find out what is being lost in the mix. That is, when mainstream media promote assumptions about pedophile priests and vulnerable children, I would also wish to ask: Are some of the most important connections between these figures getting oversimplified for the sake of capitalizing on sensational public interest? I will take on this unlikely revision of dominant assumptions by analyzing, in the second half of this essay, two modern texts that sculpt nuances between Roman Catholic religious authority figures and children into a different kind of relief from what the headlines suggest. Here I will consider Edna O'Brien's 1980 short story, "Sister Imelda," and John Patrick Shanley's 2004 play, *Doubt: A Parable,* and its 2008 film adaptation, *Doubt* (also written by Shanley and starring Philip Seymour Hoffman, Meryl Streep, and Amy Adams). In important and complementary ways, these texts prompt us to consider the common perception that priests and nuns display threatening sexual aberrance in their choice of a celibate lifestyle. By extension, these texts challenge notions that celibacy functions as a cover for sinister sexual perversions, leads to "dangerous" homo- or bisexual practices, and that the sexual corruption of children is a ubiquitous, underlying agenda of these supposed wolves in shepherds' clothing.

I begin my literary inquiry into these themes with reference to the Bettencourt–McCormack dispute because the related questions that bind "Sister Imelda" and *Doubt* also invite the consideration of lively debates in queer studies, such as those discussed by Lee Edelman in his book *No Future: Queer Theory and the Death Drive.* Edelman, among others, theorizes that defenses of the "child" proper insidiously do violence to queer lifestyles in the name of heteronormative America's sacred trinity of "the child," "the family," and "the future." This triangle represents a framework wherein "the future" is always dependent on a politically motivated definition of children. Within this analysis, it is also my goal to posit that the high-voltage charges of homophobia (or "queerophobia") that persist in America and the rest of the modern West cloud and distort interpretations of affection or caring between celibate religious figures and children. This is to posit that assumptions about the relationship of celibacy to "queerness," and anxieties about the aims of "queer" people themselves, impede opportunities to understand how mentorship by the religious might work—and do so by demonizing those who may wish to respond constructively to, and be sensitive to, the presence of disaffection or of alienation or need in the child.

Nearly a month after the disputes between Bettencourt and McCormack, a simple Google search of the term "pedophile pimp" turned up roughly 122,000 results. At least the first six pages referred to nothing other than the story outlined above. Over six years later, the Bettencourt–McCormack debate was still the first hit (of many) on a Google search for "pedophile pimp." Thus, beyond what was then last month's news, literally written in electronic record for years to come, is the intertwining of Bishop McCormack's name with the label "pedophile pimp." The connection, however, is not novel: those perceived bonds between the celibate religious life and damaging (especially homosexual) pedophilia are, in fact, yesterday's news. The media's capacity to exploit this association between celibates and abuse is, literally, limitless because of the nebulousness of the terms, situations, and characters involved. This capacity does not go completely unchecked, however. Perhaps most succinctly, a challenge to the celibacy bias appears in "Mean Men," an article by Pat Wingert published by *Newsweek* in April 2010. She leads the piece with these telling lines: "The priesthood is being cast as the refuge for pederasts. In fact, priests seem to abuse children at the same rate as everyone else" (Wingert, 1). The story's author, after alluding to general assumptions about the celibate clergy that I posited earlier, goes on to note that at the time the Catholic sex-abuse scandals were erupting (around 2002), a "Wall Street Journal-NBC News poll found that 64% of those queried thought

Catholic priests 'frequently' abused children" (1). However, Wingert backs up a counterclaim to this assumption with some significant data. For example, she cites the president of the National Center for Missing and Exploited Children, Ernie Allen, as contending that "we don't see the Catholic Church as a hotbed of this or a place that has a bigger problem than anyone else" (1).

Wingert also follows the money trail. She notes that "since the 1980's, insurance companies have offered sexual misconduct coverage as a rider on liability insurance, and their own studies indicate that Catholic Churches are not higher risk than other congregations" (1). Further, Wingert reveals that "insurance companies that cover all denominations, like Guide One Center for Risk Management, which has more than 40,000 church clients, does not charge Catholic churches higher premiums" (1). Clearly then, the 2002 public perception that Catholic priests are a dire threat to children is not confirmed by a statistical risk assessment, even when the assessors would stand to profit from connecting correlation with causation. Further, this matter is not simply one of displacing an enormous Catholic risk over a larger population to make costs manageable. As Sarah Buckley, Guide One's assistant vice president of corporate communications, explained, "We don't see a vast difference in the incidence rate between one denomination and another . . . It's pretty even across the denominations" (1). Of Wingert's compelling citations, one of the most notable is her comparison between the rates of male abusers of children in the general population and those in the clergy. She writes that the "only hard data made public by any denomination" was funded by the U.S. Conference of Catholic Bishops. It documented that between the years 1950 and 1992, 4 percent of active Catholic Priests (roughly 110,000) had been *accused* of sexual misconduct with children, "ranging from 'sexual talk' to rape" (1). Accordingly, the appearance of males in the general population who commit sexual abuse on children is estimated at 1 percent to 5 percent, leaving the Catholic demographics of accusations well within these estimates.[1] Researcher Margaret Leland Smith from the John Jay College of Criminal Justice (the institution that performed the priest study) also noted that the average person doesn't understand that child sexual abuse is "profoundly prevalent" in the general population, and thus obviously extends far beyond the realm of church-related figures or activities (1). Nonetheless, Pope Francis's recent acknowledgement that 2 percent of priests were abusers was met with shock, and news articles made calculations of the number of pedophile priests at large. One such headline, from the Los Angeles Times, incredulously queried: "Did Pope Francis Really Say 2% of Catholic Clergy Are Pedophiles?" The admission appalled as much as did the numbers it would signify, regardless of parallels with the rates in other denominations or in the general public. The BBC indignantly tabulated that "it would represent around 8,000 priests out of a global number of about 414,000" ("Pope Francis"). This "confession" by Pope Francis should be anything but a surprise: his estimate of abusers in the priesthood is in fact within the same range as abusers in the general population.

Considering the statistics, then, the idea that "the priesthood" is "a refuge for pederasts" is highly suspicious. The same can be said for nuns: celibate women also garner sexual mistrust despite the lesser media frenzy and lower rates for nun abuse cases (a phenomenon that coincides with lower statistics for women sexual abusers on the average). If celibates and men-of-the-cloth abuse children at the same per-capita rate as the average parents on the block, a typical evangelical youth minister, a teacher, the high school basketball coach, or the banker who just approved your car loan—then something is up with the bias against the priests. Enter the closet. Or, shall we say, the monastery. Or better yet, the confessional. The convent or monastery works as a substitute for the closet, and hence as metaphoric confessionals, because entering the priesthood, or any celibate religious lifestyle, is always a confession. It is a confession of "queerness," of difference, regardless of the precise sexual or mental orientation of that queerness. For both men and women, the choice of a celibate religious life is a confession that one does not desire, or seek to engage in, the quest for a heteronormal reproductive family, or "reproductive futurity" as Edelman terms it. Thus, the masses of homophobes who rage against celibacy are, to some degree, right: the priesthood and monastic life are absolutely filled with people who have chosen a "queer" lifestyle, in that they have officially opted out of a reproductive or heterosexually oriented way of living, and who do not value "reproductive futurity" in the same way the average straight, sexually active American might. Of course, religious celibates do focus on the future, a future in heaven with God. Of course, they are generally willing to deny the pleasures of the world to attain this most idyllic union. But this is not figured into public perceptions of celibate lifestyles.

The celibate's denial of key pleasures is reflected in religious rituals signifying death to the world and the flesh as one enters the monastic life: it is both a metaphorical immolation and literal self-sacrifice in terms of one's genetic (and thus biological) future. We might consider (out of context) here a passage from Gertrude Stein's opera *Four Saints in Three Acts,* in which she describes Saint Therese in a series of negations: "Not this not in this not with this," and further as "a young girl, being widowed" (588). The marriage to a dead spouse, of course, precludes the possibility of progeny; it reduces the girl's biological future to nothing. This implication of strangeness here is exponentially multiplied in the case of priestly men who also become the widows of Christ, so to speak, their queerly dead male spouse. At the same time, beyond denying biological futurity, these postmortem spiritual marriages are also the killing-off of one's ancestral lineage, family history, and any future for these two classes. Thus, unlike the official sacrament of penance, entering the "confessional closet" of religious life creates the open secret that the subject has freely chosen, feels inclined to, or even senses God's call, toward some space separate from a heteronormative lifestyle that links past and future generations. Accordingly, there is no way in which a religious celibate can be considered anything else but "queer." The queer celibate, in this sense, becomes a missing link that robs the family's future of its potential through the individual's "dying" into an alternative lifestyle. The closet that is the open confessional or cloister is also the closed pine box of the future.

I would argue that anxiety over the undeniably "queer" state of celibacy is a big part of the problem with "celibatophobia" (to coin a term). Further, it is a bias against such resistance to reproduction that seems to fuel this popular anxiety against the priesthood or monastic life. As Edelman contends, "If there is no baby and, in consequence, no future, then the blame must fall on the fatal lure of sterile, narcissistic enjoyments understood as inherently destructive of meaning and therefore as responsible for the undoing of social organization, collective reality, and inevitably life itself" (13). In addition, then, this bias is an association of the queer celibate with violence, sexual aberrance, and death. These fears and assumptions related to the priesthood are akin to what Leo Bersani cites as biases against gay men in his essay, "Is the Rectum a Grave?" In this essay, Bersani argues that gay men have been associated with AIDS in ways that connect their presumed desire for male-to-male sex with a stigmatized "feminine" and "receptive" sexual posturing that ultimately seems like a thirst for suicide; he equates the way gay men are treated with the ostracism and abuses of female prostitutes in the 19th century, depicted as lustful "vessels" of disease and the contagions of death (17–18). This suicidal thirst resonates with Edelman's concern that anyone willing to refuse the communal goals of the "cult of the child" (hence, family) is also guilty of saying "no" to the "fascism of the baby's face," and thus also willing to abort children of the past by denying their life through children of the future (19, 75). Gay men, priests, and other nonreproductive queers (even nuns), then, in accordance with the ideas of Bersani and Edelman, can be thought of as baby killers: they replace womb with tomb. How could we trust any of them with our children?

The subtext of anxiety about religious celibacy may be the disavowed realization that these religious figures are, in this way, all "queer." These queer celibates then become the scapegoats for the abundance of violence against children. We see, consequently, that the alleged sacrality of the celibate is more accurately the Church's well-veiled attempt at what Carolyn Dinshaw calls the "containment of the deviant," which here takes place by ostensibly giving these holy queers a place of elevation that is actually a circumscribed and highly scrutinized position subject to extreme regulation, objectification, and control (223). Anthropologically speaking, this control works ritualistically: it makes use of normative culture's tailings or refuse, as a sort of sacrifice to the gods; it parades the (contextually) unholy as the holy. At least, if "they" are bound to the service of the Church, perhaps some use can be made of them.

Societal regulation of queers through celibacy and religion has an important function that makes celibates' relationships with children all the more significant. Arguably, the Church has promoted a culture in which those inclined to queerness are married off to Jesus. Thus dedicated to a celibate lifestyle, religious men and women are bound to a space of pseudo-heteronormativity: they are frequently placed in communal settings that actually function like pseudofamilies. Such structural dynamics are designed with both internal and external paradigms of power that would monitor and obfuscate any of the celibate's nascent awareness of sexual difference beyond a choice designated as dedication to God through sexual self-denial. Accordingly, this lifestyle necessarily precludes any possibility of openly acknowledging their blatant disavowal of normative heteronormativity (a strange but necessary tautology here). The open secret of their celibate queerness is thus veiled by an adoption of a heterofocused discourse: monastics and clergypeople are Fathers, Brothers, Mothers, and Sisters with surrogate and metaphorical families. We know these models of nonfamilial families from world mythologies, from the Bible, from Jesus's interactions with his disciples. These familial epithets are widespread metaphors of interaction, and thus their symbolism is powerful—powerful enough to function as an enormous distraction. Immersion in this familial discourse thus ultimately gives religious queers little space for noticing their sexual uniqueness, since they are always bound to the same familial structures (and modes of address) as their heteronormative peers. They are celibate and sexually odd, but yet "married" to Christ, which is a convenient disavowal of the perversity of refusing grown-up sex. This holy marriage thus obfuscates, on the surface, any threat posed by these eternally chaste and childless figures. However, precisely because their relationships are recognized as nonreproductive in a material sense, and because of the open secrets implied in their ability to live without normative adult, heterosexual relations, the constructed and regulated sanctity of these figures disintegrates as soon as intimacy with children is brought into the picture. If these figures do not want to engage in "normal male-female sex," can we really believe they don't want any type of sex or any other sexually charged pleasure at all? And if they do, with whom or how might they want it? Since marriage to a dead God offers no satisfaction of bodily pleasures, where do these figures seek/get their fulfillment? The bottom line is that the celibacy of religious figures seems to be too much for society to accept: pledges of chastity are only taken with the suspicion that the avower is really protesting too much.

It seems that the public imagines there can be two options for the religious celibate's fulfillment, and these usually unite into a third and most frightening possibility. First, the celibate religious may seek adult homosexual liaisons. Second, they may seek pedophilic liaisons. Thus, third, and worst of all (since it combines with a twosome, of course), these people may hunt down homosexually pedophilic encounters. Therefore the "celibate" adult who self-immolates against normative earthly sexual pleasures is always a suspected transmitter of secret, aberrant pleasures. Since he or she is always infected with "sexual otherness," which cannot be fully understood or affirmed from a heteronormative reproductive framework, the religious celibate also carries a potential contagion, which could infect and kill the future of the child (and thus retrospectively, the future of their parents) in any number of ways. Through communally designated uniforms, regulated group living spaces, and those familial titles ("Father," "Sister," "Mother," "Brother"), the otherness of queer celibates is marked in a strangely appropriative manner. This implementation of a family model recodes and delimits the discourse of celibacy: the obvious rejection of heteronormativity is recoded to imply that celibates seek an ideal, Platonic, even heavenly heteronormativity—as if their aim is to be part of a spiritual "holy family." Thus no real language of queerness could ever develop for these individuals or communities because their difference is always reformed into acceptable simulacra of the dominant norms and structures, despite the radical difference that this recoding denies in the form of an open secret. These basic qualities—being denied language that would acknowledge their "queerness," and being forced to appropriate family-normative signifiers by the heteronormative-identifying adults that dominate our society—ironically pairs religious celibates with the population that they are most feared (and claimed) to harm: children.

While Lee Edelman marks "the child" as the keeper of normative culture's biological futurity, Kathryn Bond Stockton presents another perspective through which we may view the child—a view that sees all children as always and already queer (3). She further argues that

> Edelman would like to smash the social order and, along with it, the child. Perhaps most importantly for my purposes, even though Edelman makes this point in passing, "the cult of the child . . . permits no shrines to the queerness of boys and girls, since queerness, for contemporary culture at large . . . is understood as bringing children and childhood to an end." . . . There are other ways to circumvent "the child." One could explore the elegant, unruly contours of growing that don't bespeak continuance. I coin the term "sideways growth" to refer to something that locates energy, pleasure, vitality and (e)motion in the back-and-forth connections and extensions that are not reproductive. (13)

Some of these "elegant, unruly contours of growing" Stockton discusses usher forth from the important idea that "the child from the standpoint of 'normal' adults is always queer. It is 'homosexual' . . . or, despite our culture's assuming every child's straightness, the child can only be 'not-yet-straight,' since it, too, is not allowed to be sexual" (7). The uncanny parallels between the "queer" child and the "queer" celibate just don't stop. Both are rendered queer by their assumption of non-heterosexuality and by the normative adult's fears of that non-heterosexuality's potential. Further, as with the religious celibate, children are kept from linguistic articulation of their "not-yet" heterosexual state. They are denied such reflection by, as Stockton notes, the denial of their sexuality, both legally and culturally (6). In the simplest terms (since we are speaking of religion) this might be related to the idea of "reason" and the age that reason is seen to reflect a cultural responsibility: roughly and curiously, something that happens around the age of reading. Before literacy, children are commonly wrapped in a fleecy garment of sinless "innocence" marked by a restriction of language, which at a certain point is supplemented by oral traditions of normalizing storytelling. Children, then, are subversively denied sexuality until they can read and, after that, formally denied sexuality by being forced to read and write themselves as simultaneously nonsexual, presexual, and pre-heteronormative: "Someday my prince will come . . ." might be the anthem for this state of affairs among little girls in particular. As Lynda Sexson gracefully paints in her creative documentary on eighteenth- and nineteenth-century children's primers, *My Book and Heart Shall Never Part,* children are primed for both creativity and normativity as they are taught "A is for Apple." This is the dilemma of the children who, as Sexson casts it in her film, discover a "locked secret drawer" in an old dresser, where "they reached inside for the treasure" that was "not jewels," but "strange little books printed long, long ago made for children." As a little girl leafs through the faded primers and stories, she is lost in another world. She forgets "what side of the page [she is] on," while the narrator adds, "And that's called reading, finding ourselves on both sides of a page" (Sexson). The child may read and imagine, but there are also limits to this imagination that are imprinted in the letters themselves. For the letter "A," readers of the *New England Primer* were taught to remember: "In Adam's Fall We Sinned All." This rapture into the language, fictions, and imaginations of adults has thus long helped construct the image of "the child" in ways relevant to the discussions of Stockton and Edelman. It is not only the projection of a highly politicized (and arguably religious) ideal of childhood onto children that we must acknowledge and assess. Rather, we must also analyze the ways we train "children" to perform "childhood." In the Butlerian sense of a reiterative performativity, our culture has no original "child." Therefore in another parallel between religious celibates and children, the adult religious figure is marked with the aforementioned coded signifiers of a spiritually alternative heteronormative existence, while the child is bound to normativity by having no other linguistic world to connect to than the one already offered by the adults who also seek to shape them sexually, morally, and otherwise ideologically—through the symbolic primers of stories and metaphors.

It is no wonder, then, that Stockton argues that "the gay child illuminates the darkness of the child" (3). If all children are queer, then it may be those who feel most self-consciously so that go to the "secret drawer" or the "cabinet of wonders" not just to discover what is held in the darkness there but to find a mirror for the darkness in themselves—in the pieces of their identity that have not found a way into normative syntaxes and semiotics of identity construction. "Children" are accustomed to negotiating the treacherous boundaries between the mysteries of adulthood and what they, as children, are presently allowed to speak and know. Thus, they go to hidden places to share their secrets, paradoxically to give them life, light, and language. Of "children" (past or present) deprived of language, Stockton writes that "not all so-called gay adults will recognize these feelings ['haze, suspense, a fear of growing up'], since not everyone called 'gay' or 'queer' felt such feelings in their youth. . . . But for those who did, a telling kind of ghostliness hung about their growth . . . what I call the 'backward birth,' which has piercingly postmortem features" (6). Stockton's conception of "backward birth" is centered on the idea that the eventually gay-adult child is in no way "available to itself in the present tense" (6). According to Stockton then, queer children are not allowed the language through which to articulate their own sexuality (6). Thus "the protogay child has only appeared through an act of retrospection and after a death" (6). Stockton writes that, in the absence of the optional category "I am gay," for nearly all children, the "only grammatical formulation allowed to gay childhood" has been the gay adult's reminiscence that "I was a gay child"; thus, "the phrase 'gay child' is a gravestone marker for where or when one's straight life died" (7).

Significant for my study here, this moment of death to a straight future (marked by a backward glance) is a meeting point for the queer child and the adult celibate religious figure—and moves us into both *Doubt* and "Sister Imelda." Crucially, although she notes that the queer child is "unavailable to itself" in the present tense, Stockton does not deny that it seeks that availability through what often becomes a web of complicated metaphors: the boy who identified as a "'filly'—the word, he thought, for a 'homosexual seagull,'" or the "girl of nine [who] thought herself a vampire, a shadowy figure with shadowy secrets surrounding women" (6, 1). But for other children, especially Catholic children, the twisted semiotic quest to have a meaningful non-heteronormative identity in the present tense is often rooted in, and routed into, religious experience. Thus those children most self-consciously inclined to follow the road less traveled are frequently inspired to do so by taking for their role models those celibate religious figures who have managed to do just what they would like: avoid a "reproductive future" (Edelman, 147). For such children, feelings of same-sex desire can be sublimated into a desire to live in a religious community that disavows earthly pleasures in favor of that other queer love—the love of God. The image, as Stein sketched it, of "the young girl" (or boy) "being widowed" by Christ can be a convenient and perhaps unconscious way of seeking some non-heteronormative identification in the present. Therefore such children may never have to—or, sadly, never have the chance to—creatively identify as a "filly," a "homosexual seagull," or a "girl vampire," because a queer metaphor of disguise (historically, often heavy in dark woolen garments, from habits to scapulars to hair shirts) has already insidiously been set aside for them, just in case they should need it.

Doubt and "Sister Imelda" are important proof texts for issues of abuse. Both texts deal with queer children in a crisis of an unsatisfactory present in tension with an unknown future, and both deal with the popular assumptions about child abuse by celibates. These two texts are structured differently in terms of the point of view, gender, race, age—and the child's motivation to articulate queerness. But placed in conversation with each other, these texts help unravel each other and clarify key differences in what we might consider the multiple potentialities (benefits, misunderstandings, failures, dangers, and dreams) of adult–child love in a queerly religious setting. One common bond that both texts meaningfully share is that their subjects—two queer youths—seem to catch a glimpse of their own dark secrets in the religious figure they strive to emulate. These adolescents, a junior-high-aged African American boy and an Irish convent schoolgirl in her last year of studies, both recognize in their mentors (a middle-aged Irish priest and a young Irish nun, respectively) a potential for a non-heteronormative future that self-reflexively reveals and potentially validates their own non-heteronormative identities in the present. But even under the cover of the cloth, this revelation is filled with trepidation for both the celibate adults and the queer youths. These "children," then, in every way *want* to be different from the "child" Edelman disdains in *No Future*. Instead, they are the youths Stockton cites as living in limbo in *The Queer Child*. Both stories end in pain, though differently, but together they illuminate a path outside the violence of witch hunts *(Doubt)*, or conversely, actual instances of abuse ("Sister Imelda").

Contra Edelman, José Esteban Muñoz argues that giving up on a future-oriented vision of the world does not work for everyone. He writes, "I respond to Edelman's assertion that the future is the province of the child and therefore not for the queers by arguing that queerness is primarily about futurity and hope. That is to say queerness is always on the horizon" (11). Further, similar to Stockton's alertness to the way the queer child is "unavailable to itself in the present tense," Muñoz is sensitive to disparities in the way queers are permitted to experience or live out their identities, insisting that "the present is not enough. It is impoverished and toxic for queers and other people who do not feel the privilege of majoritarian belonging, normative tastes and 'rational' expectations" (27). Muñoz thus makes a case that queers need hope, that hope is not merely the province of reproductive futurism, and that "his approach to hope as a critical methodology can be best described as a backward glance that enacts a future vision" (4). Significantly, for queer children whose "present is not enough," we need a future that is not designed for the generically constructed "child."[2] For queer children (and thus really all children) "we must strive, in the face of the here and now's totalizing rendering of reality, to think and feel a *then and there*. . . . We must dream and enact new and better pleasures, other ways of being in the world, and ultimately new worlds" (1). Both *Doubt* and "Sister Imelda" show how the pleasures of the present are not enough for the queer children they depict.

Each of these texts is set chiefly in pre–Vatican II–styled Roman Catholic schools. Though rooted in the past, these settings are not irrelevant for today, because despite the ecumenical revolutions of Vatican II, the Church's doctrines on sexuality have remained remarkably consistent. *Doubt* begins in the Bronx, New York, in the late fall of 1964, while "Sister Imelda" takes place at an all-girls boarding convent school in an undisclosed location in Ireland, during what seems like roughly the same period as *Doubt* (based on descriptions of technology and pre–Vatican II religious rituals, though an exact year is not mentioned). Again, recognition and thus queer mirroring is key in both of these texts. In *Doubt*, Donald Miller is an odd member of the community from the first moment, simply because of the color of his skin (though his mother makes the clear implication that she believes being sexually queer [likely gay] is part of "the boy's nature," later in the film [Shanley n.d., 76]).[3] Donald is the first and only African American student at Saint Nicholas School, which, we are told, is attended by mostly children of working-class Irish and Italian families. He is described in the screenplay as "12, a bit chubby, black" (2). The film-as-medium helps to objectify Donald, since the story is told from a third-person limited perspective and the gaze of the viewer frequently falls on the boy when he is repeatedly depicted as the only ethnic minority in the all-white school and in church crowds. His slouched and shy posture often suggests he feels physically out of place, and early on asks a fellow altar boy, "You think I'm fat?" (3). Donald also acts passively, gently, in relation to his peers.

Very soon, however, it becomes clear that Donald is not the only character queered by his body. Father Flynn is a medium-sized man, with the same type of chubbiness we see in Donald: neither Donald nor Father Flynn is extremely masculine, because of their slight, common roundness. We first see and hear Father Flynn performing the

Mass Donald helps serve. Flynn gives a sermon on "doubt," his simple discussion of which becomes a cloud that follows him through the narrative. And as Father Flynn's queerness is also embodied, many of the doubts surrounding him are held in his hands: several scenes depict his fingernails, which the screenplay describes as "quite long and polished" (25).[4] However, one of their first scrutinized appearances comes not in image alone but in action, in a scene where Father Flynn greets students standing in line before school. He "playfully" grasps the wrist of the film's trouble-maker, William London, asking him, "You wash those hands today, Mister London?" after which, "William snatches his hand away" (11). At the same time, the school principal, Sister Aloysius, looks down to see this resistance and, taking in this sight as "her eyes narrow," her own doubt is conceived (11). From this moment, her "narrow" vision gives her the certainty to relate the "doubt" in Father Flynn's sermon to his "playful" grasp at dirty hands. For the rest of the narrative, Sister Aloysius has no doubt of Father Flynn's capacity for harm of children, and advises her fellow sisters "I want you all to be alert" (17). After the playful grasp, these suspicious hands also reappear as a suspended image in a gym scene where Father Flynn attempts to promote hygiene among the boys in Donald's class. He shows the boys his fingernails as an example of cleanliness, the simple vision of which causes London to again jerk away, in apparent disgust. If cleanliness is next to godliness, apparently in *Doubt,* both godliness and cleanliness make a peculiar triangle with queerness. Father Flynn's hands, all around, it appears, signal his otherness and signify their presumed dubious intentions and uses throughout the film.

As both man and boy are constructed as visually exceptional, odd, unmasculine, and "queer," so also any intimacy between them is constructed accordingly. Though the "doubt" sermon evokes anxiety for Sister Aloysius, Donald is affected differently. The space of "doubt" has resonated meaningfully with the adolescent who likely "doubts" his belonging in a gender-normative, white, masculine world. But he sees hope in the quiet, friendly life of the priest. After the sermon, he tells Father Flynn (who greets Donald as "champ"), "That was some sermon" (9). When Father Flynn responds playfully, "Did it mean something to you?" Donald's response is that "I want to do that. I want to be a priest" (9). Flynn does not press but tells Donald he would "make a good one" (9). Flynn then takes out a small mirrored box with a small ballerina inside, showing how the lid and mirror can be used to make the dancer spin, and after the brief sharing of boyish amusement, gives the toy to Donald. Here the identification of child-wanting-to-become-priest is reciprocated in the priest innocently partaking in an arguably girlish game, thus fulfilling the cycle of mirroring Donald had previously begun. Significantly, in this private and intimate scene in the sacristy, no erotic charge is depicted on part of man or boy; and it would seem very difficult for any of us voyeurs watching the film to make such a case. However, what comes of this moment of communion is a mutual sense of identification, a brief transcendence of time and space through the priest's "backward glance" at queer boyhood and the boy's hopeful vision of a queer, priestly future. Thus since Donald lives in the dead space of "unavailability" to himself in the "present tense," he sees a future in the priest, who is also a queer figure of death by dying to the pleasures of the flesh through the vows of his ordination. However, despite his position as a dead or ghostly adult, Father Flynn also presents the possibility of a future of belonging to an accepting community. This interaction is a strange meeting place for both Muñoz's and Edelman's theories. It is not a queer utopia, but it is a way to survive in the present that does not look toward a "reproductive future." It posits a hope that the queer child may be available through a death of the heteronormative "child" of the future. But this death is one different from the one Stockton describes when gay people look back on their past, since it does not involve a future of openly acknowledging a "gay" or "queer" past identity. Rather, it ekes out a space where one's peculiarity is potentially able to be made meaningful (though still somewhat occluded)—in an intolerant dominant religious culture that does not allow for a future that might even imagine the possibility of claiming words like "gay" or "queer." Again, it is not ideal, but here this formulation offers hope to Donald, who sees a place where he may finally fit in.

Predictably, the queer child Donald begins to have several problems at the school. It is implied that he has stolen and drunk communion wine, and he begins to be bullied occasionally by London, though his academic performance remains satisfactory. Thus beyond identification, emulation, or heroism, the relationship between priest and boy also becomes one of guardianship. But when Sister Aloysius instills

Donald's young and hopeful nun-teacher Sister James's mind with "doubts" about Father Flynn's interest in the boy, Sister James is unable to differentiate what might be signs of love and protection from signs of potential abuse—since she herself is in a mentoring, mirroring and quasi-intimate (at least through sharing of confidences) relationship with Sister Aloysius.[5] Sister James becomes the informant who acts as the eyes and ears of Sister Aloysius, whose "intolerance" and suspicion at times she finds herself mirroring in uncanny closeness: ironically it is Sister James who actually instigates the connection between Sister Aloysius's suspicions about Donald and Father Flynn; Sister James explains that in Donald's difficulties at school, he has a "protector" (31). The vague implication of impropriety as a motive for the priest's protection is all that needs to be suggested to convert doubts to certainty, and a certainty of a particular valence for Sister Aloysius. Sister James then, is also pulled into the film's crisis of hope, since as a good nun, she obediently confesses her observations to her superior. But Sister James also struggles over whether or not she has made the right decision and frequently looks to Occam's Razor, or the idea that the simplest answer will offer the most likely solution, for good-faith explanations.

Several circumstantial scenes that rely on the intimacy and confidences between Sister Aloysius and her subordinate, younger nun produce enough tension to push Father Flynn to self-sabotage when he ultimately leaves his position at the school under extreme duress. In one scene, Sister James sees the priest placing a t-shirt in Donald's locker. Though Sister James does not mention this to the principal, the suggested intimacy of the priest and boy through a touching of an undershirt still propels Sister James to enter into Sister Aloysius's confidence later. Ironically, the *suspected* inappropriate connection between priest and boy brings about an *actual* damaging connection for Sister James and her superior. In another example, after Sister James's confession that the boy has a "protector" in Father Flynn, the two nuns use a discussion of a Christmas pageant as an alibi to corner Father Flynn in Sister Aloysius's office, and for the elder nun to make accusation of impropriety. This accusation is produced by the two nuns' intimacy: Sister Aloysius goads Sister James to recall her classroom observation that Flynn summoned Donald to his office, after which the boy returned upset and smelling of alcohol.

In response, Flynn eventually confesses that the meeting with Donald was to deal with the issue of the stolen altar wine. Further, Flynn argues that he meant to preserve Donald from the shame of this information going public by keeping it a secret, thus allowing the boy to remain on the altar guild. But in this scene, any of Father Flynn's fleeting credibility in "protecting" Donald is called into question through the gaze of the two nuns: when he is offered tea, he indulgently takes three lumps of sugar (as opposed to Sister James' soft but indignant response "Never!" to the same saccharine invitation). Taking the cup, Father Flynn reveals his elegantly manicured hands to Sister Aloysius, which do not go unnoticed. In her eyes they link his "sweet tooth" with an inability to renounce the flesh, which strangely enough can only confirm him as a predatory pedophile when his gustatory appetites are combined with long nails. To her he is, of course, the hungry, gay wolf "parading" as a shepherd. In one more crucial hand-scene, Donald's books are knocked to the floor in the hallway by William London. London's motion of violence and emasculation climaxes when the mirrored-toy given to Donald by Father Flynn is crushed in the collision. Almost incomprehensibly, once again, guardianship and love of the child by the queered man is visually rendered sexually suspect when Sister James looks on at Father Flynn's attempt to help the boy pick up his things. The scene's potential scandal is punctuated with an exclamation point for Sister James, who sees Flynn end the encounter by touching Donald's face and offering a brief, comforting embrace.

Thus the function of intimacy between Flynn as teacher/priest and his student here is one of mutual mirroring, arguably through the priest's recognition of a past self through identification with the student, and the student's self-becoming through his recognition of the priest. This is a figuratively reproductive relationship, focused on hope for a future, but significantly, the relationship is not biologically reproductive (or normatively productive) in the sense that Edelman chiefly argues against. The priest–student dynamic also settles into a space that doesn't offer the full potential of utopic and nonviolating illumination that Muñoz hopes for, since the language and strictures of institution permit only a highly regulated and contained way to avoid compulsory heterosexuality. Yet here, in this time and place, this future is one to work toward, even if, in some ways, it is a future involving sacrifice or death to some freedoms in exchange for others. It is a striving for a future of identity where no apt signifiers or actions expressing what we might call some sort of "authentic queerness" seem possible (even if this class is only defined by parameters that enable discussion). And yet, despite this environment seemingly constructed to keep such open secrets, the unspoken mutual recognition of the man's and boy's queerness becomes visible enough to the community's consciousness that the pair merits extra-special supervision, regulation, and ultimately judgment. Curiously, Donald's mother—coming from a different background of race and class than the school's predominantly Irish and Italian population—is consulted and doesn't question the benefits of the relationship between priest and boy. She knows his completion of the year at Saint Nicholas School will help him get into a better high school, and this may be his only hope for a brighter future in a better class situation than the one from which he comes. As mentioned, Donald's mother is not alarmed by insinuations of a queer bond between teacher and student, and seems to juxtapose it against the boy's home life which involves severe beatings by his father, who is ultimately a real threat to the boy's actual life and who hates him because of what is openly implied and understood to be his gay "nature" (76).

In "Sister Imelda," the situation between teacher and student is different in style and effect. In *Doubt,* slander and suspicion bring about a false certainty of violence, and the story's real damage occurs when characters buy into the assumption that intimacy must indicate violation. However, for O'Brien, violence surges when tropes of propriety are used to create the appearance of boundaries. It is conforming to the rules, in large part, and exploiting their function of creating distance, that causes emotional injuries for O'Brien's protagonist and her mentor; accordingly, abuse occurs when emotional injury is employed as a surrogate for affection. The protagonist in "Sister Imelda" is a slightly older girl, living away from home at a boarding school. O'Brien never gives her subject a name or a precise age, forcing the reader to identify her in some other way. "Convent-school girl" is the most basic terminology that one might come up with, leaving analysts of the text to wonder if O'Brien wanted a psychological cloud of age ambiguity to surround "the girl" (I will refer to O'Brien's subject as "the girl" or "the protagonist" or "the subject"). This always-unnamed subject of O'Brien's "Sister Imelda" is surrounded by girls who display curiosity about the nuns' potential past relations with boys, like the subject's best friend, "Baba." Baba is a constant antagonist to the subject's affection for Sister Imelda, and in this sense is a key heteroregulatory voice in the text. Notably, Baba doesn't share the protagonist's sense of affection for the nuns or any sense of piety or humility in general—which are markers of "the girl's" queerness.

"Sister Imelda" makes some important breaks from the template offered in *Doubt.* Significantly, the perspective is through the eyes of the unnamed narrator. This structuring itself changes the dynamics of queer relations between the queer celibate and queer student. Form also comes into consideration: O'Brien's work is a short story and not a play or film. Instead of, as in *Doubt,* the audience being invited to visually share in the overlapping gazes of Sister James and Sister Aloysius, here we follow the eyes of the protagonist. Thus, instead of a relationship of pedagogical eros being projected onto a pair, here, it is imparted by the girl herself as we watch her objectify Sister Imelda's habit-covered body in a way that, we might argue, would be done chiefly by a girl with serious homosexual inclinations, especially considering how much of this woman is veiled (not even her eyebrows are allowed to show). When Sister Imelda first enters their classroom (to teach geometry), however, the girl watches the nun with her eyes lingering on Sister Imelda's few visible sensual traits. Her eyes "were blue-black and full of verve. Her lips were very purple, as if she had put puce pencil on them. They were the lips of a woman who might sing in a cabaret, and unconsciously she had formed the habit of turning them inward, as if she, too, was aware of their provocativeness" (2239). Further, beyond the pleasures of her body the girl responds to the excitement of Sister Imelda's bearing, "Some days, when her eyes were flashing, she looked almost profane and made me wonder what events inside the precincts of the convent caused her to be suddenly so excited" (2340). These words are not the words of a youth pressured into queer desires by the lack of boys in a convent school: her friend, Baba, seems completely immune to the romance the protagonist finds in Sister Imelda's charms. Responding to the girl's question of "Hasn't she wonderful eyes" (noting to herself that they were "like blackberries, large and soft and shiny"), Baba looks at the nun more critically, noting that there is "something wrong in the upstairs department," but pragmatically adds that "with makeup Imelda would be a cinch" (2340). Baba confirms her lack of romantic influence by later asserting that Sister Imelda "was a right lunatic" to return to the convent after attending the university (2340). But the protagonist is unswayed in her growing attraction to the nun. She watches her, she emulates her. She describes her "almost like a ghost who passed the boundaries of common exchange and who crept inside one, devouring so much of one's thoughts, so much of one's passion, invading the place that was called one's heart" (2340–41). Recognition here works differently than in *Doubt*. The girl's vision of Sister Imelda is not chiefly centered on the idea that, through emulating her, she might belong to an accepting, albeit undercover and unspoken queer community, however much the girl claims she wants to enter the convent. Rather than a queer companion on a journey to an acceptable celibacy, she views Sister Imelda directly as a queer object of desire: she is the penetrating ghost that perhaps the girl feels or wishes herself to be. It is not just Sister Imelda's position as nun, but contact with her as a queer woman that the girl begins cautiously and painfully to pursue.

Ironically, the girl notices Sister Imelda's extreme piety, which manifests through religious masochism: one morning she sees that one of the nun's "eyelids was red and swollen, as if she was getting a sty. [She] reckoned that she over-mortified herself by not eating at all" (2341). This role model is nearly the opposite of Donald Miller's then, and presents a different motivation toward religious celibacy. Donald Miller might eventually take three lumps of sugar and live a satisfactory, nonsexual life. O'Brien's protagonist, on the other hand, doesn't just see the restrictions and denials of the convent as a cover for queerness, but rather, they are a necessary sacrifice that could facilitate her approach of the object of her desires: "I saw in her some terrible premonition of sacrifice which I would have to emulate" (2341). Notably, the girl has not yet spoken of a religious vocation, and in the next breath observes, the way Sister Imelda "absently held the stick of chalk between her first and second fingers, the same as if it were a cigarette" (2341). Such a sudden and acute redirection of attention further connects the girl's incipient path toward religious life with an attraction, a hyperawareness, and a sensitivity to the movements and postures of her teacher's body. Unlike Donald, she does not seek a place of quiet, "queer" belonging; she wants to approach the source of her desires, despite the increasing pain that becomes associated with tension that separates them. During the sacrifices of Lent, for example, the girl explains that "yet in the thick of all these dreads I found myself becoming dreadfully happy. I had met Sister Imelda outside of class a few minutes and I felt there was an attachment between us" (2341). Here, the relationship and the sentiments directed from the nun toward the girl are filtered through the girl's recollection. Not only is Sister Imelda desirous, she is also careless and arguably manipulative of the girl's lack of power. For instance, the girl describes Sister Imelda cautiously searching out opportunities for contact with her. Clearly, the girl realizes that the nun actively desires her presence and is even willing to be cunningly indiscrete to forge their interactions, and even to show affection. The student recollects an instance where "once it [the feeling of mutual attachment] was on the grounds, when she [Imelda] did a reckless thing. She broke off a chrysanthemum and offered it to me to smell" (2341). Innocent as this gesture may seem, the girl clearly notes a breach in decorum that would usually prohibit girls and nuns from even from such simple acts. As she notes later, "Mostly the nuns were on silence and only permitted to talk during class" (2342).[6] Curiously, with the offering of a flower, Sister Imelda uses the ambiguous space of religious silence with her student to further a relationship of psychologically painful desire. This is not the only such moment the girl cites, and thus a reciprocity of intimacy develops between the two. It is an active, mutually sought, and arguably romantically charged connection, completely unlike the queer yet apparently nonerotic guardianship between Father Flynn and Donald Miller.

In the case of Flynn and Miller, their relationship is generally structured around the priest's response to the boy's need for protection and belonging. Violence in their sphere comes from the outside, whether through the boy's beatings by his rough father or in his being bullied by William London; likewise, Father Flynn experiences persecution, suspicion, and apparently libel by Sisters James and Aloysius for showing care for the boy (which in turn also causes the boy pain when Father Flynn is ousted from Saint Nicholas School and Parish). But in "Sister Imelda," violence comes from inside the relationship. As the aim of this teacher–student intimacy seems to be an almost unavoidable mutual attraction, which truly is taboo—unlike Father Flynn's queer paternalism toward Donald, these women are in a much more precarious and forbidden place when it comes to demonstrating any attachment. Almost as unavoidable as their attraction, then, is the violence that is attached to their resistance to it. This violence does not appear as intentional abuse or incitement of pain, but rather is the natural consequence of being in a situation where bodies and minds respond to each other in ways that are desired but forbidden and deprived of any means of expression. Thus as the student becomes "dreadfully happy," her happiness becomes grafted onto dread, pain, and deprivation, which substitute for union in moments when union is not possible. Though at times the girl suspects the Mother Superior has warned Sister Imelda about intimacy with students, the regulation and scrutiny of teacher–student proximity in "Sister Imelda" is largely self-enforced by the nun herself or, in rare cases, by the girl who longs for her but also fears the approach of her beloved nun.

Sister Imelda, who clearly does show the girl extra attention and develops an attachment, seems to enact this self-regulation by responding to the girl in ways that can only generate pain. When pain is the only potential for connection to the beloved, pain becomes eroticized. In "Sister Imelda," this equation makes for an almost unbearable incremental mounting of agony for the girl, who remains devoted to her nun regardless of the degree to which she is afflicted, or the "nothing" she frequently gets in return. O'Brien shows this peculiar dynamic on one occasion when Sister Imelda realizes that the girl lacks certain skills in geometry, the girl saying that it was "my worst subject, indeed a total mystery to me. [Sister Imelda] had not taught more than four classes when she realized this and threw a duster at me in rage. A few girls gasped as she asked me to stand up and make a spectacle of myself" (2341). After this attempt at humiliating the girl, the teacher "fled from the room" herself, with the other students calling the situation "a disgrace" and telling the protagonist to "write home and say [she] had been assaulted" (2341). However, the nun has clearly felt her own shame from the shame she inflicted, as indicated by her flight from the class. Additionally, the girl's response is one that quite maturely (and perhaps sadly, and clearly masochistically) puts the particulars of her humiliation aside, saying that instead of reporting an infraction, "all I wanted was to run after her and say that I was sorry to have caused her such distemper, because I knew dimly that it was as much to do with liking as it was with dislike . . . . there came a sort of speechless tenderness for her, and I might have known that I was stirred"

(2341–42). Baba harbors none of this romance and suggests getting Sister Imelda "defrocked" (2342).

The nun displays her own shame and regret in a cautious but fairly direct way later when she slips a "new holy picture" into the girl's prayer book on the sly, attached to her as a token of apology only by its surprise appearance and the clue on the back of "her beautiful ornate handwriting," which composed a quatrain about trusting "Him" in the midst of "dark doubts" when "to simply trust Him / Seems the hardest thing of all" (2342). Thus the relationship settles into a rhythm of fasting and feasting, of engagements in the most subtle pleasures that are still followed up with some type of penance or mortification. Pleasure, here, ensures pain.[7] But pain also stands in for love. Waxing mystical, O'Brien always presents these exchanges with the subtext, as with any test of faith, that affection between lover and beloved is present even when it appears to be absent (and even when it is between the queer pair of a convent-school girl and a nun).

As in *Doubt,* the relationship between the queer child and the queer celibate is, in some way, related to a surrogacy for a same-sex parental influence and affection. In one scene of "cookery class" with Sister Imelda, the girl watches the nun "sitting on the edge of a table swaying her legs" in what the girl again terms a "reckless" manner (2343). Here, the scene of baking, the aroma of the kitchen, prompted the girl to realize, as she says, "how hungry I was" (2343). Though she claims to be reminded of baking at home with her "mother testing orange cakes with a knitting needle and letting [her] lick the line of half-baked dough down the length of the needle," she also "wondered if [Sister Imelda] had supplanted [her] mother" (2343). Just as in *Doubt,* however, the association of pleasure-seeking and "sweet tooth" is made as Sister Imelda "bets" the girl has one, and pulls out some little tarts as a treat (2343). We might say (playfully) that there is a strange "communion" between the two in this scene, where the girl is hungry and the nun not only provides but, as the girl says, "watched me eat as if she herself derived some peculiar pleasure from it, whereas I was embarrassed about the pastry crumbling and the bits of blackberry jam staining my lips" (2343). As a parallel, we may recall the significance of "communion" in *Doubt,* and the disruption of the Communion proper, and along with it, the metaphoric communion that takes place when Donald is removed from the altar guild and taken out of Father Flynn's protection. However, unlike the (arguably false) assumptions of predations in *Doubt,* both of O'Brien's characters dabble in the predatory, but being masochists restricted by their strict religious context, stop short of an actual pounce. If the reader recalls the earlier scenes where the girl describes Sister Imelda's lips as "stained" and her eyes as "berries," we can easily view this scene as one of mutual, though immaculate, consumption. But part of the consequence of the hands-free union is that, as the moment passes, the girl has an epiphany: "It was clear to me then that my version of pleasure was inextricable from pain; that they existed side by side and were interdependent, like two forces of an electric current" (2343). Despite this epiphany, scenes of approach and reproach, union and separation, continue throughout the story. The pair continues to exchange symbolic and metonymic gifts. These vary but include actions of potential erotic interpretation: a religious item "slipped" someplace secret, like a medal into the girl's pocket. Or, conversely, they include gifts with some phallic, yonic, or otherwise potentially erotic signification themselves, like bananas or chocolate given by the girl to her nun. At another point, Sister Imelda's gift of a pencil sharpener and an orange to the girl (who is in the sick ward with the flu) recalls again the citrus associated with her mother, but as the girl sits in bed smelling the peels she has saved as relics, she daydreams of communicating with her nun and not her mother (2349).

It is no surprise that neither of these stories end well for the queers. Despite the fact that they take on radically different trajectories, both stories depict queer youths looking for a mirror, a place to belong, and some type of love and nurturing in a way that validates what they sense—beyond language—to be their oddness. Both Donald Miller and "the girl" therefore struggle against their ill-fitting present that is, in both cases, filled with the subversive and obvious lessons on how to become straight, or at least to avoid being queer in any sense that cannot be accounted for or appropriated by the language or religious environment at hand. Donald Miller in *Doubt* is surrounded by hormonally charged, early teens who are all instructed in boy–girl dancing lessons. The boys are routinely set down to have "man-to-man" talks with Father Flynn over snacks, about growing up and getting girls—while other subversive instructions toward heteronormativity come with scenes of kids busy flirting on the sly, like William

London or Noreen Horan (who insists on breaking dress codes by wearing a barrette and can't be kept away from the boys).[8] Donald is set apart in this environment and benefits from his identification with Father Flynn, but ultimately Sister Aloysius is able to intimidate the priest out of the school and parish with her "certainty" over his guilt, despite the doubts of everyone around her (85). If anything, it robs Donald of this queer mentor. Thus he is also potentially robbed of his queer future as a priest. This loss displaces Donald from the non-heteronormative space he had begun to establish for himself as a vulnerable black boy in the Bronx in 1964, a space Father Flynn had helped to fill with the validation and love that Donald was unable to get from his own father.

Likewise, O'Brien's girl is obviously constantly badgered by Baba, being teased over giving too much attention to Sister Imelda. Like Donald, O'Brien's protagonist plans to enter religious life. Though unlike him, as she plans to become a nun (interestingly, at the suggestion of Sister Imelda), she also knows there is something insufficient about this life for her and the love she seeks. Instead of seeking a place of belonging, as Donald does, she feels overcome with the need for romantic fulfillment. For her, the convent just seems to place her in too close of proximity to the thing she desires but can also never really have. Sister Imelda is not offered much of a voice in defending her attachments, nor, like a good nun, does she take one. Other than her gifts to the girl, and the secret revelation that her hair color is black as a reward for the girl's completing work in geometry after the last exam, Sister Imelda's only direct statements on the issue are to tell the girl "You know it's not proper for us to be so friendly" and "We must not become attached" (2346). Of these painful rejections, the girl reminds us, "I could not say we already were [attached], no more than I could remind her of the day of revels and the intimacy between us" (2346). We can argue the girl is not harmed maliciously by this mentorship or her intimacy with her teacher. It seems apparent that her understanding of the violence this tense relationship entails is mature and patient enough, since most romances involve pain of some sort. But ultimately, when she decides not to enter the convent, we can infer that it may be because she realizes that this space that had nurtured her identification with and discovery of queer desires also sadly precludes their fulfillment at any material level.[9] Just so, she goes off to the university with Baba after their graduation, with implications of her growing into a state of heteronormativity after abandoning her correspondence with Sister Imelda by the end of the summer. Thus without the language to identify as queer, without a discernable subculture to enter, and with the hurt of being robbed of both dreams and love, these children are both introduced to and denied queer identities and alternative potentialities of being by the Church. But in each case, their pain comes from a sort of a doctrinal tease, where they seek to crack the code of the open secret and are both punished for their precocity, innocence, and love—all of which run contrary to that which is allowed for "the child" or the always-queer celibate, who are expected to always couch their identities within an imitation of the normative, reproductive family.

Significant to the rhetoric of the Church is that the preservation and elevation of the non-heteronormative sanctuary of monastic or clerical life may control "the deviant" to some extent, but considering that deviance is statistically not related to deviant harm of children but is undoubtedly related to the rejection of a heteronormative lifestyle, this method of control ironically forces the translation of non-heteronormative impulses into the language of religious vocation—or calling from God. Queer marriage to Jesus offers the holiest and most revered (if not also the most precarious) positions in the church. And yet, in these stories, it leads to pain and humiliation because these marriages to Jesus seem to have multiple possibilities in how they can extend to other forms of love that, because of their lack of heteronormativity, result in suffering for those who dare to attempt them. Yet Sister Imelda specifically instructs the girl along these lines when she tells her that "humiliation was the greatest test of Christ's love, or indeed *any* love" (2348).

Thus it is fitting when in the end of *Doubt,* in Father Flynn's last Mass (offered during the Christmas season), the choir sings the hymn "Ubi caritas." This hymn is traditionally sung on Maundy Thursday when the priest washes the feet of his parishioners; this is the day before Good Friday, on which no Mass is offered and the Crucifixion of Jesus is commemorated through ritualized participation in the Stations of the Cross.[10] As the song (when continued past this initial line) is meant to translate to "Where love and loving kindness are, God is in their midst" (Kaldis, 37), we can also reinterpret this statement to prompt key questions: Where is love, precisely, when it comes to caring for children? Where is love when it comes to queer children and queer celibates? Is it allowed at all, and can it have a future? Speaking to Sister James, Father Flynn suggests it can, in a bold appeal for her understanding:

> FLYNN: You care about your class! You love them, don't you?
>
> SISTER JAMES: Yes.
>
> FLYNN: And that's natural. How else would you relate to children? That I can know in your face. It's your philosophy. It's kindness.
>
> SISTER JAMES: I don't know. I mean, of course.
>
> FLYNN: There are people who go after your humanity, Sister. They tell you the light in your heart is a weakness. Don't believe it. It's an old tactic by cruel people to kill kindness in the name of virtue. There's nothing wrong with love.
>
> SISTER JAMES: Love?
>
> FLYNN: Have you forgotten the message of our Savior? It's love of people. (60–61)

However, because of the fact that it is the regulation, surveillance, and prejudgment of open (and queer) adult–youth expressions of affection that seems to be the root of violence in these texts, it would seem that the overall answer about whether queer celibates can hope to freely and supportively show care for children without suspicion is no. But this answer, at this time, appears to be based on popular fears of "queers" that ignore the data that shows there are just as many queerly celibate and religious adults who do not hurt children as there are "safe" adults in the general population. Thus perhaps celibates are not the root of society's child abuse problems; in fact society's child abuse problems may flourish because of biases that give celibates inordinate attention. The two stories discussed here each contain a different tragedy. "Sister Imelda" shows how institutional violence manifests itself as pain as a result of internalized homophobia, especially when pain is substituted for pleasure. "Sister Imelda" suggests that the potential for sexual abuse does undeniably exist for religious celibates, as it does for anyone. *Doubt,* on the other hand, reveals that accepting violence as the only end to celibate–child relations is a mistake—and that projected, externalized "queerophobia" and "celibatophobia" are equally a problem that is dangerous and harmful to children. Indeed, there are queer children who seek, and can safely benefit from, the identification with these queer adults, no matter what choices these children may make in the future. In any case these texts show, in both beautiful and painful ways, how entering the closet of the confessional or convent does not necessarily result in a pine box. Rather, such spaces can have at least the potential to be places where a child's unusual difference can play out safely—allowing for hope for a personal future based on his or her own uniqueness.

Hailey Haffey is a Steffensen Cannon Fellow and PhD candidate at the University of Utah, where she received the College of Humanities Graduate Research Award in 2016. Her dissertation focuses on the relationships between childhood, sexuality, and religion in Modernist literature. She has published essays in *Cultural Critique, Joyce Studies Annual,* and *The Year's Work in Medievalism.*

Notes

1. According to Wingert, Allen said a "conservative estimate is one in 10," while "Margaret Leland Smith . . . says her review of the numbers indicates it's closer to 1 in 5. But in either case, the rate of abuse by Catholic priests is not higher than these national estimates" (1).

2. The "ghostly gay child" whom Stockton describes shows that "the figure of the child does not fit children" (6).

3. Also note here that direct quotations from the film are taken from Shanley's screenplay. Stockton discusses children "queered by color" extensively in *The Queer Child* in "Chapter 5: Oedipus Raced, or the Child Queered by Color" (183).

4. Here, "polished" seems to indicate a type of manicured buffing; they are not literally colored in the film, or likely intended to be in the screenplay. Regardless, they are consistently and unsettlingly feminine to onlookers.

5. The additional queerness imparted to Catholic monasticism and clergy—by nuns who frequently adopt masculine names like "Sister James," or priests who go by names like "Father Mary Michael," etc.—is something that likely deserves more attention in another study on celibacy and queerness.

6. The vow of "celibacy" in the Catholic Church is generally taken to mean a refraining from all intimate relationships, not only those of a sexual or romantic nature, so that the individual can privilege their relationship with God above all earthly relations.

7. This seems to run opposite of a key point from Gilles Deleuze, who contends that for masochists the deferral of pleasure through pain is an assurance of pleasure to come: "The masochist must undergo punishment before experiencing pleasure. It would be a mistake to confuse this temporal succession with logical

causality: suffering is not the cause of pleasure itself but the necessary precondition for achieving it" (89).

8. It doesn't take too careful of an ear to pick up on the idea that Horan's name sounds a lot like "whore," and thus the film also advocates normative sexual development as it cautiously notes that even "normative" development must be bound by the restraint of sexual appetites. Another reading might look at the "queering" of the precocious "Miss Horan," but this is outside the scope of my study here.

9. This ending is akin to what Stockton describes as the finale of masochism: "It starts with a dream and ends with the end of a cycle of sufferings—a cycle that stops when the sufferings become *too much* for masochism" (73).

10. All of this preparation is part of the Lenten cycle that leads up to the celebration of Christ's Resurrection on Easter Sunday.

Works Cited

BBC News Europe. 2014. "Pope Francis: 'About 2%' Catholic Clergy Paedophiles." July 13. http://www.bbc.com/news/world-europe-28282050.

Bersani, Leo. 2010. *"Is the Rectum a Grave?" and Other Essays.* Chicago: University of Chicago Press.

Deleuze, Gilles. 1991. *Masochism.* New York: Zone Books.

Dinshaw, Carolyn. 1994. "A Kiss Is Just a Kiss: Heterosexuality and Its Consolations in *Sir Gawain and the Green Knight.*" *Diacritics* 24, nos. 2–3: 205–26.

Edelman, Lee. 2004. *No Future: Queer Theory and the Death Drive.* Durham: Duke University Press.

Kaldis, Cynthia. 1999. *Latin Music through the Ages.* Vol. 1. Reprint. Wauconda, Ill.: Bolchazy-Carducci.

Love, Norma, and Holly Ramer. 2011 "D. J. Bettencourt: Bishop McCormack a 'Pedophile Pimp.' *Huffington Post,* April 1. https://www.huffingtonpost.com/2011/04/01/dj-bettencourt-bishop-joh_n_843911.html.

Muñoz, José Esteban. 2009. *Cruising Utopia: The Then and There of Queer Futurity.* New York: New York University Press.

O'Brien, Edna.1993. "Sister Imelda." In *The Norton Anthology of English Literature.*Vol. 2. 6th ed. Ed. M. H. Adams. New York: W. W. Norton. (Orig. pub. 1981.)

Raab, Laruen. 2014. "Did Pope Francis Really Say 2% of Catholic Clergy Are Pedophiles?" *Los Angeles Times,* July 13. http://www.latimes.com/world/europe/la-fg-wn-pope-francis-pedophile-priests-20140713-story.html.

Sexson, Lynda, dir. 2008. *My Book and Heart Shall Never Part.* Corona Productions.

Shanley, John Patrick. 2005. *Doubt: A Parable.* New York: Theatre Communications Group, Inc.

Shanley, John Patrick, dir. 2008. *Doubt.* Godspeed Productions; Scott Rudin Productions.

Shanley, John Patrick. N.d. *Doubt.* Screenplay. millarprescott.com/screenplays/doubt.pdf.

Stein, Gertrude. 1990. *Four Saints in Three Acts.* In *Selected Writings of Gertrude Stein,* 577–612. New York: Vintage Books. (Orig. pub. 1928.)

Stockton, Kathryn Bond. 2010. *The Queer Child, or Growing Sideways in the Twentieth Century.* Durham: Duke University Press.

Wingert, Pat. 2010. "Mean Men." *Newsweek,* April 10. http://www.newsweek.com/2010/04/07/mean-men.html.

THE OUTLAW-KNIGHT

LAW'S VIOLENCE IN *THE FAERIE QUEENE, THE MAN WHO SHOT LIBERTY VALANCE,* AND *THE DARK KNIGHT RISES*

Cynthia Nazarian

In Christopher Nolan's 2012 film *The Dark Knight Rises,* the hero begins as an outlaw, and an outlaw masquerades as a hero. Their names, Wayne and Bane, rhyme; they belong to the same secret martial order; both wear masks and love the same woman. As the plot unfolds these figures move between the same spaces, appropriating each other's weapons and motivations. Although the film embeds them in an allegorical discourse in which one represents justice and the other uncontrolled violence, their differences are often surprisingly minor. Legal and political theorists as varied as Walter Benjamin, Robert Cover, and Giorgio Agamben have asserted the inseparability of law and violence. In the modern state, Benjamin claims, "all violence as a means is either lawmaking or law-preserving" (287). How, then, does the state's violence distinguish itself from others, and how does it come to legitimize its own vision of law as "justice"?

The problem is far older than Nolan's film. This essay explores a figure I term the "outlaw-knight," a curious hybrid who reappears from the early days of modern statehood to uncover a fundamental indeterminacy at the heart of state-sanctioned law and violence. The outlaw-knight is a fantasy of political nostalgia, one that reifies the processes and problems of modern state formation by turning to an idealized form of feudalism. This figure marks periods of political change with a backward-looking critique of modern statehood through the figure of the individual aristocratic hero. It appears in the early modern period notably as the Knight of Justice in Edmund Spenser's *The Faerie Queene* (1596), written at a pivotal point of nostalgia for a feudal aristocratic past amid the centralization of the sixteenth-century Tudor monarchy. The outlaw-knight persists in modern cultural forms like the

American Western and superhero films, reifying the conflicts between violence and the law in the modern democratic state. A look at Book 5 of Spenser's *Faerie Queene*, John Ford's *The Man Who Shot Liberty Valance* (1962), and Christopher Nolan's *The Dark Knight Rises* (2012) will illustrate how, in varied historical and political circumstances, the outlaw-knight returns to mediate clashes between rival laws, rival forms of violence, and rival symbolic interpretations, asserting the hybridity and indeterminacy of the state's means for dealing with threats to its sovereignty.

As an early modernist, I want to argue for the importance of addressing precursors and histories of both political concepts and aesthetic figurations in modern cultural forms. Parsing their politics without also examining the past that these works call up and strategically idealize or misrepresent provides only a partial view of their artistry and political maneuvering. Although there are other examples of the outlaw-knight, I have chosen these three very different texts because of fundamental similarities in their genre and mode. First, all three of these works politicize nostalgia, idealizing a premodern past in order to criticize their contemporary politics. Furthermore, they romanticize the *same* past, the European chivalric Middle Ages. Second, these three works rely on fundamental similarities in genre and narrative technique, which they derive from that premodernity. They are nostalgic not only in their themes and figures but, much more intrinsically, at the level of their form. The epic-romance genre of *The Faerie Queene*, shared by the two films, particularly suits reflection on statehood in transition or under threat. Combining the wandering narratives, amorous escapades, aristocratic subjects, and heroic ascendancies of romance[1] with the nation-building, collectivizing concerns of epic, *The Faerie Queene*'s mixed genre is inherently backward looking.[2] The heroism of the aristocratic individual is the central drama of all three works considered here, told in the form of quest narratives that deliberately project modern political concerns onto medievalized but equally politically freighted narrative landscapes. Third, all three of these works write epic-romance in the allegorical mode: their narratives follow emblematic dynamics in which characters are clearly referential, figuring larger social and political ideas.[3]

I propose that Ford's and Nolan's films ought to be read not as mythographic or as symbolic, but as distinctly allegorical—a mode that saw its heyday in medieval and early modern texts such as Spenser's *Faerie Queene*. American Westerns have often been read as mythologizing, based on André Bazin's influential work in the early 1950s (140–57). However, these films do not generally share the central characteristics of myth, which are the supernatural or divine. Their protagonists are often heroic and self-sacrificing, but they are also distinctly human. Furthermore, Ford and Nolan's heroes are fundamentally flawed and ambiguous in crucial ways that belie their suitability as symbols. There is an obviousness, even an inevitability in the connection between the symbol and its referent that is lacking here. In contrast to the symbol's intelligibility, allegory traffics in deliberate obfuscation. Spenser famously described his poem as "a continued Allegory, or dark conceit," emphasizing the opacity and artificiality that link allegory to the enigma or the parable (2007, 714). I want to suggest that Ford and Nolan, like Spenser, build neither myths nor symbols but allegories, and that this allegorical mode is crucial to the theoretical claims that all three works make about law, violence, and justice.[4] Examining the techniques of allegorical image-making in Spenser's long poem alongside them unlocks parallel strategies in the two modern films.

It is the distance between tenor and vehicle within allegory that creates the potential for counterinterpretation.[5] This instability in possible meanings is central to the outlaw-knight's function of revealing the confusion at the heart of legal violence. This essay suggests that in a world of conflicting claims, the state monopolizes interpretation and creates symbolic images to distinguish its force from ones it has termed "outlaw." In short, it is with the outlaw-knight's help that the victor's law rewrites itself and its violence as "justice"—not simply law, but an ethically anointed vision of it. However, the knight's very methods of counterinterpretation will be turned against him when the state seeks to wash its hands clean of the violence employed on its behalf. Thus, as the works under discussion here progress further and further away from the feudalism they idealize, the fantasy of the outlaw-knight will become more and more politically nostalgic, and tragic, mourned in the present of centralized state authority and its problematic fictions.

The outlaw-knight acts as an agent of the state that will eventually destroy him; in this way, he represents a double-pronged critique, from within and without, of the costs of modern state formation to aristocratic (and liberal) models of heroism and agency. Although there are other examples of the outlaw-knight, *The Faerie Queene*, *The Man Who Shot Liberty Valance*, and *The Dark Knight Rises* highlight the utility of the outlaw-knight figure in conceptualizing and critiquing state violence at moments of transition or threat. Each emerged in periods of war and internal as well as external political stress. Book 5 of Spenser's *Faerie Queene* was published late in Elizabeth I's reign, when domestic economic pressures were at a peak and conflicts with Spain and in the Netherlands and Ireland had taken their political and financial toll. Ford's *The Man Who Shot Liberty Valance* appeared during the American Civil Rights Movement, in the midst of the Cold War, following the Bay of Pigs Invasion and in the early days of U.S. military escalation in Vietnam. Nolan's *The Dark Knight Rises* opened during U.S. combat operations in Afghanistan, a few months after the final withdrawal of American troops from Iraq. Furthermore, the screenplay was written amid the Arab Spring uprisings and the Occupy Wall Street movement of 2011. References to these surrounding conflicts appear in all three works. This suggests that cultural forms call up the outlaw-knight in times of political pressure, to evaluate statehood that appears threatened or in transition. The outlaw knight materializes to rescue the nascent or threatened state, supplying the sword with which to impose its otherwise impotent law.

THE KNIGHT'S SAVAGE JUSTICE

Spenser's *Faerie Queene*, published in two installments in 1590 and 1596, was dedicated to England's Elizabeth I, whom it figures as its titular Faerie Queen. The poem comprises six books, each about a knight who embodies a particular virtue: holiness, temperance, chastity, friendship, justice, and courtesy respectively. The focus of my study is Book 5, which is alone in exploring a public, political virtue. Titled "The Legend of Justice," Book 5 is particularly fraught with foreign conflict. Numerous Spenserian scholars have maintained that Irish politics shape *The Faerie Queene*, and Book 5 in particular. The poem's natural landscape closely resembles sixteenth-century Ireland, where Spenser was a landowner and farmer. He also served as secretary and later as apologist for Arthur Grey, 14th Baron Grey de Wilton, Elizabeth I's Lord Deputy of Ireland from 1580–82, who was responsible for some of the most brutal repressions of the Irish populace resisting Tudor rule during the Desmond Rebellion. In their evaluations of the violence in Spenser's poem, scholars have generally sought to downplay or else to lament the poet's apparently unsavory positions.[6] However, violence haunts Book 5 in part because Spenser ties it inseparably to the practice of justice itself. As I will argue, violence is not only the outcome of lawlessness in *The Faerie Queene*; it is in fact central to legal thought and practice.

It is no coincidence that the particularly bloody Irish landscape of Book 5 introduces our outlaw-knight, a hybrid of savagery and justice, and his role in marshaling an indeterminate, ethically questionable violence on behalf of the state's law against the "lawless" forces that threaten it from without. The Knight of Justice turns to symbolic representations to cement the state's vision of rule against those of its rivals. However, like the allegorical mode of *The Faerie Queene* itself, these remain equally murky, equally reinterpretable by the very forces that the state seeks to exclude in establishing its supremacy.

The Faerie Queene privileges the aristocratic agent over the state; furthermore, its nostalgia is specifically and politically medievalizing: an absentee Faerie Queen allows her knights to carry out the tasks of government in a feudal vision of devolved rule. However, by the time of the poem's composition, Britain was well on its way to acquiring most elements of modern statehood, and an increasingly centralized monarchy supported by a robust bureaucracy challenged the upper nobility at the levers of power. In short, a "knight of justice" was already obsolete, a figure of melancholic fantasy. In Spenser's world, the form of devolved, aristocratic governance the poem idealizes was already a practical impossibility. Nonetheless the poem's feudal nostalgia functions as a trenchant critique of centralized Tudor statehood.

This critique is crystallized in the figure of Sir Arthegall, the Knight of Justice, who is the subject of Book 5.[7] His story opens with a long discussion of the decline and corruption of the present age, in which virtue and vice have changed places. The poet defends his turn toward the past and an 'antique' age, when men sought virtue for its own sake. Even in this idealized past, however, the Knight of Justice is a deeply ambiguous figure. Raised by the goddess Astraea in the wilderness, he first learns to practice judgments "upon wild beasts" (5.1.7.8). Faerie lond's uncultivated terrain embodies the Hobbesian state of nature—unregulated and ungovernable, it harbors monstrous beings in its depths. The poem's knights must push back that lawless frontier in order to enforce the queen's justice. Sir Arthegall, however, simultaneously occupies both the world of the court and the untamed terrain of Faerie. His shield is emblazoned with the ambiguous motto *Salvagesse sans finesse* (4.4.39.9), which can be interpreted as "wildness without guile" but also as "barbarity without discretion." Furthermore, Arthegall is accompanied on his quest by an "yron man" named Talus who carries an iron flail and executes much of the violence that the knight's justice requires. An embodiment of the uncompromising *lex talionis,* Talus must often be restrained from wholesale slaughter. Nonetheless, he is a necessary companion to the Knight of Justice, a reminder that Spenser himself advocated extremely unsavory practices, including mass starvation, to keep the Irish populace in line in his political treatise, *A View of the State of Ireland*. In the *Faerie Queene,* Spenser also ties his concept of justice especially closely to the violence that enforces and preserves it. Sir Arthegall must be especially well armed, as justice is impotent "Unlesse it be perform'd with dreadless might. / For power is the right hand of Justice truly hight" (5.4.1.8–9).

It is generally held that the Knight of Justice's armor, overgrown with foliage and moss, marks him as a threshold figure between wilderness and courtly politics, between savagery and civilization.[8] His hybridity magnifies the multivalence of allegory itself. Rather than demonstrating the *discordia concors*—the reconciliation of disparate elements in harmonious union—that Spenser uses elsewhere in his poem, Arthegall's appearance is deliberately jarring and instead highlights its own ambiguity and the potential for competing interpretations. Book 5 blends savagery and civilization, villainy and heroism in Arthegall because it depends on the deep ambiguity of his chivalric violence.[9] For all its talk of "justice", its knight enforces law with a brutality that often mimics that of his enemies. Although Spenser's poem posits no distinction between justice and the Faerie queen's law, its nostalgic fantasy of the devolved Faerie state works to suggest the alienation of justice from law in the real politics of Elizabethan England. Andrew Hadfield's recent biography of the poet, building on a rich body of criticism exploring *The Faerie Queene*'s politics,[10] emphasizes Spenser's lifelong polemical engagements with powers that be (2012). The Legend of Justice questions the means by which the state's law is imposed, through telling moments that indicate other possible interpretations, alternative laws overwritten with the language of lawlessness.

For example, early in Book 5, Arthegall defeats the Saracen Pollente, who preys on knights who wish to cross his bridge; he fights and drowns those who refuse to pay his toll in the river beneath.[11] Hearing of this grave injustice, the Knight of Justice arrives to defeat Pollente. He does so by using the latter's very own tactics against him. Arthegall drops the villain through his own trapdoor, battles him in the water, and throws his corpse just where Pollente cast his knightly victims. Spenser deliberately blurs distinctions between the Knight of Justice and the villain, since in destroying Pollente, Arthegall in fact imitates him. After he has disposed of the Saracen, Arthegall and Talus find the Saracen's beautiful daughter and kill her too, severing her hands and feet, which they "nailed on high, that all might them behold" (5.2.26.9). Munera's dismemberment echoes an earlier episode, one in which Arthegall killed an evil knight named Sanglier to punish him for decapitating a lady. Thus, Arthegall's bloody judgment of Munera mirrors the crime committed by one of *The Faerie Queene*'s evil figures. In this way, the poem asserts a crucial confusion between the forces in conflict: the Knight of Justice's violence appears for all intents and purposes indistinguishable—both ethically and practically—from the outlaw's.

In *The Faerie Queene,* violence is necessary not only for the maintenance of justice; it is also central to legal *practice.* Robert Cover argues that legal judgment "takes place in a field of pain and death" (1992b, 203). In every act of legal interpretation, a judge must "kill off" alternate understandings of law in order to assert one above them; Cover terms this the "jurispathic" nature of legal judgment (1992a, 155). Although Book 5 repeatedly describes its evil characters as lawless, every judgment that Sir Arthegall renders showcases what is in fact a conflict between competing authorities, each lawmaking, each proposing a distinct vision of rule. In fact, Arthegall's every legal interpretation is brutal, and his every act of brutality is a legal interpretation. In this light, the specifics of Pollente's crime are revealing: "Over his Bridge, albee he rich or poor, / But he him makes his passage-penny pay: / Else he doth hold him back or beat away" (5.2.6.3–5). Pollente infringes on the state's monopoly on taxation by levying an unauthorized charge "according to the custom of [his] law" (5.2.11.7). The very existence of this other law is the problem: rather than a fight against lawlessness, Arthegall's violent judgment is in fact a jurispathic act—it destroys Pollente's law in order to affirm its own.[12] Telling moments such as this one, his encounter with the Egalitarian Giant, the Amazon Radigund, and the allegedly "lawless" Souldan, all point to what are alternative laws deliberately characterized by the state as lawlessness. In each of these cases, Arthegall performs an act of simultaneously lawmaking and law-destroying violence, which forces these figures and their older laws out into the landscape, past the frontiers of the *civitas*. Like this violence, law in *The Faerie Queene* is fundamentally agonistic; the outlaw-knight's combat embodies the competition between rival visions of rule that appear ethically indistinguishable.

How, then, does a single vision of law among others rise to the ethical order of justice? Spenser's poem points again to an ambivalent and unruly solution: a retrospective process of symbolism and interpretation that is constantly vulnerable to counter. When he has killed Pollente, Arthegall throws the body into the river but keeps the head, pitching it on a pole, "Where many years it afterwards remained, / To be a mirror to all mighty men / In whose right hands great power is contained, / That none of them the feeble overrun, / But always do their power within just compass pen" (5.2.19.5–9). Turning Pollente's head into a potent sign, Arthegall's jurispathic violence reinterprets itself as justice retrospectively. Similarly, after his defeat of the Souldan, Arthegall hangs his weapons on a tree "To all 'mongst whom this story should be spoken / [. . .] / To be a monument for evermore" (5.8.44.4–45.3). The "monument" made of Souldan's arms, like Pollente's head, cements a particular interpretation of the knight's violence as just. The episode once more showcases the state's lawmaking violence that prevails by violent force, followed by an *after-the-fact* legitimation through symbols of "justice" that are fundamentally artful and artificial.

It is difficult to imagine how messages as complex as these can be read in a decapitated head, or in suspended weaponry. Rather than supporting its knight's violent image-making, Book 5 instead draws attention to their vulnerability to counterinterpretation: in them it preserves traces of the indistinguishability of the state's violence and the criminal's, just as it does in the symbolism of Arthegall's own appearance. The instability and questionable ethics of this interpretive process coalesce in the figure of Malfont, whose tongue is nailed to a post for having slandered, ironically, a ruler named Mercilla:

> Thus there he stood, whilst high over his head,
> There written was the purport of his sin,
> In cyphers strange, that few could rightly read,
> BON FONT: but *bon* that once had written been,
> Was raced out, and *Mal* was now put in.
> So now *Malfont* was plainly to be read. (5.9.26.1–6)

A war of legal interpretation takes place over the "monument" of the poet's brutalized body. One explanation "in cyphers strange" has been crossed out and another written over it. Carl Schmitt famously declared, "Sovereign is he who decides on the exception" (5); in *The Faerie Queene,* sovereign is he who interprets violence. Faerie lond's battles are fought by rival warriors doubling as rival poets. Nonetheless, in the process of overwriting—of replacing one interpretive vision with another—the allegorical poem uncovers the extent to which visions of law built on violence, rather than establishing ethical clarities, are in fact strangely indistinguishable.

The outlaw-knight draws attention to this ethical murkiness and also to the role of the heroic individual in cementing the state's interpretation above others. As a mixed state and nonstate actor, the outlaw-knight's dual position as royal envoy and aristocratic free agent allows him to cement the state's law by lending it his sword. His doing so allows the state to maintain a distance from the deeply ambivalent brutality on which it relies. Arthegall's armor, covered in vegetation, marks his simultaneous existence inside and outside the *civitas,* distinguishing him as the guardian and interpreter of that vulnerable boundary. That the large majority of his battles should pit him not against other knights but against tyrants and usurpers highlights his role in testing feudalism against alternative visions of centralized government. Indeed, as a figure of politicized nostalgia, he reflects on the processes and failures of modern state formation occurring, as Max Weber famously suggested, through the monopolization of the "legitimate" use of violence ("Politics as a Vocation").

The outlaw-knight is both complicit in and victimized by these processes. In the end, Arthegall receives no hero's welcome in Faerie lond but instead "ere he could reform it thoroughly, / He through occasion called was away, / To Faerie Court, that of necessity / His course of Iustice he was forst to stay" (5.12.27.1–4). Once the outlaw-knight has used his sword to impose and establish the state's vision of law as "justice", his violence must be expunged. Book 5 shows the ways in which the Knight of Justice is ultimately discredited, once he is no longer useful to the state, by the very means he had employed on its behalf. On his way back to the seat of royal power, Arthegall falls victim to the Blatant Beast, an allegorical embodiment of slander, which accuses the Knight of Justice of cruelty and bloodthirstiness.[13] The Blatant Beast is the only undefeated evil in *The Faerie Queene*. It is no coincidence that Book 5, filled with the lawmaking violence that imposes the state's governance, should leave unscathed an ungovernable foe whose power is its rival ability to counterinterpret the state's self-serving fictions, the Legend of Justice foremost among them.

BEYOND THE PICKETWIRE: NOSTALGIA AND COUNTERINTERPRETATION

The formal affinity between American Westerns and the romance genre has often been noted.[14] Their narratives are wandering rather than linear, and their characters fall into stock types imbued with metaphorical meaning: outlaw, lawman, homesteader, and so on. John Ford's *The Man Who Shot Liberty Valance* (1962) is especially true to romance form; it also shares *The Faerie Queene*'s epic concerns with founding the nation, and situates its narrative both in a heroic past and in a present time of mourning. Virtually every critic has remarked on the film's heavy freight of nostalgia; produced late in Ford's career and late in the history of the form, *Liberty Valance* is often read as an elegy for the Western itself. Yet, as in Spenser's poem, the melancholy of Ford's film also channels political critique, shedding harsh light on the self-serving fictions on which statehood relies. Here, the outlaw-knight reappears specifically at a moment of transitioning models of statehood (from "lawless" frontier to incorporation and statehood for the territory) to highlight the state's traffic in legends and the extent to which it proceeds by destroying the outlaw-knight and the independent heroism and aristocratic self-determination he represents.

The film's frame narrative establishes nostalgia as its primary method: it is recounted as a flashback by "the man who shot Liberty Valance," Senator Ransom Stoddard, who arrives in the town of Shinbone with his wife for the funeral of a forgotten man. When the local newsmen demand his reasons for returning, Stoddard recounts how, as a naive young lawyer from the East, he acquired heroic standing for having beaten a violent thug, Liberty Valance, in a gunfight. Contrary to his reputation, Stoddard reveals that it was the newly deceased man, a tough local rancher named Tom Doniphon, who really shot the outlaw and selflessly allowed the credit to go to him. Stoddard, profiting from his "heroic" killing of Valance, married Doniphon's sweetheart and went to Washington, eventually becoming senator of the newly created state. When present-day Stoddard asks the editor of the Shinbone Star whether he will publish the truth of who really shot Liberty Valance, the editor refuses and speaks the film's most famous line: "This is the West, sir. When the legend becomes fact, print the legend."

A comparison with Spenser's *Faerie Queene* highlights the deeply allegorical structure of Ford's film. The original short story by Dorothy M. Johnson contains none of the symbolic social engagements of Ford's version, such as Stoddard's legal career, Valance's attack on his law books, the involvement of the characters in the territory's bid for statehood, the calls for press freedom, and the rapid political and technological development of the town. Ford endows Johnson's characters with larger conceptual implications, and repeatedly provides clues for their interpretation. Lines such as Dutton Peabody's "Liberty Valance taking liberties with the liberty of the press" and his drunken embrace of the printing press "Wait for me, old servant of the public weal: our shining hour is yet to come" alongside the motto on the school's chalkboard "Education is the basis of law and order" signal the film's allegorical depth by inviting deeper interpretation.

A number of exciting studies have examined the politics of *The Man Who Shot Liberty Valance* in the context of the Kennedy administration, in particular in the wake of the Bay of Pigs Invasion of 1961. Alan Nadel points out the similarities between themes and narratives in western films and the crafting of U.S. foreign policy regarding Cuba (193–94). John McClure highlights Kennedy's own deft use of themes from both romance and the popular western genre in his New Frontier campaign (40–45). Kent Anderson also argues that "*Liberty Valance* encapsulates the spirit of a highly evolved mode of cinematic articulation, deconstructing the iconography that Kennedy was invoking" (11). It is perhaps not coincidental that after his assassination, further legend-making around the dead president should have also invoked the medieval fantasy of Camelot. In the wake of the disillusionment that was the Bay of Pigs incident, Ford's *Man Who Shot Liberty Valance* exploits the fundamental ambiguity of allegory not only in imagery and form but also at the level of its argument: as I will propose, it is at heart an exploration of competing legends, one that asserts the same uncertainty within the concepts of law, justice, and violence as Spenser's poem.

Joshua Foa Dienstag has recently explored the democratic state's reliance on extralegal acts of exclusion in Ford's film. He reads Stoddard as the initially impotent figure of the law, Liberty Valance as unrestrained outlaw violence, and Tom Doniphon as extralegal power that must cede its authority to Stoddard in the process of democratic state formation. As Dienstag notes, the figure of "the man who shot Liberty Valance" is an amalgam: "The talents of Stoddard and Doniphon have been combined into a single figure . . . a self-executing law—a self-sustaining sovereign—who now, with the face of Ransom, can continue the project of statehood" (304).[15] The process by which this single, combined figure comes into being, however, is not so evenhanded as Dienstag's reading implies. As an outlaw-knight, Doniphon is not joined with Stoddard, but appropriated and destroyed by him and the state he represents.

Like Arthegall with his overgrown, weedy armor, Doniphon unites the heroic individual enforcer with the horse rancher who lives apart from the *civitas* in the wilderness.[16] As such, he is another feudal fantasy opposed to a nascent centralized state that threatens his independence and livelihood, but must rely on his violence in order to establish itself. The violence of "the man who shot Liberty Valance," like Arthegall's, is lawmaking and law-selecting in character: his force "civilizes" the landscape and constitutes the town, establishing the state through a violent elimination of any rival forms of rule. This violence does so, again like Arthegall's, through its indistinguishability from the outlaw's brutality: Doniphon and Valance are both gunmen, both occasional visitors to the town rather than residents, both figures of authority, albeit with differing agendas. The film emphasizes how evenly matched they are in repeated standoffs. Although Valance is evidently a villain, Doniphon's gun is as difficult to differentiate from the outlaw's as Arthegall's sword was from Pollente's. As an outlaw-knight, "the man who shot Liberty Valance" covers the ruthless violence of the outlaw with the thin veneer of the state's civilizing justice.[17]

The outlaw's "lawlessness," like the knight's "justice," is again open to debate. As I have argued, Pollente, the Egalitarian Giant, Souldan, and the other rival rulers of Spenser's *Faerie Queene* assert what are in fact alternative laws that must be forced out in the conflict between barely distinguishable state and nonstate violence. However, Ford's film, unlike Spenser's poem, clearly separates law from justice, repeatedly emphasizing the ineffectual buffoonery of Shinbone's marshal. At the same time, it lays bare the law's impotence without the violence needed to impose and legitimate it. Like Spenser's poem, the film complicates distinctions between "lawless" landscape and "lawful" *civitas*. The newsman Peabody's speech nominating Ransom Stoddard to the territorial convention describes the area's evolution from

> the vast herd of buffalo and savage redskin roaming our beautiful territory with no law to trample them except the law of survival, the law of the tomahawk and the bow and arrow. And then with the westward march of our nation came the pioneer and the buffalo hunter, the adventurous and the bold. And the boldest of these were the cattlemen who seized the wide-open range for their own personal domain, and their law was the law of the hired gun.

Just as a close look at the language of Spenser's poem uncovered the alternate laws obscured by the state's accusation of "lawlessness," Peabody's contradictory formulation "no law . . . except the law" is revealing: what he terms "lawlessness" is in fact an older, rival law that the new order seeks to eradicate through a retrospective counterinterpretation. Liberty Valance is an outlaw only from the perspective of Shinbone's nascent statehood. In the eyes of the older law—the cattlemen's law—he is a Knight of Justice himself. The battle over Shinbone therefore rages not between Stoddard's law and Valance's violence, as the legend of "the man who shot Liberty Valance" implies, but rather between Doniphon's violence and Valance's law.

These two titans—one hired by the cattlemen, the other lending his might to a weak lawyer from the East—are the only ones on equal footing. The political fate of the town is decided by their combat. Both represent an older regime, another idealized feudalism that opposes the centralizing state: they are aristocratic free agents who marshal their own forces, but ally themselves with other interests. They are thanes, knights—feudal (Doniphon, who owns a small ranch) vs. errant (Liberty Valance, who lives "where I hang my hat").[18] Furthermore, each one embodies one of the halves of Arthegall's appearance: Valance is the unruly, uncontrollable knight of the feudal anarchy, whereas Doniphon is the honor-driven, self-governing knight of chivalric ideal. The rise of the modern state will require one of these knights to willingly collaborate with it, lend it his force, and allow himself to be destroyed by it.

As in Spenser's poem, the crucial battle in Ford's film is the one that rages between competing interpretations of violence. Although Ransom Stoddard rises to the status of hero by killing a man, at the moment of his nomination as territorial delegate, Dutton Peabody attempts to wipe that defining violence away. He does so by proposing a new symbolic interpretation: "He is a man who came to us *not packing a gun* but carrying instead a bag of law books. . . . He is a man who has come to be known throughout this territory in the last few weeks as a great *champion* of law and order" (emphases added). Peabody erases the very reputation for violence that brought Stoddard to prominence. Instead, he rewrites Stoddard as an allegorical Knight ("champion") of Justice, washed clean of outlaw violence.

As we saw, Spenser's allegorical poem highlighted the indeterminacy of lawmaking violence and its susceptibility to counter-interpretation; a closer look at Ford's work alongside Spenser's raises the parallel question of just who controls meaning in Shinbone. Although several scholars have raised doubts about Stoddard's reliability, on the whole, scholarship on *Liberty Valance* accepts Stoddard's tale at face value.[19] However, as many critics acknowledge, the film raises important questions about him and his narration. In addition to his unreliability and disagreeableness, this character tells his tale in especially suggestive circumstances: Stoddard mentions three times that he goes off with the newsmen to "talk politics." The whole story of Tom Doniphon is narrated not only retroactively but also in a deeply politicized setting, and behind closed doors: Stoddard leaves his wife and Doniphon's loyal servant, Pompey—the other witnesses to the events of the past—behind with the casket, entering a separate room with the newsmen and shutting the door between them before speaking.

However, the film's most important doubts about its own fictions are cast at the level of the camera's lens. In the shootout between Stoddard and Valance, the camera repeatedly alternates between their points of view in the technique called shot–reverse shot. Robert Ray argues that by later revealing that Doniphon was the real shooter, the film "discredited the most basic figure in Classic Hollywood's formal paradigm—the shot–reverse shot. The audience's acceptance of this figure had always depended on the tacit guarantee that nothing narratively important lay outside the seam of significance isolated from the larger space by shot–reverse shot patterns" (229). By placing Doniphon's revelation in the space excluded by the shot–reverse shot, Ray contends that Ford undermined the technique itself, and emphasized Stoddard's gains at Doniphon's expense (233). However, Ray's account of this cinematic sleight-of-hand cannot fully account for Ford's frame narrative: the rupture of the shot–reverse shot sequence could function identically if the story were told from a third-person, omniscient viewpoint. The combination of the frame narrative and the void created by Ford's disruption of the shot–reverse shot signals a deeper tear in the fabric of legend. It is crucial to note that the key scene that in which Doniphon reveals that he was the one who killed Liberty Valance is the only scene in which Doniphon and Stoddard are alone, with no witnesses to their interaction. Ford's opening frame narrative, and the sequence of narration in which a pompous politician "talks politics" and tells a well-known story only to undermine it, after the fact, with a key revelation excluded by the shot–reverse shot, proposes a different possibility.

I have suggested that Ford's film exhibits the formal characteristics of allegory. As such, its figures embody but simultaneously obscure their own deeper meanings. I would therefore like to argue for taking the film's doubts seriously, and to propose that Ford's film deliberately and repeatedly raises the possibility that Stoddard's retelling is a lie. *The Man Who Shot Liberty Valance* is first and foremost about the process of making legends: what if Senator Stoddard has returned to

Shinbone, the originating site of the "man who shot Liberty Valance" legend, in order to launch a counterinterpretation of the violence that founded the state? What if, like Arthegall who retroactively interpreted the violent symbols he made of his victims, Stoddard is attempting to rewrite murder as justice? What if the "fact" that Tom Doniphon was the shooter—revealed in the film's only unwitnessed encounter—is really his (and the democratic state's) attempt to wipe his hands clean of the brutality that propelled him to power?

Reading Ford's film as a counterinterpretation of lawmaking violence highlights other suggestive details. When Senator Stoddard first views the body, he becomes angry that Doniphon is being buried without his boots. He demands that the undertaker dress the dead man not only in his boots, but also in his gun belt and spurs.[20] The scene resembles the "monuments" that Arthegall creates from the bodies of his victims: by clothing him in symbolic arms and armor, Stoddard costumes Tom Doniphon as the outlaw-knight. However, the film emphasizes the artificiality of this staging with the former marshal's interjection, "He didn't carry no handgun, Ranse. He didn't for years."

Ford's narrative framework cues us to the deliberate ambiguity of his allegory, transforming his film into an exploration of competing interpretations of violence and its place in the state. The conflict here is not between legend and fact as the famous line suggests, but rather between legend and legend. On the one hand, accepting Stoddard's tale at face value suggests that it was Doniphon who, by shooting Liberty Valance, created the legend that brought the territory to statehood. On the other hand, in the reading I have suggested, the film offers the possibility that Stoddard is attempting to cover up the fact that he killed Valance himself by retroactively and posthumously staging Tom Doniphon as an outlaw-knight. Ford's narrative framework transforms everything said into reported speech, reinforcing what Tad Gallagher has noted as a bias toward Stoddard's point of view in the portrayal of characters and the camera's positioning (408–9). Although critics generally read Liberty Valance as evil and lawless, he too is an exaggerated caricature so shaped by Stoddard's narration, and the film often hints at similarities between him and Doniphon.

Beginning with its title, Ford's film draws attention to the fictions—the legends—that the state employs in legitimating its law over others. If we acknowledge the possibility that Stoddard may be attempting to turn Doniphon into a "monument" for his own ends, thus reifying the modern democratic state's need to exclude and overwrite the violence that founded it, then Ford's film goes beyond using nostalgia for mood; the film identifies it as a central method of propaganda. Spenser's poem used the outlaw-knight to argue for the devolution of the queen's power onto aristocratic agents, nostalgically idealizing a feudal power-sharing framework. It simultaneously examined the self-serving fictions on which the centralized state relies, aided by the outlaw-knight who collaborates with and then is destroyed by it. In Ford's film, nostalgia emphasizes the loss to the outlaw-knight and to the feudal vision of individual heroic agency that he represents, both ruined through his self-sacrifice on behalf of the state. Even if Doniphon did not kill Valance, he nonetheless gave up his fiancée, his social standing, and his way of life—a sacrifice that enables the territory's accession to statehood.

Through him, Ford's film highlights not only the political efficacy of legends, but more importantly the ways in which each new symbolic fiction overwrites and excludes a prior one, which it uses, then disavows. Stoddard's redressing and burial of Doniphon is an attempt to disavow the extralegal violence on which the senator's fame and the nascent state were based. In the present of narration, few know Tom Doniphon. It is Senator Stoddard who names him, stages his body, and attempts to overwrite the legend of "the man who shot Liberty Valance" by charging the corpse with the weight of its originary violence. Nostalgia also becomes the primary tool of this reinterpretation by not only legitimating a new legend but also establishing its appeal as a replacement for "fact." In the reading I have proposed, Stoddard's melancholy in the final scene on the train might be interpreted not as private mourning, but as political failure. The senator's decision not to pursue the vice presidency and to return instead to Shinbone shows how tenaciously old legends and old violence can cling.

GOTHAM'S LAWS AND OUTLAWS

Superhero stories often follow the formal narrative and thematic features of epic-romance discussed above. Their actions also have larger implications for the cities their violence protects: figures such as Superman, Spider Man, and Batman deploy an extralegal but state-sympathetic violence to combat disorder that the state itself cannot ever seem to adequately control. These are hybrid figures like Arthegall and "the man who shot Liberty Valance,"[21] at once outside the law and agents of it, susceptible to straying too far into the landscape. In *The Dark Knight Rises,* Jonathan and Christopher Nolan's script interrogates problems of law, violence, and sovereignty, offering insights into the role of violence and allegory in the maintenance of the modern state. Like John Ford, the Nolans recast existing Batman storylines into an allegorical mode. They turn the comic books' Bane into a nightmarish figurehead spouting the populist rhetoric of the Arab Spring and Occupy Wall Street movements of the early 2010s. The film gives Bane a new backstory of selfless love and self-sacrifice. The Nolans' Bane is brutal, but also thoughtful and complex, and visibly referential. The film provides clues for its own allegorical interpretation in references to Dickens's *Tale of Two Cities* and scenes that recall the *Terreur* courts of the French Revolution.

The film opens with Batman as an outlaw, falsely accused of murdering district attorney Harvey Dent. However, Dent himself is the criminal, whose murders the judicial authorities have covered up with Batman's help. While the police hunt Batman, they lionize Dent; the city passes laws in his name to repress crime and deny prisoners parole. With Batman tarred by the authorities as a criminal and murderer, the injured Bruce Wayne has turned recluse. From the depths of a foreign prison called "the Pit" carved deep in mountainous rock, a villain named Bane brings an army of fanatical mercenaries to Gotham, ostensibly to free its people from elite oppression and to wipe out corruption. He imprisons the police in the sewers and isolates the city, turning Gotham over to its inhabitants. Revealing the administration's deceit and cover-up of Harvey Dent's crimes, Bane opens Gotham's Blackgate Penitentiary and frees all the prisoners, most incarcerated under the Harvey Dent Act. He holds the city hostage by threatening to detonate a nuclear bomb, which he has stolen and repurposed from Wayne Industries.

I have suggested that Sir Arthegall reinterprets violence as "justice" retroactively, and that Ransom Stoddard has returned to Shinbone to similarly rewrite the legend of "the man who shot Liberty

Valance." Bane goes significantly further: he announces himself as a counter-interpreter of the state's symbols, a canny allegorical reader who sees through the city's self-serving fictions, on which its authority is built and without which it will crumble. Once Bane reveals the deceit at the heart of the city's law, the regime disintegrates; indeed, Nolan's villain asserts counterinterpretation as a central tool for political change. In the wake of his revelations, private property is abolished and administration figures are condemned in kangaroo courts. A disastrous first attempt against Bane leaves Batman crippled and imprisoned in the Pit; after two failed tries, Wayne escapes and returns to Gotham, freeing the imprisoned police. In their final confrontation, Batman defeats Bane but is stabbed by his lover, Miranda Tate, who is revealed as Bane's accomplice. Bane and Tate die, but Batman cannot disarm the bomb. Instead, he flies it out of the city into the watery horizon that surrounds Gotham. The explosion presumably kills Batman, although Wayne reappears anonymously at a café in Florence, indicating his survival. Gotham erects a statue of Batman, its new state hero, in city hall.

Like Spenser's Knight of Justice, Batman is a hybrid of "salvagesse" and lawmaking violence—but so is Bane. Nolan's hero and villain are both bandits exiled by the state; both are imprisoned in the Pit, the subterranean prison that parallels the Batcave.[22] Furthermore, at important moments the film hints that hero and villain employ the very same violence. Although Nolan's Batman claims not to kill, he allows others to kill for him and refuses to rescue those he condemns. When the bomb is being carried out over Gotham, police officer John Blake warns a group of orphans to "Put your heads down, this is it!" "No, No," one replies, "that's Batman." The mistake is easy to make; the rhyming of "Bane" and "Wayne," their masks, and their love for Miranda Tate also emphasize the similarities between the figures of "lawlessness" and "justice." Furthermore, Bane and Wayne share the same weapons: the bomb threatening Gotham City is a Wayne Industries invention, and Bane takes over the city by raiding Wayne Industries' store of military equipment. Committed to a romanticized feudalism in the form of its chivalric hero, the film does not question the right of an individual capitalist (Wayne) to amass uncontrollable military power entirely apart from the state. In fact, this private capacity for violence defines him as a knight, and the film explicitly names him as such. Nolan's Batman deploys a politicized chivalry that opposes Wayne's personal heroic code to the state's corrupt power. Bane, for his part, possesses the same standing and powers despite his populist rhetoric. Both he and Wayne were trained in Ra's al Ghul's exclusive League of Shadows, which Nolan figures in the first two films of his trilogy as a kind of chivalric corps. Bane also arrives with his own mercenary army, and lays siege to the city Batman protects. He is the errant knight to Wayne's feudal champion: once again, the aristocrat who collaborates with the modern city-state is the one who owns property rather than the errant, landless knight.

Like *The Faerie Queene* and *The Man Who Shot Liberty Valance*, Nolan's film reveals that what most endangers the state is not "lawlessness" but the threat of competing law. Bane arrives from "a more ancient part of the world." His courts are courts; his law replaces another admittedly corrupt law. Standing outside of Blackgate prison, Bane recalls Spenser's Egalitarian Giant, weighing all on scales to reestablish equality for the masses. His unmasking of the lie at the heart of the Dent Act is jurispathic; his violence is as law-destroying and lawmaking as that of the state, which will eventually prevail.[23] Exposing Dent as a criminal and murderer, Bane uncovers the violence at the heart of all law and the instability of justice as a symbolic concept. As Benjamin contends, "In the great criminal this violence confronts the law with the threat of declaring a new law, a threat that even today, despite its impotence, in important instances horrifies the public as it did in primeval times. The state, however, fears this violence simply for its lawmaking character" (283). Is Bane's rule so different from Gotham's? To Gordon's accusation, "No lawyer, no witnesses. What sort of due process is this?" Bane's appointed judge answers, "More than you gave Harvey's prisoners, Commissioner." Is Gotham worth saving? If so, it must be saved by the very means it seeks to expel.

In Gotham, Bane becomes sovereign by declaring the exception: he isolates the city, even enlisting the army to ensure that Gotham remains isolated.[24] Within Gotham-as-exception, Bane's violence declares new law over the city-state's sovereignty, which, like the civilization of Shinbone and Ransom Stoddard, remains impotent without a heroic nonstate actor, a Doniphon whose violence will rescue it.[25] Although Batman's violence is equally jurispathic, his attempts to overthrow Bane succeed only when he combines his extralegal force with the appearance of the city-state's legitimacy. When Batman escapes from the Pit and returns to Gotham, he leads the trapped city police out of the sewers. In so doing, he mobilizes his private force *as state violence,* thereby becoming the hybrid figure of "salvagesse" and chivalry who can reimpose the state's law over the one declared by Bane. This final battle pushes Bane's violence (his bomb) out into the landscape and away from the city. In his last act Batman sacrifices himself, as Doniphon did, and resecures state sovereignty.

Like *The Faerie Queene* and *The Man Who Shot Liberty Valance,* the allegorical mode of Nolan's film draws attention to problems of symbolic figuration within it: like Faerie lond and Shinbone, Gotham City imposes its law by writing ethically suspect legends. The film opens with Commissioner Gordon standing before a poster of Harvey Dent, praising him as "a hero. Not the hero we deserved—the hero we needed. Nothing less than a knight, shining . . ." In the end, the city-state replaces the portrait of its first (and corrupt) symbolic knight, Dent, with the statue of Batman. Nolan brings us full circle on the state's reliance on symbol and counterinterpretation to impose law. After Bane's "liberation" of Blackgate prison, Officer Blake accuses Gordon of basing the Dent Act on a lie. The police commissioner explains, "A lie to keep a city on fire from burning to the ground. Gotham needed a hero. Someone to believe in." The line identifies this figure of justice as central to the state's legitimacy, but also as fraudulent. As Bane declares, "You have been supplied with a false idol to stop you tearing down this corrupt city. Let me tell you the truth about Harvey Dent . . ." Counterinterpretation is central to Bane's rule as well: he proposes his own fictions, rereading the city-state's. Announcing his new law at a football game, Bane characterizes himself as a liberator. He explains that he has given over control of the bomb to a citizen, who will detonate it should anyone attempt to escape. He refers to this individual as "this anonymous Gothamite, this unsung hero." Bane's symbolic everyman overwrites the state's fiction of the hero Dent: the contest of rival laws and rival forms of violence hinges on a contest of equally false Legends of Justice.

Nolan's film provides another example of counterinterpreted legend. In the Pit prison, Bruce Wayne hears of a child who once escaped it. The story drips with pathos: the child was born in the Pit to a warlord's daughter, who sacrificed herself to spare her husband. When the mother dies, a "protector" rescues and raises the child. One of the prisoners recounts the tale, emphasizing its sympathetic appeal: "Innocence cannot flower underground. It must be stamped out. But the child had a friend, a protector." The world within the Pit promotes the child as a symbol of innocence, and the "protector" as self-sacrifice. When the film reveals that these figures are Miranda Tate and Bane respectively, the conflict between them and Batman becomes not only a violent combat between competing laws but also a struggle between rival legends. It thereby becomes more difficult, and all the more necessary, to counterinterpret. The film (and the state) must find a way to reframe Bane and Tate as lawless evil and to overwrite their pathos with that of their orphaned outlaw-knight.

Nolan's nightmarish vision of Gotham-as-exception foregrounds the basic arbitrariness of all fictions of justice proposed by the state. All morally bankrupt, all deceptive and decaying, the film's competing visions of law often appear unstable, interchangeable, and formulaic. The twin "monuments" of Dent's photo and Batman's statue—one lionizing a murderous criminal, the other now mourning the very man it had blamed for the former's killing—signal a repeating cycle of false legends whose exposure only supplies new fiction.

LEGENDS AND THE GOOD OLD WAYS

For *The Dark Knight Rises,* as for *Liberty Valance* and *The Faerie Queene,* competing interpretations of lawmaking violence model competing visions of statehood. Spenser's Arthegall is an aristocratic agent of a feudal state, which the poem nostalgically romanticizes in opposition to the authoritarian Tudor monarchy. Ford's film translates this politicized medievalism as the heroic, individualist frontiersman left behind by the "civilizing" process of statehood, although scenes like Stoddard's multicultural classroom simultaneously idealize the promise of democracy. In *The Dark Knight Rises,* that communitarian promise becomes a nightmare of democracy as mob rule, emblematized by the populist, uncontrollable Bane. His Gotham-as-exception recalls Slavoj Žižek's critique of conservative, law-and-order responses to Hurricane Katrina: "What if the tension that led to the explosion in New Orleans was not the tension between 'human nature' and the force of civilisation that keeps it in check, but the tension between the two aspects of our civilisation itself?" (2008, 95–96). Like Žižek, Nolan despairs of the prospects of civilization, although from the opposite end of the political spectrum. Instead, his film embodies in Bane not only a neoliberalist critique of economic "redistribution" but also a deep cynicism regarding the populace's capacity to organize and effect political change, a cynicism that emphasizes what some have seen as the failure of the Occupy movement. Nolan's Gotham answers Žižek's question: "What if, in endeavoring to control explosions like the one in New Orleans, the forces of law and order were confronted with the very nature of capitalism at its purest, the logic of individualist competition, of ruthless self-assertion, generated by capitalist dynamics, a 'nature' much more threatening and violent than all the hurricanes and earthquakes?" (96). Nolan's Bane succeeds utterly in imposing terror in Gotham through the "fiction" of economic equality, and demonstrates the utter failure of the citizenry and the government of Gotham City to organize against him. In response, Nolan's Batman nostalgically transforms the moneyed capitalist into the chivalric hero, figured as the necessary bulwark of the corrupt and dysfunctional democratic state. *The Faerie Queene*, *The Man Who Shot Liberty Valance*, and *The Dark Knight Rises* all mourn their knights and the aristocratic agency and autonomy they embody. They also highlight the costs paid by these figures and their self-sacrifice on behalf of the state that uses and discards them.

Whereas Sir Arthegall, slandered by counterinterpretations that strip him of his reputation as Knight of Justice, is victimized by a force from deep within the lawless landscape, in Ford's film, counterinterpretation originates instead from the state itself. Although Stoddard's attempt at rewriting the legend fails, the loss is nonetheless still borne by Doniphon, who dies nameless and abandoned, at the cost of the reputation he once held as a skilled fighter and law unto himself. Doniphon repeatedly protected Stoddard from Valance, fortifying Stoddard's impotent law with his private violence. He also eventually gave up his fiancée and his way of life, and in so doing advanced the nascent state's interests. I have argued that by portraying Senator Stoddard as a self-important politician, the film offers the possibility that even Doniphon's dead body is appropriated to further the state's self-legitimation, turned into a symbol weighted with the responsibility for its violence in much the same way as Spenser's Sir Arthegall turned the bodies and weaponry of his victims retroactively into questionable symbols of "justice." Spenser's Legend of Justice drew attention to the state's ingratitude at the knight's sacrifice; Senator Stoddard goes even further by counterinterpreting in order to make appropriation appear as self-sacrifice, bloodguilt as nostalgia. Similarly, Nolan's Batman, who begins as a bandit abandoned by the state, marshals his nonstate violence on behalf of Gotham City, and sacrifices himself to it in the end. Batman dies, and Bruce Wayne is exiled, stripped even of his ancestral home, which he gives over to the city for an orphanage. Allowing the state to use his legend to legitimate itself, Batman martyrs himself and thus becomes its new Knight of Justice.

Sir Arthegall, Tom Doniphon, and Batman are all abandoned by a state that relies on their strength. It enlists them for legend, but abandons what remains—their humanity in all its pathos—not because they are external to the state, but rather because they are *prior to it*. These hybrid outlaw-knights belong to the old feudal, aristocratic order that the modern state has replaced. Furthermore, the same is true of the villains: Pollente, the Egalitarian Giant, the Souldan, Liberty Valance, and Bane are all aristocratic free agents. The modern state forms itself directly at their expense, through other knights who collaborate with it, but whom it also destroys. Benjamin's great criminal, feared by the state for his lawmaking potential, is no less than the old knight—the previous aristocratic power on which it once relied, then criminalized and exiled. As I have argued, what the modern state views as lawlessness is in fact rival law: the great criminal threatens the state not by proposing new law, as Benjamin suggests, but by threatening a return to the old ways.

In *The Faerie Queene,* the existence of rival rulers that the Knight of Justice must repeatedly overthrow reveals the fact that the centralized Tudor state is just one possibility among many, which only triumphs by violently extinguishing and then delegitimizing rival laws. The outlaw-knight serves the state but also reifies a critique of it through the nostalgic idealization of feudal aristocratic individualism. In Ford's film, the outlaw-knight's sacrifice and erasure highlight the state's reliance on self-serving fictions, even as these empower the community on behalf of which he fights and to which he must give way. Its politicized nostalgia allows the film to monumentalize his sacrifice for the democratic good, but it also provides Stoddard with the means for the state's exploitative reinterpretation. *The Dark Knight Rises* offers the sharpest critique of the centralized state, which appears demonstrably divorced from its citizens, collapsing morally as well as militarily. Nolan portrays a failed state in the midst of the total breakdown of institutions and institutional trust. Like Spenser and Ford, Nolan turns at a moment of political change to a time *before* modern statehood. In stark contrast to Ford's inclusive, supportive townsfolk, Nolan's unleashed citizenry is a mob threat to an idealized capitalist individualism, figured through private property rights. In the midst of Bane's populist anarchy, Selena Kyle pauses over a family photograph in an abandoned house, once again nostalgically lamenting, "This was someone's home once." Her friend resentfully replies, "Now it's everyone's home." In short, Nolan's conservative nostalgia returns its semifuturistic Gotham to a premodern worldview more at home in Faerie land: his Bane is the Egalitarian Giant overthrown not by deliberative debate but by brute force. Nolan's film seems to despair of the project of civilization itself. Ray notes that *Liberty Valance* suggests "that the civilizing process rested on a lie at its beginnings" (243). Nolan's film goes further to indicate that the democratic state itself is a lie, perpetuated through a progression of false symbols that decay only to be replaced by others. The statue of Batman that closes the film is, after all, only another lie. Batman is not dead, Gotham City is no less corrupt, no less incapable, and one senses that another crisis is certain. The outlaw-knight's sacrifice, while it saves the state, does not redeem it.

When Senator Stoddard tells his story and asks whether the reporters will expose the alleged fraud behind 'The Man Who Shot Liberty Valance', the newsman answers, "this is the West, Sir. When the legend becomes fact, print the legend." In this final scene, the press—Shinbone's poets—becomes complicit in the state's fictions, taking on their propagation. Cover wrote, "It will not do . . . to insist on the violence of strong poetry, and strong poets. Even the violence of weak judges is utterly real—in need of no interpretation, no critic to reveal it—a naive but immediate reality" (1986, 818). However, he and numerous others have recognized the "sacred narratives," "social cues," "interpretive models," or "aesthetic representations" required to legitimate law's violence (respectively, Cover 1984–85, 182; 1986, 819; Derrida 993, 1041). Even Spenser's contemporary Michel de Montaigne identified the *fictions légitimes* on which justice relies (537). Spenser's *Faerie Queene,* Ford's *The Man Who Shot Liberty Valance,* and Nolan's *The Dark Knight Rises* exploit the obfuscation and multivalence of allegory to highlight the fictions at the heart of the state's law and its violence. There is no "fact" in Shinbone, nor in Faerie land, nor Gotham City—only legend, the most enduring of which is justice itself.

Cynthia Nazarian is assistant professor in the Department of French and Italian and affiliated faculty of the program in Comparative Literary Studies at Northwestern University. She is the author of *Love's Wounds: Violence and the Politics of Early Modern Poetry* (2016).

Notes

I would like to thank Bonnie Honig and Patricia Fumerton for their insightful comments and suggestions, from which this paper has benefited greatly.

1. On romance, see Auerbach; Frye; Parker.

2. David Quint argues that the march toward absolutism of late Renaissance states coincided with the fall of epic. "Dying as a generic form, epic . . . looked back to its origins and to its preference for Achilles over Agamemnon: for the heroism of the individual distinct from the power of the corporate state. These nostalgic visions of aristocratic autonomy, moreover, characteristically employed the motifs and narrative structures of romance" (10). See also Burrow.

3. On allegory, see Fletcher; Jameson; Teskey.

4. My claim applies to the works as a whole: although Spenser's poem and the two films each contain important symbols and occasional references to myth, the works themselves are allegories.

5. Teskey suggests that allegory proceeds by a violent process of "capture" by which an image is forced to bear a meaning previously foreign to it.

6. The cultural context of Spenserian violence has been fruitfully explored by, among others, Hadfield (1997); McCabe (2002 and 1989); Shuger.

7. Among scholars, Sir Arthegall is often thought to represent Lord Grey in Spenser's poem.

8. See, for example, Hadfield 1997, 138; McCabe 2002, 98.

9. Arthegall's appearance offers its own counterinterpretation, a medieval counternarrative to a nostalgic early modern chivalry. As knight, he embodies the virtues of aristocratic heroism romanticized by the Elizabethan court and such figures as Sir Philip Sidney and the Earl of Essex. As savage, he reflects an older vision of unruly, uncontrollable knightly violence, which can ultimately be traced back

to the "feudal anarchy" of the tenth and eleventh centuries that followed the collapse of the Carolingian empire. Richard Kaeuper has traced the role of chivalric codes in curbing individual heroic violence in favor of centralizing monarchical authorities and their monopolization of warlike violence (1999). As he notes, whether in spite of these attempts or because of them, violence and knighthood remained inseparable throughout the Middle Ages and beyond.

10. See, among others, Hadfield 1997; Helgerson; Maley; McCabe 1989; 2002; McEachern, 34–82; Norbrook, 97–139; Montrose.

11. I examine this episode with regard to the interplay between sympathy and violence in *The Faerie Queene* in Nazarian 2016.

12. Bradin Cormack has argued that episodes such as these allegorize the conflict between English common law and native Irish Brehon law (133–76).

13. The likeness between Arthegall and Lord Grey is particularly clear in the episode of the Blatant Beast, as Spenser defends Grey's violence and laments "that good Lord blotted with the name of a bloody man" in his *View of the State of Ireland* (103). Grey was recalled from Ireland by Elizabeth I ostensibly because of his excessive brutality.

14. See Cawelti; Ray, 56.

15. See also Pearson; Pippin, 61–101.

16. See Budd.

17. Robert Ray posits an "outlaw-hero" whom he opposes to an "official hero" in the American Western. The outlaw-knight differs from Ray's outlaw-hero by uniting private violence and cooperation with the state. The outlaw-knight is an aristocratic agent, a figure of feudal nostalgia who precedes the modern state but is nonetheless implicated in a network of obligations tying him to it (58–59).

18. Doniphon and Valance both exhibit the central characteristics of the medieval knight: they are armed and appear mounted on horseback, both follow a specific code of violence and justice, they have servants/followers and wealth, and both hold the power of life and death over others around them. Doniphon further acts as a protector of the weak in his initial encounter with Ransom Stoddard, and his service to his lady, Hallie, embodies courtly service.

19. Both Scott Eyman and Tad Gallagher note how unsympathetic Stoddard appears in the present; they characterize him respectively as a "bloviating windbag" and as "pompous, . . . a caricature of a politician" (Eyman, 491; Gallagher, 409). Barry Langford further notes "the capacity for dissimulation embodied by Stoddard's livelong lie, a capacity that neither Doniphon nor Valance possess" (30). However, even Robert Pippin, who briefly suggests the possibility that Stoddard's tale might be false, quickly moves on and asserts his belief instead (83, 91). Sue Matheson also raises the question "How sincere is Stoddard's story?" but soon answers, "It is impossible to tell" (364).

20. See Matheson, 361.

21. Slavoj Žižek notes affinities between Nolan's earlier film, *The Dark Knight* (2008), and Ford's *The Man Who Shot Liberty Valance* (2012).

22. The Pit prison is Nolan's orientalist invention, located in an indeterminate Middle Eastern setting, surrounded by desert. The film appeared in the midst of the U.S. war in Afghanistan.

23. "One of the paradoxes of the state of exception lies in the fact that in the state of exception, it is impossible to distinguish transgression of the law from execution of the law" (Agamben, 57).

24. In the figure of Bane, who tells his enemies and followers alike that "you have my permission to die," we might see a critique of the Schmittian definition of sovereignty from the perspective of Foucauldian biopolitics: he is equally capable of declaring the exception, and the state (the city-state as well as federal state) is powerless in the face of his allegedly lawless violence. See Foucault, 241.

25. I disagree with Žižek's contention that "[Batman's] transgression here is purely formal: it lies in acting on behalf of the law without being legitimized to do so. In his acts, he never violates the law" (2012, n.p). In my view, Batman is consistently outside the law, outside of the *civitas* (deep in the Batcave); the extralegal character of his violence is what defines its efficacy.

Works Cited

Agamben, Giorgio. 1998. *Homo Sacer: Sovereign Power and Bare Life*. Trans. Daniel Heller-Roazen. Stanford: Stanford University Press.

Anderson, Kent. 2006. "John Ford: The Man Who Shot Liberty Valance." *Journal of Popular Culture* 39, no. 1:10–28.

Auerbach, Erich. 2003. *Mimesis: The Representation of Reality in Western Literature*. Trans. Willard Trask. Princeton: Princeton University Press.

Bazin, André. 2004. *What Is Cinema?* Vol. 2. Trans. Hugh Gray. Berkeley: University of California Press.

Benjamin, Walter. 1986. "Critique of Violence." In *Reflections*. Ed. Peter Demetz, 277–300. Trans. Edmund Jephcott. New York: Schocken Books.

Budd, Michael. 1976. "At Home in the Wilderness: Visual Imagery in John Ford's Westerns." *Cinema Journal* 166, no. 1: 62–75.

Burrow, Colin. 1993. *Epic Romance: Homer to Milton*. Oxford: Oxford University Press.

Cawelti, John. 1976. *Adventure, Mystery, and Romance: Formula Stories as Art and Popular Culture*. Chicago: University of Chicago Press.

Cormack, Bradin. 2007. *A Power to Do Justice: Jurisdiction, English Literature, and the Rise of Common Law, 1509–1625*. Chicago: University of Chicago Press.

Cover, Robert. 1984–85. "The Folktales of Justice: Tales of Jurisdiction." *Capital University Law Review* 14:179–203.

Cover, Robert. 1986. "The Bonds of Constiutional Interpretation: Of the Word, the Deed, and the Role." *Georgia Law Review* 20:815–33.

Cover, Robert. 1992a. "Nomos and Narrative." In *Narrative, Violence, and the Law*. Ed. Martha Minow, Michael Ryan, and Austin Sarat, 95–172. Ann Arbor: University of Michigan Press.

Cover, Robert. 1992b. "Violence and the Word." *Narrative, Violence, and the Law*. Ed. Martha Minow, Michael Ryan, and Austin Sarat, 203–38. Ann Arbor: University of Michigan Press.

Derrida, Jacques. 1990. "Force of Law: The Mystical Foundation of Authority." *Cardozo Law Review* 11:990–1045.

Dienstag, Joshua Foa. 2012. "A Storied Shooting: Liberty Valance and the Paradox of Sovereignty." *Political Theory* 40, no. 3: 290–318.

Eyman, Scott. 1999. *Print the Legend: The Life and Times of John Ford*. New York: Simon and Schuster.

Fletcher, Angus. 1964. *Allegory: The Theory of a Symbolic Mode*. Ithaca: Cornell University Press.

Foucault, Michel. 2003. *Society Must Be Defended: Lectures at the Collège de France, 1975–1976*. Ed. Mauro Bertani and Alessandro Fontana. Trans. David Macey. New York: Picador.

Frye, Northrop. 1976. *The Secular Scripture*. Cambridge, Mass.: Harvard University Press.

Gallagher, Tad. 1986. *John Ford: The Man and His Films*. Berkeley: University of California Press.

Gallagher, Tad. 1994. "Spenser, Ireland, and Sixteenth-Century Political Theory." *Modern Language Review* 89:1–18.

Gallagher, Tad. 1997. *Edmund Spenser's Irish Experience: Wilde Fruit and Savage Soyl*. Oxford: Oxford University Press.

Hadfield, Andrew. 2012. *Edmund Spenser: A Life*. Oxford: Clarendon Press.

Helgerson, Richard. 1992. *Forms of Nationhood: The Elizabethan Writing of England*. Chicago: University of Chicago Press.

Jameson, Fredric. 2001. "From Metaphor to Allegory." In *Anything*. Ed. Cynthia C. Davidson, 24–36. Cambridge, Mass.: MIT Press.

Kaeuper, Richard W. 1999. *Chivalry and Violence in Medieval Europe*. Oxford: Oxford University Press.

Langford, Barry. 2003. "Revisiting the 'Revisionist' Western." *Film & History* 33, no. 2: 26–35.

Maley, Willy. 1997. *Salvaging Spenser: Colonialism, Culture, and Identity*. Basingstoke: Macmillan.

Matheson, Sue. 2012. "John Ford and the Cold War: Stetsons and Cast Shadows in *The Man Who Shot Liberty Valance*." *Journal of Popular Culture* 45, no. 2: 357–69.

McCabe, Richard. 1989. "The Fate of Irena: Spenser and Political Violence." In *Spenser and Ireland: An Interdisciplinary Perspective*. Ed. Patricia Coughlan, 109–20. Cork: Cork University Press.

McCabe, Richard. 2002. *Spenser's Monstrous Regiment: Elizabethan Ireland and the Poetics of Difference*. Oxford: Oxford University Press.

McClure, John A. 1994. *Late Imperial Romance*. London: Verso Books.

McEachern, Claire. 1996. *The Poetics of English Nationhood, 1590–1612*. Cambridge: Cambridge University Press.

Montaigne, Michel de. 1998. *Les Essais*. Paris: Presses Universitaires de France.

Montrose, Louis Adrian. 2002. "Spenser and the Elizabethan Political Imaginary." *ELH* 69, no. 4: 907–46.

Nadel, Alan. 1995. *Containment Culture: American Narratives, Postmodernism, and the Atomic Age*. Durham: Duke University Press.

Nazarian, Cynthia. 2016. "Sympathy Wounds, Rivers of Blood: The Politics of Fellow-Feeling in Spenser's *Faerie Queene* and *A View of the State of Ireland*." *Modern Philology* 113, no. 3: 331–52.

Norbrook, David. 2002. *Poetry and Politics in the English Renaissance*. Oxford: Oxford University Press.

Parker, Patricia. 1979. *Inescapable Romance: Studies in the Poetics of a Mode*. Princeton: Princeton University Press.

Pearson, Sidney A., Jr. 2007. "It Is Tough to Be the Second Toughest Guy in a Tough Town: Ask the Man Who Shot Liberty Valance." *Perspectives on Political Science* 36:23–28.

Pippin, Robert B. 2010. *Hollywood Westerns and American Myth: The Importance of Howard Hawks and John Ford for Political Philosophy*. New Haven: Yale University Press.

Quint, David. 1983. *Origin and Originality in Renaissance Literature: Versions of the Source*. New Haven: Yale University Press.

Ray, Robert B. 1985. *A Certain Tendency of the Hollywood Cinema, 1930–1980*. Princeton: Princeton University Press.

Schmitt, Carl. 2005. *Political Theology*. Trans. George Schwab. Chicago: University of Chicago Press.

Shuger, Debora. 1997. "Irishmen, Aristocrats, and Other White Barbarians." *Renaissance Quarterly* 50:494–525.

Spenser, Edmund. 1997. *A View of the State of Ireland*. Ed. Andrew Hadfield and Willy Maley. Oxford: Blackwell.

Spenser, Edmund. 2007. *The Faerie Queene*. 2nd ed. Ed. A. C. Hamilton, Hiroshi Yamashita, and Toshiyuki Suzuki. Harlow: Pearson Longman.

Teskey, Gordon. 1996. *Allegory and Violence*. Ithaca: Cornell University Press.

Weber, Max. 2004. "Politics as a Vocation." In *The Vocation Lectures*. Ed. David Owen and Tracy B. Strong, 32–94. Indianapolis: Hackett.

Žižek, Slavoj. 2008. *Violence: Six Sideways Reflections*. New York: Picador.

Žižek, Slavoj. 2012. "Dictatorship of the Proletariat in Gotham City: Slavoj Žižek on 'the Dark Knight Rises.'" *Blog da boitempo* (blog), August 8. http://blogdaboitempo.com.br/2012/08/08/dictatorship-of-the-proletariat-in-gotham-city-slavoj-zizek-on-the-dark-knight-rises/.

Review Essays

EDWARD W. SAID AND JOSEPH BOONE'S *THE HOMOEROTICS OF ORIENTALISM*

Joseph Massad

Since the passing of Edward W. Said in September 2003, a plethora of books engaging his scholarly and political legacy have cropped up in academe. Ranging from the excellent to the moderately competent, the few that attack Said and his work often belong to that not-so-rare type of monographs whose authors exhibit, or sometimes seem to courageously boast of, their theoretical and empirical illiteracy.[1] Attacks on Said and his oeuvre, of course, predate his untimely death; but in this posthumous era, it is a different crowd of academics, ones who had closely guarded their secret criticisms of Said when he was alive but felt compelled to avow them publicly following his demise.

Criticizing Said's scholarship and politics or the legacy of both certainly has no statute of limitations; however, it is most interesting that some of the recent attacks on his scholarship and politics issue not only from the traditional American (and Israeli) liberal and conservative right wing (ranging from Michael Walzer and Judith Miller to Bernard Lewis and Emmanuel Sivan), or from apologists for Zionist and Israeli colonialism (ranging again from Michael Walzer and Judith Miller to Bernard Lewis and Emmanuel Sivan), but from left–liberal academics and journalists who want to claim an affiliation with Said as they disavow his work and legacy. Some of them, like the proimperialist parvenu Christopher Hitchens, who made a clean break with their leftist anti-imperial past and embraced the more profitable side of a neoliberal imperial power with abandon, had been friends and allies of Said until (in the case of Hitchens, a few months before) his death—what would their proper designation be, one wonders: *nouveaux droitistes*, neocons, or quite simply neoliberals?

A number of attacks on Said have come from a new corner that is still under construction, one invested in what it calls "sexuality" *in*

"Islam" (or in the "Middle East," or the "Islamicate" world), from a new discipline that *dare* speak, indeed shout, its name from the high rooftops of academe, namely, "Queer Middle East studies." But before exploring these Johnny-come-latelies, we must turn to the earlier critics of Said in order to grasp the limited innovativeness and the amount of indebtedness of his more recent critics to them.

Said's Orientalist critics had accused him, inter alia, of "demonizing" Orientalists, or indeed the "West" itself (Bernard Lewis, but more recently also Robert Irwin, inter alia), and of ignoring German or Dutch Orientalists (e.g., Maxime Rodinson). While the first claim is baseless given Said's evident attentiveness to the rich multifacetedness of many of the Orientalists he studied, the problem with the second is that neither Rodinson nor his second-rate chorus line ever bothered to demonstrate how Said would have reached different, let alone opposite, conclusions had he subjected the Germans and the Dutch to his critical eye (something he himself had remarked on in responding to his critics in 1985 [Said 1985, 1]), especially as the more recent scholarship of Susanne Marchand has shown that Said would have found very little in the German context that would have altered any of his major findings about French and British Orientalisms (though Marchand, who too often misunderstands Said and Foucault and is hostile to discourse analysis, would argue that Said's view was too totalizing and "binarist" in the German case) (Marchand 2009).

In addition to academic Orientalists, Said's right- and left-wing American and Israeli critics describe/d him as "savage," "angry," and "rageful," indeed as a "terrorist," and his left–liberal academic critics (the Israeli Jewish academics among them were, as Ella Shohat has shown, pioneers in this regard), worried about what they deemed to be his "inflexibility," "fixity," "staticness," attachment to "binarisms" and "dichotomous" thinking, lack of "nuance," and inattention to "subtlety."

Adopting the most right wing of postcolonial scholars, Homi Bhabha, as their patron saint of choice, these leftists celebrated the latter as "going beyond" Said.[2] But as Shohat has painstakingly uncovered, it is the aversion to Said's anticolonialism and Bhabha's ambivalence about it that made the latter a coveted safe alternative to Said, especially among Israeli Jewish leftist academics. Perhaps leftist Israeli Jewish columnist Nir Baram's description summarizes this finding in declaring that Bhabha "unlike Said redeemed the Orient from the ultimate role of the victim and the slave, understanding that the imagination is not one-way but two-way: in other words, the Orient also imagines the West and imitates it. Bhabha, speaking about two creatures that move in a constantly changing dynamic space, perfected Said's frozen thesis, and led the way into a much more fascinating discourse."[3]

This claim of "going beyond Said," as Shohat has revealed, is fraudulent, not only in Israeli "post-structuralist" circles but also among Said's U.S. left–liberal academic critics who "seem to displace Said's deconstruction of the binarism of colonial discourse onto Said's own text, as if Said, and not colonialism and racism, were binarist" (2004, 66).

Bhabha himself is an active participant in these trends (both the liberal and conservative American and the Israeli procolonialist stance and its post-structuralist *ambivalent* successors who want to claim the anticolonial mantle without disavowing colonialism) when his courage, which was well ensconced during Said's life, erupted with force following the latter's death. Suddenly clad with this long-lost virtue, Bhabha boldly declared that "Said's rage sometimes drives him toward a dark two-dimensionality," and that Said's "polemical outrage" had "led him, at times, to pass over distinctions, to resist shades of meaning and interpretations."[4] We have thus arrived at the realm of "nuance," "fluidity," "mobility," "shades of grey," which Said allegedly lacked but, luckily for us, Bhabha and his left–liberal Israeli and American peers seem to possess in abundance.

This is where the nascent field of scholarship that wants to call itself "Queer Middle East studies," populated mostly by junior missionary academics, joined the attacks on Said and his *Orientalism* as disabling the kinds of politics they wish to inflict on the "Islamicate" world. One claim has it that Said and Saidean-derived analysis produce a "Queer discomfort" and a politically correct straitjacket and/or that Said got it all wrong and that his analysis needs to be thrown out in order for politics, or even cross-racial forms of sexual pleasure, to proceed (Shalakany, 125–29). Another critic insists that "the Orientalism paradigm privileges the power of the West's discourse to a degree that obscures resistances to this discourse, other competing discourses, and material realities" (Amireh, 645). Another still finds resistances to Orientalist epistemology as "arguing for the clarity of the distinction of the East/West divide in ways that resonate with the very Orientalism [one] critiques" (Al-Kassim, 304). These newcomers who are pushing for "Queer Middle East studies" (a good number of whom are not even Middle East studies specialists but Europeanists and Americanists attempting to colonize an already colonized discipline) are joined by some who want to create "Sinophone" queer studies and who insist that an analysis that uncovers how Orientalist and colonial knowledges were instituted in the colonies is one that engages in "full-blown self- or re-orientalisation" (Chiang, 634). They complain of lack of "nuance" and of "simplicity" in what they identify as Saidean analyses, à la Bhabha, compared to claims of complexity that they believe they offer instead.

In a 1995 inaugural article that deals specifically with European Orientalist representations of homoeroticism in the Orient titled "Vacation Cruises, or The Homoerotics of Orientalism," by Joseph Boone, who teaches English at the University of Southern California, cited Bhabha as a scholar from whom he takes a "cue" of "the continually 'unfixing' propensities of the colonial stereotype" (2014, 91). In his informative article, Boone wants to supplement Said's description of the Orientalist strategy of rendering the Orient as female to be penetrated by a Western male by clarifying that the feminine role of the Orient need not always be that of a female. This addition aside, little if anything would change in Said's conclusions as a result of this informative article, which adds more examples of and is in tune with what Said had provided and addressed in his book, namely Said's contention that Orientalism functions as a discourse that creates and interprets its object, and one that is embedded in structures of imperial power.

Orientalist scholarship, as Said had explained, is full of contradictions and not always or often a coherent body of work. For example, Arab men are both rendered supermasculine and ultrafeminine simultaneously compared to the moderate civilized masculinity of Occidental men, something I explore in my first book, *Colonial Effects* (Massad 2001). But Said's book was not intended as a comprehensive encyclopedia of Orientalist representations, as some of his critics seem to want the book to be, but as a discursive analysis of the production of Orientalist knowledge and Western colonial power. In this early and welcome essay, Boone announced that he was working on a book on the "*homoerotics of orientalism* (from which this essay is excerpted)." But that was in 1995; two decades later, the book has finally been published.

In his new book, Boone seeks to put into "dialogue" the Western and the so-called Islamicate archives on homoerotics. He tells us that this has been made possible for him, as a Europeanist who knows no "Islamicate" languages whatsoever, by the new scholarship in the field of Middle East studies on sexuality. It is in basing himself on these studies, a good number of which are not of optimal academic quality and merit, that he feels confident he can now read both archives, one in translation to European languages and the other in the original European languages to achieve this dialogue, or, what he sometimes calls in claiming an affiliation with Said, "contrapuntal" reading (2014, xxii, xxvii).

In contrast with literary and feminist scholars whose critiques of Said's *Orientalism* in the last three and a half decades aimed to expand and elaborate on his work, in *The Homoerotics of Orientalism*, Boone is most interested in and more sympathetic to Said's conservative and Orientalist critics, like Robert Irwin for one, who claim that Orientalism was a benevolent exercise of knowledge that Said demonized. In his new book, Boone has joined the anti-Saidean neoconservative chorus by claiming without originality that Said had allegedly created a "Manichean view of West versus East" (24). While in his earlier, less hostile essay, written when Said was alive, Boone did criticize Said's inattention to Gustave Flaubert's sexual excitement over the Egyptian dancer/catamite Hasan el-Belbeissi (1996, 92) (though Said had of course noted Flaubert's interest in "almehs and khawals, dancing girls and boys respectively" [Said 1978, 186]), he did not list any of the other unseemly sins committed by Said and which seem to have suddenly been identified in his new book. It is true that Said did not possess the sharp appetite for discussing these homoerotic representations that Boone wants him to have had, but this need not lead to a poverty of analysis. Said stated rather clearly in relation to Flaubert:

> Why the Orient seems still to suggest not only fecundity but sexual promise (and threat), untiring sensuality, unlimited desire, deep generative energies, is something on which one could speculate: it is not the province of my analysis here, alas, despite its frequently noted appearance. Nevertheless, one must acknowledge its importance as something

> eliciting complex responses, sometimes even a frightening self-discovery, in the Orientalists, and Flaubert was an interesting case in point. (1978, 188)

Said further spoke of "Flaubert's own voyages in and obsession with the Orient" and the association Flaubert made "between the Orient and the freedom of licentious sex." Said concluded that "the Orient was a place where one could look for sexual experience unobtainable in Europe. Virtually no European writer who wrote on or traveled to the Orient in the period after 1800 exempted himself or herself from this quest: Flaubert, Nerval, 'Dirty Dick' Burton, and Lane are only the most notable" (190). One could say that whereas Said had sought to signal these representations as important, they were not as central to his own book project. Boone, however, and in line with the Bhabhaesque critics of Said, refers to "nuance" and what is "subtle" and "more flexible," ad infinitum, as what his own work offers in contrast to Said's.[5]

Boone notes "the degree to which the heterosexual tenor of Said's metaphors occlude alternative forms of eroticism underlying the Orientalist enterprise. . . . Pace Said, the template for Flaubert's erotic experience of Egypt turns out to be less based on gender opposition than of polymorphous perversity" (194). But how is any of this a "corrective" to Said's account of Orientalism? Said discusses sexual metaphors only fleetingly and insists that while this is an important project, it was not the one he was undertaking. Indeed, Said was clear on the contradictions of Orientalist representations of Oriental men: "An Oriental Arab is that impossible creature whose libidinal energy drives him to paroxysms of overstimulation—and yet, he is a puppet in the eyes of the world, staring vacantly out at a modern landscape he can neither understand nor cope with" (1978, 312).

The attempt here to depict Said's understanding of Orientalism as not complex (à la Bhabha) is so disingenuous that one only notes it because it is part of the accumulation of accusations against Said's project by "Left" academics as not sufficiently nuanced, if nuanced at all, and that it presents Orientalism as fully coherent without any internal contradictions. But Said's *Orientalism,* as Said announces at the outset, had sought to identify "changes, modulations, refinements, even revolutions [that] take place within Orientalism" (1978, 15). Aside from the fact that Said was always careful to note the contradictions within Orientalism as a body of thought, but one which coheres in the service of political and economic imperial power in certain ways, what exactly does Boone, being the latest (though by no means the most astute) of such critics, aim to say? That Orientalism has the good and the bad and it is wrong to present it all as "bad." Would anyone doubt that academic, literary, artistic, and anthropological studies inspired and inspiring anti-Black racism, anti-Jewish anti-Semitism, sexism against women, or homophobia targeting homosexuals do not fully cohere as systems of thought, that they are riven with internal contradictions that show blacks as weak and as strong simultaneously, as human and as not-human, as repulsive and as sexy; that women are virtuous and the agents of vice, weak yet strong, more cunning yet less intelligent than men; that Jews are capitalists and communists; that Jewish men are effeminate and lascivious, chasing after gentile women, as cowards yet as killers of Christian children; that male homosexuals are effeminate weaklings and predatory manly pedophiles, and so on? How does any of this lead to the conclusion that the representational discourses of racism, sexism, homophobia, and anti-Semitism have the good and the bad and it would be wrong to portray them only as bad? Such views are not accepted as correctives to our understanding of racism, sexism, anti-Semitism, and homophobia, yet they are increasingly legitimized as "correctives" to Said's analysis of Orientalism.

The ontology and epistemology that Said theorized as constituting the "West" and "Western subjectivity" disappear, however, in Boone's and his cohort's understanding of the Saidean project. While Boone poses as someone who understands Said's project, he claims to counter it though providing a study of a "large number of Anglo-European (and later U.S.) writers and artists, travelers, and thinkers—by and large men—who over the centuries *have found themselves gripped by and compelled to attempt to represent*, what, to their eyes, has seemed to be the relative openness, to say nothing of abundance, of erotic relations between men in the Islamicate world" (Boone 2014, xxi, emphasis added). But Said's project has uncovered how these artists and writers did *not wake up one day* to "[find] themselves gripped and compelled to attempt to represent . . . erotic relations between men in the Islamicate world," but rather were constituted as the European (and later, Euro-American) artists and writers whose very constitution leads and "compels" them to represent the Orient as the other, and often, as the opposite, of the Occident. Said asserts how "the Orientalist, poet or scholar, makes the Orient speak, describes the Orient, renders its mysteries plain for and to the West" (1978, 20–21). It is this basic lack of grasping Said's project, rather than the unpersuasive attempt to go beyond it, that dooms Boone's project from the outset. The twenty-year lag in publishing his book, alas, does not demonstrate that Boone has acquired more robust interpretative and analytical skills, let alone more progressive politics than his 1995 essay, rather the opposite seems to be true.

In 2014, the now-conservative Boone accuses Said, without presenting any evidence, of "manipulation of sources and tendency to find evidence that supports a preformulated thesis" (2014, 24) and then proceeds to claim that not only Said's "sympathetic" readers, but "nearly everyone agrees that his thesis at times creates and reifies a monolithic 'Orient,' one that in its vast singularity is all the more easily dominated by an equally monolithic 'Occident' whose all-seeing, all-knowing discursive mastery come to seem universal and irreversible" (25). But this is an outright fabrication; most of Said's "sympathetic," much less his unsympathetic, readers do not agree on this at all, and Boone provides no evidence that they do.

Mistaking Said's views of Orientalism as a transhistorical phenomenon rather than as a modern Enlightenment and post-Enlightenment discourse, which is how Said presented it, Boone attempts to disprove a fictional Said, who allegedly conflated "the West and empire." To do so, Boone informs us that it is not the Orient but "Europe" which was "living in fear of Islamic domination, rather than the reverse, beginning with the spread of Arab rule and empire from the eighth century through the reign of the Egyptian Mamluks, including the 400-year Moorish habitation of Iberia." (25). I fear Boone's conflation of Christendom with Europe (the latter, as we saw, he posits as having existed in the eighth century, no less) and with the "Occident" and "Empire," is one of many egregious errors that he commits (not to mention that he arbitrarily subtracts three centuries from the length of the "Moorish habitation of Iberia," which lasted from 711 to 1492). For the ahistorical Boone, as we will see, not only has "Europe" always existed but so has "sexuality."

Whereas in his new book, Boone cites Bhabha sparingly as one of those alleged "sympathetic" critics of Said who "queried essentializing aspects of [Said's] theory in order to expand its reach and utility" (25), he seems to have taken this Bhabhaesque cue and followed it all too well throughout the book. Ultimately, his disavowal of Said while claiming to embrace his work is intended, as we will see, as a launching pad for Boone's project of putting into "dialogue" the Western and "Islamicate" archives on homoerotics.

Boone gets this impulse for a "dialogue" from another Europeanist, Valerie Traub, who was invited to intervene in a project of two Iranian scholars who called for "Islamicate" sexuality studies or for "queering" Middle East studies, which Boone tells us he "shares" with them. Like Boone, Traub does not know any of the languages or histories of the "Islamicate" world, a fact that does not stop either of them from writing about it. Moreover, whereas Boone acknowledges that he has nothing new to say to Middle East specialists, since he relies on their work entirely, he hopes that "the specific angle of vision I bring to this body of literature by putting it in proximity to European perspectives, projections, and representations inspires continued conversation between our disciplines and fields of expertise" (xxvii). It doesn't.

Boone clearly does not have an original project; he borrows the argument of yet another scholar who, like him, is also an interloping tourist into Middle East studies—namely, Dina al-Kassim. Al-Kassim, as Boone cites her and echoes her, wants to negotiate a space between the projection of modern Western historians of sexuality of *their* own sexual ontology onto desires expressed in the archive of their own past and onto the archives of the past and the present of *other* cultures. Al-Kassim in turn wants to negotiate a way between understanding what those desires were and are and how to name them while at the same time not letting her or anyone else's vigilance, of refusing to recognize and name these desires as knowable from a presentist perspective, to stand in the way of reading those desires in ways that could clearly be "legible" to them. Unfortunately, Boone, like Al-Kassim, seems most invested in reducing the impact of colonialism and its Orientalist epistemology in this operation to come up with a simplistic balanced and liberal outcome, whereby those who claim colonialism and Orientalism were all-encompassing and all bad are one kind of extremists and those who think them all good are equal extremists.

In the name of nuance and liberal critique, Boone and a small cohort of like-minded scholars want to tell us that it was a bit of both. In this context, the target of their criticisms, if not their attack, is not colonial and Orientalist voices, but rather and specifically their enemies, hence the focus on Edward Said and his book *Orientalism* as the primary culprits in this saga of excavating and saving the "homosexual" from the past of Europe and from the past and the present of the Orient.

True to this simplifying liberal project, Said is not just maligned and vilified in the name of a politically correct "nuance," or to be more precise, a "more nuanced" approach (an adjective that has become the alibi behind which anyone attempting to impose contemporary Western perceptions of sexual identities and desires on the past of Europe and on the present and the past of the rest of the world barricades her or himself); Said and his project are presented as constituting elements of both the good and the bad (Boone 2014, xx). The risks involved in this modestly learned liberal approach of "on the one hand and on the other" do not seem to deter Boone, who announces with vigorous, if inexcusable, confidence that "crossing such boundaries is a risk that this project is willing to take" (xx). He even has Said authorize him to generalize even where "generalizations seem impossible to make" (53). Except that Said was not speaking of generalizing about cultures and peoples as Boone does, but across the representational strategies and methods used in different disciplines and genres, such as literature, "which is supposed to be subjective and powerless," and journalism, which is supposed to be "objective and powerful," and even between photography, sociology, the novel, and positivism, as he put it (Said 1983, 157). Said's call, as Boone presents it, would allow Boone to generalize across one thousand years of literatures and arts produced by Muslims in myriad languages and geographies, none of which Boone knows—something totally antithetical to Said's method.

Boone begins by declaring several caveats: his new book, he insists, is not a Middle East studies book, and it is not part of the literature on transnationalism and globalism. It is also not an example of transnational queer theory or a work of history, or even of art history. Also, it is not a work about the representation of women (xxvii–xxviii). Many more caveats follow.

Nonetheless, the fact that Boone is studying four and a half centuries of Western representations and a millennium of "Islamicate" representations (he takes us as far back as the eighth–ninth century poet Abu Nuwas) does not mean, he tells us in a defensive posture, that his project can be criticized for "essentialism, Orientalism, and monolingualism." But even this defensiveness, he again borrows from an Israeli scholar (Dror Ze'evi), who, like Boone, also wants to shield his work from many of these key charges (Boone 2014, xxviii). Also, while Boone realizes that even within Middle East studies there are Ottomanists, Persianists, and Arabists, he misrepresents a quote from Khaled El-Rouayheb to defend himself against the charge that he ignores differences, which can "obscure continuities that extend over time and region." But, again, this is not what El-Rouayheb is discussing in the quote. El-Rouayheb in fact acknowledges the legitimacy of concerns expressed over "undifferentiated statements about attitudes in 'Islam' or 'Islamic civilization.'" He argues, however, that those who want to maintain social divisions between religious scholars, Sufis, poets, and the upper classes as "distinct groups" are caricaturing "social reality" (El-Rouayheb, 11). Unlike Boone who wants to generalize about the Ottoman, Persian, and Arab worlds, El-Rouayheb, being the meticulous learned scholar who is literate in the languages whose literatures he researches, studies exclusively the "Arab-Islamic world" between 1500 and 1800, and not the entire "Islamic" world for over a millennium without knowing any of its languages.

Finally, Boone again borrows from Al-Kassim, who alleges without a shred of empirical evidence that the biopolitical state was not imposed by colonial rule but rather emerged in the West and the Orient at the same time without the help of colonialism. Al-Kassim caricatures those who see a role for colonialism in this as "rejecting" interactions with the "foreign" in the name of some "cultural authenticity" (Boone 2014, xxix). One wonders if this is a case of the unlearned leading the unlearned.

Boone cites some Middle East scholars who are displeased that when they use Orientalist methods of analysis they are accused of Orientalism. He does so as a way to fend off his potential attackers and more insidiously to legitimize his uncorroborated claim that people who work on homosexuality in the Middle East are condemned for their work when more often than not they have in fact been celebrated. Countering this alleged charge as a way to delegitimize any potential criticism of his own project, Boone, without hesitation, labels such critics as homophobes. He contends that the alleged extra attention that "gay-focused work on the Middle East" gets and how it is labeled as "especially exploitative" is motivated by "a degree of unconscious homophobia" (xxx)! But when has gay-focused scholarship on the Middle East been seen as especially exploitative by academics? Who has ever made this charge? Boone cites no one. Furthermore, how can such a claim coexist with Boone's own claim that the homoerotics of Orientalism had been ignored and marginalized in the field, including allegedly by Said himself, who is faulted for having only addressed the heteroerotics of Orientalism?

Now that Boone has instructed the reader of what the book is not and what it cannot be criticized for, he proceeds proleptically to delegitimize all potential critics. Quoting a friend in the academy who calls for "an academic ethos of critical generosity" (xxxii) (whose advice Boone does not follow), Boone, borrowing U.S. imperial lingo that dismisses its opponents as always already "extremists," identifies and dismisses the perspectives of those who object to Orientalist projects and methods like his and his cohort's as "extreme," "paranoid" and "suspicion-laden" (xxxi). Such "extremists" are accused of denying "human agency," which, he tells us, *even* gay Western (read: white) pornographic photographers do not deny their Arab subjects (xxxi).

Boone's commitment to universalism is such that he speaks of universal "human desires," especially "the deep human desire present in most, if not all, cultures to travel to strange lands in order to encounter the unknown and unfamiliar, most often experiences in the form of cultural difference" (xxiv). This is by way of defending his "human desire" to travel to past Oriental and Occidental times and geographies and present ones as universal. His hope is that the two terms of his title—Orientalism and homoeroticism—which he seems not to realize are English and French terms that were later Europeanized beyond France and England but which still resist universalization, will be "refigured" through their travel and engagement with one another and with "the ever-ongoing process of cross-cultural exchange" (xxiv) something that is never evinced in this book.

Sexuality seems to occur everywhere and is never historicized. While historians of sexuality as a Western European taxonomy trace its emergence to the late eighteenth and the nineteenth century, Boone does not agree. In the last four and a half centuries, he tells us, contact by European writers and artists with the Orient seems to have exposed them to "alternative understandings of sexuality" (xxi). In reading an English and an Ottoman document from the seventeenth century containing what Western classifications refer to now as homoerotic themes, Boone concludes that the two documents "illuminate the history of sexuality" (6).

Boone understands that "heterosexuality" and homosexuality" are a "modern, Western-based binary" but not "sexuality" itself, which he thinks has "distinctions varying widely *over centuries* and geographic regions" (16, emphasis added). This central error of ahistoricity is evident throughout the book. Thus, Boone speaks of "Judeo-Christian and Islamic cultures" across time, not realizing that both "the Judeo-Christian" and the "Islamic" are modern and recent inventions, let alone the notion of "culture" itself, which also emerges in the nineteenth century (17).

For the ahistorical Boone, sexuality has always been there, including in sixteenth- and seventeenth-century Europe and the Ottoman Empire. He declares that French and Ottoman authors of the sixteenth century "share an explicit interest in Ottoman sexuality and both share an obsession with ordering systems—taxonomies are not solely, as Foucault's distinction between *scientia sexualis* and *ars erotica* would have it, a product of the modern West." But what Foucault addressed were the new "scientific" taxonomies (Foucault 1973), some of which also begin for him in the sixteenth century, but not pornographic types of which Foucault was well aware as extant in ancient Greek literature.[6] Still Boone thinks he is cleverer than Foucault when he declares how the Ottoman sixteenth-century courtier and poet Ghazali "presents an alternative classification of boy-lovers into *three* types (evincing, pace Foucault, identity categories)" (119). But Foucault understood that the ancients spoke of a multiplicity of sexual desires and sexual positions, what he noted as quintessentially different in modern scientific sexual taxonomies was that one's sexual desires and practices became constitutive of one, that they tell the inner *truth* of one, that they are indeed her and his very identity—having become part of a new regime of truth (Foucault 1980). Boone's inattention and lack of understanding of Foucault, just like his failure to understand Said, betrays an ideological agenda and an insistent theoretical illiteracy that seeks to attack those aspects of Foucault and Said that run counter to Boone's commitment to sexual geographical universalism as well as to the ahistoricity of sexuality.

Boone's ignorance of Ottoman, Persian, and Arabic literatures is such that he thinks that the treatise written by the Ottoman sixteenth-century Ghazali is akin not to the eighth-century Arabic treatise by al-Jahiz, *Mufakharat Al-Jawari wa al-Ghilman,* but to Plato's *Symposium.* That al-Jahiz might have been influenced by Plato's *Phaedrus,* not primarily the *Symposium,* and more importantly by Plutarch's *Erotikos,* is noted in the literature, but how would the Europeanist Boone know this upon his sudden reincarnation as an Ottomanist, Persianist, and Arabist (Boone 2014, 119, 446n18)? Boone's analysis that this was a sixteenth-century reflection of contemporary Ottoman society rather than an author's use of a classical piece of literature from the eighth century to comment on the sixteenth is another of the many errors he commits, resulting from his ignorance of the field.

In line with his ahistorical approach, Boone discusses Flaubert (who wrote immediately before or on the cusp of the new age when homo- and heterosexuality were invented) as if adhering fully to the later regime of sexuality that was still in formation at the time of his writing (Flaubert visited Egypt in 1849–50). It seems that Boone's ahistorical sense of what and when sexuality became the new regime of truth accounts for much of his analysis and for the many errors in it, leading him to jump from an analysis of the writings of Flaubert to Lawrence Durrell and Norman Mailer seamlessly, as he need not account for sexuality as historical, let alone for the history of sexuality itself. It turns out that Boone's accusation that Said reifies the Orient is more apt as a description of Boone's own project of conjuring up a reified "homoerotics of Orientalism" as an unchanging transhistorical phenomenon.

Boone provides no criterion for the selection of the texts and artwork he includes in his book—books and documents are selected from the sixteenth century to the twenty-first without any explanation of how and why these texts were selected and not others, and whether these are being presented as comprehensive or representative texts or as esoteric ones, and so on—Carl Benjamin Klunzinger and Flaubert, for example, are included after a discussion of Norman Mailer,

Richard Burton, and the contemporary U.S. television series *Rome*! The subsequent coverage of André Gide and Somerset Maugham, like Mailer before them, tells us nothing that we did not know nor does it offer anything more than extra examples of the same. Yet all of this is presented as a corrective to Said.

Temporal peregrinations between ancient Egyptian myths and contemporary American gay appropriations dot Boone's text. For example, Norman Mailer's novelistic fancies merge together and suddenly lead to the strangest conclusions of all, wherein the rhetoric by contemporary Egyptian conservatives that homosexual practices come from the West are identified by the author as "displacing and repressing the more distant centuries of non-European invasion and conquest in which institutionalized homoerotic relationships among men formed an intrinsic aspect of Muslim Egyptian life" (180). Note the wording "institutionalized homoerotic relationships" and "intrinsic aspect of Muslim Egyptian life," all of which Boone bases on the evidence of French colonials who believed that the unnatural vice of homosexuality was widespread among poor and rich Muslim men of Egypt (one wonders if Egyptian Christian and Jewish men escaped it, and if so, whether this was on account of their not being Muslim). Assuming such evidence is credible, would it not be more circumspect to speak of these times as ones in which same-sex desire was expressed in different literary and artistic genres that were not "intrinsic" to Muslim life but rather genres that sometimes flourished and were often not banned by the authorities? Unfortunately, Boone's lack of vigilance and circumspection coupled with his carelessness in choosing words and arriving at unjustified conclusions parallel his unfamiliarity with the actual histories and languages of the region.

Relying on the journalist Thomas Dworzak, who invents, appropriates, and most likely stages a trove of photographs of "Taliban men" in a Kabul conquered by U.S. troops, examples of which are included in Boone's book (to titillate readers, perhaps?), Boone declares peremptorily and relying on Western Orientalist sources (including Ahmed Rachid, a Pakistani journalist whom Boone misidentifies as a "historian,") that in Afghanistan "the tradition of male sexual apprenticeships and relationships is still widely practiced" (301).

Boone's Euro-American centrism is so intense that he defends it with a surprising ferocity for someone who claims to be a critical scholar. Anticipating the accusations of Dworzak's possible staging of the photographs for a Western Orientalist audience, Boone launches a diatribe against anticipated critics: "So intent on uncovering a narrative of Western appropriation, Dworzak's critics failed to see these images for what they are, revealing, once again, how easily homosexuality can be used as a political weapon to reinstate a reductively West–versus–Middle East binary. Seeing these images 'as they are' does not mean their unintended viewers will ever know with certainty the precise nature of the desires inspiring these photographs or the relationships they recorded. But it does mean that viewers can open themselves to the 'contradictory cultural context of these oddly beautiful photographs'" (301).

This outrageous diatribe seems uninterested in identifying the "viewers" as Western and European and not "Afghani" and seems to forget that Boone had just finished telling us how these photographs should be viewed with solid certainty as part of what he identified as "the tradition of male sexual apprenticeships and relationships" in Afghanistan. That he proceeds to quote a reviewer from the Gay Internationalist publication *The Gay and Lesbian Review Worldwide,* who posed the question, "How can one pose with flowers, arm around your buddy, kohl highlighting beautiful young eyes, and yet be a foot soldier for those who would punish you severely for such an abomination" (Boone 2014, 302) as evidence of lack of "certainty" of how to view the photographs demonstrates Boone's commitment to the very Orientalist homoerotics he claims to subject to critique. Yet and without any hesitation, Boone is on the march, declaring in conclusion that these Western-staged photographs that are marketed for a Western audience force "viewers to resist simplifying the complex, unstable, combustible, relation of sexuality and the phenomenon we call Orientalism" (303). Perhaps had Boone considered that sexuality itself might be an Orientalist construction, he would have been forced to abandon his subject position altogether and investigated the phenomenon of the "homoerotics of Orientalism" for the sheer redundancy that it is.[7]

Manifesting an orthodox, perhaps even a fundamentalist, commitment to universalism across the history and geography of the world is most evident in Boone's refusal to consider history and historicity as factors, let alone, differing geographical, linguistic, and visual and artistic traditions as expressions of the local, as opposed to expressions of one universal code. Hence and without an ounce of hesitation, in comparing visual representations of a male athlete in seventeenth-century Iran versus representations of male muscularity in 1950s United States as one and the same, Boone declares: "This smiling youth forms a seventeenth century equivalent of the 'beefcake' models featured in American physique magazines in the 1950s" (318).

Nothing seems to stand in the way of such anachronisms. In describing an Ottoman pictorial representation from the mid-eighteenth century, Boone states that "it is interesting that the percussion instruments, being played by the voyeurs have, since [ancient] Egyptian times, been associated with heightened sexual ecstasy, thus potentially implicating them in the *jouissance* of the scene" (75). Thus his presumably Said-authorized generalizations continue from the time of the pharaohs in Egypt to the mid-eighteenth-century Ottoman Empire!

The expert knowledge Boone claims to have at present in attacking Said and his *Orientalism* by claiming that what he offers is a corrective to it, however, is nowhere in sight. Take this other important example, namely his discussion of Dutch author Jacob Israel de Haan. Strangely, Boone, who claims such mastery over "Islamicate" material, although it is not part of his academic expertise, pleads ignorance in this European case, which presumably is. His alleged expertise in Europe and the Orient suddenly disappears as he approaches the subject of Zionism, its anti-Arab bigotry in its pre-state heyday period (let alone its post-state legally institutionalized racism), when it also fought against Orthodox Jews.

De Haan was a Dutch Jewish writer and activist who moved to Palestine in 1919. When Boone speaks of de Haan's activism in Palestine, which most likely led to his murder by Jerusalem operatives of the Zionist militia (the Haganah)—there is evidence that Zionist anti-homosexual prejudice was also an operative factor in his assassination—Boone tells us that "De Haan grew disillusioned with what he perceived as the Zionist party's *[sic]* antagonism toward Orthodox Jews and Arabs alike" (286). Boone never identifies the Zionist criminals who killed de Haan, nor does he mention the fact that his assassination was ordered in 1924 by none other than Yitzhak Ben-Zvi, who would later become Israel's second president. Rather, Boone declares that the "consequence [of his activism] was De Haan's political assassination at the age of 43," presumably at the hands of extraterrestrials! Most surprising is Boone's insistence on denying any rights to the Palestinian people, especially as he identifies de Haan as an activist trying to "forge alliances between Zionist hopes and Palestine *[sic]* rights," whatever "Palestine rights" are (290)!

Whereas de Haan visited Russia and wrote on the conditions of Russian political prisoners under the Czarist regime, Boone has him interested in some alleged "mass imprisonment of Jews in Tsarist Russia," which should come as a shocking revelation to historians of Russia, let alone historians of Russian Jews, who have not documented such "mass imprisonment." In fact, de Haan visited Russian prisons in 1912 and published a book about Russian political prisoners of all religious and political persuasions in 1913. Finally, and in the recent tradition of homosexual essentialism, Boone identifies de Haan as a "homosexual" and as a "gay man" rather than a man who manifested heterosexual and homosexual desires and practices, especially as Boone acknowledges that the man had been married.

Overall, Boone provides a litany of examples of Orientalist writings that reveal nothing new in terms of epistemological or ontological differences from familiar Orientalist accounts, yet he seems to think that what he offers might "transform previous understandings of Orientalism" (298). How it might do so is never made clear.

The overwhelming number of basic mistakes that Boone commits in this book stare one in the face, starting from the opening page, where Boone informs us that "'Zab' is Arabic for penis." In reality, *zub* is Arabic for dick (xvii). The numerous errors in Arabic transliteration are everywhere—*mukhannath* is sometimes rendered "*makhannath*" (30) "majnum" instead of majnun (31). He claims that Abdelwahab Bouhdiba's book *Sexuality in Islam* was "the first major Arabic-language study of its kind," except that Bouhdiba's book was written in French (46),[8] not in Arabic, and was published in 1975, not in "1985." He provides a nonsensical assertion that the "Prophet [Muhammad] nowhere names *liwat* . . . in the list of grave sins against God" without noting that the word did not even exist at the time of the Prophet but is a later coinage (46). The nineteenth-century ruler of Egypt, Muhammad Ali, is referred to in an ignorant shorthand as "Muhammad," who is identified *not* as of Albanian Muslim origins as he indeed was, but as "in fact Armenian" (179), which exposes Boone's lack of even elementary knowledge of facts about the "Orient." Boone, it seems, is not only ignorant of the Middle East but also of Europe, where he claims expertise. *Beur,* which overwhelmingly refers to French-born Arabs whose parents are immigrants from North Africa or to North African–born Arabs who immigrated as children to France, is wrongly defined by Boone as "a racial term designating a man of mixed French and North African descent" (407). He speaks of how Andalusian "Arab poets . . . memorialized the charms of Jewish lads," as if Arabic-speaking Jews were less Arab than the Arabic-speaking Muslim poets, and constituted a nationality in the modern Zionist sense (63).

Boone's attempt to show expertise in the region extends to comical levels when he incessantly seeks to exhibit his (faux) knowledge of Arabic. In the course of proving that an Orientalist European book of erotica that claims to be of Ottoman origins is a fraud, Boone asserts, in response to the Orientalist author's claim of a pun between the French *chic* and the alleged Arabic word "*sik,*" which "is Arabic slang for 'cock'"! But there is no such word in classical Arabic or in the many Arabic slangs that refers to "cock." Most likely the author is confusing the Turkish words *çük* (pronounced *chük*) and *sik,* both of which mean "cock" in Turkish. Yet Boone's proof that the book was indeed of European provenance was not based on the European author's ignorance of Arabic but rather, according to Boone, that the alleged "pun" between French and "Arabic" of this allegedly Arabic word "only works if one is speaking in French" and not that in reality no such pun exists in the first place, whether one were speaking French or Arabic (269), or even Turkish.

In addition to misidentifying de Haan as a homosexual, Boone also seeks to out a well-known Egyptian film director, Youssef Chahine, as "bisexual," something the heterosexually married director never declared or avowed. But Boone is able to extract that *truth* from Chahine's cinematic oeuvre. Indeed, Boone goes as far as asserting that Chahine's use of cinematic language implies "homosexuality's existence as part and parcel of Egypt's heritage, as well as part of his personal identity and politics" (237). How he reaches such conclusions remains a mystery. He also misunderstands some of the subplots in Chahine's films and seems not to know the correct chronology of his film releases (*The Return of the Prodigal Son* was released in 1976, two years before *Alexandria . . . Why?* not "the same year as *Alexandria . . . Why?*" [252]). His seeming ignorance of the context and background of Chahine's films is such that he identifies *The Return of the Prodigal Son* as a film about "the Arab-Israeli conflict" rather than about the political situation in Egypt itself and the betrayal of a dreamy President Nasir by his own power-hungry regime men during and after the 1967 War.[9]

Lack of knowledge of Arabic makes Boone state that "one might hypothesize that the adult male [in a Safavid pictorial representation] being sodomized is supposed to represent the ubnah, a man who takes pleasure in being penetrated and poses a definitional problem in Islamic medical and ethical discourse." But *ubnah* refers to a medical *condition* afflicting men that causes them to seek and enjoy being anally penetrated by other men, and does not refer to such a man himself, who would be called *ma'bun*. This condition was only diagnosed by the twelfth-century Ibn Sina in a little known medical treatise and remained mostly unknown in other "Islamic" medical treatises (though specialized medical references to it continued in medical books). How a sixteenth-century Safavid pictorial representation is related to the twelfth-century *ubnah* diagnosed by Ibn Sina is something Boone never tells us.

Boone's intent on proving the homosexual investments of European travelers to the Orient, who write of its sodomitic practices, focus on their detailed descriptions of Oriental male bodies and their beauty, betraying their own fixated and erotically charged gaze. One, however, could say the same about Boone's book, which is full of a large number of Orientalist homoerotic paintings and photographs, most of which are gratuitous and not essential for the points he wants to make. Their main purpose seems to be to tantalize and excite the contemporary reader, and less so to provide the critique that Boone purports to offer. But not all Orientalist photographs are intended to exploit, he insists; rather, the photographic genre of ethnographic types, as far as Boone is concerned, "rang[es] from the exploitative to the legitimate" (386)! How their legitimacy is established, only Boone can decide.

When he speaks of Paul Bowles's sexual exploits with Moroccan men in Tangiers, especially his relationship with Mohammed Mrabet, the presentist Boone is most sympathetic. Bowles's portraits of the half-naked Mrabet "not only record a fantasy of desirable otherness but document the lasting relationship between American expatriate and Moroccan writer" (392). Contrast this conclusion with Boone's more learned understanding in his 1995 essay, where he states that

> the story of many Western men's encounters with the Near East, whatever these tourists' putative sexual orientations, has also been the story of a crisis in male subjectivity—the crisis that by definition is occidental masculinity itself. Every rereading of this story may help Western readers re-orient their perceptions of the complex undercurrents of those fantasized geographies of male desire that depend on, even as they resist, the homoerotics of an orientalizing discourse whose phallocentric collusions and resistant excitations this essay has just begun to uncover. (1995, 104)

In his book, Boone volunteers that the photographs of Charles Roffey are also not objectifying because the Arab men he photographed "seem to take pleasure in being admired: their agency remains intact" (2014, 394). Michel Giliberti's objectification of Tunisian men (Giliberti was born in Tunisia in 1950 and left with his *pied noir* family to France in 1961) is seen by Boone as indicative of intersubjectivity, evidenced by the men who "smile back at the camera," which renders Giliberti, who now lives in Normandie, "a reciprocal subject of shared ethnic origins and language." One is not sure here if Boone knows that the majority of Tunisians are not ethnic Italians or French colons and that their native language is Arabic and not French (395). Boone's strange interpretations are such that he asserts in a most serious manner that Giliberti's "representing his male [Tunisian] subjects as cheerful and open, rather than mysterious and closed, becomes a political statement that, in shattering an Orientalist stereotype, engages and rewrites the homoerotics of Orientalism in an affirmative vein" (395). Boone's fantasy that it is only classic Orientalism that masculinizes the European and feminizes the Oriental and that when contemporary Western pornographers reverse this polarity they are being subversive is a most shallow assertion, further exposing his limitations as a scholar of Orientalism (403–4).

Boone's book is a synthesis of the work of others, though at times the author wants to claim equal credit for the analysis that he offers, even if and when he acknowledges that others have offered it years before him. Thus, rather than acknowledge that his analysis of two Egyptian novels is based on the analysis of a work published seven years before his book, he concedes simply that a previous work "also argues" the same points he is offering now (233).

The major problem of Boone's book is its lateness, which, however, is related to a tautology: he tells us that he could not write his book had it not been for the recent books that have come out about the so-called "Islamicate" world, which allowed him to write his "contrapuntal" account, while at the same time he offers nothing conceptually or analytically new, and very little that is empirically novel. But this indeed is the point: studies of Orientalist representations of sexuality of Arab, Iranian, and Ottoman depictions of sexual desires and practices have already provided all this information and more, and made many of the arguments, for better or worse, that Boone wants to push on his readers now. The synthetic basis of the book is not its major shortcoming, however, but rather its utter redundancy and lack of originality. As another late enemy of Said, Christopher Hitchens, once said, "The one unforgivable sin is to be boring." That is a sin of which Boone's book is most guilty.

This is not to say that the question of sexuality and Middle East studies is not a worthy topic of scholarship. As I have argued in my last two books, the problem with the methodology of "Queer Middle East studies" is its central liberal imperial universalizing gesture that seeks to impose sexuality as a universal and a transhistorical category. The fact that many of those writing in this nascent field may claim to oppose imperialism politically while being epistemologically and ontologically committed to it is not necessarily a contradiction, as what they fail to do is performatively counteract imperial epistemological and ontological particularism, which they insist is a form of universalism, even as they insist on being anti-imperialist. I argue in *Islam in Liberalism* that

> it is the production of Islam in sexuality that needs to be studied so that we can understand the emergence of a field that seeks and insists on the need to study an object it calls "sexuality in Islam." What is required is a Foucaultian investigation into the conditions of possibility for truth

> statements about "Islam." Instead of assuming and seeking to uncover the mechanisms by which something called sexuality operates inside the category Islam, scholars must begin with the "positive mechanisms" that generate this Western will to know. . . . The outcome of this kind of approach will reveal much about how Western scholarship on sexuality not only constitutes something it calls "Islam" but also how it constitutes "Europe," the "West," as an always already racialized normativity. (Massad 2015, 272–73)

The revisionism among some liberal–left academics of Said's work did not emerge in a vacuum, but rather in the context of the Iranian Revolution, the rise in Islamisms, 9/11, the subsequent U.S. invasions of Muslim-majority countries, and the U.S. war against actually existing "Islam" as a threat to U.S. interests. The rise of Islamophobia and of threats identified as "Islamofascism" and "totalitarian" Islam are also important factors in this context.

In addition to the U.S. imperial campaign to allegedly "save" Muslims from Muslim despots and help them establish liberal democracy, we must add the related liberal crusades to rescue Muslim women and Muslim homosexuals from the grip of "Islam," or at least the grip of the "Islamofascists." It is in this context that Said's *Orientalism* has become an obstacle to these moral crusades that have become dear to liberal academics steeped in the U.S. campaign for "human rights" around the world.[10] Their alleged moving "beyond" Said is nothing short of a cover for their wish that Said's *Orientalism* had never been written.

If in his 1995 essay Boone astutely worried that "the homoerotics of orientalism constantly threatens to become another name for occidental homophobia" (96), the politics, ideology, and substandard scholarship he offers us in his 2014 *The Homoerotics of Orientalism* constantly threaten to become another name for occidental Gay Internationalism and homonationalism, both of which being subsets of the new white imperial cultural supremacy that opposes itself to a medieval Orient and to an Islam that it seeks to enlighten.

Joseph Massad is professor of modern Arab politics and intellectual history at Columbia University. His most recent books include *Desiring Arabs* (2007) and *Islam in Liberalism* (2015).

Notes

1. This is indeed very different from earlier learned critics of Said, like James Clifford (255–76). For an engagement with Clifford's important critique, see Brennan, 74, 77–78.
2. See Shohat 1992, 121–43; 2004, 55–75.
3. Cited in Shohat 2004, 65.
4. Bhabha, 20. See my response to Bhabha in Massad 2010, 40–42.
5. See, for example, Boone 2014, xxiv, xxv, xxxii, 5.
6. See Foucault 1988.
7. On this, see Massad 2015.
8. What is odd is that Boone cites my own criticisms of the book in my own book, *Desiring Arabs*, and cites the very pages where I discuss the bad Arabic translations of Bouhdiba's book from the French!
9. On Chahine, see Massad 1999.
10. For the history of the rise of "human rights," see Moyn.

Works Cited

Al-Kassim, Dina. 2008. "Epilogue." In *Islamicate Sexualities: Translations across Temporal Geographies of Desire*. Ed. Kathryn Babayan, and Afsaneh Najmabadi. Cambridge, Mass.: Harvard Center for Middle East Studies.

Amireh, Amal. 2010. "Afterword." *GLQ* 16, no. 4: 636–47.

Bhabha, Homi K. 2004. "Untimely Ends." *Artforum*, February.

Boone, Joseph A. 1995. "Vacation Cruises, or the Homoerotics of Orientalism." *PMLA* 110, no. 1: 89–107.

Boone, Joseph A. 2014. *The Homoerotics of Orientalism*. New York: Columbia University Press.

Brennan, Tim. 1992. "Places of Mind, Occupied Lands: Edward Said and Philology." In *Edward Said: A Critical Reader*. Ed. Michael Sprinker, 74–95. Oxford: Blackwell.

Chiang, Howard. 2010. "Epistemic Modernity and the Emergence of Homosexuality in China," *Gender & History* 22, no. 3: 629–57.

Clifford, James. 1988. *The Predicament of Culture: Twentieth-Century Ethnography, Literature, and Art*. Cambridge: Harvard University Press.

El-Rouayheb, Khaled. 2005. *Before Homosexuality in the Arab-Islamic World, 1500–1800*. Chicago: University of Chicago Press.

Foucault, Michel. 1973. *The Order of Things: An Archeology of the Human Sciences*. New York: Vintage Books.

Foucault, Michel. 1980. *The History of Sexuality, Volume I: An Introduction*. New York: Vintage Books.

Foucault, Michel. 1988. *The History of Sexuality, Volume 3: The Care of the Self*. New York: Vintage Books.

Marchand, Suzanne L. 2009. *German Orientalism in the Age of Empire: Religion, Race, and Scholarship*. Cambridge: Cambridge University Press.

Massad, Joseph. 1999. "Art and Politics in the Cinema of Youssef Chahine." *Journal of Palestine Studies* 110:77–93.

Massad, Joseph. 2001. *Colonial Effects: The Making of National Identity in Jordan*. New York: Columbia University Press.

Massad, Joseph. 2007. *Desiring Arabs*. Chicago: University of Chicago Press.

Massad, Joseph. 2010. "Affiliating with Edward Said." In *Emancipation and Representation: On the Intellectual Meditations of Edward Said*. Ed. Hakem Rustom and Adel Iskander. Berkeley: University of California Press.

Massad, Joseph. 2015. *Islam in Liberalism*. Chicago: University of Chicago Press.

Moyn, Samuel. 2010. *The Last Utopia: Human Rights in History*. Cambridge, Mass.: Belknap Press of Harvard University Press.

Said, Edward W. 1978. *Orientalism*. New York: Pantheon Books.

Said, Edward W. 1983. "Opponents, Audiences, Constituencies, and Communities," In *The Anti-Aesthetic: Essays on Postmodern Culture*. Ed. Hal. Foster, 135–59. Seattle: Bay Press.

Said, Edward W. 1985. "Orientalism Reconsidered." *Race & Class* 27, no. 2: 1–15.

Shalakany, Amr. 2007. "On a Certain Queer Discomfort with Orientalism." In *Proceedings of the Annual Meeting*, 125–29. N.p.: American Society of International Law.

Shohat, Ella. 1992. "Antinomies of Exile: Said at the Frontiers of National Narrations." In *Edward Said: A Critical Reader*. Ed. Michael Sprinker, 121–43. Oxford: Blackwell.

Shohat, Ella. 2004. "The 'Postcolonial' in Translation: Reading Said in Hebrew." *Journal of Palestine Studies* 33, no. 3 (Spring): 55–75.

IN THE CONJUNCTURE

Conjuncture: from the Latin *conjungere* (to bind together, to connect, to join). A combination of circumstances, a convergence of events, an intersection of contingencies and necessities, a complex, overdetermined state of affairs—usually producing a crisis, leading to a breaking point, driving to a historic crossroads . . .

"In The Conjuncture" is a new thematic section of *Cultural Critique,* consisting of short pieces meant at once as soundings, interventions, and provocations regarding a cultural and political phenomenon of urgent and topical interest. Straddling the seldom-crossed border between critical–theoretical scholarship and op-ed journalism, this section will focus, each time, on a singular historical conjuncture, whose salient features may resonate with other situations elsewhere, and whose aftershocks may be felt rippling across the global terrain. In this section, we invite public intellectuals to write in the conjuncture.

The editors welcome proposals for this thematic section, which should be addressed to *Cultural Critique,* Department of Cultural Studies and Comparative Literature, 235 Nicholson Hall, 216 Pillsbury Drive S.E., University of Minnesota, Minneapolis, MN 55455, U.S.A., or via email to cultcrit@umn.edu.

CASTRO, OR COMMUNISM IN THE VANISHING PRESENT

Fidel Alejandro Castro Ruz died on a Friday last November. That night in and around the Versailles Restaurant on Eighth Street (Calle Ocho) and Thirty-Fifth Avenue in Miami, crowds gathered to supplement their typical dining (Versailles has long characterized itself as the "most famous Cuban restaurant in the world") with an impromptu festival.

As predicted. A friend, present and aghast, put it bluntly: "Yes, but what exactly were they celebrating?"

Our question is the reverse: What exactly has been lost?

Perhaps an unbearable urgency has been given to this question by the arrival and slow passing of the past year, 2017, the year during which those of us who still care will mark the one hundred–year anniversary of the two revolutions (the dates vary depending on the calendar one consults) that brought Lenin and the Bolsheviks to power in the former Soviet Union. "Former" here marks precisely the source of the urgency brought to Castro's death, and this despite all of the nuances and subtleties called for by bringing this man and that movement into intimate contact.

The conjoined pieces that follow (we solicited "essays, aphorisms, fragments") variously engage "Fidel" as a portal (had he not given the word *gusano* its unique, non-zoological meaning, "wormhole" might also work here), the portal through which to ponder, not so much his legacy (although Nimtz, Beverly, and Karl touch on this) but what those of us committed to the cause of the Left risk losing in surrendering such a legacy to the swarm of populisms actively rethinking contemporary global politics in the absence of a concept of revolution (passive or otherwise).

Because Nimtz draws attention to the film *Maestra* ("teacher" in the feminine), and because, for better *and* for worse, *Cultural Critique* is an academic journal, it seems fitting here to cite from Fidel's four-hour improvised speech, "La Historia me absolverá" (history will absolve me), those passages on education. They could not speak to us more resonantly than now.

> Finally, a revolutionary government would undertake the total reform of our teaching system *(nuestra enseñanza),* attuning it with the initiatives discussed earlier, to urgently prepare the generations being called upon to live in a happier country. One must not forget the words of the Apostle: "A grave error is being committed in Latin America: communities *(pueblos)* who live almost entirely off the products of the land are being prepared for an urban existence and are not being prepared for an agrarian one. The happiest people *(el pueblo)* are those whose children have been best educated both in the formation of their thought and in the guidance of their sentiments. A well-instructed people will always be strong and free."

> But the soul of teaching is the teacher, and the educators in Cuba are paid miserably, yet despite this, no one is more dedicated to his vocation than the Cuban teacher. Who among us did not learn his ABCs *(primeras letras)* in a small public school? It is clearly time that we stop paying spare change *(limosnas)* to the men and women who have in their hands, both today and tomorrow, the most sacred mission in the world, which is to teach. No teacher should earn less than 200 pesos, just as no secondary school teacher should earn less than 350 pesos if we want them to dedicate themselves entirely to their elevated task, without succumbing to every kind of penurious privation *(mezquinas privaciones)*. Moreover, we must concern ourselves with the teachers who carry out their functions in the countryside: so, the free use of the means of transportation; and to all of them, every five years at least, a six month recess from their labors *(tareas)*, on a stipend, so that they can attend specialist courses either in this country or abroad, bringing themselves up to date with the latest pedagogical insights, and constantly improving their programs and systems." (Online at bureau.comandantina.com/archivos, my translation)

Instead of tediously correcting for inflation, we simply suggest that these paragraphs, as signposts to the pieces that follow, might substitute for the line Dante famously suspended over the gates of Hell: "Lasciate ogne speranza, voi ch' intrate."

The Editors

CALIBAN AFTER COMMUNISM
THOUGHTS ON THE FUTURE OF CUBA

John Beverley

Like most Americans, I welcomed the Obama initiative to re-establish diplomatic relations and open up new commercial and travel ties with Cuba. I also welcomed the reform process in Cuba itself, though I thought it was moving too slowly. The new initiative by Trump, though it symbolically cancels the Obama accord, does not in fact change things all that much in the short run. The Cuban response to the Obama initiative was sluggish and cautious, and now with the hostility of the new administration will be probably even more sluggish and cautious. Why not? The Cubans know that while there is much to be gained from making a transition out of Communism, there is also much to be lost: consider the cases of Hungary and Poland, for example, now both moving towards right-wing authoritarianism. And in Cuba's case there will be no EU to bail it out.

So it matters what form the transition in Cuba will take. But I think it would be fair to say that *whatever* happens in Cuba in the coming period—whether there will be a decisive shift towards economic liberalization, multiparty politics, and integration with the world market; or whether things will remain more or less the same (unsatisfactory but survivable); or whether there is a possible a "third" way, something like a Cuban version of the Chinese path—will be a disappointment.

Hungary and Poland were appendixes of the Soviet system, with regimes essentially imposed on recalcitrant populations by the Red Army in the wake of the Second World War. But Cuba made its own revolution. It was in the 1960s and 70s a powerful, vigorous, attractive example of a possible alternative secular modernity. An alternative to what? An alternative to capitalism as a model of development for Third World or postcolonial countries, but also to the increasingly sclerotic, repressive model of Soviet socialism. In this sense, Cuba could be said to have been a "world–historical" entity, in Hegel's sense of that term.

I hope I am not being too rhetorical in saying that Cuba was a beacon of hope for millions of people around the world. It was Vietnam's ally in its war against the United States. It was Cuban military forces that helped defeat the South African army in Angola, an achievement that led to the eventual collapse of the apartheid regime (whereas the United States supported that regime). It was Cuba that supported the revolutionary upsurge in Central America in the 1970s and 80s, and the Sandinistas in particular. It was Cuba that provided decisive medical and humanitarian aid to Haiti in the wake of the terrible earthquake.

But it was also the idea of a secular revolutionary modernity that the Cuban revolution represented that was compelling (an idea embodied in the great films produced by the Cuban film institute, the ICAIC). It was for my generation in the United States—the generation of the Sixties—a great inspiration, a source of enthusiasm about the possibility of change, an enthusiasm that animated the New Left, the civil rights movement, and the women's movements, for example.

We now know what many had feared inside and outside of Cuba: that despite its initial daring and originality, the revolution steered too close to the Soviet Union and was dragged down by the collapse of the Soviet bloc after 1989. Cuban socialism, which, to repeat, was the result of a popular revolution from below, and not imposed by the Red Army, as in the case of many Eastern European countries, survived. But it lost its normativity. The end of that normativity in the 1990s was expressed by the Cubans themselves in the somewhat oxymoronic concept of the "Special Period in times of peace"—Período Especial en tiempos de paz (oxymoronic because one expects states of exception in a period of war, not of peace). The idea of the Special Period was meant to signify publicly and officially that while the Communist regime itself did not collapse, as was the case in the Soviet Union and Eastern Europe, what remained was no longer, even for Cuban officialdom, a model of what an advanced, egalitarian socialist society should look like.

For Cuba simply to remain in place among the ruins of what was once a vigorous revolutionary project will be a disappointment, then. On the other hand, if as a result of the reform process and the new opening of relations with the United States Cuba now makes more decisively a transition to a mixed or even predominantly free market economy with a somewhat more open and democratic, perhaps multiparty, political system, then at best, it seems to me, Cuba may achieve in a generation or so the standard of living and economic development of, say, Costa Rica today. I do not mean to disrespect Costa Rica by saying this: it is a very pleasant and in its way successful country where many North Americans like to go to retire or vacation. And I'm sure many Cubans in Cuba today would be delighted to have the kind of freedoms and economic opportunities that Costa Ricans have as a matter of course.

It goes without saying that this prospect falls far short of the transformative importance that Cuba had in the late twentieth century. Cuba will return essentially to being what it was before 1959, a virtual dependency of the United States, with some remnant of the great social programs, especially in medicine and education, created by the revolution, and a radical nationalist cultural ethos that has become itself, paradoxically, a kind of tourist commodity, like the figure of Che Guevara or the Buena Vista Social Club. So the path of renovation via the present reform process and the resumption of relations with the United States will be disappointing, even if it is under present circumstances desirable and perhaps inevitable in any case.

My assumption, then, is that the future of whatever transformative potential the Cuban revolution possessed or continues to possess lies outside of Cuba itself (and outside too the Cuban exile community, or diaspora, whose historical role also has been and will continue to be disappointing, as was the case with the exile communities produced by the Russian revolution).

The Special Period and the subsequent sine curve pattern of liberalization and tightening up in the new century brought many new cultural and civic advances in Cuba—for example, in relation to LGBT rights, a notoriously sore point in the 1960s and 70s. (On the other hand, de facto racism against the black population and class prejudice seem to have increased.) Cultural production in Cuba is certainly much freer, more disinhibited. On the other hand, it has become more parochial and *costumbrista* (the Spanish word for "local color" art), sometimes in effect a high-end version of tourist art. The only Cuban writer who has anything like an international audience today is perhaps Leonardo Padura. The key area of film, which was one of the greatest and most influential achievements of Cuban culture during the revolutionary period—has lost both its urgency and quality. Cuba no longer sustains its own film industry: it depends on coproductions, mainly with Spain. It is as if with the removal of the heavy-handed repression of the spheres of literature and art, the intensity and originality of the Cuban culture, even dissident or antirevolutionary culture, has waned too.

So I am not sanguine about the possibilities represented in Special Period cultural liberalization, which mixes both accommodation to globalization and resistance (Elzbieta Sklodowska has studied in detail this peculiar dialectic in Special Period culture in *Invento, luego resisto: El Período Especial en Cuba como experiencia y metáfora* [2016]). Instead, I want to turn back rather to an earlier, decidedly *unliberal* or *antiliberal* cultural moment: the moment of the publication, in 1971, of Roberto Fernandéz Retamar's famous essay, *Calibán: Notas sobre arte y cultura en Nuestra América,* in the cultural journal he headed at the time, *Casa de las Américas.*

The immediate and pressing context for Retamar's essay was the so-called Padilla affair—el Caso Padilla. In 1968 the Cuban poet Heberto Padilla, at one time a supporter of the revolution, had been denied a literary prize he had been awarded in Cuba for a collection of poems titled *Fuera del juego* (Out of the game [of the revolution, that is]). Padilla was subsequently harassed and at one point even imprisoned by the revolutionary authorities for lack of political correctness and forced to produce an obviously coerced self-criticism of "errors." This provoked a widespread reaction among European and Latin America literary intellectuals who had previously been sympathetic to the Cuban Revolution, including, for example, Jean Paul Sartre and Simone de Beauvoir, Mario Vargas Llosa, Carlos Fuentes, Susan Sontag, and Hans Werner Enzensberg. Other writers, like Gabriel García Márquez, remained faithful to, although increasingly critical of, Cuba. Padilla himself went into exile in the United States in 1980.

The Padilla affair marked an emerging split between the left–liberal literary intelligentsia in Latin America and elsewhere and the Cuban Revolution, whose own official cultural policy moved in the early 1970s into a rather orthodox and repressive phase famously dubbed by the Cuban literary critic Ambrosio Fornet, a close associate of Retamar's, *el quinquenio gris*—the grey five years. Retamar wanted to propose in *Caliban* something quite different from the party-dictated, neo-Stalinist cultural mores of the Quinquenio Gris. Indeed, the essay is often seen as one of the foundational texts of postcolonialism. But willy-nilly, in Cuba itself *Caliban* became a kind of signal or symptom of the shift.

The use of the name Caliban in Retamar's essay comes of course from the character in Shakespeare's play *The Tempest*. Prospero, the ruler of Milan, has been overthrown and has taken refuge on an island with his daughter Miranda. Here by his art of magic he imposes his rule on the native inhabitants, who include Caliban, "a deformed slave" in Shakespeare's characterization, and the sprightly "spirit of the air," Ariel. Though *The Tempest* is nominally set on an island in the Mediterranean, it must have brought to mind for early seventeenth-century audiences in England the islands of the Caribbean, including Cuba, and their colonization in the sixteenth century. Caliban is an anagram of "cannibal," and "cannibal" is in turn—at least so Retamar claims—a deformation of the word Carib, or Caribe, to designate the inhabitants of the new world as savages or cannibals. Both Ariel and Caliban become the servants of Prospero, who will eventually be restored to his throne at the end of the play.

In the roughly three and a half centuries between *The Tempest* and Retamar's essay there is a long, complex, and rich history of the Caliban-cannibal-Caribbean–Latin American association, which Carlos Jáuregui (2008) has traced admirably. For our purposes here, however, it is enough to recall that in 1899 the Uruguayan intellectual José Rodó published his famous essay *Ariel*, attacking the emerging forces of U.S. imperialism—the 1898 Spanish-American War had just concluded—and trying to formulate a principle for a Latin American identity that could resist this onslaught. Latin America was Ariel, Rodó suggested, the spirit of the air, the poet. Latin American life would be ruled by a kind of aesthetic and philosophical elite, not immune to commerce but whose spiritual genealogy, via the constitution of southern or Latin Europe in the Roman Empire, went back to the classical period of Hellenic civilization. The United States, on the other hand, was Caliban, gruff, ill-spoken, utilitarian, misshapen, vigorous but crude, newborn, lacking a usable past.

Retamar's counterclaim in 1971 was that the model for the postcolonial Latin American intellectual was not Ariel but Caliban: "Nuestro símbolo no es pues Ariel, como pensó Rodó, sino Calibán." This meant not so much the opposition of the white, creole intellectual as such to a racially diverse "popular" subject, Caliban (Retamar was himself an elite intellectual and poet). It was rather the opposition of one kind of intellectual—the Europeanized man of letters, or *letrado*—to a new type of intellectual, Caliban, who represented the spirit of national liberation and postcolonial critique. The essay ends with an evocation of the figure of Che Guevara, and a speech Che gives at one of the new universities created by the revolution—the image combines political daring and pedagogy as instruments of power. Che Guevara is the new Caliban. Or rather the graduates of the new university he speaks at will be the new Calibans.

Retamar was participating in *Calibán* in the question of the formation and role of the postcolonial intellectual—a theme also raised famously by Frantz Fanon in *The Wretched of the Earth* and Edward Said, for whom the writers of the postcolonial world would be the harbingers of a "new humanism." Caliban is the "native," the colonized subject, without, however, being simply nativist or fundamentalist. He is estranged from his mother, Sycorax, who represents tradition and religious culture. He has lost his touch with his own language and past, and has been in some sense transcultured by his experience as Prospero's slave. He has learned the language of Prospero not to assimilate but, so he claims, "the better to curse you."

In Gramscian terms, Caliban is the "organic" intellectual behind the project of decolonization, whereas Ariel is the "traditional" intellectual, bound fatally to the ruling hierarchy and foreign domination. The European and Latin American writers who, like Mario Vargas Llosa, were attacking Cuba in the early 1970s, were the Ariels of Latin America. They had become, Retamar was saying more or less explicitly, the lackeys of U.S. imperialism. It did not help their cause that the journal many of the critics of Cuba, like Vargas Llosa, published in, *Mundo Nuevo,* turned out to be financed by a cultural front of the CIA.

What can we make of this today somewhat obscure debate?

First, Retamar did not understand at the time what now seems clear in retrospect: the fact that the Padilla affair and its aftermath represented the *end* of the cultural hegemony of the Cuban Revolution rather than its further expansion. Retamar expected that the Padilla debate would be subsumed in a longer-term development of Cuban and international socialist culture and prosperity as the Cold War proceeded; at the time, 1971, it still seemed possible that the force of socialism and anticolonial struggle would win out in the long run. The intellectual should put himself or herself (though, as many feminists pointed out, the figure of Caliban was problematic from a gender point of view) at the service of that possibility, which was sustained by the Soviet Union and, up to that point, China as well. That assumption on Retamar's part (as I imagine he would agree today) was part of the problem of Cuba's linking itself too closely with the Soviet Union. Perhaps the linkage seemed essential at the time, even for something like the revolution to survive; but in the long run it was unfortunate. If the central question of the Cold War was which of the two great systems—capitalism or Communism—would provide a better route to modernity in the underdeveloped world, then the answer of history has been clear: capitalism.

It has been the immense force and success of neoliberal globalization that brought to an end or impasse the project of socialism in the twentieth century. The question is whether that can be a meaningful alternative that is not itself swallowed up by the force of globalization. In this context, the idea of Caliban still retains a certain urgency and appeal, as an image of a cultural possibility that stands at the edge of globalization. It is true that we are with globalization in something like an "after" of postcolonialism, which has undoubtedly lost its appeal in the developing world; but to the extent that colonialism was essential to modern capitalism from its inception in the late Middle Ages, then globalization means not the suspension of coloniality of power but rather its putative universalization.

Accordingly, I want to recall a famous selection of passages from Antonio Gramsci's *Prison Notebooks* of the 1930s, which is known in English as *The Modern Prince*. As the title suggests, these passages have to do above all with Gramsci's own relation to Italy's greatest political thinker, Machiavelli, and his book, *The Prince,* which predates *The Tempest* by about a century. Machiavelli's argument, to recall, was that for a people or a nation to come into its own as such required a visionary leader who could endow them in their scattered heterogeneity with a new sense of identity and purpose. To be able to do that, Gramsci argued, was to create a new form of hegemony, which he defined as "the moral and intellectual leadership of the nation" (1959). For Machiavelli, the model of such a leader was Moses, who liberates the Jews from slavery in Egypt, gives them the tables of the law and a sense of identity and purpose as a "people." What Italy needed, divided in the early sixteenth century among the various rising nation-states, like Spain and France, and rival city-states, was a leader like Moses.

Gramsci understood that in modern times that function could no longer be that of the individual intellectual or leader. Instead, the modern Prince is the *party*, because it has the possibility to bring together the heterogeneous elements of Italian society and forge a new kind of society and culture out of them.

Retamar was trying to channel something like Gramsci's argument about the Prince in *Caliban* (his more direct inspiration was, of course, José Martí). Caliban is the image of someone—something—that will lead us out of bondage. But Caliban after Communism will not be the postcolonial intellectual in the mode imagined and performed by Martí, or Frantz Fanon and Edward Said, or Aimé Cesaire, or Retamar himself. Nor will it be a figure like Che Guevara or Fidel Castro (it could be perhaps someone like Chávez, but the collapse of Chavismo after his untimely death shows the limitations of the caudillo as a political focus). Nor will it be a mass party on the order of the old Communist parties of the Third International, including the Italian Communist Party that Gramsci led, all of which have either disappeared or made their peace with globalization. Nor will it be a new "vanguard party" of the sort espoused by the various forms of ultraleftism, usually Trotskyist in inspiration. It is easier to say what it will not be than what it will be. For what it is worth, I imagine something like a political party or movement of a new type, inflected ideologically and strategically by what we broadly understand as the challenges of postcolonialism and feminism, and the new possibilities and contradictions generated by globalization, which include the generalization of democracy as the ground for politics. I am thinking of a "Left" version of the kind of populism that has been articulated with dramatic success by the right in Europe and now the United States and Turkey. One could point to elements of this possibility in the Bernie Sanders phenomenon in the United States (in retrospect, it seems clear that Sanders would have had a better chance to win the U.S. election than Hillary), the unexpected success of Corbyn in the UK, Syriza in Greece, Podemos in Spain, in addition to what remains of the Pink Tide governments of Latin America.

Some would say that what I have in mind here is similar to what Michael Hardt and Antonio Negri mean by the "multitude" in their influential Empire trilogy—a new, postnational, hydra-headed radical subject summoned up by globalization and the Web, but destined to go beyond its capitalist form (Jaron Lanier has spoken, ironically, about "digital Maoism" in this sense). But the idea of the multitude notably vacates claims of nationalism and identity politics as anachronistic, whereas the idea of Caliban is founded centrally on the concept of national liberation struggle and postcolonialism and "identity."

As in the case of the Bolivian MAS, which I see as a kind of model here, such a party or movement would be nationalist but it would no longer represent the national as simply a hybrid/transcultured identity (Retamar's image of Caliban, by contrast, accepts *mestizaje*, or racial hybridity, as the essential form of socialist citizenship). Rather, the new party would be itself founded on the principle of multiculturalism and sexual and cultural diversity. It would see the principle of the national as precisely its multicultural, multiethnic character, as in the claim the MAS has inscribed in the Bolivian constitution that the country is a "multinational state." The new citizen, in turn, would be an artist, a worker, gay, afro, a slum-dweller, a peasant or small farmer, a middle-class professional woman, a poor woman, a member of an indigenous community or group, or an indigenous small entrepreneur, above all a *young* person. But that panoply of subject positions—a kind of postmodern version of the Popular Front of the 1930s—would be joined by what the late, great political theorist Ernesto Laclau (2007) called "an egalitarian imaginary." The generalization of difference, in other words, must be accompanied by a generalization of the principle of equality. We are not too far here from the ending pages of *Caliban*. (Fidel Castro anticipated something of this heterogeneity of the Latin American radical–popular subject in his 1962 Second Declaration of Havana, which bears rereading today). It is as a residue or reminder of that egalitarian imaginary that something of Cuba's world-historical significance could persist. Cuba was never strictly speaking an egalitarian society, even in the days of the revolution, but certainly it was a society deeply oriented toward egalitarianism.

A few years ago, I would have said that the new Caliban, the modern Prince, was to be found not in Cuba or what Cuba will become, but rather in those parties and now regimes of Latin America that emerged in the wake of the consequences of the defeat of the traditional Left in the seventies and eighties, the parties of the so-called Pink Tide, or *marea rosada*. I say a few years ago, because now it appears that the Pink Tide is in retreat, especially with the impeachment of Dilma Roussef in Brazil and the deep crisis (some might say collapse) of the project of Chavismo in Venezuela. Still, things may shift in the not-too-distant future (Lula remains the most powerful candidate in the Brazilian election upcoming in 2018; the center–left has a good chance in the upcoming Mexican elections too). And, in any case, despite its present slump, the Pink Tide established a new horizon of expectations among the populations of Latin America that it will be difficult to dismantle completely. In a sense, the Pink Tide has been the victim of its own success in lifting masses of people out of poverty or subsistence and integrating them into consumer culture but also into the circuits of neoliberal consumer desire.

Hopefully the Cuban transition will be guided and nourished by the reemergence at the edge of globalization of a plausible Left, rather than the right-wing nationalist–populist trend that points in the direction of something like Hungary or Poland or Turkey (or our own country) today. But that eventuality will involve a kind of a paradox. Cuba will no longer be at the forefront of the global Left. It will retain some residual esteem among progressive people, nor do I doubt its own capacity to improvise and innovate new forms of popular democracy and participation. But its destiny is to be itself transformed *from without,* in a sense, by forms of culture, technology, democracy, mixed economy, and citizen participation that the new forms of the Left are bringing forth. Cuba will no longer be a world-historical country, but perhaps a happier one.

John Beverley is Distinguished Professor of Hispanic languages and literatures at the University of Pittsburgh. He coedits the University of Pittsburgh Press series Illuminations: Cultural Formations of the Americas. He edited the collection *From Cuba* in 2002 as a special issue of *boundary 2.* His most recent book is *Latinamericanism after 9/11* (2011). Forthcoming is a collection of essays, *In the Ebb of the Pink Tide: Essays on Latinamericanism and Literature.*

Works Cited

Fernández Retamar, Roberto. 1989. Caliban: Notes toward a Discussion of Culture in Our America. In *Caliban and Other Essays,* 3–45. Trans Edward Baker. Minneapolis: University of Minnesota Press.

Gramsci, Antonio. 1959. *The Modern Prince*. New York: International.
Jáuregui, Carlos. 2008. *Canibalia: Canibalismo, antropofagia cultura y consumo en América Latina.* Frankfurt: Iberoamericana Vervuert.
Laclau, Ernesto. 2007. *On Populist Reason*. London: Verso.
Sklodowska, Elzbieta. 2016. *Invento, luego resisto: El Período Especial en Cuba como experiencia y metáfora.* Santiago de Chile: Cuarto Propio.

REFLECTIONS ON REVOLUTION AND SOCIALISM IN OUR TIMES

Rebecca E. Karl

As Fidel Castro lay dying in November 2016, the American electoral season was in the process of playing its most recent morbid joke on the world. On the one hand, Castro's death in Cuba seemed to augur the final demise of state alternatives to capitalist democracy—those alternatives historically named "socialism"—even while, on the other hand, Trump's victory in the United States seemed to ring the final death knell of precisely that very capitalist democracy, whose hovering on life support had already been signaled by the inexorable rise of Tea Party Republicans in the United States and of Far Right movements throughout Europe, the Philippines, and Japan, among others. Between the death, the demise, and the life support lurks China, an actually existing one-party Communist-led capitalist state, with nary a fig-leaf vestige of socialism remaining, despite a sometimes historical-sounding rhetoric promising a distantly attainable communist future. In critical global analyses of the past several decades, China often enough has been referred to as a "post-socialist" state,[1] joined in that grouping by Russia and the former Eastern Europe bloc, whose post-1989/1991 histories are almost uniformly configured around a paradigm of reaction: all that is done, said, and promised is (but) a reaction against the previous Communist hegemony, as well as, more recently, against the attempts by "the West" (Euro-America) to capture that reaction for profit and the postsovereign politics of "humanitarian" military intervention. The fact that China is still ruled by a Communist Party-State is little hindrance, here, to its inclusion in the normative postsocialist grouping, although caveats of course abound.

Given this muddle, I wish to inquire: What today is our "actuality" (as the 1930s Japanese philosopher Tosaka Jun called it)?[2] More precisely, does the category "postsocialist" do the work it theoretically and historically purports to do, so as to shed light on our times? Can postsocialist be a global concept rather than a delimited national or chronological marker? If so, what is its purview? In this brief essay, I argue that postsocialism can work as a global concept, albeit only in the sense that Dai Jinhua has discussed for our present moment. As Dai theorizes, we are in the "post post–Cold War era" (后冷战后时代), where the first "post" must be construed as an "anti" rather than merely a chronological "after." As she has explicated, the conceptual ambit named by the first "post" is the global problem of China-in-the-world after the Cold War and the consequent onset of a global antipolitical—a specifically antisocialist—present. First, then, hers is not the China-in-the-world articulated in the "rise of China" idiom so beloved by Chinese nationalist intellectual ventriloquists and state celebrators in the service of proclaiming that China is regaining its proper place at the center of world history. Or, that is, the dreamy triumphal assertion that China has (finally, rightfully) joined tracks with (*jiegui*: 接轨) the so-called normative history of capitalist accumulation wedded to culturalist conservatism, a path with Chinese characteristics that had been interrupted by the radicalism of the twentieth-century's revolutionary interregnum.[3] Rather, Dai's is a lesser-known immanently critical China-in-the-world conceptualization premised on recuperating the erasure of twentieth-century revolutionary histories, histories that must centrally feature the intertwined revolutionary trajectory of China and the twentieth-century world. Thus, where the normative post post–Cold War China idiom points to a presentist repression of history, in which there is no imaginary of futurity other than the banal statement that "China is the future; the future is Chinese,"[4] Dai's version has no use for this antipolitical China-in-the-world. Yet by the same token, as Dai maintains, for the critical version she advocates there are simply no historical or cultural coordinates in the mainland Chinese sphere (Dai 2016).

Indeed, as she has noted, the celebratory suppression touted by the state and its many domestic and foreign ventriloquists overlaps with the age of the internet, where history is flattened, is a conjunctural coincidence as well as a historical symptom. It provides the condition of possibility for the redemptive discourse on the crises engendered by the current moment of highly uneven capitalist accumulation to be articulated in China and elsewhere as a political unconscious not of (renewed or radicalized) socialism but of (warmed-over conservative pseudo-Confucian) imperial restoration. The appeal to a pseudo-Confucianism—now, as solution not only to China's crises, but to global crises writ large—through the advocacy of "harmony" and "harmoniousness" (*hexie* 和谐) is ubiquitously present in many of the most highly valued and viewed products of China's vast state-controlled formal educational as well as its more anarchic informal cultural spheres.[5] The following takes up this triangulated moment of our times in an attempt to think our "actuality." I first discuss the cultural idioms of revolutionary Cuba in China and then return to a discussion of "post(anti)-socialism."

THE PRODUCTION OF REVOLUTIONARY HISTORIES IN CHINA

As I have written elsewhere, the Cuban revolutions and Spanish-Cuban-Philippine-American War of the late nineteenth and early twentieth centuries—among other anticolonial revolutions of that era—were modal events not only in the Western hemisphere but also in China (see Karl 2002). From 1898 to 1905, Chinese intellectuals, for the first time involved in their own modern revolutionary organizing against the then-ruling Manchu Qing dynasty, briefly looked to what they thought were the lessons of the Cuban Revolution for inspiration and guidance. Indeed, the Cuban Revolution along with the war of independence in the Philippines—linked through their shared anti-Spanish activity and subsequent American imperialist interventions—helped Chinese intellectuals recognize and devise various strategies for combating the crushing burden of modern imperialist colonialism, particularly in its complicit alliance with Qing dynastic rule. A number of essays and a Beijing opera were written on the topic of the Cuban Revolution and were widely disseminated among the reading public. While the opera was apparently never performed on stage, its script was often reprinted in the most popular journals of the day. Entitled *The Miraculous Story of a Student Tide* (*Xuehaichao chuanqi* 学海潮传奇), penned by a certain Chun Mengsheng (an obvious pseudonym, although his identity is not known), the opera is divided into four acts: "Seduced by Literature," "Party Purgatory," "Urban Battle," and "Bloodshed." Written in the lyrical style known as "butterflies chasing flowers" (*dielianhua* 蝶恋花), this highly stylized and fictionalized opera of Cuba in the world speaks of racialized labor oppression, Chinese coolie labor, political solidarity, and revolutionary student mobilization across national and colonial borders. It is the fluidity of the latter—with Cuban student revolutionaries moving through the United States and other locations for fundraising, education, organizational support—that seemed to provide an almost-exact how-to manual for educated Chinese organizers, who were exiled from the Qing empire itself, but who continued to be vitally involved in antidynastic politics and fundraising through their transnational and translational connections in Japan, Hong Kong, London, South Africa, Mexico, India, and elsewhere.[6]

Roughly a half-century later, after Castro's revolution in 1959 and now with Mao Zedong and the Communist Party fully in control in China, Cuba reemerged into Chinese consciousness as a site of possible successful socialist revolutionary activity in the Western hemisphere. While it was not until 1962 that the Cuban revolutionary leadership proclaimed their socialist ideological allegiances, nevertheless, Castro and particularly Che Guevara were welcomed by Mao and Zhou Enlai as disrupters, at the very least, of the U.S. hegemonic hemispheric position. According to the historian Yinghong Cheng, immediately after Castro's entry into Havana in January 1959, Mao wrote an editorial in the *People's Daily* (*Renmin ribao* 人民日报) hailing his victory and the triumph of "national democracy" over U.S. imperialism.[7] Up until the 1966 split between Cuba and China—in part occasioned by the Cuban decision to side with the Soviet Union in the increasingly acrimonious Sino-Soviet ideological and border skirmishes of those years—the relations between the Cuban revolutionary movement in power and the Chinese Communist Party were aloofly cordial and at times even close. (Castro reportedly loved Chinese food and would show up late at night at the Chinese embassy in Havana, where cooks would prepare a special meal for him. This ended by 1966. Ironically, of course, most of the Chinese Cubans, many of them petty bourgeois restauranteurs who had populated Havana's one-time sizable Chinatown, had, by then, fled Havana for more hospitable business environs in Florida or New York.)

Fast forward to 2000, when an entirely new form of performative drama was staged in Beijing. Entitled *Qie Gewala* (*Che Guevara* 切格瓦拉), Zhang Guangtian's juxtapositional meditation on China's post(anti)-socialist present along with Cuba's socialist past created a cultural and political sensation (Li). As much commentary on China's promarketized calculative antipolitics of the Dengist reform era as on an idealized version of Cuba's Che-inspired socialism of the early 1960s, the play presents a series of vignettes in an almost Brechtian style known in China as "living newspaper" drama (*huobao ju* 活报剧). The overall import of the *Che Guevara* play was to present a critique of China's capitalist present through a Cuban socialist past animated by the articulated ideals of Che. As Che intones in the play (he is never seen, always heard offstage in a basso-profundo voice):

> Don't ask if the bonfire should be set
> Ask if darkness still pervades
> Don't ask if the gun should be loaded
> Ask if oppression and exploitation still dominate
> Don't ask if the just cause has a future
> Ask if injustice is still rampant.

Here, then, the logic of and for a socialist revolution is articulated as a need demanded by the past and a requirement for the present and future as well.[8]

In the aftermath of its limited-time performance, the anticapitalist message of the play somewhat faded, but one scene remained a touchstone long after the play had shuttered: the enduring image of the three empty seats offered by the director and producers to representatives of the American embassy, none of whom ever attended or responded to the invitation. The particular context and referent for this staged offstage moment was the bombing in 1999 of the Chinese embassy in Belgrade by the U.S. military in their "humanitarian" intervention in the Serbian civil war. As the producers said in an audience talk-back session on the issue: "American imperialists feel self-important, but they deceive both themselves and others. They are pleased with themselves, believing that people around the world look to them for salvation. They miscalculate. We didn't expect the American embassy to send people to the show. When the seats are empty, they are more eye-catching" (He, cited in Li). By 2000, in other words, the drama's sympathetic retrieval of Che's/Cuba's socialist lessons for China or China's socialist brotherhood with Cuba had already become more a question of cultural imagination than of actual politics: it was a nostalgic gesture receiving audience approval, albeit solely within the context of the theater itself. The critique remaining from the play was the one animated by the American bombing of the Belgrade Chinese embassy, where the U.S. pretense to "humanitarian" intervention was demonstrated to be an aggressive act of war and was seized on by hypernationalists and amplified into a nationwide anti-American movement in China. The coming dominance of the nationalistic "rise of China" popular sentiment can be dated almost precisely from this moment. (Although, of course, the play's producers were not intending to fuel that particular politics.)

Already in 1989 Castro had lauded Deng Xiaoping for his crackdown on the social movement centering on Tian'anmen in June of that year. Since that time, ChinaCuba relations have gone through a large transformation, particularly once the Soviet Union broke apart and Russian aid to Cuba was curtailed. China is now a major financier and land developer in Cuba, as well as a major importer/consumer of Cuba's sugar. Even as Castro became and remained in the 1990s and 2000s one of China's Communist Party's favorite fellow "socialists," it is evident that Cuba's position as a socialist ideal would have to be drawn from its past rather than its present. Even Huang Jisu, one of the producers of the *Che Guevara* play, notes: "We used Che Guevara . . . as a vehicle to express our thoughts and sentiments about the fate of socialism" (2015, originally in Huang Jisu 2000).

THE ACTUALITY OF THE POST(ANTI)-SOCIALIST PRESENT

Can twentieth-century figures of socialist revolution help us think our antisocialist present? Are there cultural coordinates for our current moment, our actuality? An older paradigm of potential and actual social struggle, to which political liberalism as a procedural democratic form was one historical answer (and socialism another, of course), was subsumed in the 1980s/90s, as a rhetoric, into a seemingly seamless form of the "economic" as essentially a transhistorical matter of the unfettered free market. This configuration articulates what we might name the age of the revenge of liberalism (as Karl Polyani cautioned already back in the late 1940s). In this sense, our present can often appear as a return to and reelaboration of some of the most anti- and illiberal doctrines of earlier (prewar) times: post-postliberalism as a repetitive antiliberalism, whether we call it fascist or something else. We could cast this repetition in the following idiom: previous illiberalisms propounded on the economistic relationship of value to market price so as to bypass and indeed suppress the theoretically vibrant discussions and sharp struggles over the actually existing conflictual social relationship of value to labor and the historical emergence of capitalism in its colonialimperialist forms. In the 1870s, this version of illiberalism formed the foundation of Carl Menger's consciously anti-Marxist "marginalist revolution" and the subsequent rise through the late nineteenth and into the twentieth century of the Austrian School of Economics, with its particular emphasis on aggregated individual desire and consumption as the key modalities of measuring use-value through market exchange and market equilibrium (see Karl 2017, chapter 3). In the 1930s and 1940s, parts of this set of principles were adduced, separately albeit not uncoincidentally, to the political illiberalisms of Carl Schmitt in Germany, Friedrich Hayek in Hungary/Britain, Leo Strauss in Chicago, Giovanni Gentile in Italy, and Chen Lifu in China (among others, of course) to yield the global fascist and neoconservative economic–ideological turns of that time. These attempted to displace the political and social conflicts engaged by the praxis of mass democracy—liberal *and* revolutionary socialist—as a remedy for domestic and global capitalist unevenness unto the closure of the state–market complex and its properly delegated and designated ruling elites. By the 1970s–90s, all of this reemerged, reconfigured, and updated for the Cold War era, with the revalorization by the Nobel Prize for Economics of Hayek's (1974) and Milton Friedman's (1976) advocacies for deregulated markets, aimed to push state socialism—and even more urgently, liberal Keynsianism—off the conceptual map of proper economic–ideological practice.

As Richard Seymour has argued in his analysis of David Cameron's Britain, Hayek's championing of an authoritarian liberalism was a means to meet the challenge of mass democracy; it cozily harmonized with Schmitt's critique of political liberalism and Ludwig von Mises's postwar theories of the relation between free markets and free societies in the 1981 endorsement by Hayek of Pinochet's Chile. Indeed, Hayek pointed to Chile as an exemplar of how the liberal social relations of capitalism could be effectively managed through privatization, technocracy, and antidemocratic dictatorship. This legacy of technocracy married to market deregulation and privatization of services came through the Thatcher/Reagan/Deng Xiaoping years and survives and thrives today thinly disguised as the death and demise of democracy that has yielded our current post(anti)-post-Cold War social and political crises in liberalism and socialism alike (Seymour).

In this simultaneously local and global context of the revenge of liberalism, it is no coincidence that both Strauss and Schmitt have been conjoined in contemporary China to Hayekian free market theory, yielding thereby a particularly noxious brew of antiliberal, antisocialist, hypernationalist political and economic philosophy and practice, accompanied by a culturally conservative advocacy for a "return" to Confucian values, a suppression of feminist activism, and a positively desired sociocultural hegemony of educated (male) elites and technocrats.

In 2010, the Columbia University historian of (European) ideas, Mark Lilla, bemusedly wrote of his encounters in Beijing with Chinese Schmittians and Straussians, clueless then and now about what liberalism is and might be. In his brief essay, "Reading Strauss in Beijing," Lilla paternalistically forgives young Chinese of a "conservative bent" for their admiration for both antiliberals, because, after all, the students are Chinese, and, in the end, Lilla admits, both Strauss and Schmitt had legitimate critiques of liberalism. According to Lilla, these students

> are mainly concerned with maintaining "harmony." . . . Their reading of [Chinese] history convinces them that China's enduring challenges have always been to maintain territorial unity, keep social peace, and defend national interests against other states—challenges heightened today by global market forces and a liberal ideology that idealizes individual rights, social pluralism, and international law. . . . Like Schmitt, they can't make up their minds whether liberal ideas are hopelessly naïve . . . or whether they are changing the world in ways that are detrimental to society and international order. . . . Schmitt's conclusion—that, given the naturally adversarial nature of politics, we would be better off with a system of geographical spheres of influence dominated by a few great powers—sits particularly well with many of the young Chinese I met.

Aside from his abysmal ignorance of Chinese history, one could very well ask Lilla where the challenge to liberal ideology is coming from. Insofar as many Chinese students—even more so today in 2018 than in 2010—have embraced wholeheartedly the tenets of individualism as economic and cultural self-interest (that very individualism long identified as liberalism's core cultural-ideological content) the putative Chinese "challenge" to liberalism is a product of Lilla's fantasy or preconception about the cultural collectivism of Chinese (Asiatic?) thinking. Moreover, insofar as international law has long been bent almost completely to serve the interests of Chinese (and other global) finance capitals, what could be the problem with international law, so long as the Chinese state can manipulate it to its own advantage? One could argue plausibly that the Chinese state is now the bulwark against the erosion by Trumpism of precisely the international legal regime that historically served U.S. global dominance so well.

More to the point than the self-serving attitudes of elite Chinese students—which are no more or less self-serving than those of elite American students, even if the particulars are more eruditely articulated in China (indeed, here Lilla does point to something important: the convergence of Chinese social–cultural conservatism with certain versions of this political philosophy in the United States)—yet, even more telling than this is Lilla's own somewhat positive evaluation of Schmitt and later in the essay, of Strauss. If Schmitt can be characterized merely as a skeptic of liberal "naivete," as Lilla does, then the fascism—the antiliberal outgrowth of liberalism itself—associated with Schmittian philosophy can easily be seen merely as a plausible corrective to liberalism's infantile disorder. Lilla's insistence on reading *with* Schmitt to arrive at an interpretation of politics as always and only being about national–culturalist specificities and individual self-interest—and thus as always and only about individual and/or national–cultural conflict (clash of civilizations, anyone?)—simply ignores the history of the early twentieth century to which Schmitt was responding (and the repetition with difference to which the contemporary Schmitt revival corresponds). That is, Lilla ignores the specter of domestic and global mass politics and mass democracy promised by liberalism and socialism, he ignores the solidarities of identity that are formed through such promises. In this sense, Lilla misreads Chinese students' fascination with Schmitt as a symptom of their collectivist–cultural reactions to individualist liberalism, when in fact it is posed as a repudiation of the mass politics of the Maoist socialist sort and as a rationale for the construction of a form of political hegemony under the aegis of themselves as technocratic and enabling agents of the Chinese state and of ongoing capitalist accumulation.

To this hegemonic aspiration, Straussian doctrine, with its well-known emphasis on the rule of elites, can be adduced without problem: it dovetails nicely with the repudiation of mass politics in China today and the affirmation of an elite ruling class whose education and social positions are indicators and affirmations of their natural right to govern and get wealthy. In this sense, the acceptance of Strauss is not, as Lilla would have it, attributable to some Chinese Confucian cultural predisposition toward the historical rule of *junzi* (gentleman scholars 君子). That is, Strauss does not, as Lilla claims, provide "a bridge between their ancient tradition and our own." Indeed, this kind of insistent misrecognition of Chinese people as culturally bound rather than historically formed is tiresomely predictable and always wrong in its laziness. Bypassing culturalism and returning to history, we can conclude *contra* Lilla but in keeping with our previous point that the appeal of Schmitt and Strauss in China today, as was paradoxically true among self-proclaimed leftist intellectuals in the United States and Britain at some junctures in the 1990s and beyond (e.g., Zhang Xudong),[9] is really an attempt to think politics without the masses or the people, or in short, without any notion of democracy—liberal or socialist.[10] Where the Schmittian/Straussian critique was said in U.S./British leftish circles to provide a new vantage onto a long-standing antipathy toward liberalism, we can also recognize that these antiliberal critiques can and did become naked attacks on the prospects of any radical mass politics of an alternative (noncapitalist) futurity.

It is *this* hoped-for erasure of the possibility of a radical democratic praxis that forms a core content of our "actuality," our present. The return of this particular ideological form—its repetitive appearance—is informed by a specific version of the present as a surface temporality rather than as a product of multiple mediations. It is this surface temporality to which simple chronological "post-isms" often point. This (Hegelian) eternal present expresses the neoliberal fantasy of reconquering the time of the present through the complete colonization of human life by the economic, defined through and saturated by an everyday practice limited to the pursuit of self-interest, itself knowable and realizable through the creation and potential satisfaction of consumer desire. In structure (if obviously not in particulars), this immediacy corresponds well to Pierre Bourdieu's characterization of pre-modern/pre-capitalist social life as a *habitus*, where the economic *is life itself*. As Bourdieu has it: "The *habitus* is the universalizing mediation which causes an individual agent's practices, without either explicit reason or signifying intent, to be none the less 'sensible' and 'reasonable'" (79, 83). That is, precapitalist social logic as neoliberal capitalist logic—albeit differently, of course—is aimed at constant restructuring and reproduction: in the one case, the reproduction of an unmediated set of social relations as a structure of social life, while in the other, ours, the restructuring of the complex mediations of capitalist accumulation whose global spatial horizon must be translated into the temporal immediacy of an endless reproduction of the same in the commodity form. In one recent statement of this restructuring and reproductive logic, Hayekian scholar Liu Junming states that "economic freedom is the mother of all freedoms," going on to explain that this was a lesson purportedly learned in the China of the Nationalist Party in the 1930s (the "Nanjing Decade"), forgotten under Maoism, and then relearned in the 1990s with the rejoining of China's national tracks to the supposed correct and natural historical trajectory of antirevolutionary free markets wedded to antiradical cultural conservatism (49–60).

As is clear, this form of historical reproduction and temporal immediacy dissolves effortlessly into ahistorical timelessness. It erases history at the same time as making it endlessly atemporal. It forms the lines along which the Austrian School of Economics (to which Hayek was heir) was critiqued in the 1930s–40s by Marxist economic philosopher Wang Yanan. As Wang clearly saw at that time, the theory of human nature on which the Austrian School was based—in which desire is the sole basis for the realization of economic value, where the capacity for the fulfillment of this desire in the market is the measure of the freedom of society—was essentially an ahistorical and antipolitical theory. As Wang maintained, when political economy is adduced to that theory, it becomes a "natural order" that requires no historical or political explanatory. Thus, if economics is an ontology of human nature for the Austrians, as Wang put it, then it is so because use-value is the central nervous system of its doctrines. And indeed, in Austrian School theory—very much in vogue in China today, in its Hayekian form—the marketplace is figured as the neutral arena in which various individuals' desires are coordinated and get realized in exchange as use-value.[11] In Ludwig von Mises's full articulation of this logic for the hoped-for postsocialist postliberal world (our world of antipolitics), there only exists the present time of use-value exchange: "Action is as such in the real present because it utilizes the instant and thus embodies its reality" (100). (Von Mises was part of the second generation of the Austrian School; his institute and intellectual descendants are some of the most potent sponsors of today's Republican Party antibrain trust.) The contrast between von Mises's version of "reality"–the "real present" that refers to the immediacy of action as a fulfillment of desire in the instant—and the concept of "actuality" that refers to a densely layered temporality of historical praxis and futurity (or, in short, to a possibility of mass democratic [socialist] politics), could not be more stark.

CONCLUSION

What I have been suggesting throughout this short meditation on revolution and socialism for our times is that, while the "post" of the contemporary conjuncture, whether in China or elsewhere, often refers in an uncritically ideological fashion to a temporality, where the immediacy of the "real present" as an economic principle attached to a conservative culturalism erases the necessity to think of a past or a future in favor of an exclusive focus on an ahistorical timelessness, in a critical sense, the "post" must be recognized as a form of antipolitics, whose object of repudiation is the possibility for liberal democracy *as well as* a revolutionary socialist politics of democracy that is *not reducible* to the sham of consumer choice and putative market freedom alone. That is, the death of socialism contains within it the fall of liberalism. In China, antipolitics is posed as a repudiation of and solution to the so-called fanaticisms of twentieth-century revolution and Maoist mass mobilizations ,and liberalism is eschewed in its political forms even as it is heartily embraced in its economic–cultural commodity form. Meanwhile, in Euro-America, this antipolitics has been posed—now more openly than in recent memory—as an extension of some of the most extreme political illiberalisms embedded in the liberal order from the very beginning. The convergence of these historical forms of "depoliticization," to expand Wang Hui's term, forces us to contend with a "situation where all earlier forms of political subjectivity—party, class, nation [race and gender]—face the crisis of depoliticization, [where] the search for new forms must be accompanied by a redefinition of the boundaries of politics itself" (Wang Hui, 18). Retrieving the moments when revolutions were local and global simultaneously—as with Cuba in China's cultural imaginary over the course of the twentieth century—allows us to remember a different historical time, when revolution and socialist politics defined the parameters of an abstract futurity that could be realized concretely in the present. While I am skeptical that these provide real guides today, they do remind us that we must seize the "post" away from the antipolitical ideologues and redirect it towards the elaboration and creation of a different and more democratically just future, whatever that future is called and however it is configured.

Rebecca E. Karl is professor of history at New York University–NY. She is the author, most recently, of *The Magic of Concepts: History and the Economic in Twentieth-Century China* (2017) and coeditor/cotranslator (with Xueping Zhong) of Cai Xiang, *Revolution and Its Narratives: China's Socialist Literary and Cultural Imaginaries, 1949–1966* (2016).

Notes

1. Arif Dirlik (1989) wrote one of the earliest trenchant discussions of "post-socialism" as a term of critical analysis. See also Litzinger.

2. Tosaka's "actuality" should not be confused with Italian fascist philosopher Giovanni Gentile's idealist Hegelian version. Tosaka's was a materialist philosophy of the "nowness" of events in and of everyday life. In this sense, it was both antihistoricist and antimetaphysical. See Harootunian, 129–31.

3. This is the same bogeyman China that has appeared in the past two decades to haunt the dreams of U.S. hegemonizers. Whereas previously, China was figured as a blue ant infestation overwhelming the West, now China is the disciplined behemoth ready to overtake the world. See, for immediate examples, Allison; French. For a credulous review of these books, see Shapiro.

4. An anthology of newly translated works by Dai Jinhua, edited by Lisa Rofel, will be published by Duke University Press, hopefully in 2018. The analyses referenced here are explored in those essays, some of which are available in Chinese in Dai 2015. For an extended argument about the erasure of revolutionary history in the 1990s through to the present, see Karl 2017.

5. We could certainly see the expansion of Chinese state-sponsored Confucius Institutes into the world's educational sectors as an overt proclamation of this culturalist principle. And, as Angela Zito has argued, the return to filiality as a core concern and even legal norm in the People's Republic of China is indicative of a culturalist turn intended to recall idealized norms of a dynastic past through the animation of that stagnant past in a dynamic digital present. (Zito's written work on this is forthcoming.)

6. Printed, for one example, in *Xinmin congbao,* n.p.

7. See Cheng. My account below is based on Cheng's research on the matter.

8. A full translation of the play by Jonathan Noble is available on the MCLC website: http://u.osu.edu/mclc/.

9. See Zhang, where one learns through the evocation of Schmitt more about Zhang's own authoritarian desires than those of his putative subject, Deng Xiaoping. (I thank Christopher Connery for bringing this essay to my attention.)

10. For a critique of this, see Neocleous. For an extended discussion of similar issues for China, see Karl 2010.

11. For a long discussion of Wang's critique of the Austrians, see Karl 2017, chapter 3.

Works Cited

Allison, Graham. 2017. *Destined for War: Can America and China Escape Thucydides's Trap?* New York: Houghton Mifflin.

Bourdieu, Pierre. 1991. *Outline of a Theory of Practice.* Cambridge: Cambridge University Press.

Cheng, Yinghong. 2007. "Sino-Cuban Relations during the Early Years of the Castro Regime, 1959–1966." *Journal of Cold War Studies* 9, no. 3 (Summer): 78–114.

Dai, Jinhua. 2015. *Moming zhi suo* [莫名之锁 A key with no name]. Shanghai: Fudan daxue chubanshe.

Dai, Jinhua. 2016. "Meiyou zuobiao de wenhua dixing" [没有坐标的文化地形 A cultural landscape without coordinates]. Talk delivered at University of California, Santa Cruz, Cultural Studies workshop, May 25.

Dai, Jinhua. Forthcoming. *After the Post-Cold War: Essays by Dai Jinhua.* Ed. Lisa Rofel. Durham: Duke University Press.

Dirlik, Arif. 1989. "Post-Socialism: Reflections on Socialism with Chinese Characteristics." *Critical Asian Studies* 21, no. 1: 33–44.

French, Howard. 2017. *Everything under the Heavens: How the Past Helps Shape China's Push for Global Power*. New York: Knopf.

Harootunian, Harry. 2000. *Overcome by Modernity: History, Culture, and Community in Interwar Japan.* Princeton: Princeton University Press.

He, Li, ed. 2000. "Yu guanzhong jiaoliu riji jiexuan" [与观众交流日记节选 Selection of notes of dialogues with the audience]. *Zhongguo yu shijie* [中国于世界 China and the world; special issue]. http://www.chinabulletin.com/.

Huang, Jisu. 2000. *Wenyi lilun yu piping* [文艺理论与批评 Literary theory and criticism] 5:66–71.

Huang, Jisu. 2015. "Che Guevara: Notes on the Play, Its Production and Reception." In *Debating the Socialist Legacy and Capitalist Globalization in China*. Ed. Xueping Zhong and Ban Wang, 205–16. Trans. Xie Fang. New York: Palgrave McMillan.

Karl, Rebecca. 2002. *Staging the World: Chinese Nationalism at the Turn of the Twentieth Century*. Durham: Duke University Press.

Karl, Rebecca. 2010. "The Flight to Rights: 1990s China and Beyond." *Telos* 151 (Summer): 87–104.

Karl, Rebecca. 2017. *Magic of Concepts: History and the Economic in Twentieth-Century China*. Durham: Duke University Press.

Li, Ruru. 2001. "Sino the Times: Three Spoken Drama Productions on the Beijing Stage." *TDR/The Drama Review* 45, no. 2: 129–44.

Lilla, Mark. 2010. "Reading Strauss in Beijing." *New Republic*, December 8.

Litzinger, Ralph. 2002. "Theorizing Postsocialism: Reflections on the Politics of Marginality in Contemporary China." *South Atlantic Quarterly* 101, no. 1: 33–55.

Liu, Junming. 2000. "The Intellectual Turn: The Emergence of Liberalism in Contemporary China." In *China's Future: Constructive Partner or Emerging Threat?* Ed. Ted Galen Carpenter and James A. Dorn, 49–60. Washington, D.C.: Cato Institution.

Neocleous, Mark. 1996. "Friend or Enemy? Reading Schmitt Politically." *Radical Philosophy* 79 (September / October): 13–23.

Seymour, Richard. 2011. "David Cameron's Tea Party." *Radical Philosophy* 165 (January / February): 6–9.

Shapiro, Judith. 2017. "America's Collision Course with China." *New York Times*, Book Review Section, June 15. https://www.nytimes.com/2017/06/15/books/review/everything-under-the-heavens-howard-french-destined-for-war-graham-allison.html.

Von Mises, Ludwig. 1996. *Human Action: A Treatise on Economics*. New York: Foundation for Economic Education.

Wang, Hui. 2009. "Depoliticized Politics: From East to West." In *The End of Revolution: China and the Limits of Modernity*, 3–18. New York: Verso.

Xinmin congbao [新民从报 New people's miscellany]. 1904. Nos. 46–48. February 17.

Zhang, Xudong. 2014. "Zuowei 'zhuquanzhe' de Deng Xiaoping." [作为"主权者"的邓小平 Deng Xiaoping as authoritarian]. *Guanchazhe* [观察者 The observer]. http://www.guancha.cn/zhang-xu-dong/2014_08_20_257504_s.shtml.

THE AMBIGUOUS DEBT OF COUNTERREVOLUTION TO REVOLUTION

REPLY TO A VIGILANT MELANCHOLIC

Soumyabrata Choudhury

INTRODUCTION

In the letter of invitation to write for this issue—an unusual one that does not shrink from accentuating its partisan call in the name of a certain "historical immortal" Fidel Castro, whose recent death is also an occasion to recalibrate the economy of his life between its political historicity and revolutionary immortality—a central question is posed: What is lost when the concept of revolution is lost to the thinking of politics? I don't find myself capable of undertaking the Castroist recalibration but I will attempt a compact response to the general question.

My reply to this vigilant and melancholic question is that what is also lost when revolution is lost to politics is the thought of *counterrevolution*. Why do I place a special value on this somewhat paradoxical loss? For two reasons: first, to lose the reference to counterrevolution is to be deprived of a unifying diagnostic category with which to grasp our times on a global scale; second, with the disappearance of a kind of historical consciousness of revolution and counterrevolution, what vanishes, or tends to vanish, is the ambiguous *debt* counterrevolution has hitherto felt toward revolution even in the age of its greatest triumph.

It is important to clarify, of course, that the foregoing response to the initial partisan announcement stands its ground only on the condition that "loss" is not understood to be "nonexistence". Loss is rather to be grasped in the psychoanalytic sense that when a subject is said to suffer a "loss of reality" (2001b), what is indicated is a kind of lapse of the power of the subject to *symbolize* her reality. Often the loss of reality is the measure of the very acuity, even violence, of the reality that the subject is unable to insert herself into anymore. It does not mean the empirical disappearance of that reality. However, before applying this analogy to the question of counterrevolution as a crisis of symbolization in a situation of disavowal of its originary debt to, at the very least, a *revolutionary hypothesis,* one must consider a radical, if counterintuitive, option.

Is it possible to conceptualize a *pure* counterrevolution, a counterrevolution which is not, in the words of Joseph de Maistre, "a revolution in reverse but the opposite of revolution?" (cited in Arendt, 8). When Hannah Arendt in her mid-twentieth-century classic *On Revolution* cites these words, she immediately consigns them to an "empty witticism" (8) And yet the triumphant speech of contemporary global capitalism does flicker between two registers: on the one hand, it proclaims a *historical* victory over all its erstwhile adversaries, including something like a revolutionary "left" opponent; on the other hand, it claims liberation from all past and historical moorings to, as if, be born anew. In this peculiar threshold of a new birth as well as a restoration of a truth beyond the tradition of revolutionary philosophy, which in Arendt's terms constitutes revolution as a kind of natality, as "new things,"[1] the empty witticism of a pure counterrevolutionary affirmation, which is the opposite and not the reverse of revolution, seems to come alive.

However, the real point of interest in our present moment is not merely the burden and entanglement of its paradoxes but also the mechanisms by which the paradoxes can be carried off smoothly. The point of interest is to study how the historical debt to revolution is overcome—or disavowed, as the case may be. What is of interest is how counterrevolution, without a jolt of contradiction, constitutes itself as "new things" *in* history as well as a restoration of a truth that is attached to a kind of ontological system beyond all historical contingency. In concrete terms, the investigation of a "pure counterrevolution" would consist of asking, What is the "ontological system" of something that appears in history, say, something like "capitalism," but whose doctrine of being pronounces, at the very stroke of its historical enunciation, an immemorial truth? How might we carry off this counterintuitive and contradictory move smoothly so as to give an "empty witticism" a life of ideological power?

I will state my hypothesis on the performance and content of the "ontological system" of contemporary capitalism at the end of this essay. Before that, I want to conduct two preliminary, even classical, exercises: First, I want to lay out the possible meaning of a revolutionary hypothesis that every counterrevolution logically presupposes. I want to do this in the light of Arendt's work and Alain Badiou's radical generic question vis-a-vis all philosophies of history, "Is change possible?"[2] Then, I intend to analyze the structure of counterrevolutionary debt to revolution and the peculiar ambiguity of this debt. This I will do with reference to a singular fragment from the works of the early twentieth-century Indian political thinker B. R. Ambedkar.[3] Finally, I will return to the investigation as to whether counterrevolution has indeed come into its own and overcome its historical-cum-structural debt to claim an ontological truth, to affirm a self-caused existence *(causa sui)*,or whether its triumphant speech is a twisted performance of disavowal under the twin threats of internal crisis and the continuing specter of a revolutionary hypothesis.

REVOLUTION: MEANING AND EVENT

Since everything begins in the spirit of a vigilant melancholy—What is lost when the concept of revolution is lost to the thinking of politics?—we must further enquire as to what are the elements of that concept whose traces grow fainter each day. Arendt presents three initial elements making the meaning of revolution—novelty, beginnings, and violence. She adds the fourth feature that revolutions are irresistible (40); in that sense, she speaks of the historical necessity of living in an age of revolutions.

The analytical elaboration of revolution, however, does not entail that all *acts* of revolution are the same. So for Arendt, the American Revolution and the French Revolution illustrate almost conflictual images of the act of revolution. While both are "modern" events in the sense that they are staked on radical novelty and absolute beginnings in history rather than conforming to ancient ideas of a cyclical history of constitutions / regimes (to be found, for instance in Polybius, though it has to be said that he left room for *tyché*, or "chance," in political history [Arendt, 13, 14]), the two cases do not activate these elements in the same way. In fact, for Arendt, their internal sequences are reverse images of each other: The American Revolution was an unforeseen act of founding the *speech of freedom*—not merely a regime of free speech—under historical conditions of material liberation from economic and social misery. The French Revolution, to the contrary, plunged the speech of liberty, equality, and fraternity into the real historical body of a nation divided by social and economic inequality and misery in the extreme. This inevitably led from the most exalted revolutionary speech to a kind of speechlessness of pure violence during the French Revolution (42). At least that is a part of Arendt's magisterial evaluation.

Irrespective of the correctness of the evaluation and the internal variation in the revolutionary sequences of the modern age, the latter must not be confused with the momentous happenings of past epochs. Insofar as the sequences transmit an utterly novel speech, even if scrambled with the most sordid historical materiality, they enforce a singularly modern historical necessity. To this extent, with all the variant convulsions in the several revolutions from the eighteenth to the twentieth centuries, they compose, in Proudhon's vision, just *one* revolution, the only one to ever take place.[4] Hence, it seems to me that Arendt's pioneering valorization of the modern age as an age of revolution(s) provokes us to think of the meaning of revolution along a more generic idea of *event*.

It is on the above point that Badiou's criticism of Michel Foucault applies as much to Arendt's definition of revolution, a definition that is historical, too historical. In an interview with Bruno Bosteels, significantly titled, "Can Change be Thought?" Badiou says:

> It almost seems to me as if, in some way, the discursive truth of a time comes at the price of stripping this time of its generic procedures. Finally, the situation for him [Foucault] draws out on *episteme* insofar as one first of all subtracts that which made an exception to it. (Bosteels, 256)

It seems to me that Arendt, despite her tremendous valorization of the irreducibility and irresistibility of revolution, nevertheless reduces it to a question of *historical knowledge,* of a kind of modern revolutionary *episteme*. This has the peculiar effect of making revolution the measure of the modern age while stressing the incommensurable newness of revolution as an object of knowledge. So, for Arendt, revolution does gain a certain universality, but one which is agreed on as a universal modern revolutionary *norm*. Yet the content of that norm, so precious to her, which is a new founding speech or discourse, doesn't cease to orient us toward another sort of universal—the "universal exception."[5] Badiou speaks of that which treats historical particularity with generic invention, temporal sequences with eternal ideas. Badiou says:

> It [history] is the attempt to write the history of everything, to grasp a situation outside the belabouring of this situation by the generic procedures properly speaking. That is only normal because history must treat of time without eternity. . . . I am not against the relation to our past, even less so against the presence of the past, because, on the contrary, I think that the past can convoke you with an enormous liveliness as present. But I am against this figure that apprehends situations in their time by subtracting any hypothesis concerning the way in which this time has been treated by something other than itself, that is, ultimately by subtracting the procedures of truth of which this time has occasionally been the site. (Bosteels, 256)

Is it unfair to suggest that Arendt deprives herself of a revolutionary hypothesis that treats the modern history of revolutions with a figure other than itself? Well, it is uncertain whether she permits the retroactive action of the modern ideas of freedom and equality to govern our way to look at all the premodern pasts. It is not certain that Arendt is able to conceive of a new generic invention what Badiou calls "truth-procedure/process,"[6] which would make it possible to evaluate and think of historical sequences in a revolutionary way irrespective of whether the generic procedure and the revolutionary hypothesis are born of any of those sequences.

The wavering presented above needs to be scrutinized in the light of the question as to what generic procedures of truth involve. The question can be further vivified through examining Arendt's favorite metaphor of the "birth" of the modern age of revolutions. Now it is clear that Arendt's organic or organismic metaphor is never an alibi for her to dramatize the birth of a new age to an *instant*. The birth is long-drawn and tortuous, it is, indeed, a "process" or a "procedure." For example, Arendt and Badiou would agree on the fact that the real historical break of the French Revolution comes with Robespierre and the Terror when a total—and terrible—separation with the old regime is actually accomplished (Arendt, 42–43; Badiou 2005). It is not spontaneously "born" with the July 1789 Bastille happening. Nevertheless, Arendt stabilizes this "truth" of the revolution to the immanence of the historical sequence for which the metaphor of a birth still meets the purpose of conveying the quasi-organic *passion* materializing the novelty, beginnings, violence, and irresistibility underlying the history between 1789 and 1794.

In Badiou's view, the "truth" of the revolution is a generic invention wagered by Robespierre, Saint-Just, among others, that an *event* of revolutionary magnitude, sweeping up the force of ideas of equality, freedom, and collective happiness, has taken place. The wager has a double consequence: it both enforces the event it avows in history—hence that inconsolable word "Terror"—and constructs a hypothesis that posits the event as a site transmitting ideas that are something like figures of eternity. These ideas have immanent effects in history but no historical incarnation. So Robespierre and Saint-Just were not personifications of ideas in history (as were not Lenin and Castro), and the story of the revolution is not told as an organic birth or narrative plot, with beginning, middle and end.[7]

The fundamental stakes of this contestation are divided between a generic philosophy and a philosophy of history, even if the latter is carried out by an unhappy consciousness of the price this philosophy extracts. In Arendt's evaluation, the definition of revolutionary action as free praxis remains an ideal speech-situation best approximated in the American Revolution. Otherwise the ideal functions as a shifting horizon for the only reality of revolution, which is historical. The ideal subtracted from the historical web of agents and actions leaves only discursive grids for evaluating the "truth" of revolutions—this is the unlikely point of contact between Arendt and Foucault.[8] In Arendt's language, which is far closer to the nineteenth-century tradition of Hegelian Marxism than Foucault's later-day innovations, the age of revolution is prescribed as a *historical necessity*. Hence also her reference to someone like Proudhon on there being always but "one revolution." Interestingly, when Marx himself addressed this matter, he analyzed the contemporary actuality of that "one revolution" in his times to be the bourgeois revolution and *capitalism*. By the logic of historical necessity, capitalism was judged to be inevitable, but Marx assigned himself another, more perilous task in *Capital*: that of unbinding or desaturating the analysis of the historical nodes of capitalist existence from exhaustion of all future "chances" of history—in other words, from letting the logic of historical necessity go dry and keeping its *chance* of delivering future change alive.

It seems to me that the threshold of the concept of "class" in Marx, though a tremulous one, marks the aleatory point of the otherwise necessitarian trajectory imputed to history.[9] This also marks the possible formation of, not a political subject—so dear to Arendt—but a *subject of politics*. Historically speaking, the political subject has been exhaustively distributed between the two revolutions, the American and the French, within the Western world. They set the two paradigms for rest of the world to choose from in their inevitable if late journey to bourgeois democracy. The history of revolutions, in Arendt's powerful estimation, is the modern reign of "world-history," from which there is no escaping for any society, including the colonized non-Western ones.

The thinking of a subject of politics, from Marx to Badiou, is not historical. It does not concern the privileged locus of a founding speech in conditions of some degree of actual historical equality that makes possible this discourse of politics as the circulating speech of freedom. It is not an affair of citizens in a good democracy. The subject of politics is concerned with *any* politics that is capable of constructing the revolutionary hypothesis. This brings us back to the difficulty of how to think of the concept of the event. I will not rehearse Badiou's complex formalization here but rather discuss the concept in general secular terms. It can be studied at two disparate levels: If the event is understood ontologically, then it involves a breach in a given regime of knowledges that constitutes the regime's exception; the event is a breakout from the being of entities under their signs of knowledge (their *episteme*). Studied historically, the event is a retroaction of the historical speech of its avowal. This avowal entails the generic or universal access of the event's retroactive reality for *anyone*.[10] Hence, the event is defined almost aphoristically as "the universal exception". What is essential in this distribution between the objective radicality of the breach and the subjective courage of the avowal is the divisive and emancipatory reorientation toward *new* signs of generic construction of the following hypothesis: "Universal politics exists!" Yet universal politics is not an ideal brought to earth but the existential courage and creativity that include acts of language during the thinking of this politics in new ways. Finally, the dialectical conceptualization of event doesn't prescribe a future or schematize a past based on the materiality of historical happenings. In this sense, Badiou develops a *materialist dialectic* and not dialectics applied to this material sequence or that.[11] He doesn't create an *expectation* of the event from history. Neither does he make the event impose a *debt* the future must pay for its past sins. Thus Badiou emerges quite disentangled from any utopian, messianic, or reactive strands that might exist in the different traditions of Marxism and cultures of the Left.[12]

THE AMBIGUOUS DEBT OF COUNTERREVOLUTION TO REVOLUTION

Yet counterrevolution has hitherto felt a crushing debt to revolution . . . which revolution didn't impose in the first place. Herein lies the first kind of ambiguity of the debt. The second concerns counterrevolution's desire to deny, if not disavow, that debt and pretend it doesn't exist. The irony is completed when we note that the counterrevolutionary desire attaches to a nonexistent, void object.

In an unfinished text from the 1940s called "Krishna and His *Gita*: Philosophic Justification of Counter-revolution," the political thinker B. R. Ambedkar, (who also headed the drafting committee of the Indian constitution between 1947 and 1950), writes, "With them [the counterrevolutionaries, among whom he specifically refers to the Hindu nationalist B. G. Tilak] it is a matter of honour that Counter-revolution should not be shown to be indebted to Revolution" (1987, 371). To achieve this effect, counterrevolution invents "ingenious" (371) arguments to deny the original revolution. According to me, the interest of what Ambedkar calls counterrevolutionary ingenuity lies in the "evental" conception of revolution, which such ingenuity targets. Ambedkar's object in this essay was to show that the text venerated in Indian history (up to the present moment), the *Bhagavad Gita,* was a counterrevolutionary philosophical text to ideologically justify the Hindu *reaction* to the original Buddhist revolution around the sixth to fifth century BC. The Buddhist revolution was an egalitarian repudiation of the hierarchical Hindu social order in ancient India, and its originary "evental" character lay not merely in the historical repudiation but also in its generic articulation of equality as a new thinkable universal principle.

In Ambedkar's essay, there is much historical granulation of possible evidence to show why it is reasonable to assume the *Gita* was put together at least five hundred years after the teachings of the Buddha.[13] That effort is not my concern here. I want to stress the overall stakes of the historical contestation that seem to lie in an asymmetry between the Buddhist moment and the Hindu counterrevolutionary aftermath : while the force of the former comes from the *speculative materiality* of the idea of equality in Buddha's teaching, resulting in new, small republican forms of political organization (called *gana* in old Indian languages like Sanskrit and Pali), the counterrevolution is staked on a direct reversal to despotic and hegemonic forms of political and social rule. What comes instead of the pure speculative, hypothetical—and materialist—status of the egalitarian proposition is the imposition of *dogma* in a text like the *Gita* to justify the counterrevolutionary political agenda. This agenda continues in Ambedkar's own day, and religious revivalist thinkers like B. G. Tilak—who are also nationalist—invent new "ingenious" arguments to deny the egalitarian breach in an undisturbed history of Hindu social sovereignty.[14] The procedure of denial acts also to simultaneously enforce the *Gita* as the philosophical legitimator— nay, *source*— of that sovereignty.

The dogmatic project, as a logic, reveals its tautological character (despite all the ingenious obfuscation), in the following way: The project of justifying the so-called superiority or the sovereignty of a historically particular religious, communitarian, or national identity requires the *transcendence* of that particularity through the violence of dogma. But this violence is also encoded in a particular historical text, contingently and strategically produced. To break this tautology, the text, the code, and the dogma transmitted through them must all dissimulate themselves as immemorial "truths" co-extensive with something like the order of *nature*. Thus historically specific identities will have been converted to "natural being."

To get past this insidious and violent operation, the contingency of historical discourse must be *avowed*. But this requires a subject of avowal, whose political status lies in both the act of the avowal and the universalization of that act. Ambedkar avows the materiality of a past event, whose historical particularity has a speculative life of universal possibility for *any politics*, at *any time*. Thus while the dogmatic operation obfuscates its particular historical motives by a false transcendence that denies its historical enforcement, the subject of politics avows its universalist orientation as a kind of immanent separation from history. Badiou, at one place, points out the tautological confidence in and fanaticism for national identity among those who mourn the loss of national distinctiveness in the age of globalization—or would dogmatically and terroristically reenforce this distinctiveness—forget that the birth of the modern nation had nothing to do with primordial or "natural-national identity" (Badiou and Finkielkraut). It was a result of the generic aspiration of peoples for self-determination as a universal *human* collective in a specific historical condition in Europe of the nineteenth century (and in colonized societies in both the nineteenth and twentieth centuries). "Nation" was an "evental" name for an immanent separation and its flickering universalization under particularly unstable historical conditions. In Badiou's view, the modern nation was the divisive and emancipatory creation within a revolutionary tradition, not an identitarian one—but whose time is now probably finished (1–36).

However, it is not surprising that despite its convoluted dogmatics, counterrevolution has remained anxious about its debt to revolution in the high period of modernity. It seems to me that all its efforts at philosophical justification are actually directed, from the nineteenth century onwards, at insinuating the debt into the entrails of the modern *state-power* in the name of the revolution itself. Thus after the Terror, the Thermidoreans acted in the name of the revolution while instituting revisionism—"citizenship" being the first revisionist institution—and so did Napoleon, the strange embodiment of the objective republic and the subjective empire. Thinkers of the revolution in 1789, like Abbé Siéyes, became ideologues of the state by 1794–95 (Sonenscher). But the counterrevolutionary ideology still worked in the name of the revolution—as if it were the true inheritor of the revolutionary debt, which the modern state-institutions would pay back with material happiness to the people.

This was a travesty insofar as one of the first moments of the French Revolution in 1789 was one when the people refused to pay the church *tithes* on the grounds of the right to default on their own religious and communitarian inheritance.[15] As revolutionaries, the people were willing, joyful defaulters on their own historico-communitarian identities; they were no creditors to whom the future would be bound by debt! But it was a useful travesty for counterrevolution to convert the original "defaulters" into sovereign creditors because the move ensured the institutional continuity of state-power between revolution and counterrevolution. After the Terror, once this continuity becomes a matter of political virtue, its presence is felt inexorably—even in the post-Leninist experience of the Soviet state.[16] But that delicate historical investigation I will not carry out here.

One provisional conclusion follows from the above that the locus of the state is a key path of the naturalization of the ambiguous revolutionary debt. The state functions institutionally to achieve this naturalization but it is also an *ontological neutralizer* of the debt. With new forms of government that act as new modes or dispositions of life, such as "citizenship", the partisan subjective force of the perceived debt acted out as guilt and violent resentment is greatly attenuated and displaced onto the neutral being of an impassible state, within which "citizenship," "democracy," and so on, are neither hypotheses of thought nor sites of wager; they are simply zones of deployment. In the final section, I will propose that at a certain threshold, capitalism becomes a zone of indistinction between revolution and counterrevolution, with an ontological aim that goes beyond mere statist neutralization. I will propose that capitalism increasingly seeks a new ontology of social being as *nature,* as natural universality. But before that, I want to open a brief parenthesis on the contemporary structure of globalization with an asymmetrical distribution between Western societies, where the loss of any *trace* of a revolutionary hypothesis is nearly total, and some non-Western societies, where the revolutionary hypothesis still retains a political effectivity.

When Badiou coins the phrase "communist hypothesis"—and I take my cue from him—he chooses the weakest and most profound term possible: "communist."[17] To my mind, the communist hypothesis poses the following challenge: Is it possible to affirm the most profound materiality for the *thought* of Communism at the time of its greatest historical weakness? In a global epoch of Western liberal democracy being the measure of all historical politics, including neoliberal, conservative, and nondemocratic politics, does the communist hypothesis enforce any particular subjective avowal or decision? From another angle, how *decent* is it to speak of the communist idea or hypothesis in view of the disastrous outcome of the historical Left on a world-scale? Clearly, despite these grim challenges, if the declaration of the communist idea still holds attention, that testifies to some enormous hidden strength and resources of the idea. Nevertheless we must accept that Badiou is a master who teaches his lesson in the desert of Western society, where all revolutionary sequences of history have been exhausted. Now it is perfectly possible—and heroically admirable—for some, including Badiou, to show "fidelity" to (Badiou's term in his book on St. Paul [2003], which I will not discuss), or in my vocabulary, avow, certain past sequences—for example, the sequence culminating in May 1968—but such acts only confirm the pure transparency of the past to the present viewer. So the naive "Communist" enjoys a paradoxical transcendence over its own historical destiny, when declared from the commanding philosophical heights of an Alain Badiou. Correlatively, Badiou becomes a solid philosophical alibi for "Left circles" to renew their internal sociability, or what they call with revisionist snobbery, their "culture"[18]—in other words, their "comfort zone" in the space of the university while totally disavowing the desert of which the university is a part.

When I speak of the "revolutionary hypothesis," I am mostly thinking of situations where a certain division or torsion still operates between historical sequences and speculative wagers, between historicity and truth. Much of this statement can be illustrated by what has happened in the Arab world and the Middle East, from the Arab Spring (see Badiou 2012) to the idea of an Islamic Caliphate strangely mirroring the image of globalization, in the last ten years. But instead I will limit myself to the Indian situation and its historical point of excess, from where issues a revolutionary *Ambedkarite* hypothesis with significant political effects. This hypothesis today has a singular name, which in several Indian languages reads as *dalit* and translated into English means "oppressed." But as a name, it subjectifies an objective sociohistorical condition such that the subject, which is a subject of *politics*, exceeds the object, which is a society of those segregated and outcasted as "untouchables" by Hindu dogma (Jaffrelot). *Dalit* and *Ambedkarite* appear exchangeable at this point because Ambedkar himself came from an untouchable social group. But the interesting fact is that while the thinker spoke and wrote for more than thirty years as an egalitarian militant, the name *dalit* gains currency only after Ambedkar's death in 1956. It assumes an intense historicity between the 1970s and the present, when we can speak retroactively of an Ambedkarite hypothesis underlying a *dalit* revolution, whose sequence remains indeterminate and open even as I write.

The inference I draw from the situation I have summarized is that the very fuzziness, even obscurity, of a historical sequence, testifies to its effectivity, its "enormous liveliness" (Badiou's words from the Bosteels interview) in the present. But that presence in no way disperses the speculative eternity of egalitarian thought into presentist political consideration. At the same time, the ruling classes that wield political power—the present government is ruled by the Bhartiya Janta Party (BJP) with a majoritarian nationalist and Hindu theologico-social agenda—attend to the *dalit* sequence only for presentist considerations. They must *manage* the situation by reducing its point of excess back to a peculiarly improvised ideology of "individual–social" justice completely subtracted from the thought of collective emancipation.[19] At the same time, we can observe the following equivocation on the part of the ruling classes and their state ideology: On the one hand, they must acknowledge in their bad conscience, as it were, a *dalit* debt of Indian history, and act in the spirit of counterrevolutionary strategy to assimilate and neutralize the debt in new institutional forms of the state. On the other, their dogmatics are *global*; they would rather prescribe a pure managerial life of what is called in economic jargon "governance" (or "economic government") which is, tendentially speaking, poststatist. To that extent, despite the distance from the state that characterizes both the revolutionary hypothesis and neoliberal dogma, in a non-Western society like India, the state is the last historical site of their terrible and terribly unequal battle.

CAPITALISM TODAY: LOSS OF REALITY OR THE REAL OF A LOSS?

To return to the question posed by our vigilant melancholic: What is lost when the concept of revolution is lost to the thought of politics? Gathering together the divergent series opened up by Arendt and Badiou, we might say that what is lost are even the last traces of revolution as *free action*, the *historical necessity* of the age of revolutions and the *contingent eternity* of the revolutionary idea. So the consequent query would be: If the loss is indeed real, then does the counterrevolutionary project lapse too because the question of reversing the revolution doesn't arise anymore? Or, does counterrevolution come into its own and give body to what Arendt dismissed in Joseph de Maistre's assertion as "empty witticism"—that is, give body to an *opposite* reality of the revolution?

But here an ambiguity arises such that the distinction between reversal and opposition becomes indistinct. It is not clear whether the opposite of revolution would consist in the *capture* of the thought of revolution, its principles and definition, by counterrevolutionary actors, or in *changing* those very principles. But the very thesis that there occurs an irreducible novel change (or birth, if you will) of generic forms of thought,—that is, of "principles" in the originary sense—*is* the meaning of revolution. Hence, with the event of a generic invention of new principles, the possibility of a new subject of politics arises who is not a "political actor" engaged in defeating another such actor in a game of power or deposing her from the place of sovereignty.

At this stage, we are faced with a logical impasse that can only be expressed by the phrase "loss of reality": there occurs a loss of reality of the very thought of politics when the concept of revolution is lost to it.

I started with resorting to a psychoanalytic parallel in response to the central question. In psychoanalytic terms, a "loss of reality" is what is suffered in *psychosis* insofar as the structure of this pathology involves radical disavowal of the very place or ground of this reality. In other words, reality is blocked from the patient's symbolic access, her discourse. However, Freud points out that given there still is *some* discourse—of course there can be a total catatonic, somatic expiration of discourse, but who can be sure that even catatonia is not *some* emission of signs?—the patient, in her worst delusional disavowal, seems to nevertheless calmly observe from one solitary residual corner of her mind, the rest of the scene of utter disorder, observe it like a rational vigilant spectator.[20] Interestingly, in his etiology of melancholy (or *melancholia*), Freud says that with the melancholic, it is not actually the object lost that the patient becomes pathologically attached to—it is to the *loss itself* (2001a). A type of narcissistic libido in a situation of unsuccessful mourning of the loss of the original reality, the real object of a kind of love—what else is revolution if not an affair of love!—invests the loss itself as its object. Thus we, through a risky sliding along specialized categories, move from a problematic of "loss of reality" to one of "the real of loss."

Now if I am excused the further rash move of replacing the structure of the psychotic subject with the fiction of a "vigilant melancholic," I would like to propose that with this figure we imagine a sort of rational hero fighting the complete internalization of a structure of delusion. So even if the concept of revolution is smashed to pieces against the rock of a global *economic dogmatics,* the rational or vigilant melancholic (if not a psychotic) still prepares to pick up the shards. Why do I then use the fiction of a "melancholic" at all? Because an affect threatens to overcome the figure/fiction that the old world is dead and our debts outlive the mortality of history. It is the paradigmatic counterrevolutionary affect of an *unpayable melancholic debt.* The partisans of the lost revolution, in the very passage to a counterrevolutionary affect, retain their rational vigilance—therein lies their heroism.

The other hypothesis, the "witty" one, proposes that we live in an age of pure, immaculate counterrevolution, which has no interest or stakes anymore in reversing the historical age of revolutions or opposing the generic principles of that age with its own. This counterintuitive counterrevolution can only be subjectified through a twisted figuration into a peculiar "antisubject which I will call the *narcissistic melancholic.* In Freud's scheme, narcissism provides the real support for a structure of melancholy to emerge. But in our context, the analogy points to an extreme subjective modality on a collective global scale: love of the loss of the possibility to act freely, to change historically, to think infinitely; in other words, *love of the loss of anything to live for.*

According to the present hypothesis, the objective form hosting this subjective modality is capitalism as it exists today. And like any objective form, despite being a host to the most paradoxical of nihilisms, capitalism today must present a logic, or even better, an *ontology.* If capitalism is able to present an independent ontology that is produced out of history but is itself not historically relative (in this respect, exactly like revolutionary thought) and in its production, accomplishes a finality that ends even the logic of historical necessity (exactly the goal of counterrevolution) then the paradox is resolved. A counterrevolutionary ontology becomes the highest stage of evolution, in which history, including revolutionary history, was a lower stage. And insofar as *this* was always the secret finality of the logic, history itself was masked evolution; history was the work of "the cunning of Nature."[21] So once the secret is revealed and the logic completed with the form called "capitalism" passing from mere historical necessity to laws of evolution, it is clear that any pure, independent, even affirmative, counterrevolutionary ontology must be an *ontology of Nature*.

The counterrevolutionary hypothesis then is that history is staged by the cunning of Nature as a mask and ruse of evolution; that history is a *simulacrum*. But every simulacrum dissimulates a truth, a "true being" whose restoration is at stake in the finality that governs the evolutionary scheme. This leads to a major conflation: the finality or the final restoration of an ontological truth becomes identical to an objective stage or form of *life*. Is this then the strange realization of the end of alienation of laboring life from its species-being that Marx dreamt of in the *Economic and Philosophical Manuscripts of 1844*? Of individual cognitive work from the General Intellect as thought of in *Grundrisse*?[22]

These variations on the counterrevolutionary hypothesis, some of which render it nearly utopian and communistic,[23] would deserve further consideration except for the fact that the stage or form we call "capitalism" today has changed its fundamental axiom. Unlike in the age of political economy from Adam Smith to Marx and later nineteenth-century economic sociology, capitalism today is not based on the ontological decision that the source of value is human labor. The axiom that labor is the actualization of an ontological *capacity* to create *another* life, a social one, is largely discredited today.[24]

It is true that with the early twentieth-century economic doctrines, from the Chicago school to German ordoliberalism after the Second World War, we are met with a sort of minimalist and aleatory ontology of "entrepreneurship. Enterprise is human, of course, but it lacks the substantive theory of a capacity or a power of "being"; instead it *plays* a game of chance, stakes, and wits with "life." And life, in turn, is not solely a biological substratum of creative transformations effected by human work; it is a field of multiple possibilities essentially *beyond* the locus of the human subject (Foucault). Life is self-differentiated into human and nonhuman, historical and organic intentional and aleatory or adaptive. Nevertheless it has to be said that these doctrines, though with minimized ontological weight, possessed a *political* stake outside the limits of a purely instrumental economic science. Political economy was not dead yet.

Wolfgang Streeck, in his recent book, *How Will Capitalism End?* points out that with the end of late capitalism, which is a term from 1930s, and the onset of *neoliberalism,* which carries on to date, we witness the final demise of political economy. Neoliberalism is the institution of language games that circulate commands and prescriptions to manage the loss of hitherto existing historical totalities such as "society" and "the state." Streeck observes that late capitalism, with regulatory state-policies, addressed the crises that historical nations such as Germany had to deal with in the twentieth century. Its "practical philosophy" enabled an interventionist German state to act on behalf of an approximate, even aleatory, totality, called "society."[25] But this approximation *existed* with the strategic support of a "light" biopolitical ontology.

It seems to me, following Streeck's analysis (and associated ones he refers to), that the loss of the modern lineage of the public ontology of a neutral–regulative state and the systematic–integrative function of a social totality demands a radical ontological reevaluation. What exists when nothing historical exists anymore? We must remember that the revolutionary hypothesis did not exceed historical actuality by voiding it. The battle with counterrevolution *was* historical; only the revolutionary hypothesis, insofar as it is the generic thought of politics, exceeded the battle while fighting it. But the present reevaluation consists in asking, What will be the measure of this epoch if it is not, as Arendt declared regarding the twentieth century, the world-historical measure of revolution? To this extent, the problem of neoliberal globalization is to make its ontological decision that brings the reign of world-history to an unequivocal close.

Now to state the ontological decision on behalf of a counterrevolutionary hypothesis: when nothing historical exists anymore, when no historical totality exists *as* totality, then only *nature* exists in the order of being. However, since history hitherto was understood as the site of novelty—of contingent, irreducible, and irresistible *change*—and nature is radically incommensurable with history, then it follows that nature is the immemorial regime of the Same. But we have seen, the objective form bearing the name "neoliberal capitalism" (as different from, say, nineteenth-century industrial capitalism and late capitalism of the postwar twentieth century) comes to pass as a decisive repudiating of the perspective of a world-history, a *single* bloc of historical time on a world-scale (which includes colonial history, but I will not argue the point here). So the ontological proposal forming the counterrevolutionary hypothesis becomes: what exists is nature as the immemorial, the Same, but what comes to pass in the Same is difference, only difference. In other words, nature is the being-indifferent to all difference while there is *nothing but difference*.[26] Whether this is a debased Schellingism or a vulgar Deleuzism I do not want to belabor, but the consequence of the proposal is obvious: no difference can ever be *activated* to breach the very ontological system that secures the immemorial reign of the different. No differential *opportunity* can ever come to make possible a new Same, *a new immemorial*.[27]

These abstract chains of thought, however wretched, do not have to be untrue. They can even be made to correspond with the empirical forms and experiences of a globalized world in the following way: What exists is capitalism, which itself was the finality of a masked evolution, and what comes to pass within capitalism (which is the new name of the *nature of things*, of *rerum natura*)[28] is the never-ending difference of individuals, communities, cultures, mores, and sign-systems. Capital is absolutely indifferent to these differences as long as none of them is *activated*, no difference becomes an *event*. But the circle closes in with the reiteration of the ontological axiom—the only being is that of Nature and this order of being admits of no events or subjects; nothing happens and no one thinks in Nature.

All this one would still bear as a hallucinated but coherent or possible hypothesis but for two objections: First, how can a finalism be introduced into an evolutionary scheme? Even by the standards of natural history and a general Darwinism, where is the place for a *theology* of final causes in a story of mutation, variation, and adaptation?[29] The most one can achieve with an evolutionary imaginary is an effective *myth* of the famous "survival of the fittest" in the sphere of capitalism, but that would still be a structural, theoretical myth.[30] The immaculate counterrevolutionary ontology of endless difference at eternal rest does not hold even as an evolutionary fiction.

Second, the central *philosophical* fallacy of the axiomatic method in this case is that it is contradictory to both ontologically *decide* in a singular, subjective gesture, as to what is the name of being *and* assert that this name denotes a natural necessity. If capitalism is a natural necessity, then its contingent naming as "neoliberal," "globalization," even "capitalism" itself, has no ontological weight. But the very thesis that capitalism is the true reign of Nature *is* ontological. The only way back from this philosophical failure is through the knot of history and evolution—and as we have seen, only theology or dogmatics can adjudicate in favor of the latter.

CONCLUSION

If the narcissistic melancholic has failed to hold his gaze on the real of his loss, what exactly is his failure? It is the failure to *live* the loss subjectively, a failure sought to be compensated by the transformation of the loss into an object of love—a failed move because the very object form is ontologically unsustainable.

But this does not necessarily mean that we have to be loyal to the vigilant melancholic and the rational psychotic by holding on to a residual place of sanity. The loss may well be real but with two qualifications: First, it may be that the intensification of a crisis of neoliberal capitalism leads the latter to present a *fantasy* of its immemorial, a historical unchallengibility. In other words, the entire counterrevolutionary hypothesis is an ideology of crisis. Second, it is possible that the loss of world-historical reference to a politics of emancipation and the collapse of the revolutionary hypothesis is a *regional* problem of Western societies. For instance, Streeck shows how, in the era of neoliberal crisis after crisis till the markets crash in 2008, the simultaneous rule of something like "absolute capitalism" (my phrase) is, in reality, not a complete evacuation of the great totalities of society and the state in the West, but their *wavering*.

Streeck argues that Western societies today, under the onslaught of the debt crisis in particular, operate as "less-than-societies" (13–15). These "less-than-societies" live under weakened sovereignty and institutional environments, to improvise an ad hoc groupist social existence instead of a systematically integrated one. Every state, in its turn, is a detotalized partisan actor on behalf of global oligarchies; states are increasingly being "privatized," including such hallowed state institutions such as the military.[31] In effect, there is a "de-coupling" (20–24) between capitalism and political democracy that in the eyes of both modern political philosophy and political economy were eternally betrothed. Paradoxically, this loss of the democratic partner renders capitalism that much more self-referential, absolute, and *exposed to crises.*

Finally, suppose the loss is a specific social transformation of the West but is distributed asymmetrically on a global scale: For instance, in a non-Western but global context like India, we observe a hierarchical arrangement of social gradation, whose temporal depth is deeper than both modernity and colonialism but is articulated with the same economic dogma that prescribes the eternal truth of capitalism (in India it is called "development"). In this milieu, the Indian prime minister, Narendra Modi, in November 2016, through a classic performative speech act, demonetized the economy by declaring 80 percent of its currency henceforth invalid. This was an act of the state, both peculiarly Keynesian and Goebbelsian, objectively fiscal and subjectively delusional.[32] India thus presented—or presents, since the scene is still unfolding—the double articulation of "less-than-society" and "a-lot-of-state" but with a crucial difference from the West: All of these acts or moves are taking place with an acute consciousness on the part of every actor, including the prime minister, that India is a *historical* society. And like any historical society, it's still subject to the ambiguous debt counterrevolution—which is sweeping the country—feels toward revolution.

Yet that is to say a specter of the revolutionary hypothesis haunts a society like India today. But what kind of a society is India? It is a "less-than-a-society." Now India is "less-than-a-society" in a different way from those developed Western nations, who have become so ("less-than-a-society") as a *result* of their neoliberal capitalist direction. With a case like India—alternatively described as Third World, developing, emerging global power, and so on—the inegalitarian and graded nature of society that prevents a life of the "common" (Ambedkar 1989, 50–51)makes "less-than-a-society" the very social *condition* for capitalism to exist. The strategic question then is: How might we invest and capitalize the contradictory conditions of real social inequality and formal political democracy in its march? Even while in other sectors of the global order the same system leads to an effective decoupling of itself with its formal condition, which is political democracy, and results in the degradation of society to being "less-than-a-society". It is as if in the West, society is experiencing its last days, while in a country like India, society has never existed and is struggling to come into being *for the first time*. The political and existential response to an asymmetrical distribution of systemic effects of the neoliberal global order seems to be the following: In certain parts of the world today, the frantic management of crises of capitalist society and the imminent *loss* of the social object itself leads either to an ontological glorification of this loss—recall Margaret Thatcher's verdict that society doesn't exist, only individuals and families do[33]—or a heroic pessimism that doesn't give up on critically *thinking* about this loss even while submerging in it. In other parts, the contradictions of history appear with greater violence each day. Here counterrevolution makes desperately ingenious and brutal moves to deny the ontological as well as historical debt it so ponderously carries—thus testifying to the existence not of a wavering between one kind of melancholy and another but of an *enthusiasm*[34] that activates a subject of generic politics, whose arguments with history are still not over.

Soumyabrata Choudhury is associate professor at the School of Arts and Aesthetics at Jawaharlal Nehru University. He has authored *Theatre, Number, Event: Three Studies on the Relationship of Sovereignty, Power, and Truth* (2013) and articles on ancient Greek liturgy, the staging of Ibsen, psychoanalysis, Nietzsche, Schiller, and Hegel. His new book, *Ambedkar and Other Immortals: An Untouchable Research Program*, is due to be published in April 2018.

Notes

1. For *novus ordo saecleum* and eagerness for "new things" *(navarum cupidi)*, see Arendt, 24, 28.

2. See Bosteels. It might be noted that in Arendt's usage "change" is not of the order of the unprecedented or the new, it is closest to the meaning of "mutation" (for instance in Cicero's *mutatio rerum*).

3. For a political and intellectual biography of Ambedkar, see Keer.

4. For Proudhon's coinage of the "permanent revolution,"' which is "self-same and perpetual," see Arendt, 44.

5. The definition of the event as the universalizable exception to a situation, but immanent to it, must be distinguished from the image of an event as "sovereign exception" along the lines of a philosophy of politics like Carl Schmitt's.

6. In the English translation of Badiou's concept, both these words have been employed. Though it is "procedure" that is more commonly used, as in the phrase "truth-procedure," it is interesting to note that "process" involves a more subjective as well as historical sense than "procedure," which is more "logical" and objective.

7. It is noteworthy that Arendt, among her several metaphors, also frequently uses the language of theatre. She often speaks of "actors" and "spectacles" when she narrates the twists and turns of history. More to the point is the fact that Arendt brings a self-conscious analysis to bear on how revolution and revolutionaries use the image of theatre— for instance, the image of persona, mask, embodiment, and so on. But she goes on to diagnose how the revolutionary also desires to unmask the lies and alienations of history to reach the "natural" human being. See Arendt, 102–3.

8. Though it has to be kept in mind that Badiou, in the conversation with Bosteels, acknowledges Foucault's real passion for the "singularity of the present" while expressing his reservations about the great discursive enclosures of the past created by the master.

9. The literature here is vast; I will instead acknowledge my debt to Anup Dhar of Ambedkar University, Delhi, who pointed out at a recent conference that Marx, in *Capital,* occasionally uses the verb "make" for the concept of class—as in "making a class" rather than simply stating that a class is. In my view, such "making" cannot be the reverse of necessitarian thinking (i.e., a voluntarism) but might involve the play of chance and thought.

10. With this egalitarian address "for anyone" in mind, we might understand why Badiou privileges mathematics as the pursuit of generic truths as opposed to more particularized approaches, such as language-systems, sign-systems, cultural discourses, etc.

11. One might also simplify the implications of this by saying that, for Badiou, there is no dialectical significance of merely "reality," its constitutive sequences . . . the dialectic pertains to the juncture of division in reality. This is Badiou's "Maoism" and mathematicism—and both are centered on the thinking of the "event." Commentators (like Alenka Zupancic) take a distance from this so-called eventual concentration. However, it cannot be overlooked that, for Badiou, the event doesn't find its extraordinary interest outside the elements of "ordinary reality."

12. In its most serious philosophical consequence, this noneschatological, nonmessianic project keeps Badiou at a resolute distance from the singular thinker of these things: Walter Benjamin. In less systematic terms the project reveals a robust antiutopian temperament of the philosopher.

13. This is surely the place to put on record that in his last year of life, 1956, Ambedkar converted to Buddhism and composed his own "rational" gospel shorn of several Buddhist legends, *The Buddha and his Dhamma.* See Ambedkar 1992.

14. An obvious reference, though essential to the context of the argument, must find a minimal response: M. K Gandhi's attachment to the *Gita* was inimitable, and he gave a strange "protestant" turn to the history of reading this text by making it an ethical affair. The mainstream Hindu reading was no doubt an "orientalist" imitation of the congregational ritual and dogmatic–philosophical reading that came with the Bible and the Christian Church.

15. For an analysis of the crucial citation of Jules Michelet's *History of the French Revolution* invoking the "right of the default of heirs" in the context of the end of the *tithes* in August 1789, see Choudhury, 202–9.

In this earlier monograph I propose a certain concept of liturgical debt and apply it along the following schematic lines:

1. Liturgical debt on a limited citizenship-determined scale is to be originally found in the ancient Greek city of Athens. The subjective side to this debt is the obligation of the citizen to participate in civic spaces and activities; the objective side is to provide liturgies (public services) for the city's activities on behalf of the city itself.
2. This relationship is rendered semiprivate in the Roman context and the liturgical debt is now actualized under a patron-client matrix. While the client can be an individual or a section of the Roman society and not the entire city, the patron is often a rich aristocrat who performs charity to gain individual reputation. This is also called "eurgetism" in the Roman context.
3. With global imperial Christianity the individual is drastically minoritized and, subjectively speaking, anyone can be Christianized and can feel the Christian debt to serve God and the church. Objectively, the debt is more and more tokentistic (for example, tithes) and symbolic (being part of the Eucharistic congregation, for instance).
4. In capitalism the liturgical debt is the debt of human labor as ontological service. Objectively, labor is transformed into capital/dead labor (living labor's obligation to die!) and its power of accumulation and reproduction on an extended scale. The debt/obligation to participate in capital is also the power to participate in the political forms of capitalism (democracy being the foremost form).
5. Revolutionary interruption or defaulting is the idea of a willed defaulting on the debt and power of participation in hitherto existing historical regimes. Thus the French Revolution was a defaulting on religious debt/power, while Communist revolution ideally is a defaulting on the socio-ontological inheritance of human being as labor.
6. Following Wolfgang Streeck, whom I refer to in this essay, a crisis of the liturgical logic can be diagnosed. The rational order of capital as debt, obligation, and power leading to a regime of a subjective capitalistic conduct (Max Weber's protestant conduct) to which another revolutionary rationality of freedom and debtlessness can be opposed—

> this dialectic is in crisis because the right of defaulting has entered the objective structure of neoliberal debt. Private debt-defaulting will be protected by public institutions as of now. So the counterliturgical axiom of the French Revolution that society has a sacred debt to the perpetual defaulters that is the poor is now changed to the following: society has a profane duty to cover up for the oligarchy of the rich debtors-defaulters, whose objective right seems to be to default if necessary, and it is a right established as a privileged condition of the borrowing itself.

16. At the same time I want to clarify that this is an analysis of a contingent historical process and does not fall into Francois Furet's influential revisionist schema of an inherent totalitarianism that is incarnated in history from the Terror to Bolshevik state.

17. For the "communist hypothesis," see Badiou and Finkielkraut, 107–25.

18. In this respect many old oppositions have become increasingly blurred: the liberal and the Left, the revisionist and the progressive democratic, and so on. In this process the historical "Left" hides its failure under a cloak thrown to it by the cultural "Left", a cloak originally fabricated by the revisionist denial of the event of the French Revolution by Francois Furet's culturalist thesis. It was famously—or notoriously, depending on your taste—predicated on the word "sociability" as substituted for "equality."

19. I coin this oxymoron "individual–social justice" to convey the point that in a country like India, two logics are intertwined. A neoliberal global logic emerges in our times that works by the elemental form of the "individual" (the aspirational agent of neoliberal economics has created a denser psychology for the economic actor than the nineteenth-century postulate of the rational individual). But the individual is not a free being but she is always already corporatized. At the same time the logic of society runs in the direction of total social control over all individual agency (particularly that of women) by hidebound communitarian traditions. However, the tradition of hierarchical society leads to a radical absence of any principle of society as a totality. In the circumstances all programs of "social justice" adopted by the state are a way of satisfying the desire for social improvement without risking a social revolution. So the programs invariably speak of opportunities for individuals from disadvantaged groups who can then become "role models." However, there can never be the slightest opportunity for the true liberation of individuality, which would be a political liberation from corporate subjugation.

20. For Freud's startling analysis of psychosis from *An Outline of Psycho-Analysis* and an excellent reading in the light of Lacan, see Regnault, 107–8.

21. This perverse reference to Hegel and his "cunning of Reason" indicates that much of what I improvise is an attempt to insert a Hegelian logic of dialectic and philosophy of history anonymously into an overnamed and over-deconstructed milieu.

22. *The Grundrisse* is, of course, one of Antonio Negri's, and the Italian autonomists', favorite texts. For an original interpretation of the General Intellect in relation to Arendt and Deleuze, see Virno.

23. This indiscernibility between the global capitalist mode of production and the alter-global ontology of the insurrectionary "multitude" (according to Negri et al.) is always attractive in so far as the multitude is an ontological "leap of faith" (Kierkegaard). But the mode of production is "objective" while a "leap of faith" is subjective. This leads to a further indiscernibility between first politics and ontology, then ontology and religion.

24. The rejection of the axiom of productive human labor today is corrosive and conveniently inconsistent. However, the thinker to have stepped back from the axiom and into a space of creative but strictly unproductive human action (following the Aristotelian distinction between *poiesis,* or instrumental production, and *praxis* as self-referential public action) was Hannah Arendt. Today she would appear to have been the last and the rarest of philosophical liberals.

25. I am reading Streeck in light of Foucault's *Birth of Biopolitics*—a text to which Streeck refers, though marginally. For the crisis of disintegrating society and deindividualizing individuals in neoliberalism, see Streeck, 14.

26. For the equation of difference and pure indifference, in the static image of multiplicity themselves serving a fixed image of thought in the readings of the philosopher Schelling (the first problematic reader being Hegel), see Deleuze, 276–77.

27. For the construction of "new truths" as new immemorials that possess historicity but no history (and no philosophy of history adequate to their historicities), see Choudhury.

28. The reference to Lucretius here also indicates a travesty, when a materialist ancient philosophy serves the cause of a dogmatic naturalism. See Lucretius, *The Nature of Things* (London: Penguin, 2007).

29. In a conscious imitation of capitalist corrosion of being, I use the terms "finalism" and "final causes" corrosively. For a profound investigation of these notions in philosophy and evolutionary biology, see Ruyer.

30. One can join the economic myth that underlies capitalism—"myth" because no one ever defined competition and fitness transparently, as monopolies and oligarchies do not win in the market struggles, they control the market—with the myth of the "state of Nature" in Thomas Hobbes that underlie the theory of the modern state.

31. Streeck refers to works that show that in the wars in Afghanistan, Iraq mercenaries have been included in the American ground forces employed by private firms. Apart from the logistical scrambling, such information also scrambles the notion of a patriotic military as well as a professional–public one (28).

32. It was pointed out by some astute commentators (See Mehta) that the Indian prime minister's announcement of demonetization, in effect, commanded a total population into obedience (since currency concerns everyone). The context of the command was not important; the sheer act of doing so was a subjective subjugation of the people. On the other hand, the objective context is oddly

Keynesian, where demonetization is meant to propel *digital* demand as well as transactions on a total macroeconomic scale. In fact, after the 2008 global crisis, Left-leaning economists like Paul Krugman advocated a Keynesian response on the part of the state rather than prescribe austerity. See Streeck, 18 n.24.

33. Streeck, 40 n.67. In a context like India's, the Thatcherite pronouncement ("ontological decision") would run like this: Society doesn't exist, only individuals, families, and castes do.

34. "Enthusiasm" is an evocation delivered to the spectacle and thought of the revolution by Immanuel Kant in *The Conflict of Faculties*. According to Kant, the French Revolution generates enthusiasm when you contemplate it like a spectator or a thinker does—abstracted from real history. Jules Michelet, in contrast, speaks of the partisan enthusiasm of the historical actors of the French Revolution. In our times, Badiou calls enthusiasm the affect of generic emancipatory politics.

Works Cited

Ambedkar, Babasaheb. 1987. "Krishna and his *Gita*: Philosophical Justification of Counterrevolution." In *Writings and Speeches*. Vol. 3. Ed. Vasant Moon, 357–80. Bombay: Education Department, Government of Maharashtra.

Ambedkar, Babasaheb. 1989. "Annihilation of Caste with a Reply to Mahatma Gandhi". In *Writings and Speeches*. Vol. 1. Ed. Vasant Moon, 23–96. Bombay: Education Department, Government of Maharashtra.

Ambedkar, Babasaheb. 1992. "The Buddha and His Dhamma". In *Writings and Speeches*. Vol. 11. Ed. Vasant Moon. Bombay: Education Department, Government of Maharashtra.

Arendt, Hannah. 2016. *On Revolution*. London: Faber & Faber.

Badiou, Alain. 2003. *Saint Paul: The Foundation of Universalism*. Trans. Ray Brassier. Stanford: Stanford University Press.

Badiou, Alain. 2005. "What Is a Thermidorean?" In *Metapolitics*, 124–40. Trans. Jason Barker. London: Verso.

Badiou, Alain. 2012. *Return of History: Time of Riots and Uprising*. Trans. Gregory Elliott. London: Verso.

Badiou, Alain, and Alain Finkielkraut. 2014. *Confrontation :A Conversation with Aude Lancelin*. Trans. Susan Spitzer. Cambridge: Polity Press.

Bosteels, Bruno. 2005. "Can Change Be Thought? A Dialogue with Alain Badiou." In *Alain Badiou: Philosophy and Its Conditions*. Ed. Gabriel Riera, 238–61. Albany: State University of New York Press.

Choudhury, Soumyabrata. 2013. *Theatre, Number, Event: Three Studies on the Relationship of Sovereignty, Power, and Truth*. Shimla: IIAS.

Deleuze, Gilles. 1994. *Difference and Repetition*. Trans. Paul Patton. London: Athlane Press.

Foucault, Michel. 2010. *The Birth of Biopolitics: Lectures at the Collège de France, 1978–1979*. Trans. Graham Burchell. London: Palgrave Macmillan.

Freud, Sigmund. 2001a. "Mourning and Melancholy." In *The Complete Psychological Works of Sigmund Freud.* Vol. 14. Ed. James Strachey, 243–58. London: Vintage Classics.

Freud, Sigmund. 2001b. "The Loss of Reality in Neurosis and Psychosis." In *The Complete Psychological Works of Sigmund Freud.* Vol. 19. Ed. James Strachey, 183–87. London: Vintage Classics.

Jaffrelot, Christophe. 2004. *Dr. Ambedkar and Untouchability: Analysing and Fighting Caste.* London: C. Hurst and Permanent Black.

Keer, Dhananjay. 2009. *Dr. Babasaheb Ambedkar: Life and Mission.* Mumbai: Popular Prakshan.

Lucretius. 2007. *The Nature of Things.* London: Penguin.

Marx, Karl. 1977. *Economic and Political Manuscripts of 1844.* Moscow: Progress.

Pratap Bhanu Mehta. 2016. "You Have Been Warned." *Indian Express,* November 17.

Regnault, Francois. 2014. "The Emperor's Heron." Trans. J. W. Stone. *Lacanian Ink* nos. 43–44: 107–8.

Ruyer, Raymond. 2016. *Neofinalism.* Trans. Alyosha Edlebi. Minneapolis: University of Minnesota Press.

Sonenscher, Michael. 2003. "Introduction." In *Sieyes: Political Writings.* Ed. Michael Sonenscher, vii–lxiv. Indianapolis: Hackett.

Streeck, Wolfgang. 2017. *How Will Capitalism End? Essays on a Failing System.* Trans. Tessa Hanswedell and Rodney Livingstone. New Delhi: Juggernaut.

Virno, Paolo. 1996. "Virtuosity and Revolution: The Political Theory of Exodus." In *Radical Thought in Italy: A Potential Politics.* Ed. Paolo Virno and Michael Hardt, 189–212. Minneapolis: University of Minnesota Press.

FIDEL AND THE TRICONTINENTAL IMAGINATION

Aditya Nigam

Recently a Left-wing music group from Delhi, *Parcham,* uploaded a Hindi version of the song "Guantanamera," the Cuban folk song revolutionized by the poetry of Jose Marti. In part, it was an exercise in nostalgia about what we had left behind, but in equal measure it was still a longing for a future that many of us had come to associate with the Cuban Revolution and the figures of Fidel Castro and Che Guevara. If Che was the perennial revolutionary, the figure of Fidel increasingly embodied for us, in our youthful revolutionary days, the "tricontinental" imagination—that is, the coming together of the oppressed peoples of three continents: Asia, Africa, and Latin America. In this imagination the small Caribbean island offering dogged resistance to the big bully in the North appeared as a powerful voice of support and solidarity for us all.

We knew that "Guantanamera" was not just a plaintive love song, it was a song that embodied the fighting spirit of Cuba. And clearly its resonances were felt in similar ways elsewhere in the three continents as well. In October 2016, some of us were in Johannesburg for a workshop on Democratic Marxism. The Rhodes Must Fall movement, begun in Cape Town, had galvanized the very air of Johannesburg—and indeed all of South Africa. Acquiring massive dimensions, the struggle had transformed into the militant Fees Must Fall campaign for the democratization of higher education. One evening, after the workshop, our hosts took us to a restaurant with live music. Well into the night, as we were preparing to leave, the band suddenly started singing "Guantanamera," and the effect was electrifying. Almost everyone present joined in, we were singing an inspiring collective anthem.

What does this have to do with Fidel? And why talk of him today, in 2017?

To my mind, the tricontinental spirit embodied the spirit of decolonization and was part of a process that has acquired newer dimensions today. It has been noted by analysts that it was the first Tricontinental Conference that not only brought together towering figures like Amilcar Cabral, Salvador Allende, and Fidel Castro, but also helped, along with unwavering Cuban support, the Palestinian cause enter into Latin American consciousness. At one level, we could say that even today, in 2018, the "colonial matrix of power" (Quijano; Escobar) continues to structure our world, and imperialist bullying across the three continents continues unabated. That legacy of decolonization, therefore, continues to be important for us today.

But that perhaps does not tell us the whole story.

For too long have we labored under the illusion that while we fight imperialist bullying and domination we can happily continue to build capitalism "in our own way" in our respective societies. Capitalism, after all, was also supposed to be about liberating ourselves from so-called backwardness and underdevelopment. For it was the agent of history just as colonialism—its overseas adventure—was an "unconscious tool of History." Even though there were theorists who proclaimed "underdevelopment" at one pole to be structurally linked to "development" at the other, the fascination for capitalism continued to hold its seduction through the desire for development.

It is only in recent times that the realization has started dawning among some sections of the Left that capitalism, *in any form,* is antithetical to the very existence of humankind. It is perhaps time to recognize that "capitalism" is not just an economic system (or a mode of production) ordained by history to unite the whole world into a modern cosmopolitanism. Rather, "capitalism" and "the economy" are Euro-America's poisonous gifts to humanity, for it is through the institution of bourgeois private property and the idea of "the economy" as an autonomous domain with its own self-fulfilling logic that the hegemony of the West is established over our minds. It is only now that we have seriously begun to appreciate how deeply and constitutively this hegemony is tied to the genocide of indigenous populations and racial slavery— tied to the idea that these are merely accidental by-products of an otherwise emancipatory discourse through which the West colonized the world.

The tricontinental imagination and new global solidarities across the colonized world, however, emerged through a *political* rupture, a break in the logic of the economy. The October Revolution in Russia (whose centenary falls this year), along with the Chinese and Cuban Revolutions, make possible the emergence of this subjectivity through a decisive break in the overarching logic of the "economy" and its apparently inexorable, objective logic.

The theoretical import of this moment of emergence was, however, little understood and appreciated even by the protagonists of this epic drama themselves. Thus it happened that through the 1950s, '60s and '70s, they debated industrialization and dependency, with Marxists joining in to "explain" why capitalism continued to be "retarded," and development "arrested," in the peripheries. Capitalism and the overall logic of the economy never really came to be interrogated seriously.

Among Indian Marxists and Leftists in general, the figure of Fidel Castro (as of Che Guevara) remained an inspirational figure and an idea that was the very embodiment of the revolutionary spirit itself. Fidel was the leader of the small island state that was challenging the mighty United States of America in its own backyard. Fidel was a leading figure of the Non-Aligned Movement, whose iconic photograph with the then Indian Prime Minister Indira Gandhi, everyone was familiar with. And yet, to the best of my knowledge, there is little evidence to show that anyone on the Left seriously engaged with Fidel's ideas theoretically or ever took the notion of triconcontinentalism as a way of rereading Euro-Marxist discourse and repurposing it for the non-European world.

The unfinished business of decolonization then, entails dismantling this hegemony at the level of thought itself. It urges us to take the logic ushered in by the Tricontinental Conference to its logical end, which alone can illuminate to us the fallacies of privatizing nature and its "resources"—land, water, and air. Proposals for "delinking" once enunciated at the purely economic level, need to be taken forward into the very domain of thought. That is where ideas of *political* "economies of sharing" and notions like *buen vivir* are being articulated, drawing on entirely different cosmologies and ways of being and thinking.

In a sense, Fidel stands at the cusp of this transformation, steering the Cuban economy in the face of long years of economic blockade, in the direction of a less wasteful and more ecologically sensitive economy.

Now that Fidel is no more, Fidel has become an idea—an idea that embodies the relentless struggle for justice against imperialist domination and the coloniality of power; an idea that calls on us to ceaselessly carry on the battle of decolonization. Indeed, Fidel is the idea of tricontinental solidarity.

Aditya Nigam works at the Centre for the Study of Developing Societies, Delhi. He is currently engaged in a study of capital and democracy from a non-Western perspective. He is author of *The Insurrection of Little Selves: The Crisis of Secular Nationalism in India* (2006) and *After Utopia: Modernity, Socialism, and the Postcolony* (2010), among others.

Note

This tribute develops on certain ideas I have earlier elaborated in Nigam 1999; 2011.

Works Cited

Escobar, Arturo. 2004. "Beyond the Third World: Imperial Globality, Global Coloniality and Anti-Globalisation Social Movements." *Third World Quarterly* 25, no. 1: 207–30.

Nigam, Aditya. 1999. "Marxism and the Postcolonial World: Footnotes to a Long March." *Economic and Political Weekly* 34, nos. 1–2: 33–43.

Nigam, Aditya. 2011. *Desire Named Development*. New Delhi: Penguin Books.

Quijano, Aníbal. 2000. "Coloniality of Power and Eurocentrism in Latin America." *International Sociology* 15, no. 2: 215–32.

UN HOMENAJE A FIDEL (AN HOMAGE TO FIDEL)

August Nimtz

The following talk was delivered by August Nimtz on December 15, 2016, at Plymouth Congregational Church in Minneapolis. The occasion was a public program to celebrate the life of Fidel Castro, sponsored by the Minnesota Cuba Committee. Nimtz is co-coordinator of the committee as well as professor of political science and African American and African studies. The committee has organized solidarity work for the Cuban Revolution in Minnesota since 1990 and is part of the National Network on Cuba that organizes similar activities in other cities. Nimtz is also coeditor along with Gary Prevost of *Race in Cuba: Essays on the Revolution and Racial Inequality by Esteban Morales Dominguez*. The talk has been slightly edited for the sake of clarity.

Two years and two days ago a momentous development took place that many of us in this room thought unlikely: Presidents Raul Castro's and Barack Obama's announcement that both of their governments would begin the process to restore diplomatic ties and the normalization of other relations.

In case you might have concluded from that announcement and the discussions between both governments since then that the ruling class in the United States had now finally come to its senses and has finally come to accept the existence of the Cuban Revolution, you're probably having second thoughts. The coverage of Fidel Castro's death by the big business media has likely been a rude awakening for you. From the conservative to the liberal end of the continuum of the media you have been offered a sobering lesson in capitalism's unrelenting hostility to the Cuban Revolution. Exactly because Fidel epitomized the very essence of the revolution is why the coverage of his death was so hostile.

What animates that hostility? How to explain?

First and foremost it has to do with what took place on the island more than half a century ago—one of those rare moments in human history when the subjects or the subjugated in society become the protagonists. To fully appreciate what happened, it is necessary to think historically, big history.

Not long after the birth of the modern working class—yes, that class whom the pundits have just discovered owing to the recent election cycle—it sought to take political power in order to improve its life chances. The first insurrection it staged, in 1848, went down to bloody defeat in Paris. It tried again in 1871, also in Paris, and for the first time ever workers were able to actually take power—but were only able to hold power for two and a half months. It too was drowned in blood.

It would take almost a half century before the working class—this time in alliance with the peasantry—would again be successful, in Russia in 1917, the Bolshevik Revolution. But by at least a decade later it was increasingly clear that a counterrevolution was under way in the Soviet Union. By then a bureaucratic social layer headed by Stalin had usurped political power; the product of another bloody overturn. To understand what happens in a counterrevolution, think the Arab Spring in Egypt and how it was hijacked.

The history of the insurrectionary working class teaches, therefore, that it is one thing to take power; it's another to hold on to it. Never has the working class been in power as long as it's been in Cuba—more than half a century! How was that possible?

The Cuban Revolution teaches that a real revolution can't be brought into existence by elections; it teaches that even mass demonstrations aren't sufficient. A real revolution involves the actual taking of power by the masses themselves.

Once the rebel army of about three thousand combatants headed by Fidel had broken the back of the U.S.-backed army of dictator Fulgencio Batista after two years of fighting, the Cuban masses in the tens and hundreds of thousands became the architects of history beginning with the general strike of January 1, 1959. Nothing made clearer that this wasn't just a general strike when the masses, in coordination with the Rebel Army and the underground movement, took over virtually all of the police stations on the island and, therefore, put an end to one of the most sanguinary police forces in the hemisphere. For Black Lives

Matter activists and supporters who want to put an end to police brutality, look to what the Cuban masses did. It's a matter, literally, of life and death.

And then the peasantry went into motion—spontaneous expropriations of the land of the landlords, domestic and international. The new revolutionary government began to organize and institutionalize those expropriations with the Agrarian Reform Law of May 1959. As Raul Castro put it, that law did more than anything until then to convince Washington why the Cuban Revolution had to be overthrown.

And then in 1960 the working class went into motion. When the capitalist bosses fled to Miami and elsewhere, workers realized that the only way to keep the factories and other work places running was to take them over. Thus began what they called "interventions," the origins of the nationalization of the means of production, the beginning of the socialist phase of the revolution.

Again, revolutions can't be voted into power. All elections can do is to register preferences for either candidates or policies. Power has to be taken—exactly what the toilers of Cuba began doing on January 1, 1959. And unlike anywhere since the Bolshevik Revolution, the toilers had a government that supported and helped organize the taking of power.

Using that governmental power to arm the masses to secure their conquests was indispensable. That's what made it possible to defeat Washington's mercenary-supported invasion of the island in April 1961. The mercenaries met an armed people who were willing to die to defend their new conquests. That's the fundamental reason why they were defeated at the Bay of Pigs, or Playa Giron, only seventy-two hours after their invasion—the first defeat U.S. imperialism had ever suffered and, thus, another reason for Washington's implacable hatred for the revolution.

And in the midst of that victory, the socialist course of the revolution was proclaimed; the bourgeois forces in the government had long fled to Miami and elsewhere.

In that proclamation Fidel explained that because the first socialist revolution in the Americas was made ninety miles from the shores of U.S. imperialism, "right under their noses," as he put, "they will never forgive us." The Cuban Revolution was Washington's Don Corleone problem. Washington, in other words, got disrespected in its own back yard. If the Cuban toilers could get away with it, others in the hemisphere could be inspired to do the same. Cuba, in other words, was a bad example for Washington. That's the essential reason for the hatred of the Cuban Revolution that was so uniformly on display in the capitalist media's coverage of Fidel's death. It remains a bad example.

But it's not enough, as history has shown, for workers to take power; it has to be kept and that means the toilers will have to actually run the new society. That's what made the literacy campaign of 1961 all so important. Bringing up all of Cuba's workers and peasants to at least an elementary-grade reading and writing level was necessary, and that was achieved in that defining moment of the revolution—the same year in which the mercenary expedition at the Bay of Pigs was defeated.

Most crucial in the literacy campaign was how both the teachers—largely young women—and their students, largely peasants, were themselves transformed in the process. Yes, learning to read and write is of enormous importance. But doing that through voluntary labor was transformative for both teachers as well as students. In the patriarchal world of that era the tens of thousands of young women who participated were forever marked by that experience. If you haven't seen it, I encourage you to see and share with others Catherine Murphy's wonderful documentary about the literacy campaign, *Maestra.* The literacy campaign, I contend, was a decisive moment in understanding why the Cuban Revolution was able to survive in the face of Washington's six-decade-long unrelenting hostility.

The entire process in those first three years of the revolution revealed two indispensable requirements for making a revolution—the conquest of state power and having the kind of leadership that Fidel provided. Without a Fidel in that most crucial stage in the revolution its survival, I'm convinced, would not have been possible. The Arab Spring illustrates tragically what happens when a revolutionary movement lacks the kind of leadership Fidel provided.

Some of the more savvy voices of the capitalist media did mention—almost in passing—some of the social gains of the revolution, such as Cuba's internationally well-known health-care and education systems. But what that media went out of its way to ignore is Cuba's decades-long and proud record of proletarian internationalism. Nelson Mandela captured it best when he visited Cuba not long after coming out of prison in 1990, when he told a mass rally in Matanzas, Cuba, that "were it not for what you did in Angola in 1988, I would not be able to be here today with you." He also said: "What other country can point to a record of greater selflessness than Cuba has displayed in its relations with Africa?"[1]

When the last Cuban contingents returned from Angola in 1991, Raul was most prophetic. What the Cuban volunteers had done in Angola, he said in a welcoming speech, specifically, the selflessness that they practiced there, is exactly what would be necessary for the revolution to successfully confront the gravest crisis in its history—the collapse of the Soviet Union and the resulting "special period." "Thanks to Angola," Raul said, "we understand in all its dimensions Comrade Fidel's point that when a people like the Cuban people have been capable of fighting and making sacrifices for the freedom of another people, what wouldn't they be capable of doing for itself?" In other words, Angola saved the Cuban Revolution.

Perhaps the most noble and self-sacrificing moment of the revolution's proletarian internationalism is what it did in West Africa in the summer and fall of 2014, when 256 volunteers, at the request of the World Health Organization, went to fight the Ebola epidemic. They were selected out of 12,000 who had volunteered to go. That's 12,000 out of a population of 11 million! The fact that the number of U.S. citizens who volunteered to go to fight the epidemic never reached more than 2,800—I'm just referring to those who volunteered and not those who actually went—out of a population of 325 million, speaks volumes about the different values that prevail in the two countries.[2]

No other government in the world made such a contribution to fighting the Ebola scourge; again, what state power makes possible. All of us owe a debt to the Cuban Revolution, whether we are aware of it or not. Unless scourges like Ebola are controlled at the source we are all unsafe. In a world in which such a pestilence is only an airplane fight away, to think that controlling the borders of the United States or any country against Ebola is effective is naive at best.

If the Obama project were to be successful, the bringing of capitalism back to Cuba—and that's what its normalization of relations with Cuba was really about—the values of proletarian internationalism, sharing one's limited resources with the most oppressed in the world, would be undermined. Capitalism would begin to erode such values. Capitalism is about what its ideological defenders call "self-interest," or what the rest of us call "selfishness," or "I-got-mine- and-you-get-yours, or "what-have-you-done-for-me-lately" thinking.

The enmity for the Cuban example is especially rabid at this moment—and not just because of the new administration that's about to take office. The Trump election, rather, registers a deeper problem for capitalism—its increasing inability to ensure prosperity for working people. That's what his election registers. What's deplorable is not that some of our fellow workers may have voted for Trump in the belief that the demagogue would provide jobs; as Marx once said, a drowning person will grab hold to a twig for salvation. Many an African American worker voted for Obama thinking that their lives would improve and have since learned otherwise. Just ask the citizens of Flint, Michigan! No, what's deplorable is an economic/political system in which workers think that the only way in which they can have a job, put food on the table for their families, or pay a mortgage note is to vote for a blatantly racist/sexist/xenophobic candidate. That's what's deplorable and truly irredeemable. It was capitalism that gave us Trump, and why anyone would want to see capitalism's return to Cuba is a discussion we urgently need to have.

Until the very end Fidel gave political instructions—how to bury a hero of the working-class revolution. For those of us who have longed wish that Lenin's corpse be removed from the tomb that Stalin constructed to turn Lenin, against his wishes, into a mummified icon, Fidel has now set a standard. As Raul revealed in Santiago de Cuba, at the end of the nine-day commemoration, Fidel's last wish was that "after his death, his name and likeness never be used to designate institutions, plazas, parks, avenues, streets, or other public spaces, nor monuments, busts, statues, and other such tributes be erected. In accordance with Compañero Fidel's decision, during the next period of sessions of the National Assembly of People's Power we will present necessary legislative proposals to ensure his will is upheld."

In other words, Fidel to the end wanted no Stalinist cult of personality.

To have lived in the era of Fidel is a privilege. Fidel is irreplaceable. At certain and rare moments in history such individuals appear and all of us, all of working-class humanity, have been privileged to have been in the same world he inhabited.

I suspect the only thing Fidel would not have agreed with is the postponement of Bastion 2016 until the following month. As some of you know, every December 2, the day the *Granma* landed at the end of 1956, the entire population of the island mobilizes for military preparedness. It sends a message to its unforgiving enemy ninety miles away that the Cuban people are not lowering their guard; they are prepared to defend their revolution by any means necessary. Fidel, I think, would have said: "My funeral can be postponed; more important is letting our enemy know that preparing to defend ourselves if necessary cannot be postponed." But that's my humble opinion.

I say that to stress that the Cuban Revolution has survived exactly because the Cuban masses are prepared to defend it; without that readiness there is no way the revolution could have survived ninety miles from the shores of the most powerful state in history that unceasingly seeks its overthrow.

No word was uttered more in the capitalist media's coverage of Fidel's death than "dictator." Yes, there is a dictatorship in Cuba, but not of an individual or a couple of brothers in their eighties but rather of the Cuban working class that took power six decades ago and continues to keep power by imposing its will. That was the real target of the media's hostility, and I think we should defend the right of the Cuban masses to take whatever measures they deem necessary to defend their revolution against Washington's unrelenting aggression, including in the new "Obama-let's-play-nice" rendition.

Please read, if you haven't already—we've made it available here [at the door]—Raul's speech that he gave in Santiago, where Fidel's remains were interned on December 3. It's very educational. After recounting key moments in Fidel's life, he said:

> This is the undefeated Fidel who brings us together through his example and demonstration that, yes we could, yes we can, and yes we will! I repeat, he demonstrated that yes we could, yes we can, and yes we will overcome any obstacle, threat, or turmoil in our determined efforts to build socialism in Cuba. Or to say it another way, which is the same thing: to guarantee the independence and sovereignty of our homeland!

The spirit of the speech underscores, I think, that Fidel's death is an important moment for the revolution. The exact opposite of what the enemies of the revolution had hoped for. The nine days of commemoration in Cuba marked a strengthening and deepening of the commitment of Cubans of all ages throughout the island to defend their revolution.

A student in my Cuban Revolution class this semester who's in close contact with her family in Cuba confirmed this assessment.

Also in his speech, Raul said, echoing the president of Algeria [one of the foreign leaders who spoke at the commemoration], that one of Fidel's great assets was his ability to see into the future. Raul mentioned specifically Fidel seeing in 1989 the possible collapse of the Soviet Union and the affiliated bloc in Eastern Europe. And if that should happen, he said, Cuba was prepared to uphold the banner of socialist revolution—exactly what Cubans did.

Another foresight of Fidel was what he said when Cuban revolutionaries, the Cuban Five, volunteered to infiltrate terrorist groups in South Florida and were arrested in 1998: "Volverán"— "they will return"—exactly what happened when the last of them returned on December 17, 2014. I confess that not all of us were so confident that would happen. Not only did Fidel live long enough to see that victory but also a longtime defender of the revolution and member of our Cuba Committee who led our work to free the Five, Frank Forrestal, who died almost a year later.

Fidel made another prediction that Raul could have also mentioned—a claim that all of us should seriously ponder, especially in the moment in which we find ourselves. In a speech in the context of increasing U.S. hostility toward the revolution, a few weeks before the Bay of Pigs, or Playa Giron—the first defeat for U.S. imperialism—Fidel said: "There will be a victorious socialist revolution in the U.S. before a victorious counterrevolution in Cuba." I'll repeat. "There will be a victorious socialist revolution in the U.S. before a victorious counterrevolution in Cuba."

On this coming January 1, the working class in Cuba will have been in power for fifty-eight years—six times longer than the working class in the Soviet Union. Despite the plans of the Obama administration and no doubt his successor, there has been no victorious counterrevolution. We, therefore, still have time to prove him correct.

Fidel's revolutionary optimism, his unwavering confidence in the working class, what his words captured—and what his enemies so hate—is the real Fidel.

For those of us still trying to absorb the significance of the Trump election, and who may have fallen into a bit of pessimism, never forget that moment after the *Granma* landing at the end of 1956, when the eighty-two fighters who were on the yacht were shipwrecked and the vast majority had been killed or captured by Batista's army. Never forget Fidel's reaction when after a couple of weeks, twelve of them—only twelve!—were able to regroup in the in the Sierra Maestra. Twelve of them and seven rifles: in Fidel's immortal words, "Now we will win the war." When Raul recounted that moment at the mass rally in Santiago, the crowd erupted with shouts of: "Fidel, Fidel: That's Fidel!"

That's the Fidel we celebrate tonight. That's the Fidel who should inspire us to realize what he predicted: Again, "There will be a victorious socialist revolution in the U.S. before a victorious counterrevolution in Cuba."

August H. Nimtz is professor of political science and African American and African studies and Distinguished Teaching Professor at the University of Minnesota and co-coordinator of the Minnesota Cuba Committee. He is coeditor along with Gary Prevost of *Race in Cuba: Essays on the Revolution and Racial Inequality* by Esteban Morales Dominguez (2013). His most recent book is the two-volume *Lenin's Electoral Strategy* (2014).

Notes

1. Between 1975 and 1988 more than three hundred thousand Cubans volunteered to go to Angola to prevent the racist South African regime's attempt to overthrow its government. The decisive battle took place in the spring of 1988, at the small settlement of Cuito Cuanavale. A combination of mainly Cuban and Angolan forces dealt South African troops a major defeat and paved the way, as Fidel predicted, to the negotiations that brought about the end of Apartheid.
2. This data comes from the U.S. Agency for International Development website, where volunteers could post their applications.

BOOK REVIEWS

Cultural Critique's commitment to cultural and intellectual debate and discussion is bolstered by the regular inclusion of reviews of both new and not-so-new books. Generally, books reviewed will have appeared within the past three years, although reviews of older books that are emerging or reemerging in intellectual debates are also welcome. As an academic publication, *Cultural Critique* sees itself as having a responsibility to devote space to authors whose work may not be otherwise reviewed. For *Cultural Critique*'s special issues, book reviews should share the issue's thematic focus. *Cultural Critique*'s book review editors solicit writers, books, and ideas for future contributions to this section of the journal. Please contact the book review editors at cultcrit@umn.edu or *Cultural Critique,* Department of Cultural Studies and Comparative Literature, 216 Pillsbury Drive S.E., 235 Nicholson Hall, University of Minnesota, Minneapolis, MN 55455–0229.

CROWDS AND POWER

NOTES TOWARD A PERFORMATIVE THEORY OF ASSEMBLY

BY JUDITH BUTLER

Harvard University Press, 2015

Jodi Dean

In the opening decades of the twenty-first century, crowds have disrupted the settings given by capital and the state. Breaking with the suffocating reflexivity of contribution and critique in the mediated networks of communicative capitalism, insistent crowds impress themselves where they don't belong. Their very presence challenges the privatization of ostensibly public places from São Paulo, to Istanbul, to New York. Intense and temporary aggregations in multiple locations now appear as one struggle. We see Montreal connected to Athens connected to Cairo connected to Madrid connected to Oakland. Instead of the incommunicable strikes of a multitude of singularities, crowds and riots in place after place communicate the collective movement of the people, pushing questions of similarity, meaning, and alliance: Of what politics will the crowd have been the subject?

Some contemporary crowd observers claim the crowd for democracy. They see in the amassing of thousands a democratic insistence, a demand to be heard and included. Others recognize that the crowd exceeds democracy. Communicative capitalism reconfigures the relation between crowds, democracy, capitalism, and class. "We are the 99%" is a slogan of class war. On the one hand, the democratic reading of the crowd blocks this reconfiguration from view. It harnesses the crowd into the service of the very setting that the crowd disrupts. On the other hand, the democratic reading reveals a struggle over the subject of politics: the contest over whether a crowd is the people or the mob.[1]

The association of crowds and democracy has a long legacy. In the nineteenth and twentieth centuries, the crowd appeared as the quintessential political expression of the people. Commentators wanting to keep the people in their place depicted crowds as brutal, primitive, and criminal mobs. Commentators seeking to overthrow the elites championed the crowd's political vitality: workers, peasants, and commoners of every sort were asserting their sovereignty. Marx famously describes the crowds of the Paris Commune as the people "storming heaven." For nineteenth- and twentieth-century observers, crowds and popular democracy are intertwined. The issue is whether the sovereignty of the people can be anything other than mob rule.

The democratic reading of the crowd turns on the alternative: the mob or the people. Even as the crowd forces the possibility of the intrusion of the people into politics, whether the people is the subject of a crowd event is up for grabs. The crowd opens up a site of struggle over its subject. A crowd might have been a mob, not an event at all. It might have been a predictable, legitimate gathering, again, not an event but an affirmation of its setting. And it might have the people rising up to emancipate themselves. Which a crowd event is, or, better, which it will have been, is an effect of the political process the crowd event activates. The crowd does not have a politics. It is the opportunity for politics. The determination whether a crowd was a mob or the people results from political struggle.

The most influential early crowd theorist was Gustave Le Bon. His widely reprinted and translated book, *The Crowd: A Study of the Popular Mind,* laid the groundwork for twentieth-century theorization of crowds. Le Bon presents the crowd as a distinct form of collectivity. The crowd is a temporary collective being. It holds itself together affectively via imitation, contagion, suggestion, and a sense of its own invincibility. Because the crowd is a collective being, it cannot be reduced to individuated bodies. On the contrary, the primary characteristic of a crowd is its operation as a force of its own, like an organism. The crowd is more than an aggregate of individuals. It is individuals changed through the torsion of their aggregation, the force aggregation exerts back on them to do together what is impossible alone.

Democratic governments justify themselves as rule by the people. When crowds gather in opposition, they expose the limits of this justification. The will of the majority expressed in elections stops appearing as the will of the people. That not all of the people support this government or those decisions becomes openly, physically, intensely manifest.

Disagreement and opposition start to do more than circulate as particular contributions to the production of nuggets of shareable outrage in the never-ending flow of clickbait in which we drown one another. They index collective power, the affective generativity that exceeds individual choices, actions, and opinions. Many press back, using the strength of embodied number to install a gap in the dominant order. They make apparent its biases, compromises, and underlying investments in protecting the processes through which the capitalist class accumulates wealth. They expose the fragility of the separations and boxes upholding electoral politics. The crowd reclaims for the people the political field democracy would try to fragment and manage.

In her new book, *Notes Toward a Performative Theory of Assembly,* Judith Butler also attends to the excessive dimension of popular sovereignty manifest in recent years in the amassing of many in streets and squares. Rather than presenting this excess in terms of the power that accrues through aggregation, Butler considers the contestations enacted through strikes, assemblies, vigils, and occupations in terms of "plural and embodied performativity." She writes, "When bodies assemble on the street, in the square, or in other forms of public space (including virtual ones), they are exercising a plural and performative right to appear" (11). The presence of bodies, or the expressive function that bodies exert, "delivers a bodily demand for a more livable set of economic, social, and political conditions no longer afflicted by induced forms of precarity" (11). The argument seems to be (and I say "seems" because the book is presented as "notes toward" a theory, thereby accommodating the strings of questions and qualifications that suggest an ongoing process of reflection more than an actual theory) that the multiple and repeated assemblies of people in contemporary protests is best understood via an emphasis on embodiment. These are embodied actions, which means they cannot be reduced to speech acts. Embodied actions point to conditions of possibility for speech acts, conditions of livability. For Butler, this placing of livability at the forefront of politics is both the crucial element of contemporary political enactments and a link to the generalized precarity characteristic of the present. The bodies assembled in protest are the bodies imperiled by accelerating precarity.

I can imagine that many readers will appreciate Butler's meditations on performativity and precarity. Some will benefit from her articulation of threats to trans bodies and lives and the unlivable conditions faced by refugees and prisoners. Others will share her criticisms of Hannah Arendt and, like Butler, nevertheless continue to draw from Arendt's emphases on plural and concerted action. I admire Butler's attention to the ambiguity, limits, and conflicts involved in any invocation of the people, whether that invocation comes from bodies assembled in protest or elected officials justifying their own authority. This attention enables Butler to bring out the performative dimension of popular sovereignty, its reliance on multiple, repeated, and contestable enactments. Given that the people can never fully assemble themselves, that the divisions within and between them are constitutive, "the people" names the battle over the name "the people" (167).

Given that the book places itself in the context of the mass assemblies in Tahrir Square and Gezi Park and Zuccotti Park, I found myself returning to Butler's focus on precarity. Why at the moment of global demonstrations of collective strength—revolutions, riots, protests, strikes, and blockades—is she emphasizing precarity, vulnerability, exposure, and grievability? By way of contrast, one might observe how the Marxist tradition always couples precarity with strength. The capitalist conditions that make the situation of individual workers economically precarious produce at the same time conditions for the development of political power: the centralization and concentration of the workforce, the vulnerability of production to stoppages and strikes. Is the best that can be said about recent movements is that they are "enacted by bodies under duress or in the name of duress," that they are claiming "we are not disposable," that they are gatherings of the ungrievable in public space? What about standing up and fighting back, changing the system, being the people united who will never be defeated? Where are the militants, the organizers, and the agitators? Where are the Indignados, the temporary and unemployed workers who are not just precarious but also angry and willing to assert the power of their collective anger in the streets? What happened to the blockades and the channels of active neighborhood support for those who are tear-gassed and pepper-sprayed? Why did the crowd's sense of power and invincibility get lost?

There are at least two explanations for the omission or loss of collective power. The first stems from Butler's characterization of precarity as a general condition. In contrast with proletarianization, a process of economic immiseration and dispossession associated with capitalism's production of a class of unemployed, underemployed, and waged workers, precaritization accompanies neoliberalism's dismantling of social services and expansion of market logics. Butler explains:

> "Precarity" designates that politically induced condition in which certain populations suffer from failing social and economic networks of support more than others, and become differentially exposed to injury, violence, and death. . . . Precarity is thus the differential distribution of precariousness. Populations that are differentially exposed suffer heightened risk of disease, poverty, starvation, displacement, and vulnerability to violence without adequate protection or redress. Precarity also characterizes that politically induced condition of maximized vulnerability and exposure for populations exposed to arbitrary state violence, to street or domestic violence, or other forms not enacted by states but for which the judicial instruments of states fail to provide sufficient protection or redress." (33–34)

Precarity designates less an economic effect than it does a relation to the state. Insofar as Butler refers to "failing social and economic networks of support," she implies prior success or adequacy, as if capitalism were not a system reliant on crises, unemployment, inequality, and exploitation. That Butler approaches precarity from the perspective of the state manifests in the language of "population," a category of demographics and biopolitics. The "differential distribution of precariousness" invites measurement and comparisons, risk assessment and determinations of adequate redress. Butler poses such questions directly, noting that the "point of view of the unequal demographic distribution of precarity" leads us to ask, "Whose lives are cut short more easily? Whose lives are plunged into a greater sense of transience and early mortality?" (48). From a state perspective, militant crowds dissolve into precarious populations that need to be managed. The strength of number dissipates into the vulnerability of individuated bodies.

Butler offers "precarity" as an alternative to the limitations of identity politics. "Precarity is the rubric that brings together women, queers, transgender people, the poor, the differently abled, and the stateless, but also religious and racial minorities: it is a social and economic condition, but not an identity" (58). I agree with Butler on the limits of identity as a political category adequate for the Left today. And I agree that a sense of precarity is a feature of lives exposed to the harsh competition of capitalist markets. My concern is with the kind of political rubric "precarity" provides. It doesn't name the strength that comes from collective power. It persists in seeing people as vulnerable, insecure, and suffering bodies. It notes their appearance in space, but sees this as the appearing of the destitute and ungrieved, not as the opening salvo of an insurgent force. Instead of identifying and amplifying emancipatory possibilities, Butler emphasizes the psychic effects of precaritization: "This process acclimatizes populations over time to insecurity and hopelessness" (15). Coming together, assembling, in Butler's version, expresses freedom and exercises a right. But it does not constitute a new power with revolutionary potential.

In contrast, the Marxist tradition emphasizes the power of the producers. The strength of the oppressed comes from their role in production. When we organize, when we stand together, the proletarianized are strong enough to fight back against the forces of capital and the state and sometimes win. We take back what is ours. In what consists the strength of the precarious? What sort of counterforce do and can they constitute? Butler's emphases on vulnerability and livability sideline these questions of collective power. For her, those who take to the streets "are working to ward off the prospect of oblivion" (181). Rather than recognizing the crowds in streets and squares as fighting for the abolition of capitalism, racism, exploitation, and oppression, Butler places them in a struggle against precarity "lived as slow death, a damaged sense of time, or unmanageable exposure to arbitrary loss, injury, or destitution" (69). The struggle is against a shared condition rather than a ruling class, state formation, or economic system. The cause of this condition—the *crime* of it—does not appear. When the goal is a livable rather than an emancipated life, identifying an enemy, even an opponent, becomes less significant than, say, finding employment or getting some kind of protections from the state.

Butler's emphasis on precarity, particularly from the biopolitical perspective on populations, is the first explanation for her omission of collective power. Emphasizing vulnerable bodies rather than an invincible crowd, she's attuned to risk rather than courage, uncertainty rather than confidence, grief rather than triumph. The second explanation comes from her distrust of collectivity and insistence on the individual. Throughout the book, Butler writes thoughtfully and well about sociality, interdependence, and relationality. Discussing action in alliance she observes that "alliance is not reducible to a collection of individuals, and it is, strictly speaking, not individuals who act" (84). The "I" is always bound up in norms, practices, and expectations that come from outside it, that produce it, although never fully or without remainders. Bodies, too, cannot be understood "as completely distinct from one another" (130). And yet, in a book inspired by and engaged with the politics of the mass assemblies and demonstrations that have drawn the world's attention over the last decade, Butler presses an individualized question of the good life: How ought I to live?

Butler recognizes the embeddedness of this question in politics and the social distribution of livability, in broader arrangements of power and critique. That is her point. But why this question here and why phrased in terms of the "I" who critically evaluates her life and setting? In the very moment when Butler gestures toward a vision of the good life as plural, embodied, and lived in struggle, she holds on to the "I." She writes, "If I am to lead a good life, it will be a life lived with others, a life that is no life without those others; I will not lose this *I* that I am; whoever I am will be transformed by my connections with others, since my dependency on another, and my dependability, are necessary in order to live and to live well" (218). What underlies the assurance that the "I" will not get lost? Why is such assurance necessary? The implication is that politics follows from an individual orientation, an individual's concern with her own life, its conditions, whether it will be grieved. So even as Butler insists on the social constitution of the "I," rightly extending this account beyond human sociality to encompass environments and the nonhuman, she renders the basic question of the good life in terms of "one"—how ought "one" live, how ought "I" live.

This is not the question posed by the new cycle of struggles. They push past and through contemporary preoccupations with the individual and her ethical dilemmas. The many exert a press and intensity. Crowds expand, forcing themselves where they don't belong. Militants, agitators, and organizers work ceaselessly and, often, sacrificially. They hold nothing back, giving themselves over fully to the struggle. What matters is justice, the abolition of racism, capitalism, incarceration, and fossil fuels. For many, these struggles exceed life and livability. They are the "more than life" worth dying for. The power of collectivity derives from this excess: together we are stronger than we are apart, and we are stronger together because we push each other to do and be more than we could ever do or be alone.

The years of capitalist resurgence currently associated with neoliberalism have been difficult for the Left. But this is changing, and the changes are being led by the people in the streets. The challenge for Left theorists is to develop concepts, ideas, analyses, and arguments that can strengthen these struggles, helping to push them in an emancipatory, egalitarian direction. Judith Butler consistently endeavors to meet this challenge, to model the kind of critical engagement through which theory becomes action. Her attunement to vulnerability provides solace to many who feel their lives to be unlivable and fear their deaths will be ungrieved. Perhaps her opening to the strength that accrues to those assemble will inspire her to continue to forward the power of the many as they unite in collective struggle.

Jodi Dean is the Donald R. Harter '39 Chair of Humanities and Social Sciences at Hobart and William Smith Colleges. Her most recent book is *Crowds and Party* (2016).

Note

1. For a detailed discussion of the political opening produced by crowds, see Jodi Dean, *Crowds and Party* (Verso, 2016).

ANALYSIS TERMINABLE AND POSTPONED

ILLUSIONS OF A FUTURE: PSYCHOANALYSIS AND THE BIOPOLITICS OF DESIRE

BY KATE SCHECHTER

Duke University Press, 2014

Christopher Lane

"What *is* psychoanalysis, if what one's colleagues are doing, always, is *not* it?" (10). One of several questions driving Kate Schechter's sharp critique of psychoanalysis, especially as it's been taught and practiced in Chicago for several decades, *Illusions of a Future* puts psychoanalysis in the context of a "biopolitics of desire" involving managed care, medication, and the neoliberal expectations often tied to both. The "illusions" in the book's title are chiefly those of the analysts, Schechter concludes, with a strong implication that the future of psychoanalysis in the United States might itself become quixotic and illusory, given a multitude of changes in treatment, including in the "quick-fix, medication-centered world of managed behavioral health" (1).

Schechter—herself a psychoanalyst, psychotherapist, and medical anthropologist at Rush University Medical College, Chicago—builds her critique and intervention on the compromises that the analysts she interviewed feel compelled to adopt and the predicaments in which they report finding themselves, among them "an atmosphere of scarce work" and the need to maintain a regular practice, for themselves as for their patients (3). This in turn raises questions as to whether what they facilitate clinically may still be thought psychoanalytic, in the sense of involving free association and several sessions per week, to practice a treatment with national protocols, specialty textbooks, and a long, complex history, not least in Chicago itself. Building on both archival and ethnographic research, Schechter's book examines the broader implications of those adjustments for psychoanalysis nationally, including in its relation to psychiatry, to patients, and to biopolitics more generally.

Schechter's intervention, described by her as "rethink[ing] biopolitics with renovated psychoanalytic resources" (8), draws heavily on the work of Jacques Derrida and of Michel Foucault, in ways that might initially surprise, given a long-inherited assumption that especially Foucauldian and psychoanalytic perspectives on desire and biopolitics are inimical and impossible to resolve. Yet as Schechter helpfully underscores, with support from Foucault's extensive references to psychoanalysis, including his clear, repeated differentiation of Freudianism from the normalizing aims of biological psychiatry, Foucault "granted psychoanalysis . . . [an] axial position . . . in the transition from classical sovereignty to liberal governmentality" (8). The approach to "reading psychoanalysis in terms of biopolitics" is thus in one sense a significant adjustment for critical theory in the United States, holding considerable promise as a way of engaging empirically with what Schechter terms "local catalogs of resistances," including in the consulting room (10).

Quite surprisingly underexamined in her book, Schechter herself "underwent training in psychoanalysis" in the same community of analysts she writes about ethnographically, and she continues to serve as a faculty member of the Chicago Institute for Psychoanalysis, an institution of which she is rather critical in the book (14). It therefore isn't clear if the analysts interviewed were also former teachers or remain her colleagues. It would have been fascinating to read a fuller account involving her own self-definition as an analyst and theorist, including the ways that she navigates this complex terrain, with and without patients.

Schechter's ethnography of psychoanalysis in Chicago—as represented chiefly by its Institute for Psychoanalysis and Psychoanalytic Society, two organizations with a long-standing, seemingly intractable rivalry—is nonetheless made analogous to shifts in a more abstract but inescapable "biopolitics of desire" that for several decades has been reshaping the country as a whole. Problems and deficiencies in the local are thus given much wider implication in *Illusions of a Future,* including for psychoanalysis nationally. "So how do today's analysts maintain themselves as analysts," Schechter asks rhetorically of the gauntlet she lays down at the outset, "when they do not—cannot—practice what they preach?" (179).

Her contention is forceful, at times withering, but finally incomplete; it points to difficulties in the United States (perhaps especially the Midwest) that work less successfully as examples for, say, Europe, Asia (including Australia), and South America: "They give up *analysis* precisely in their efforts to maintain themselves *as psychoanalysts*, substituting an imaginary of objective need and its real satisfaction for an imaginary of wishful fantasy and its interpretative resolution, playing up the relationship and down the transference, maintaining themselves as analysts who do not *analyze* but instead *provide* vital emotional supplies" (179, emphases in original).

The judgment is made broadly from the premise that her colleagues' approach to treatment is insufficiently psychoanalytic, rather than, say, that it is psychoanalytic at all. It amounts to a lament about how psychoanalysis has been taught and practiced in Chicago, but the aim of the critique is, if anything, that we need *more* psycho*analysis*, not less. On that count at least, it seems difficult to imagine that her colleagues wouldn't strongly agree.

The environment in which psychoanalysis operates in the United States clearly is changing, and rapidly. *Illusions of a Future* opens with a brief vignette about Digital Diagnostics, a company advertising on its website a "new 3-minute psychoanalytic diagnosis that integrates seamlessly into busy clinics" (19). Stark questions inevitably arise from this rash, unlikely promise, including about the reliability of such "diagnoses"—generated in minutes from information volunteered over the internet. At the heart of such questions lies the type of transference that might develop unconsciously and the intensity of analysis that might then be possible, especially if "3-minute" diagnoses and "seamless integration" govern broader expectations for the actual treatment.

But the ad's very premise of a "busy clinic," in Schechter's hands, also unwittingly stresses an anxiety voiced by several of the psychoanalysts she interviewed, who are said to "grimace" when asked how many analysands they have—a number often quite different, it should be noted, from the number of patients that they treat overall. One analyst asserts that he's a net "donor not a recipient" (56); another, that she has "four and a half" patients in analysis (61), with the "half" apparently representing a patient who for financial reasons had scaled back to one session per week. The analyst nonetheless still considered the treatment to be psychoanalytic.

A third analyst Schechter interviews—representing, it must be said, the sum total of interviewees in the book—responds to the same question by explaining: "You'll want to know that I'm doing less and less transference work, more and more interrupting, more talking, [and] more direct shaping of behavior" (59). Yet here, too, he views himself as chiefly proactive and adaptive, in adjusting to his patients' particular needs and availability. Schechter views his reply as self-consciously adopting a "commanding stance" (59), while the previous analyst quoted apparently "exemplifies a common defensiveness brought on by a redefinition of the status of psychoanalysis in the field of psychiatry" (56).

Illusions of a Future examines these challenges with a view to watching the analysts themselves try to make sense of them professionally, while explaining how they function clinically, in ways that might seem anathema to a classically Freudian treatment relying heavily on a patient's transference. Schechter's approach here is promising and the paradox that drives it vitally important to consider, even if the compromises the analysts find aren't too surprising. In some respects, especially when involving careful assessment of a patient's needs, the adjustments even seem commendable. That the analysts (and patients) sometimes chafe against the constraints of time and health insurers seems quite understandable.

For Schechter, however—and here some exegesis on her own practice would have been invaluable, not least in demolishing a sometimes-false distance in her book between author and interviewees—the analysts are, unbeknownst to themselves, colluding in a broader shift toward "neoliberal medicine" that deprioritizes (when it doesn't ridicule) analysis of the unconscious and the intensification of transference (68). As a result, the treatment apparently becomes overly preoccupied by discussion of costs, benefits, and goals. Concerning one of the analysts' rueful statements about the apparent need to be flexible, risk-taking, yet consistently "nice" with her patients, Schechter writes unsparingly: "In [her] ontology of psychoanalysis, we are now firmly in a world of *need* and *provision* rather than a world of wish and defense" (68 emphases in original). Yet the actual dynamic of the consulting room may be less schematic—more open to nuance and complexity than such snapshots imply. As one of the analysts notes of an obviously well-considered position, "I am not hanging back in the background [of my sessions], silently waiting for the patient's fantasies and then pointing out how she's distorting her image of me. I am actively sussing out her emotional needs, actively meeting them. Our relationship is front and center" (173). Even more generally, a treatment leaning strongly to psychotherapy or other psychodynamic approaches, given a patient's time pressures, isn't in itself an axiomatic avoidance of psychoanalytic technique, even if the latter is practiced less obviously or frequently.

In light of such distinctions, Schechter's opening question, "What *is* psychoanalysis, if what one's colleagues are doing, always, is *not* it?" (10), seems slightly awry at the outset, especially in that ubiquitous and damning "always." Clearly, psychoanalysis *is* still taking place, if in conditions its practitioners consider far from optimal. It seems fairer to advance Schechter's adjusted assertion, later in the book, that because of larger, impersonal changes within medicine and psychiatry, including their almost wholesale embrace of biopolitics, the analysts "are contending with competing imperatives while trying at the same time to maintain themselves as both moral persons and successful professionals" (179).

Observations such as these brought to mind Janet Malcolm's well-titled book from 1982, *Psychoanalysis: The Impossible Profession,* originally a series of articles in the *New Yorker* outlining Freud's late thoughts on treatment and technique. Just as Schechter's title alludes to Freud's famous treatise on religious belief, *The Future of an Illusion* (1927), so Malcolm's book stems from Freud's near-final work *Analysis Terminable and Interminable* (1937), in which he bluntly concedes: "It almost looks as if analysis were the third of those 'impossible' professions in which one can be sure beforehand of achieving unsatisfying results. The other two, which have been known much longer, are education and government" (v).

In this half-century retrospective, Freud wrestles with the challenge and unpredictability of transference in analysis, with Malcolm calling the term and concept his "most original and radical discovery"—more so, apparently, than even infant sexuality and the death drive—in that it determines the contours of romantic love, while helping to explain how, in analytic treatment as in close relationships, "we all invent each other according to early blueprints" (Malcolm, 6). The transfer of affect involved is by definition complicated, since it tends to repeat itself unconsciously. "We overcome the transference," Freud remarked in his *Introductory Lectures,* "by pointing out to the patient that his feelings do not arise from the present situation and do not apply to the person of the doctor, but that they are repeating something that happened to him earlier. In this way," he concludes, "we oblige him to transform his repetition into a memory" (8).

Like some of the Chicago analysts she interviews, Schechter isn't sure if this process is still tenable or whether it was ever so clear-cut. On the question of what patients continue to *want* from analysis, as from the analyst, she quotes one colleague as suggesting, "It's a strange situation: the *meaning* of their suffering doesn't seem important to people to understand in the way it used to" (20).

Generalities such as these will frustrate those wanting sharper, more compelling lines of evidence in *Illusions of a Future,* while nonetheless piquing interest. Comparable anecdotes in Malcolm's earlier book suggest that trends identified several decades ago have if anything intensified in the years since: "There are," she writes of the early 1980s, "few analytic patients who can free-associate easily, if at all." Consequently, "analysts today don't expect the free-association process to take hold until well into the analysis; in fact, some regard the appearance of true free association as a signal to terminate the analysis" (17). Malcolm also touched on issues integral to the investigative interview that Schechter is likely to have experienced even more acutely, given her ties to the institution examined: "The analysts I had seen," notes Malcolm, "so far had dealt with me as they habitually deal with patients on first meeting—courteously, neutrally, noncommittally, reservedly, 'abstinently'—and had also shown a certain wariness at being in the presence of a journalist" (5–6) or, in Schechter's case, an interviewing colleague and former student.

But if *Illusions of a Future* is neither exhaustive nor entirely persuasive in documenting trends in psychoanalytic treatment beyond Chicago, the book is stronger when revisiting the protracted division separating the city's two major training organizations, the Chicago Institute for Psychoanalysis (founded in 1932 by Franz Alexander) and the Chicago Psychoanalytic Society (founded the previous year by his former analysand, Lionel Blitzsten). The long-standing disputes that have determined relations between these institutions, stemming from conceptual differences often masked as their founders' personal rivalry, form almost the entire second half of Schechter's book (chapters 3 to 6), and read quite differently from those of the first. The issues come alive in the retelling, and Schechter can point more confidently than elsewhere to the acrimonious, sometimes bizarre effects of a professional transference gone spectacularly awry.

The intrigue begins with Blitzsten himself, who, according to Schechter, "always claimed to have been analyzed by Freud, while Freud denied 'ever having known anyone by that name'" (77). In his subsequent appointment at Northwestern University's Department of Psychiatry, Blitzsten represented the first psychoanalyst to work in the United States west of New York, and Schechter paints a vivid picture of his evening seminars as "glittering avant-garde affairs attended by the Chicago intelligentsia during the 1920s and 1930s, welcoming philanthropists, academics, medical colleagues, artists, students, [and] writers . . . to explore the world of Freudian ideas" (77).

Meanwhile, Alexander, "the man Freud would call 'my best pupil in the United States,'" arrived in Chicago in 1931, his faculty appointment at the University of Chicago designating him officially as the nation's "first professor of psychoanalysis" (77, 78). Comparisons were doubtless inevitable. A rivalry intensified when, after Alexander's contract at the university was terminated (despite Freud's best efforts at restoring it), he set up the Chicago Institute for Psychoanalysis with an emphasis at odds with that of Blitzsten, his former analysand.

In the pages that follow, we learn why Alexander was subsequently accused of "manipulating" the transference rather than "analyzing" it (83), including by trying to accelerate psychoanalytic treatment and make it available to a greater number. We also track intense institutional debates about what constitutes the "proper place of psychoanalysis," including when its techniques appear "formulaic" or helpfully "genetic," heterodox or hopelessly normalizing (84, 90). Schechter also traces the dramatic and contentious rise of self psychology in Chicago when Heinz Kohut, a prominent member of the Chicago Institute, broke in the late 1960s with ego psychologists over drive theory and instead represented narcissism and associated grandiosity, incredibly, as "positive, growth-seeking phenomena to be welcomed" (136).

Although the minutiae of these debates can read today like inside-baseball, of interest largely to the participants themselves and their historians, the longer-term trends capture part of Schechter's thesis. Especially in Chicago, psychoanalysis has at times veered wildly from forms of treatment and teaching that rely on orthodox concepts such as transference, with the consequence today that in their distance from classical psychoanalysis they appear aligned with the very biomedical forces that view psychoanalytic terms and concepts with disdain. A running national narrative puts psychodynamic therapy—and, even more, psychoanalysis—as more costly and less effective than psychopharmacology, despite a wealth of evidence in fact indicating the reverse (see, for instance, Shedler, 98).

According to Schechter, the analysts she interviews misplace their frustration professionally by misidentifying its cause: "The psychoanalysts in Chicago do not sit around proclaiming the horrors of dealing with Blue Cross Blue Shield to get reimbursed for their work. Rather, they turn their situation into a debate between ancestors and a complicated theoretical battle about the status of the therapeutic relationship" (184).

Perhaps the analysts' frustration with health insurers surfaced in other conversations to which Schechter simply wasn't party. The turn to ancestors and to theoretical battles from decades past may nonetheless be an effect intensified by Chicago's unique history in having training institutes that straddle classical psychoanalysis with self psychology and thus, according to many associated with those fields and organizations, "mutually exclusive positions" (92). The city's unusualness in that regard doesn't quite corroborate Schechter's larger claim about biopolitics, neoliberalism, and "managerial optimism" (106): "I see psychoanalysis unwittingly contributing to the biopoliticization of contemporary U.S. society" (181). A wider focus, involving not just the nation's East and West Coasts, but also Europe and South America, would have deepened the evidence while complicating the argument. Meanwhile, the psychical difficulty that transference continues to pose raises important questions about not just effective treatment but also the terms of a "cure" and the broader possibility of rescuing desire from a myriad neoliberal and biomedical constraints.

Christopher Lane teaches English and intellectual history at Northwestern University. His books include *Shyness: How Normal Behavior Became a Sickness* (2007), which was awarded the Prescrire Prize for Medical Writing in 2010, *The Age of Doubt: Tracing the Roots of Our Religious Uncertainty* (2011), and, most recently, *Surge of Piety: Norman*

Vincent Peale and the Remaking of American Religious Life (2016). He is currently writing a book about citizenship in the age of neuropolitics.

Works Cited

Malcolm, Janet. 1982. *Psychoanalysis: The Impossible Profession*. New York: Vintage.

Shedler, Jonathan. 2010. "The Efficacy of Psychodynamic Psychotherapy." *American Psychology* 65, no. 2: 98–109. https://www.apa.org/pubs/journals/releases/amp-65-2-98.pdf.

BOOKS RECEIVED

Adamczak, Bini. *Communism for Kids*. Trans. Jacob Blumenfeld and Sophie Lewis. Cambridge,Mass.: MIT Press, 2017.

Adorno, Theodor W. *An Introduction to Dialectics*. Ed. Christoph Ziermann. Malden, Mass.: Polity, 2017.

Adrian, Kim. *Sock*. Object Lessons. New York: Bloomsbury Press, 2017.

Alexandrova, Alena. *Breaking Resemblance: The Role of Religious Motifs in Contemporary Art*. New York: Fordham University Press, 2017.

Anker, Elizabeth S., and Rita Felski, eds. *Critique and Postcritique*. Durham: Duke University Press, 2017.

Atkinson, Meera. *The Poetics of Transgenerational Trauma*. New York: Bloomsbury Press, 2017.

Bellacasa, Maria Puig de la. *Matters of Care: Speculative Ethics in More than Human Worlds*. Minneapolis: University of Minnesota Press, 2017.

Bernes, Jasper. *The Work of Art in the Age of Deindustrialization*. Stanford: Stanford University Press, 2017.

Born, Georgina, Eric Lewis, and Will Straw. *Improvisation and Social Aesthetics*. Durham: Duke University Press, 2017.

Brown, Rebecca M. *Displaying Time: The Many Temporalities of the Festival of India*. Seattle: University of Washington Press, 2017.

Bucar, Elizabeth. *Pious Fashion: How Muslim Women Dress*. Cambridge, Mass.: Harvard University Press, 2017.

Campt, Tina M. *Listening to Images*. Durham: Duke University Press, 2017.

Capshaw, Katharine, and Anna Mae Duane, eds. *Who Writes for Black Children? African American Children's Literature Before 1900*. Minneapolis: University of Minnesota Press, 2017.

Chemla, Karine, and Evelyn Fox Keller, eds. *Cultures Without Culturalism: The Making of Scientific Knowledge*. Durham: Duke University Press, 2017.

Cheney-Lippold, John. *We Are Data: Algorithms and the Making of Our Digital Selves*. New York: New York University Press, 2017.

Corbett, John. *Vinyl Freak: Love Letters to a Dying Medium*. Durham: Duke University Press, 2017.

Crossley, Alison Dahl. *Finding Feminism: Millennial Activists and the Unfinished Gender Revolution*. New York: New York University Press, 2017.

Davalos, Karen Mary. *Chicana/o Remix: Art and Errata since the Sixties*. New York: New York University Press, 2017.

Davis, Heath Fogg. *Beyond Trans: Does Gender Matter?* New York: New York University Press, 2017.

Delanda, Manuel, and Graham Harman. *The Rise of Realism*. Malden, Mass.: Polity Press, 2017.

Dryhouse, Carol. *Heartthrobs: A History of Women and Desire*. New York: Oxford University Press, 2017.

Duckert, Lowell. *For All Waters: Finding Ourselves in Early Modern Wetscapes*. Minneapolis: University of Minnesota Press, 2017.

Fish, Jennifer N. *Domestic Workers of the World: A Global Movement for Dignity and Human Rights*. New York: New York University Press, 2017.

Fleiner, Carey. *The Kinks: A Thoroughly English Phenomenon*. New York: Rowman and Littlefield, 2017.

Flores, Glenda M. *Latina Teachers: Creating Careers and Guarding Culture*. New York: New York University Press, 2017.

Gagliano, Monica, John C. Ryan, Patricia Vieira, eds. *The Language of Plants: Science, Philosophy, Literature*. Minneapolis: University of Minnesota Press, 2017.

Gaines, Malik. *Black Performance on the Outskirts of the Left: A History of the Impossible*. New York: New York University Press, 2017.

Germano, William. *Eye Chart*. Object Lesson. New York: Bloomsbury Press, 2017.

Grebowicz, Margret. *Whale Song*. Object Lesson. New York: Bloomsbury Press, 2017.

Gullette, Margaret Morganroth. *Ending Racism, or How Not to Shoot Old People*. New Brunswick: Rutgers University Press, 2017.

Hall, Stuart, and Bill Schwartz. *Familiar Stranger: A Life between Two Islands*. Durham: Duke University Press, 2017.

Hamilton, Clive. *Defiant Earth: The Fate of Humans in the Anthropocene*. Malden, Mass.: Polity Press, 2017.

Han, Byung-Chul. *The Agony of Eros*. Trans. Erik Butler. Untimely Meditations Series. Cambridge,Mass.: MIT Press, 2017.

Harriss, M. Cooper. *Ralph Ellison's Invisible Theology*. New York: New York University Press, 2017.

Harvey, Robert. *Sharing Common Ground: A Space for Ethics*. New York: Bloomsbury Press, 2017.

Horton, Jessica L. *Art for an Undivided Earth: The American Indian Movement Generation*. Durham: Duke University Press, 2017.

Jones, Kellie. *South of Pico: African American Artists in Los Angeles in the 1960s and 1970s*. Durham: Duke University Press, 2017.

Kidd, Dustin. *Social Media Freaks: Digital Identity in the Network Society*. Boulder: Westview Press, 2017.

Klossowski, Pierre. *Living Currency*. Ed. Vernon W. Cisney, Nicolae Morar, and Daniel W. Smith. New York: Bloomsbury Press, 2017.

Koschorke, Albrecht. *On Hitler's "Mein Kampf": The Poetics of National Socialism*. Trans. Erik Butler. Untimely Meditations Series. Cambridge, Mass.: MIT Press, 2017.

Leahy, Anna. *Tumor*. Object Lessons. New York: Bloomsbury Press, 2017.

Lee, Christopher J. *Jet Lag*. Object Lessons. New York: Bloomsbury Press, 2017.

Letzler, David. *The Cruft of Fiction: Mega-Novels and the Science of Paying Attention*. Lincoln: University of Nebraska Press, 2017.

Love, Erik. *Islamophobia and Racism in America*. New York: New York University Press, 2017.

Mahmood, Saba. *Religious Difference in a Secular Age: A Minority Report*. Princeton: Princeton University Press, 2016.

Margaroni, Maria, Apostolos Lampropoulos, Christakis Chatzichristou, eds. *Textual Layering: Contact, Layering, Critique*. Lanham,Md.: Lexington Books, 2017.

Marso, Lori Jo. *Politics with Beauvoir: Freedom in the Encounter*. Durham: Duke University Press, 2017.

Mattfeld, Monica. *Becoming Centaur: Eighteenth-Century Masculinity and English Horsemanship*. University Park: Penn State University Press, 2017.

Maxwell, William J., ed. *James Baldwin: The FBI File*. New York: Arcade, 2017.

Merish, Lori. *Archives of Labor: Working-Class Women and Literary Culture in the Antebellum United States*. Durham: Duke University Press, 2017.

Morris, Catherine, and Rujeko Hockley, eds. *We Wanted A Revolution: Black Radical Women, 1965–85, A Sourcebook*. Durham: Duke University Press, 2017.

Murray, Janet H. *Hamlet on the Holodeck: The Future of Narrative in Cyberspace*. Updated ed. Cambridge, Mass.: MIT Press, 2017.

Nassar, Maha. *Brother's Apart: Palestinian Citizens of Israel and the Arab World*. Stanford: Stanford University Press, 2017.

Nesbitt, Nick, ed. *The Concept in Crisis: Reading Capital Today*. Durham: Duke University Press, 2017.

Newton, Matthew. *Shopping Mall*. Object Lessons. New York: Bloomsbury Press, 2017.

Perry, Samuel L. *Growing God's Family: The Global Orphan Care Movement and the Limits of Evangelical Activism*. New York: New York University Press, 2017.

Price, Marshall N. *Nina Chanel Abney: Royal Flush*. Durham: Nasher Museum of Art at Duke University, 2017.

Prins, Yopie. *Ladies' Greek: Victorian Translations of Tragedy*. Princeton: Princeton University Press, 2017.

Rangan, Pooja. *Immediations: The Humanitarian Impulse in Documentary*. Durham: Duke University Press, 2017.

Robbins, Bruce, and Paulo Lemos Horta, eds. *Cosmopolitanisms*. New York: New York University Press, 2017.

Rockhill, Gabriel. *Counter-History of the Present: Untimely Interrogations into Globalization, Technology, Democracy*. Durham: Duke University Press, 2017.

Rowe, Christopher. *Michael Haneke: The Intermedial Void*. Evanston: Northwestern University Press, 2017.

Roybal, Karen R. *Archives of Dispossession: Recovering the Testimonios of Mexican American Herederas, 1848–1960*. Chapel Hill: University of North Carolina Press, 2017.

Russert, Britt. *Fugitive Science: Empiricism and Freedom in Early African American Culture*. New York: New York University Press, 2017.

Sappol, Michael. *Body Modern: Fritz Kahn, Scientific Illustration, and the Homuncular Subject*. Minneapolis: University of Minnesota Press, 2017.

Scott, David. *Stuart Hall's Voice: Intimations of an Ethics of Receptive Generosity*. Durham: Duke University Press, 2017.

Silva, Noenoe K. *The Power of the Steel-Tipped Pen: Reconstructing Native Hawaiian Intellectual History*. Durham: Duke University Press, 2017.

Smith, Shawn Michelle, and Sharon Sliwinski, eds. *Photography and the Optical Unconscious*. Durham: Duke University Press, 2017.

Solomon-Godeau, Abigail. *Photography After Photography: Gender, Genre, History*. Ed. Sarah Parsons. Durham: Duke University Press, 2017.

Srnicek, Nick. *Platform Capitalism*. Malden, Mass.: Polity, 2017.

Stavans, Ilan. *I Love My Selfie*. Durham: Duke University Press, 2017.

Steinweg, Marcus. *The Terror of Evidence*. Trans. Amanda Demarco. Foreword by Thomas Hirschhorn. Cambridge, Mass.: MIT Press, 2017.

Traber, Daniel S. *Culturcide and Non-identity across American Culture*. Lanham, Md.: Lexington Books, 2017.

Tsing, Anna, Nils Bubandt, eds. *Arts of Living on a Damaged Planet: Monsters of the Anthropocene*. Minneapolis: University of Minnesota Press, 2017.

Tuhus-Dubrow, Rebecca. *Personal Stereo*. Object Lesson. New York: Bloomsbury Press, 2017.

Vee, Annette. *Coding Literacy: How Computer Programming Is Changing Writing.* Cambridge, Mass.: MIT Press, 2017.

Waldschmidt, Anne, Hanjo Berressem, Moritz Ingwersen, eds. *Culture–Theory–Disability: Encounters between Disability Studies and Cultural Studies.* Bielfeld: Transcript Verlag, 2017.

Waltham-Smith, Naomi. *Music and Belonging between Revolution and Restoration.* New York: Oxford University Press, 2017.

Wellmann, Janina. *The Form of Becoming: Embryology and the Epistemology of Rhythm, 1760–1830.* Trans. Kate Sturge. New York: Zone Books, 2017.

Zakaria, Rafia. *Veil.* Object Lessons. New York: Bloomsbury Press, 2017.